The MEGAYACHTS USA

VOLUME ONE ★ 2000

A BOAT INTERNATIONAL PUBLICATION

THE MEGAYACHTS USA.

is published by
EDISEA LIMITED
a subsidiary of
BOAT INTERNATIONAL PUBLICATIONS LIMITED
5-7 Kingston Hill, Kingston-upon-Thames, Surrey KT2 7PW England
Tel: +44 (0)20 8 547 2662   Fax: +44 (0)20 8 547 1201

Copyright © 1999 Edisea Ltd.

ISBN 1 898524 85 8

*All rights reserved. No part of this book may be
produced or transmitted in any form or by any means,
electronic or mechanical, including photocopying, recording,
or by any information storage and retrieval system, without
permission in writing from Boat International Publications.*

Great care has been taken throughout this
book to ensure accuracy, but the publishers
cannot accept responsibility for errors
which may occur.

★ ★ ★

PUBLISHER	Christian Chalmin
EDITOR	Chris Caswell
MANAGING EDITOR	Jill Bobrow
EDITORIAL ASSISTANT	Deborah Wolfe
COPY EDITOR	Janet Hubbard-Brown
DESIGN/PRODUCTION	Bonnie Atwater/Atwater Design
PHOTO EDITOR/PRODUCTION	Dana Jinkins/Dana Jinkins Photography
GENERAL ACCOMMODATION DRAWINGS	Don Beeck
SALES DIRECTOR	Malcolm Maclean
ADVERTISEMENT MANAGER	Paul Cave
ADVERTISEMENT SALES	Marc Caudron
	Debbie MacLaren
ADVERTISEMENT DESIGNER	Janin Drumm
ADVERTISEMENT CO-ORDINATOR	Amy Merrigan
PRODUCTION MANAGER	Francis Ransom
PRINTING & BINDING	Star Standard, Singapore

EDMISTON:
THE RIGHT YACHT
IN THE RIGHT PLACE
AT THE RIGHT TIME.

Edmiston is dedicated to providing the very best in yachting. We buy, sell, charter, arrange to build or refit, the finest yachts in the world. Our experience takes in superyachts of every persuasion, from the latest in modern technology to Classics that grace the oceans. Each client and every yacht has a distinct personality and we will find the perfect yacht to charter for a cruise in the Mediterranean, or to purchase for the ultimate in privacy. Only the best yachts stand the test of time and that is why, at Edmiston, we make a point of distinguishing the best from the rest.

edmiston

EDMISTON & COMPANY LIMITED
51 CHARLES STREET
LONDON. W1X 7PA. UK
TELEPHONE: +44 171 495 5151
TELEFAX: +44 171 495 5150
E-MAIL: edmiston@btinternet.com

EDMISTON & COMPANY
9 AVENUE D'OSTENDE
MONTE CARLO, MONACO
MC 98000
TELEPHONE: +377 93 30 54 44
TELEFAX: +377 93 30 55 33
E-MAIL: edmiston@infonie.fr

http://www.yachtworld.com/edmiston

CONTENTS

FOREWORD 9
INTRODUCTION 11

THE YACHTS

AERIE	36	*Tim Pawsey*	*photos by Neil Rabinowitz*
ALLEGRA	42	*Roger Lean-Vercoe*	*photos by Dana Jinkins & Shaw McCutcheon*
ANDROMEDA	50	*Chris Caswell*	*photos by Dana Jinkins & Sandra Williams*
DARE TO DREAM	58	*Tim Pawsey*	*photos by Neil Rabinowitz*
DISCOVERY	66	*Cynthia Kaul*	*photos by Martin Fine & Neil Rabinowitz*
HYPERION	72	*Alessandro Vitelli*	*photos by Dana Jinkins & Louis Psihoyos*
JANET	82	*Chris Caswell*	*photos by Dana Jinkins & Mike Whitt*
KATRION	88	*Roger Lean-Vercoe*	*photos by Bill Muncke*
LA BARONESSA	94	*Roger Lean-Vercoe*	*photos by Bill Muncke*
LADY GRACE MARIE	102	*Christina Di Martino*	*photos by Donna & Ken Chesler*
LADY LINDA	108	*William Brooks*	*photos by Dana Jinkins & Donna and Ken Chesler*
MARLENA	116	*Alessandro Vitelli*	*photos by Shaw McCutcheon*
MIA ELISE	122	*Reg Potterton*	*photos by Gary John Norman*
MONTANA	128	*Roger Lean-Vercoe*	*photos by Bugsy Gedlek*
SAVANNAH	134	*Alessandro Vitelli*	*photos by Dana Jinkins & Guy Gurney*
SHERIFF	142	*Chris Caswell*	*photos by Bugsy Gedlek & Bruce Miller*
TIGRESS	148	*Chris Caswell*	*photos by Martin Fine & Mike Whitt*
UBIQUITOUS	154	*Roger Lean-Vercoe*	*photos by Neil Rabinowitz*
VARSITY JACKET	162	*Christina Di Martino*	*photos by Donna & Ken Chesler*
WEHR NUTS	170	*Chris Caswell*	*photos by Dana Jinkins*
WILD HORSES	178	*Alessandro Vitelli*	*photos by Dana Jinkins*

DESTINATIONS

Arctic Passage	198	*Rob Johnson*	*photos by Onne van der Wal*
Cruising the Turkish Aegean	208	*Roger Lean-Vercoe*	*photos by Roger Lean-Vercoe*

THE LUXURY YACHT MARKET

Builders 232
Designers 252

DIRECTORY 264

INDEX 284

PHOTOGRAPHERS & ADVERTISERS 288

INTRODUCING THE NEWEST DELTA, THE 151' *AFFINITY* ~ DELIVERED OCTOBER 1999

DELTA

Delta Marine 1608 South 96th Street Seattle Washington 98108 USA T: 206 762 2282 F: 206 762 2627 info@deltamarine.com

CAMPER & NICHOLSONS
INTERNATIONAL
YACHTING SINCE 1782

www.cnconnect.com

The right people
worldwide

SALE & PURCHASE   YACHT MANAGEMENT   CREW SELECTION
CHARTER MANAGEMENT   CHARTER   NEW CONSTRUCTION

Miami Tel: +1 305 604 9191   Palm Beach Tel: +1 561 655 2121

Foreword

What makes a boat deserve the label yacht? To me, it is directly related to its level of refined conveniences. If one can live on a boat for an extended period, in an isolated part of the world, with all of the conveniences normally associated with a well-equipped home, it deserves to be called a yacht. If these conveniences are put in a beautiful and efficient shape and are sufficiently refined in function, form and aesthetics, it then deserves the label megayacht.

The list of required basic amenities is long: refrigeration, air conditioning, cooking facilities, food storage capacity, watermakers, engines, generators, bedrooms, living rooms, dining areas, entertainment facilities, bathrooms, waste management facilities, smaller boats to get ashore, and so on. Sailing yachts add more requirements in the rigging, lines, winches and sails. Add to this the need for a crew to keep all of these things continuously maintained in one of the most hostile environments on earth, plus the essentials required to make their full-time living environment comfortable, and it is no wonder that most people associate yachting with size and expense.

Anyone who has ever gone through the design and construction of a yacht with their own personal stamp of taste and functionality knows both the pain and satisfaction that comes from doing it. In building *Hyperion*, I personally made over sixty trips to Amsterdam in a period of four years. My project was made more difficult for the Royal Huisman Shipyard due to my requirement that it include a completely untested and new monitoring and control system, which was designed and implemented by a small team of engineers working with me in California. I wanted everything on the boat that could be controlled to be controllable via flat-panel display touch screen—the same touch screens on which everything measurable had to be displayed. Over seven thousand things were to measured and displayed in real-time, from rig loads to engine parameters, as well as entertainment media. Twenty-four such screens, 24 computers, a computer room, two servers, and a new crew member to maintain them were also required. With few exceptions, the people at Huisman trusted that we could meet the schedule and deliver a working system. The project was a resounding success but, in the end, I am thankful that Wolter Huisman and his team even talk to me.

Your motivation for reading this book is no doubt driven by your romance with the sea and the beautiful vessels crafted to ply it. In reading it, respect the craftsmen, designers, and artists who dedicate themselves to the continuing art of producing these functional, reliable, beautiful ships.

Without them, this romantic world would be lost.

Jim Clark

FRASER
YACHTS
WORLDWIDE
www.fraseryachts.com

Newport Beach, CA
3471 Via Lido
(949) 673 5252
Fax.(949) 673 8795
frasernb@frasernb.com

San Diego, CA
2353 Shelter Island Drive
(619) 225 0588
Fax.(619) 225 1325
frasersd@frasersd.com

Sausalito, CA
320 Harbor Drive
(415) 332 5311
Fax.(415) 332 7036
frasersf@frasersf.com

Seattle, WA
1001 Fairview Avenue North
(206) 382 9494
Fax.(206) 382 9480
frasersea@frasersea.com

Visit our website for the very latest yacht listings. Updated three times daily, you'll find our full inventory of brokerage and charter yachts worldwide

Brokerage, Sales & New Construction

137' Paolo Caliari design, 1990

127' Delta Tri-Deck, 1989

Worldwide Charters

Yacht Management

115' Custom Crescent Beach, 1994

95' Admiral Marine, 1990

Yacht & Marine Insurance

FRASER YACHTS,
a company with worldwide vision!

Offering clients unparalleled attention in a full range of yachting services. For further information, contact your nearest Fraser Yachts Office.

Introduction

Gather together a cross-section of the yachting industry—builders, naval architects, designers, stylists, and owners—and ask them to define a megayacht. You're likely to get as many definitions as you have experts.

Some would set a size minimum, saying that nothing under a certain length would qualify. Others with an engineering bent might choose to define it by volume, while those involved on the appearances side might require it to meet the highest levels of styling and decor. Owners, of course, would probably think first of costs.

All would be right. And all would be wrong. The essence of a megayacht combines all of those parameters—size, style, and cost. But it is something more, too, and that is what we have attempted to define in this first edition of *MegaYachts USA*. As you may know, our parent company also produces the *The Superyachts* book but we have, to use the nautical term, taken a different tack here.

First of all, every yacht in this book has a direct link to the American market, either through builder, designer, or owner. That threshold eliminated many interesting yachts, which you are likely to find in *The Superyachts*.

Second, we set an entirely arbitrary size minimum of 85 feet or 26 meters. (We made one exception for the 76ft daysailer, *Wild Horses*) How did we come to that particular number? As we gathered our nominations for the yachts to be included, that length seemed to keep reappearing magically, as if on a Ouija board. With the luxury yacht market growing exponentially both in numbers and in length, that number is likely to be much higher for our next volume.

Third, we set one final benchmark. Each yacht must excel in a particular field, such as craftsmanship, design, or styling. With that last hurdle for the candidates to cross, we were able to winnow out our final selection. There were, I have to say, a number of yachts that met both our size and our geographic link. But they were yachts about which we simply said, "Nice yacht," rather than "Wow!"

So I hope you enjoy our selection of "Wows." Each has been carefully photographed to provide you with a guided tour of the yacht and, in separate sections, you'll find a report entitled "The Luxury Yacht Market" that profiles a cross-section of builders and designers, and previews new projects, as well as a "Directory" of companies in the megayacht field.

I have one caveat to make—this book, as with anything in a field growing as fast as luxury yachting, is by no means complete. We have attempted to include a cross section of yachts that we find exceptional, but not every yacht, builder, or designer could possibly fit within these pages.

With that in mind, I look forward to using the first year of the new millenium to uncover an entirely new selection of yachts and services to present in Volume II.

Chris Caswell

YOU MAY WANT TO GIVE YOURSELF
A MOMENT TO CATCH YOUR BREATH.

Hatteras

9 2 C O C K P I T M O T O R Y A C H T

For more information call Hatteras Yachts at 1-252-633-3101 or www.hatterasyachts.com

BURGER

F U L F I L L I N G   D R E A M S   S I N C E   1 8 6 3

BURGER BOAT COMPANY
1811 Spring Street, Manitowoc, WI 54220

TEL
920-684-1600

FAX
920-684-6555

www.burgerboat.com

La Baronessa, the largest private yacht built in the USA since 1930, has been heralded as the best of modern-day technology rendered with old-world craftsmanship. It's the latest in a long line of world-class yachts to have quietly emerged over the past 80 years from our Wisconsin shipyard, where engineering artistry is passed from one generation to the next. And bare hulls are forged into masterpieces.

PJ Hull 228 La Baronessa 59m (195ft) motoryacht
Powered by twin 1,950hp Caterpillar diesels, it has a range of over 10,000 miles
920 743 4412   www.palmerjohnson.com

© Palmer Johnson 1999

The world's finest yachts all have one thing in common...

...our name
MEGA YACHT

New construction

Refitting and repairs

Custom interiors

At Mega Yacht Services International, we do one thing and we do it well: we service mega yachts. We handle all aspects of construction, maintenance, repair and refitting, including exterior painting and refinishing.

With an on-site yacht-quality interior construction shop there is less delay, as our craftsmen have total control over all aspects of your project. This ensures our ability to meet your high standards.

Our operations have recently expanded to include a new location in Tampa, Florida.

We are now teaming up with the world renowned Westship Yachts for an even higher level of perfection in new construction.

Contact us at our new U.S. office in Tampa, Florida for more information or to discuss the possibilities.

Phone: 813.835.8283
Fax: 813.835.7372
e-mail: Mega-yacht@att.net

MEGA YACHT SERVICES INTERNATIONAL
FULL SERVICE YACHT FACILITIES

EXPERIENCE COUNTS

Excellence II
L.O.A. 47.50 meters (156 ft.)

Drawing upon the owner's experience and continual desire for excellence, Feadship delivers a return on investment that goes beyond elegance, comfort and enjoyment. Feadship's experience means uncompromising quality. Perhaps that's why more Feadship owners build their next dream with us.

Feadship Holland
Tel. +31 (0)23 - 524 70 00
Fax +31 (0)23 - 524 86 39

Feadship America
Tel. +1 (954) 761-1830
Fax +1 (954) 761-3412

Feadship France
Tel. +33 (0)4 93 34 28 77
Fax +33 (0)4 93 34 71 60

www.feadship.nl
info@feadship.nl

PHILBROOK'S
BOATYARD LTD.

OVER 50 YEARS OF BOATBUILDING EXPERIENCE
Philbrook's Boatyard Limited is recognized for building performance vessels. Those dedicating the time and money to build a luxury yacht will want to talk to a Philbrook's Representative.

PHILBROOK'S BOATYARD LIMITED performs quality renovations, refits and repairs. ~ In-water or in-yard service. ~ Superior, state-of-the art facilities accelerate year round structural and cosmetic repairs. ~ On-site capabilities for large boats. ~ Facilities for skippers and crews. ~ Two marine ways accommodate most vessels — 150 tons or 130 feet. ~ **Philbrook's has the experience & knowledge to build luxury yachts.**

PHILBROOK'S ~ BOATBUILDERS OF THE PACIFIC NORTHWEST.

PHONE: 250-656-1157 ~ FAX: 250-656-1155 ~ E-MAIL: philbrooks@pinc.com ~ http://www.philbrooks.com
2324 Harbour Road, Sidney, B.C., Canada, V8L 2P6

CHRISTENSEN

Available for Delivery Late Fall 2000

Christensen has established itself as the world leader by building more composite mega-yachts over 120' than any other shipyard in the world.

LOA: 150 ft.
Beam: 28 ft.
Draft Half Load: 7'2"
Powered by Detroit Diesel 8V4000

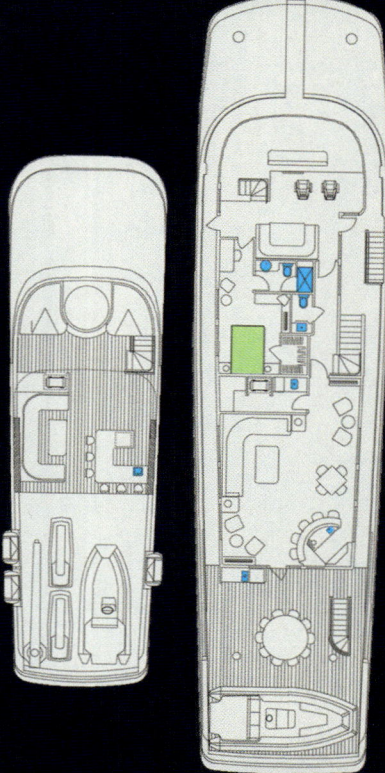

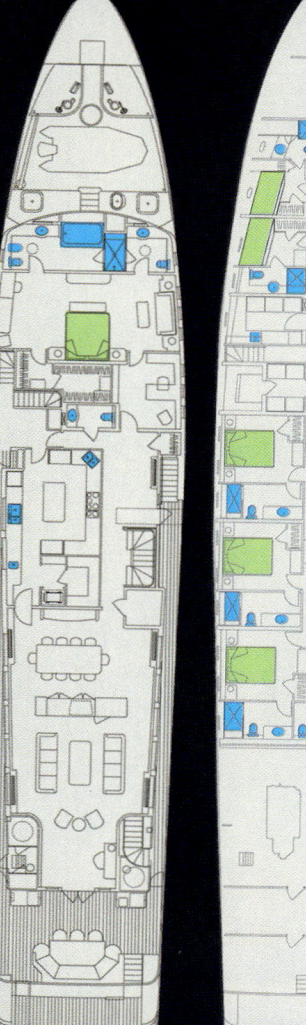

Shipyard & Main Office:
(360) 695-3238 Fax (360) 695-3252 Vancouver, WA
Sales & Service:
(954) 766-8888 Fax (954) 766-8889 Ft. Lauderdale, FL
Visit our website: www.christensenyachts.com

The Eastbay 43's beautiful teak interior shows its Grand Banks heritage.

49 Hardtop Express

Fast boats have always had their attraction. But until recently, those who wanted to go fast had to settle for plastic looking, "Euro-Styled" boats with questionable seakeeping abilities. Eastbay, by Grand Banks, has changed the way fast boats look and behave. Starting with an authentic C. Raymond Hunt hull design, Eastbays are capable of running offshore in rough weather. Like her pilot boat sisterships, her modified deep V-hull can punch through heavy seas, keeping her crew comfortable and dry. And thanks to the legendary Grand Banks reputation for boat building, the Eastbay looks and feels like a real boat. Featuring beautiful, handcrafted teak interiors and meticulously finished fiberglass, they are the envy of knowledgeable yachtsmen everywhere. Available as the 38 Express and Hardtop Express, 43 Express, Sedan and Flybridge Sedan and the 49 Hardtop Express, Eastbays are for those who've been waiting to fly first class.

38 Express

EASTBAY®

DESIGNED BY RAY HUNT. BUILT BY GRAND BANKS

Grand Banks Yachts, Ltd., 26 Pearl Street, Norwalk, CT 06850
Phone: (203) 845-0023 • Fax (203) 845-0024 • www.grandbanks.com

FLY FIRST CLASS.

Eastbay 43 Flybridge Sedan cruising at 24 knots.

HEESEN SHIPYARDS,
WHERE CENTURY OLD TRADITIONS

MEET 21ST CENTURY TECHNOLOGY.

NO ESCAPE
BUILT BY HEESEN SHIPYARDS
THE NETHERLANDS

DIASHIP North America
1535 S.E. 17th Street, Suite 103
Fort Lauderdale, Florida 33316
Tel: (954) 459-9996, Fax: (954) 459-9997
Email: diaship@gate.net

DIASHIP Asia
204-B Blok "K", MK. 12, Batu Maung
11960, Penang, Malaysia
Tel: (60) 4-626-2628, Fax: (60) 4-626-2688
Email: ksoh@pc.jaring.my

DIASHIP International
Watapanastraat 1
Oranjestad, Aruba
Tel: (297) 82-0388, Fax: (297) 82-6018
Email: diaship_aua@yahoo.com

HEESEN Shipyards
Rijnstraat 2, P.O. Box 8
5340 AA, Oss, The Netherlands
Tel: (31) 412-665544, Fax: (31) 412-665566
Email: heesen.diaship@tip.nl

FULL SERVICE YACHT REPAIR & REFIT ON THE SAVANNAH RIVER.

CONTACT: DONALD ANSLEY OR MICHAEL BACH (912) 234-6579 • 301 N. LATHROP AVENUE, SAVANNAH, GA

July 1, 1997: China Takes Rule of Hong Kong From the U.K. Good for Us.

Business is booming in Hong Kong and Cheoy Lee Shipyards is taking advantage of it.

By 2001, China's shipbuilding industry is expected to produce more than 10% of the world's commercial shipping tonnage, and Cheoy Lee will contribute significantly.

Shipbuilder to the world since the family run business began in 1870, Cheoy Lee has consistently produced some of the finest luxury yachts and commercial vessels.

Today, due in part to the succession of Hong Kong from the British to the Chinese, Cheoy Lee is entering an unprecedented era of growth. A new state-of-the-art manufacturing facility will help meet world-wide demand and keep Cheoy Lee at the forefront of yacht and ship construction.

Cheoy Lee's extensive line of motoryachts are expertly crafted specifically for the American market and priced competitively. The yachts range in size from the 50' Sportsfish to 150' Megayachts. Reap the rewards of Cheoy Lee's 130 years of shipbuilding.

CHEOY LEE
SHIPBUILDERS TO THE WORLD FOR OVER A CENTURY

Cheoy Lee Shipyards, Ltd.
89 + 91 Hing Wah St. West
Lai Chi Kok, Kowloon, Hong Kong
(852) 2-307-6333 • fax (852) 2-307-5577
cheoylee@hkstar.com

Cheoy Lee Shipyards North America
1497 S.E. 17th Street
Fort Lauderdale, FL 33316
(954) 527-0999 • fax (954) 527-2887
info@cheoyleena.com

Compass Point Yachts, Inc.
809 Fairview Place N., Ste. 150 • Seattle, WA 98109
(206) 625-1580•Fax (206) 682-1473
compasspt@aol.com
San Diego Office: (619) 523-5490 • Fax (619) 523-5493
scoveyachts@earthlink.net

YACHTASIA
B40 Club de Mar
E 07015 Palma de Mallorca, Spain
+34-971-699-040
Fax +34-971-691-802
info@yachtasia.com

WAYNE C GROUP

*. . . years of dedication
presenting quality investments to buyers,
for builders and owners of
premium Sportfisher, Sailing and Motor Yachts . . .*

• Brokerage • Charter • Construction • Consultation • Management •

**625 Lucerne Avenue • 2nd Floor • Lake Worth • Florida • 33460
Telephone 561-588-8135 • Facsimile 561-588-8136
www.waynec.com**

Work with lenders who understand your needs . . .

George J. Shull & Associates

- **PERSONAL YACHT AND JET FINANCE ARRANGEMENTS**
- **TAX - QUALIFIED OFFSHORE PROGRAMS AVAILABLE**
- **PRIVACY ENSURED**

Bahia Mar Yacht Center • 801 Seabreeze Boulevard
Fort Lauderdale, FL 33316
954.463.4546 • Fax: 954.463.5531

PHOTO BY JIM RAYCROFT

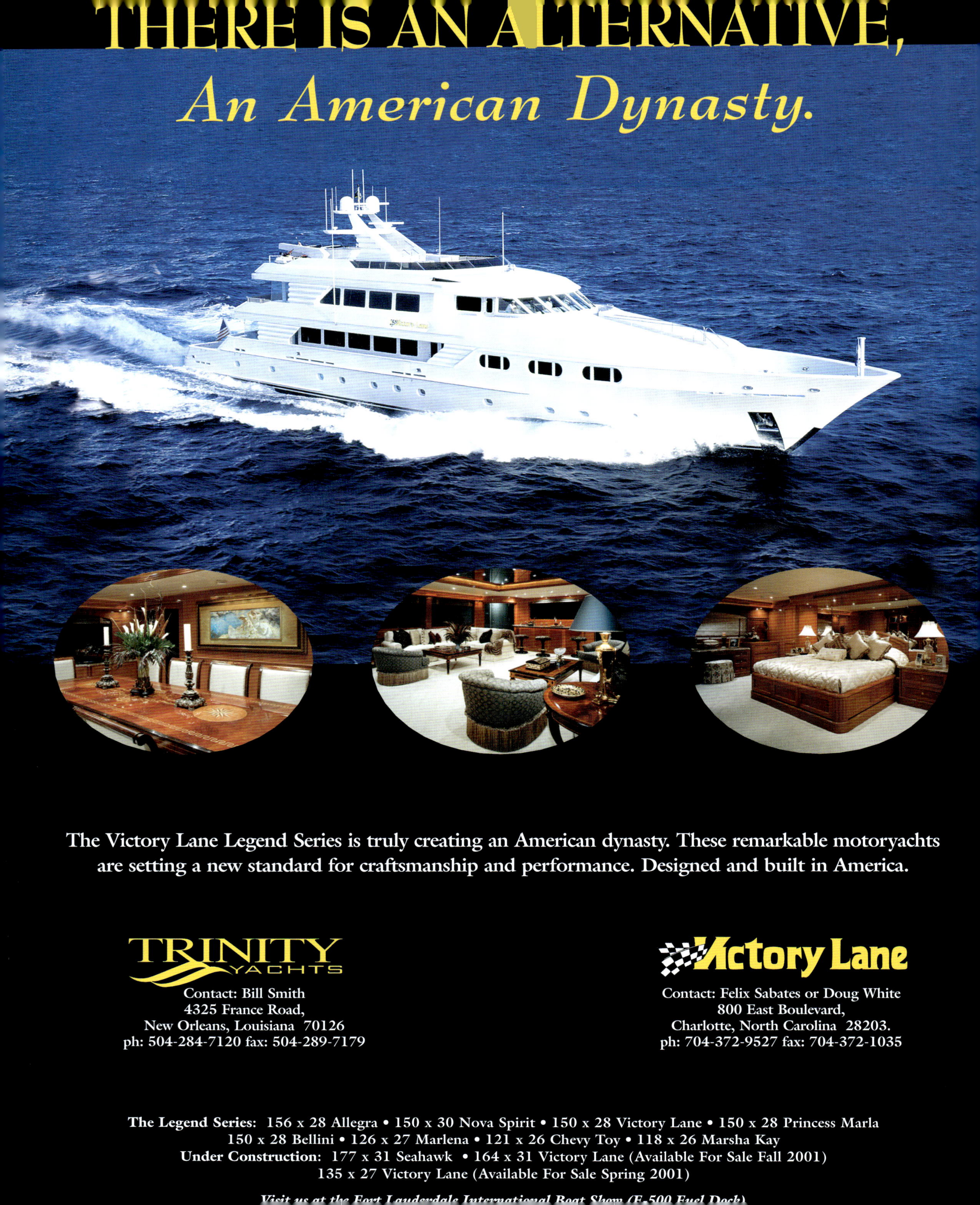
THERE IS AN ALTERNATIVE,
An American Dynasty.
The Victory Lane Legend Series is truly creating an American dynasty. These remarkable motoryachts are setting a new standard for craftsmanship and performance. Designed and built in America.
TRINITY YACHTS
Contact: Bill Smith
4325 France Road,
New Orleans, Louisiana 70126
ph: 504-284-7120 fax: 504-289-7179
Victory Lane
Contact: Felix Sabates or Doug White
800 East Boulevard,
Charlotte, North Carolina 28203.
ph: 704-372-9527 fax: 704-372-1035
The Legend Series: 156 x 28 Allegra • 150 x 30 Nova Spirit • 150 x 28 Victory Lane • 150 x 28 Princess Marla
150 x 28 Bellini • 126 x 27 Marlena • 121 x 26 Chevy Toy • 118 x 26 Marsha Kay
Under Construction: 177 x 31 Seahawk • 164 x 31 Victory Lane (Available For Sale Fall 2001)
135 x 27 Victory Lane (Available For Sale Spring 2001)
Visit us at the Fort Lauderdale International Boat Show (E-500 Fuel Dock)

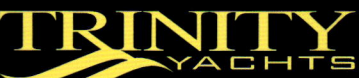

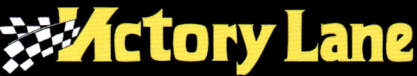

SELL YOUR YACHT

Like Brazil sells coffee
Like Germany sells steel
Like Boeing sells airplanes

COUNTERTRADE

www.strikerpacific.com

Striker Pacific Corporation
Seattle, WA United States

give yourself a piece of freedom

For over 20 years we have given our clients magic moments of excitement and freedom.

If you really want the motor yacht you have always dreamed of, catch our wave and feel the style and quality of the right **board**.

C.B.I. NAVI

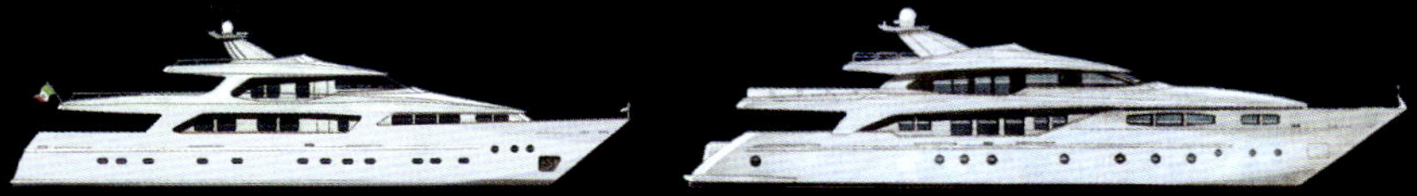

115'   135'

C.B.I. NAVI SPA - 55049 Viareggio ITALY - Via Giannessi Via Pescatori - Tel. +39-0584-388192 - Fax +39-0584-388060
COMPAGNIA BRESCIANA INVESTIMENTI SPA - Cap. Soc. Lit. 86.600.000.000
E-Mail: info@cbinavi.com - Internet: http://www.cbinavi.com

PATRICK ★ KNOWLES DESIGNS

YACHT • AIRCRAFT • SPECIALISTS

M/Y Dare To Dream

M/Y Varsity Jacket

1650 Southeast 17th Street Causeway, Suite 210 • Fort Lauderdale, Florida 33316 • 954-832-0108 Fax: 954-832-9951

Simrad has built its name on products which do what they are designed to do, whatever the conditions. Built on the

SIMRAD MARINELINE

same principles as the company's sophisticated electronics for the demanding commercial and fisheries market, Simrad offers a complete range of high quality systems including autopilots, instruments, radars, VHF, DGPS chartplotters and echo sounders. A worldwide sales and service network is available to you.

...marine electronics to improve boating

CHARTPLOTTERS

The new professional range of Simrad DGPS chartplotters offers a choice of models with 6", 10" and 14" displays in bright TFT colors which can be viewed from any angle. User friendly and intuitive to operate via the windows type menu system, split screen dual chart scale and navigation information are easily accessible.

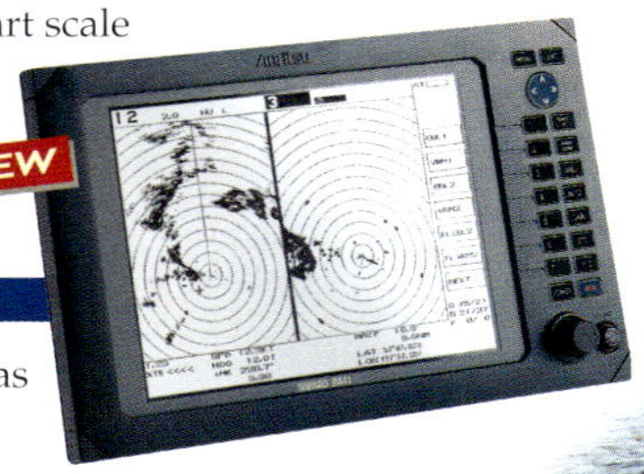

RADARS

Radar technology has taken a major step forward with the Simrad RA41 and RA42 which incorporate features that have previously not been available even on large high seas Radars. These benefits include widescreen, continuous range and the unique dual range facility that allows two ranges to be viewed on one screen simultaneously.

AUTOPILOTS

When buying a Simrad Autopilot you are assured of equipment which will constantly maintain the desired course and provide accurate steering whatever the weather, allowing the helmsman to relax and navigate while still keeping a watchful eye. Simrad Autopilots have been designed to adapt to to a boat's steering characteristics in varying sea states, automatically.

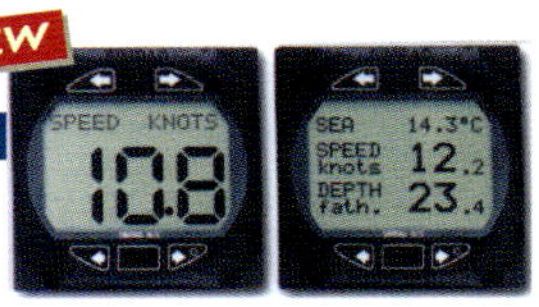

INSTRUMENTS

The new Simrad IS15 instrument range has been developed to be the easiest to fit, and easy to use, a major advance in economical stand alone and integrated systems. In the stand alone system the transducer and power cable are connected directly to the instrument. The IS15 will determine which transducer is connected and configures automatically to the input - and you're ready to go.

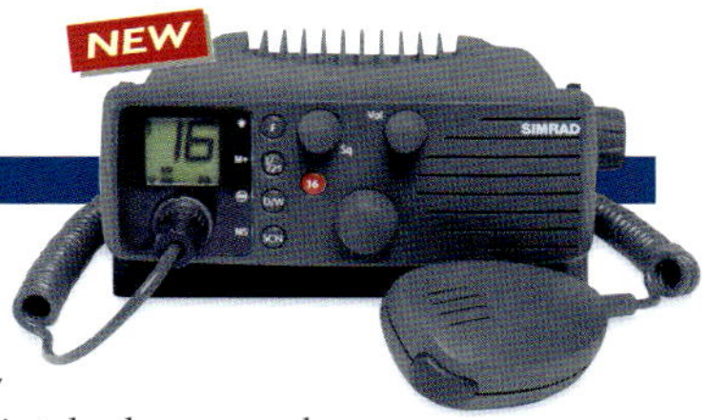

VHF

The new rugged compact, VHF radiotelephone can be installed in cockpit or fly bridge. Either fistmike or handset, with or without DSC unit, can be selected.

Call for the new Simrad MarineLine catalog or visit our web site, www.simrad.com, information about Simrad products

For a free brochure and a list of Simrad dealers near you, call:
Simrad, Inc. 19210 33rd Ave. W. • Suite A • Lynnwood • WA • 98036 • USA
Tel: (425) 778-8821 • Fax: (425) 771-7211   www.simrad.com

SIMRAD
A KONGSBERG Company

WORLDWIDE MANUFACTURER OF MARINE ELECTRONICS

At Richard Bertram, excellence has been a time honored tradition since 1946.

For over fifty years, Richard Bertram has been catering to the needs of yachtsman around the world. Today, they can offer their clients the best that Italy has to offer... *Benetti*.

Richard Bertram is the exclusive North American representative for Benetti's new *Classic Series* of fiberglass motoryachts.

AZIMUT

RICHARD BERTRAM, INC.

Benetti CLASSIC

MIAMI, FL
(305) 633-9761 • Fax (305) 634-9071

FORT LAUDERDALE, FL
(954) 467-8405 • Fax (954) 763-2675

DANIA, FL
(954) 925-9070 • Fax (954) 925-9540

Web Site: www.bertramyacht.com • E-mail: rbi@bertramyacht.com

YACHT BROKERAGE • MARTY A LOWE INTERIORS • YACHT FINANCING AND INSURANCE • FULL SERVICE YARD • CHARTER SERVICES

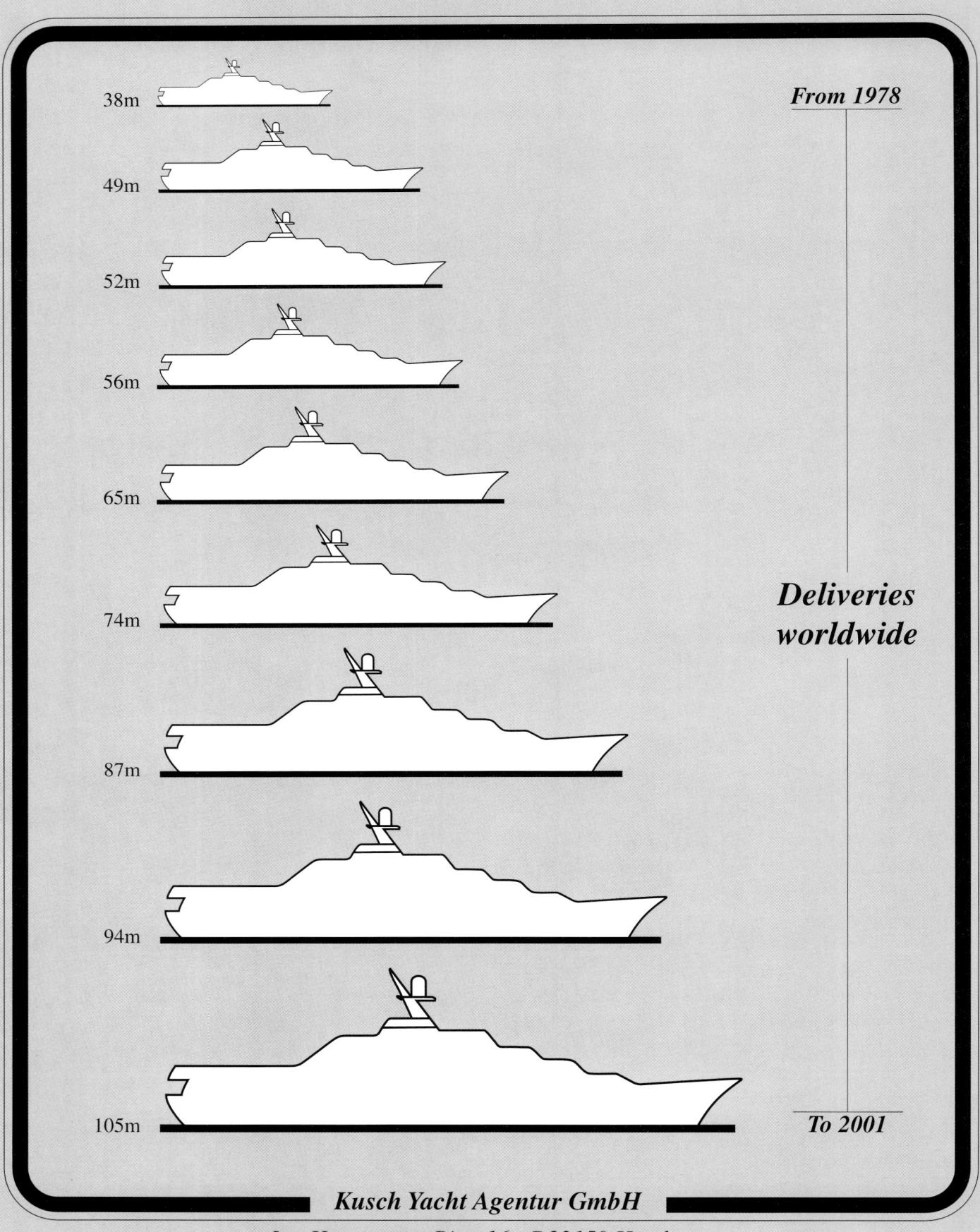

The YACHTS

Aerie

100-foot Nordlund Motoryacht

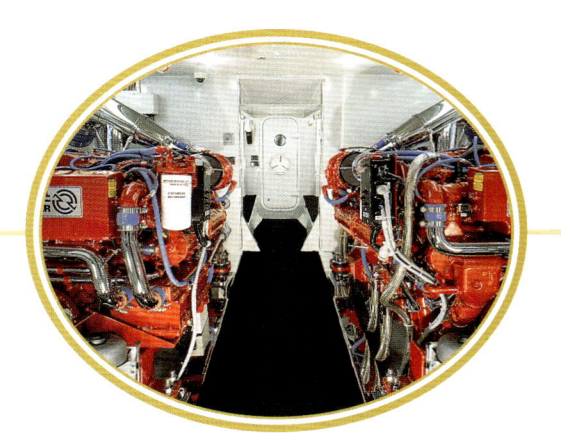

The anchor of strong design is that rare ability to simultaneously present elements of contrast and harmony with form and function. Such is the achievement embodied in *Aerie*, a newly-launched, 100ft custom motoryacht from Nordlund Boat Company that ingeniously marries sleek, contemporary lines from Ed Monk N.A. with the welcoming but also discriminating personality of Pokela Design. Owners Gordon and Sally Nordlund (not related to the builder), wanted *Aerie* to be a home away from home as well as a luxury yacht. The result is a paragon of understated elegance and industrial-strength efficiency.

One day, the Nordlunds were enjoying the view from their Pacific Northwest shoreline home (named Eagle's Nest) when they saw a large Nordlund yacht motoring down the channel. Shortly thereafter, they decided it was time to upgrade from their 63ft Nordlund to a new vessel. Discussions ensued with Nordlund and Pokela Design. After a two-year planning and construction period, the owners took delivery of their new aptly-christened *Aerie* (eagle's nest).

The second vessel always allows a better understanding between shipyard and owner, says builder Paul Nordlund. He worked closely with *Aerie*'s skipper, who was present throughout construction. "The skipper's degree of knowledge makes a big difference," says the builder. "He (or she) gets to know where everything is, plus our employees learn a lot when they meet the people who'll be running the vessel. Not many owners are willing to commit the time and money to include their captain, but it is a definite advantage for this size vessel."

No doubt it was also critical, considering the owner's unwavering, fastidious approach to every detail. "I knew what I wanted right down to the water pumps," notes Gordon Nordlund, whose background in heavy industrial construction has given him a keen understanding of the need to blend beauty with precision and practicality.

Entered aft, the main saloon yields a bright, open-plan arrangement that also accommodates a 270-degree panorama, viewed through extensive smoked glass. Blinds are recessed in channels and the room's working components (a Lexicon-controlled surround sound, home-entertainment center with satellite TV) are closeted in madrona burl. The simplicity of design allows full appreciation of the outside surroundings, as well as allowing the owners' collection of contemporary jade and glass art to be showcased within.

From the saloon, two steps lead up to the dining room, which features a custom oblong glass table on a polished marble and stainless steel frame. The table and maple cabinetry—which divides the room from the main saloon—is cleverly partnered by a madrona burl and stainless steel overhead dining light. A large abstract painting of poplars picks up the aquamarine tones of the water outside; and discrete, inlaid strips of A-Look ceiling mirror parallel the room's proportions.

In planning, the owners invited interior designer John Pokela to view their home, to give him a sense of the space and ambience they sought to transpose to their motoryacht. Across the board, his interpretation instills a sense of seamless comfort and quality, through a constant weave of different textures and surfaces. Burled maple, madrona, marble, stainless steel, and glass are

Porthole ❋ *Aerie*'s first-class engine room, painted in red, white, and blue, may well be the most detail-oriented ever to come from the Nordlund shipyard.

Above ❋ The lines of *Aerie* are classic Ed Monk, with full walkaround side decks, raked pilothouse windows and eyebrow. For cruising in the Pacific Northwest, the cockpit is protected by the bridge overhang.

Left ❋ The teak-planked cockpit features a transparent bait tank that can hold either fresh or salt water fish and, with moving phosphorescent lights, becomes a soothing distraction at night.

★ AERIE 37

Main picture ★ The madrona burl cabinet to port in the saloon conceals a television and entertainment center.

Opp. bottom left ★ The informal galley surrounds an island that houses a radiant heat cooktop.

Opp. bottom right ★ The dining room features an oblong glass table with a madrona and stainless steel light fixture overhead.

individually orchestrated with careful measure to present a truly balanced décor in a continuum that enhances the vessel's modern lines.

In the galley, a desire to entertain with ease and informality resulted in a well-equipped space that boasts a Sub Zero fridge and freezer and an island with Dacor radiant heat cook-top. Padded stainless steel stools provide for informal dining, while the galley's practical layout and size allows the chef plenty of movement and easy access to an ash-burl-encased wall of drawer lockers. Extractors are concealed in a custom-made, stainless steel, three-light fixture. For formal occasions a set of Waterford awaits, neatly stored in maple cabinetry that emulates the square pattern employed throughout the port side of the vessel.

The pilothouse, despite functional form, still exudes a

sense of comfort and warmth. Fully digitalized instrumentation (including centrally-located radar easily viewed from twin, Italian-crafted chairs) is uncluttered and housed in rich madrona burl. Maple cabinetry to port of the pilot station conceals plotter, computer, and printer while a separate area around a compact table allows the guests to sit in comfort behind the skipper. Under the pedestal's shallow platform, a pair of drawers permits storage for a double set of charts on either side, while behind, an A-Look mirror adds depth and continues the theme from the saloon.

In all, careful use of space allows a total of five separate day areas on the main deck, including a covered aft cockpit with day-head, Gaggenau stove and barbecue, fridge and ice maker.

Closed circuit TV permits the skipper to monitor activity aft, but the main attraction is a clear-sided, fresh-or-salt-water bait tank that provides gentle nocturnal distraction with its revolving phosphorescent lights. Fishing rods are stored out of sight in full length, easily-accessed ceiling bins above the bulwark companionways.

Above, on the spacious hardtopped flybridge, guests lack for nothing, rarely having to move from their perch to enjoy considered comforts. These include wraparound seating, wet bar, grill, sink, ice maker, and a two-drawer Sub Zero refrigerator/freezer.

"It's the perfect party area," says Nordlund. But there's a working side, too. All navigational electronics are duplicated and added controls include twin remote side docking stations (and one aft). An extendable davit launches a 17ft Grady White or 13.5ft Rendova runabout.

Below, a separate midship-paneled stairway to the full-width master stateroom allows privacy from guest and crew accommodations. Here, a sculpture of polished,

★ AERIE 39

Above ❋ The master suite has a shoji-style natural ash burl headboard and sliding screens over the ports.

Right ❋ Access to the bridge is made easy because the inside stairwell leading from the pilothouse.

Below ❋ The pilothouse features digital instrumentation and a central radar screen easily viewed from the twin Italian-made helm chairs.

burl hardwood made specially for the vessel (and one of a number which resides in the owners' other homes) provides rugged contrast to the room's otherwise symmetrical lines that feature a shoji-style natural ash burl headboard. For added comfort, the full-size bathroom with Jacuzzi™ tub also boasts a heated green serpentine-patterned marble floor.

The crew's quarters (reached by a forward stairway off the pilothouse) reflect the same comfort as the rest of the vessel. A three-bunk, bulkhead crew cabin with Whisper Wall track system doubles as overflow accommodation when required for visiting grandchildren.

Aft of the skipper's quarters and head, two guest staterooms (furnished in maple burl and stainless steel, each with full head) provide flexible accommodations, one a double and one with twins and a bunk. All staterooms feature shoji-style screens, whose diffused natural light picks up the fine wood grains; and all have TV and VCR combinations with individual multi-links and thermostatic controls.

Air-conditioned for comfort, the engine-room gleams like a hot-rodder's dream. Piping and engine mounts are all of highly-polished stainless steel and the twin 1110hp Detroit Diesel 12V92TA Penske special diesels are painted red, with casting seams machined smooth to eliminate sharp edges. In full flight, *Aerie* cruises comfortably at around 15 knots, with a maximum to 22 knots, but the owners prefer a more sedate pace of around 10 knots to better appreciate the scenery.

"I wanted a first-class engine room," owner Gordon Nordlund said. Indeed, suggest *Aerie*'s builders, it may well be the most detail-oriented of its kind ever to come from their shipyard. While the owner's requested engine color-scheme called for red throughout and stainless steel, the tubing had to stay blue. The result, unquestionably, is that this power plant is not only spotless—in its gleaming, bone-white compartment—but also, quite likely, the most patriotic engine room afloat. Here, as throughout, practicality is key, with oil filters easily accessible on the aft bulk head.

"Of course," says Nordlund, "In my opinion, the engine room is the nicest part of the boat." On a vessel already swathed in detail, that's saying something. Moreover, if cleanliness is next to godliness, then this is about as close to Heaven on earth as one can get. "Oil collects dust," says the owner. "But wash it down once a year and it won't. I want this engine room to look like this ten years from now." Somehow, you just know it will.

This is a boat that shines stem to stern—literally. The stainless steel pulpit, custom-machined and polished at Nordlund's insistence, is a reflection of the detail that follows throughout, and probably as fine a quality as you'll find anywhere, according to the builder. And the owner is quite satisfied.

The primary goal in building a custom boat, suggests Paul Nordlund, is to reflect the owners' taste. Gordon Nordlund concurs, "There were no surprises and not really too much that I would do differently. I knew about everything that was going in and that makes all the difference."

SPECIFICATIONS

Length	100ft (30.48m)
Beam	21ft (6.4)
Draft	5ft (7.62m)
Displacement	170,000lbs
Power	Twin 12V92 Detroit DDEC
Speed	22knots/15knots
Naval Architect	Edwin Monk & Son
Interior design	Pokela Design
Builder/Year	Nordlund Boat Co., Inc. /1998

★ AERIE

ALLEGRA

175-foot Trinity Motoryacht

In 1997, *Victory Lane*, a brand new American-built superyacht, was unveiled at the Fort Lauderdale Boat Show. Built as a speculative project by Felix Sabates' company Victory Lane Enterprises, her style and quality captivated visitors at the show—especially the person who bought her for a cool $16 million or so on opening day. The first of the Legend series to be built at Trinity Yachts, she has now been renamed *Princess Marla*; but visitors to the 1998 show might be excused from thinking they were experiencing *déja vu* when they saw the new *Victory Lane* being featured at the Trinity Yachts' display. This yacht, too, was sold on the opening day of the show and renamed *Allegra*.

The timing of show-stopping publicity announcements aside, this was certainly no mystical experience. The combined talents of Trinity Yachts and the balanced mix of ingredients specified by Felix Sabates and his team, which includes project manager John Posgay and interior designers Dee Robinson and Carolyn Sabates, have certainly produced yet another notable motoryacht.

One of the prime requirements of a successful speculative yacht is good looks, and the exterior styling and general arrangement of the interior created by Ward Setzer of Paragon Design provide *Allegra* with an abundance.

Starting at her high bow, the sheerline sweeps aft towards the pilothouse, encompassing the three oval portlights of the full-beam master suite before dropping to main deck level behind a fashion plate which conceals and protects the stairs uniting the two decks. From here it follows the main deck bulwark, running aft along the side deck past the huge picture windows of the main saloon, and then drops down to the fishing cockpit in the stern.

The descending tiers act as a counterpoint to the line of the superstructure, which climbs gently upwards over the pilothouse to the sun deck where it continues well aft into an overhang, as does the line of the bridge deck just below. This substantially increases the area of valuable deck space, the second vital ingredient of a successful yacht, available to the owner.

In addition to being spacious, *Allegra*'s decks are also well planned. Even though the bridge deck saloon is built out, making this universally popular room as big as possible, the side decks are preserved at main deck level. This leaves an easy route from stern to bow (important for the crew, especially during docking operations) along

Porthole   Delightful touches, like the antique desk in the main saloon, abound throughout *Allegra*.

Opp. left   This night photo shows off the shaded aft deck with built-in dining table, as well as the sitting area on the upper bridge deck that is protected behind glass side screens.

Above   An aerial view accentuates *Allegra*'s powerful lines and clearly shows the recessed crew walkway from the Portuguese bridge to the foredeck.

Left   The sundeck is complete with a spa pool and an outdoor living space that includes a wet-bar adjacent to a casual dining area.

ALLEGRA   43

Above ★ The main deck lounge provides a comfortable atmosphere for conversation.

Left ★ The bridge deck lounge has a Dakota granite-topped bar, two conversation areas, and sliding doors to the semi-enclosed aft deck.

Opp. right ★ The formal dining area seats ten. *Allegra* was delivered with a full complement of Lenox bone china and Waterford crystal.

the side decks, up the stairs to the Portuguese bridge forward of the pilothouse, and then down a central walkway over the superstructure to the foredeck.

The yacht's single tender, a splendidly classic 21ft, 6-seater Packard "Gentleman's Launch" that blasts a 50-knot performance from its inboard V-8 diesel, is stowed on the aft part of the sundeck, along with a pair of wetbikes. On a yacht of this size a single tender is insufficient to serve both crew and owner's needs, so the suggested solution is to tow a larger tender astern. This has been accomplished on earlier Victory Lanes, even when cruising as far afield as the southern Caribbean, although it would not be a serious option for oceanic passages. A third tender, for general purpose use, can be carried in the lazarette, but this must be small and of the fully inflatable variety. Forward of the tender's storage, a spa pool nestles between the twin legs of the mast, while forward again is a spacious outdoor living area, with lounge-chairs and a horseshoe arrangement of seats around a casual dining table, and an adjacent wet bar and forward-facing bench seats behind the windscreen near the yacht's flying bridge control station.

An added level of formality is found one deck down on the aft end of the bridge deck. Laid with teak and pleasantly shaded by the deck above, this area is united with the adjacent sky lounge through a pair of glazed doors, creating a splendid inside/outside area, comfortable yet not over-casual in its decoration, where guests will feel relaxed no matter what the hour or dress code.

Inside, in air-conditioned comfort, the view through the panoramic windows is almost as good as from the deck, while subtle lighting combined with the warmth of the sapele paneling's quarter-matched grain and intricate decorative inlay does wonders for the room after dark. Two conversation areas, a superb bar topped in rich Dakota mahogany granite, and an entertainment center with a 45-inch television and a karaoke machine all flanked by bookshelves, complete this self-contained comfort zone.

The last of *Allegra*'s three comprehensive guest areas is found at the aft end of the main deck. Again luxuriously decked in teak, it has a dining table set against the aft rail, together with a spacious fishing cockpit and an external bathing platform and adjacent exercise room/diving store just a few steps below. Thus it combines all the functions of a watersports park—viewing platform, beach, dock, and the yacht's main outdoor dining area, complete with its own barbecue.

Another vital ingredient of a speculative yacht is an interior with the widest possible appeal. Florida-based designers Dee Robinson and Carolyn Sabates, masters of this art with over 15 projects behind them, have created a comfortable style for *Allegra*, which weaves understated sophistication with an open invitation to relax and enjoy. Fabrics and furnishings of muted color combine with rich woods and marbles whose detailed finish has created a unifying thread throughout the vessel. The final touch is an attractive selection of artwork, including a Remington bronze horseman, high-quality Lenox bone china and Waterford crystal, all of which is included in the turnkey price of the yacht.

Allegra's main entrance is through doors from either side deck to an impressive amidships lobby that is floored in Sicilian perlato marble inlaid with rich red breccia coral. This is the crossroads of the yacht. Delicately bannistered stairs lead up to the skylounge and down to the guest accommodations; aft is the dining saloon and main deck lounge; forward is the master stateroom; while further doors open to the day head and the galley.

Although the basic layout of this yacht bears a strong relationship to the previous Trinity-built *Victory Lane*, the new model has many significant changes. Apart from the exterior addition of a fishing cockpit and open aft deck (in contrast to the enclosed stern deck of the earlier yacht), the main deck lounge and dining saloon have been completely remodeled. The former includes a handsome bar across the aft bulkhead and two distinct groups of seating, while the dining saloon now fills the full beam of the deckhouse, rather than being a separate compartment opening off a starboard side passageway. Access to the dining room is much more convenient, with four sliding doors glazed with bevel-edged glass opening into a splendid room that is furnished with a handsome 10-seater table and chairs that were custom-built for the yacht in Spain by Lopez Negro.

Conveniently positioned directly across the lobby, the galley is laid out for efficiency with the servery well separated from the chef's domain by a marble-topped counter. The chef has been spared nothing in terms of equipment—an eight-burner commercial quality stove with two griddles and three ovens, two warm drawers, twin microwaves, two pairs of Delfield fridges and freezers, two Miele dishwashers, a pair of trash compactors, twin sinks with built-in garbage disposal, and acres of work surface. Few custom yachts come so well equipped, let alone one which has been speculatively built.

The master suite, too, has been provided with every convenience that could be desired. Entered through a private office, the full beam stateroom offers a king-size bed together with settee, vanity desk, and audio/visual entertainment center. Forward of the bed are a pair of cedar-lined walk-in wardrobes while his and hers bathrooms, one with a huge shower and the other with a two-person spa pool, are positioned aft. High quality pearwood and madrona burl cabinets made by Stultz Manufacturing of Kansas City, the sub-contractors for all the yacht's woodwork, are joined by spectacular marbles and beautifully matched carpets and fabrics. Guests are

Above ✦ One side of the spacious his-and-hers bathrooms in the master suite features a two-person spa pool.

Opp. left ✦ The master suite, entered through a private office, is the ultimate retreat.

Right ✦ Guests aboard *Allegra* are treated well with two double and two California-twin staterooms, all with shoji blinds, Jacuzzi™ tubs, and cedar-lined closets.

★ ALLEGRA 47

accommodated in similar style in two double and two California-twin staterooms of equal size which open from a spacious lower deck lobby that is laid with a combination of delightful *crema marfil* and *breccia pernice* marble and brought to life with vivid paintings. Shoji blinds covering the portlights project soft light onto the warm tones of the cabins, all provided with Jacuzzi™ tubs and cedar-lined closets. The owners can rest assured, whatever the status of their guests, there will be no complaints about their rooms.

Among the yacht's working areas, guests will only get to see the bridge during the course of their visit. It is well designed to receive them, and includes a semi-circle of leather seating positioned to give a comprehensive view of the facia panel which boasts an array of the latest equipment. Screens dominate: twin ARPA radars from Simrad; the Caterpillar control screen which can call up the engine instrumentation, diagnostics and historic information; and a pair of computer screens which can display information from chart plotter to ship's accounts, and even offer up television programs.

Unseen aspects of the yacht live up to its overt quality. The aluminum hull has ABS design certification and incorporates five watertight bulkheads. Crew quarters in the bow have a good-size mess room and three twin-bunked cabins, although the laundry area could be improved by enlarging it enough to allow for an ironing board. The captain has a pleasant cabin aft of the bridge, while the chief engineer is very sensibly quartered aft, alongside the dive room in the stern and adjacent to his engine room.

Building on experience from last year's *Victory Lane*, water tank capacity has been increased and the Kilopak generators have been mounted fore and aft on either side of the engine room entrance to permit the watermakers to be positioned alongside. Otherwise the immaculate layout of the room, dominated by its red-painted 2,250hp Caterpillar 3512B diesels, remains much the same. Fresh from her launch they provided a top speed of 27 knots on early trials, but with her interior fitted and at half-load condition, the top speed is now a realistic 24 knots and continuous cruise 20 knots. Cruising at 11 knots, her 17,161gal

Opp. top (inset) — Allegra moves with grace through the water.

Opp. bottom — The pilothouse on *Allegra* is designed to accommodate guests, with a curved leather lounge overlooking the helm.

Left — The engine room is spacious, and has twin generators, twin watermakers, and red-painted Caterpillar 12-cylinder diesels that push *Allegra* to a top speed of 24 knots.

fuel tanks permit an impressive 6,500nm range.

One reason for Sabates' outstanding success is that when he builds a yacht he acts much as an owner, making demands of the yard and taking on the often difficult decisions on layout and function himself. Of course a yard can also make such decisions, but the subtle difference is that a yard is often tempted to choose the easier, less costly solution when a conflict or problem arises, which can compromise the finished product in the eyes of a potential owner. Sabates sells yachts because, in general, they were not built under such compromises, and because his experience of the market, along with that of John Posgay, allows him to incorporate the best mix of layout, features, design, and equipment at an attractive price.

Because of the time taken to build a superyacht of this quality, visitors to the next Fort Lauderdale Boat Show will not see a new *Victory Lane* of this size, but you can bet that in the year after, not only will an enhanced *Victory Lane* be gracing the show, but it will be sold by the end of it!

SPECIFICATIONS

LOA	156ft. (47.54m)
Beam	28ft (8.53m)
Draft (half load)	7ft (2.13m)
Engines	2 x 2,250hp caterpillar 512B diesels
Gearboxes	ZF BW465
Shafts	2 x Aquatech 22HS
Propellers	2 x 5-blade Nibral
Speed (max/cruise)	24/20 knots
Fuel capacity	17,161 gallons
Range at 11 knots	6,500nm
Electricity generation	2 x 90KW Caterpillar 3304
Stabilizers	Naiad 505
Bow thruster	American Bow Thruster
Owner and guests	3 x double and 2 x twin staterooms
Crew	Captain and 6 crew
Construction	Aluminum hull and superstructure
Classification	ABS ✠ A1, AMS Yachting Service
Interior design	Dee Robinson/Carolyn Sabates
Exterior styling	Paragon Design/Victory Lane
Naval architecture	Trinity Yachts
Builder/Year	Trinity Yachts, New Orleans, LA /1998

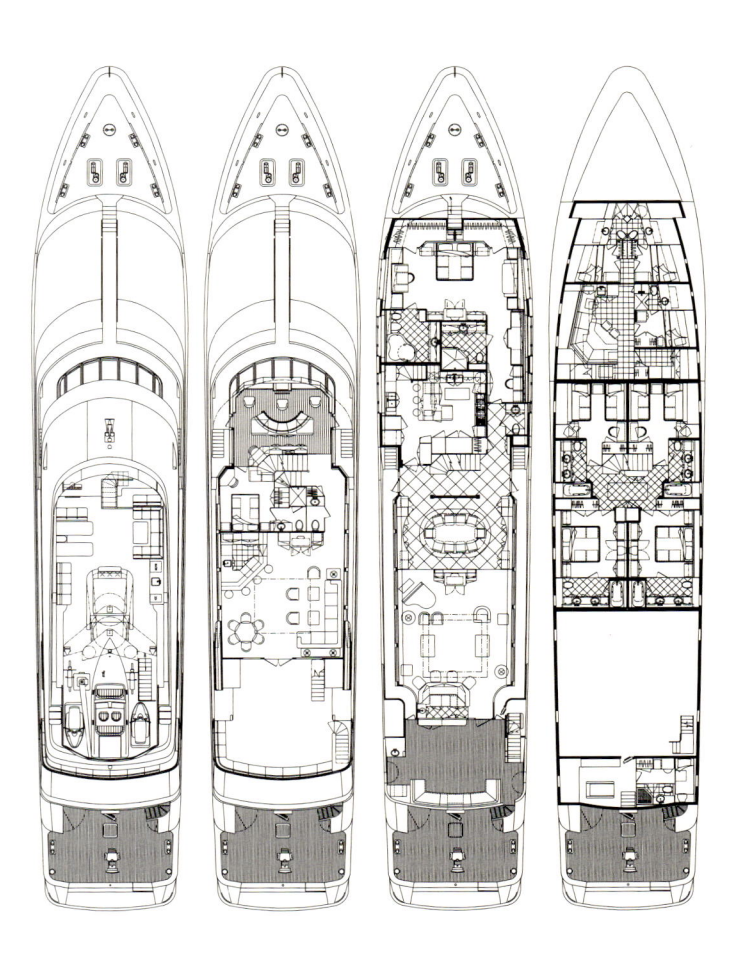

THE STARSHIP ANDROMEDA

115-foot Staysail Schooner

Faced with a maze of marina piers while looking for this big schooner, I stopped a salty-looking fellow to ask for directions as he walked past. "*Andromeda*?" I asked. Tossing his head toward a far corner of the marina, he replied with a grin, "You can't miss her!"

And he was right. With more than 35 years poking around every sort of yacht on the waterfronts of the world, I can honestly say that I've never seen anything quite like *Andromeda*.

And, like most new-tech, high-tech, cutting-edge projects, *Andromeda* polarizes anyone who visits her. You will either love her or you'll hate her: there is absolutely no gray area in between.

Either way, however, you will come away impressed by the superlative craftsmanship on this yacht. Every detail, including those that will never see the light of day, has been painstakingly crafted and every system is designed and assembled specifically for *Andromeda*. In fact, as I was being given a tour of the yacht, it became almost a game to see if I could find a single item — a cleat or perhaps a turning block — that was an off-the-shelf purchase. I didn't win. Everything from the custom masts to the smallest deck fittings was fabricated for a place and a purpose aboard this yacht.

For most builders, a business card serves as an introduction to new clients. Omega Marine Developers, on the other hand, chose a 115-foot, 90-ton calling card as a way of showing off their talents to potential customers. And, whether you love or hate *Andromeda*, you can't fault the superb quality throughout the yacht.

In many ways, *Andromeda* is a blend of old and new. With a traditional full keel, attached rudder, and long (32ft!) overhangs, the steel hull has a classic sweep to her sheer. Yet from the wales up, she is straight out of a George Lucas sci-fi thriller with a small aluminum pilothouse that sports a sweptback New Millennium look. The staysail schooner rig is not just traditional, but a throwback to an era before the advent of electric winches and roller furlers that eliminated the need for small and easily handled sails. *Andromeda* has all the sophisticated furlers and sail trim systems, of course, but on a classic rig. And that may well be an advantage, since the staysails require neither booms nor the towering masts of today's mega-sailing yachts, and the staysail schooner has always proven to be fast upwind.

Omega Marine Developers is a new company which, without any preconceived notions of what many might consider impossible, simply set out to build a yacht

Porthole If you're looking for a thrill, the lounge seats on the mastheads are sure to provide it, particularly under sail.

Opp. left The aft lounge area has twin marble tables linked hydraulically to gimbal for comfortable dining at any angle of heel.

Above Under sail, *Andromeda* has a classic staysail schooner rig, but a sci-fi deck and superstructure.

Right A sheet block is a good example of the "boat jewelry" made from flawlessly welded and highly polished stainless steel.

★ ANDROMEDA

THE MegaYachts USA ★ 2000

Opp. top left The saloon features a semi-circle of seating that are also used for dining.

Opp. bottom left The entire saloon lounge area can be converted into a dining area with a Corinthian burled elm table that turns and expands to 11ft.

Left The stainless steel and granite galley has every possible amenity, including cleverly designed nesting storage for utensils.

unlike any other. Starting with a blank sheet of paper, I can imagine the principals sitting around a conference table throwing out ideas for the new project.

"Wouldn't it be great if we could have elevators that went up the masts?" one would ask, only to have another suggest mounting comfortable lounge seats at the mastheads.

"How about using the whole midship deck area as a disco dance floor and party area?" says one designer, and another points out that it could also provide plenty of space for on-deck storage of tenders.

"With a schooner," someone points out, "We could hang a circus net between the spreaders that would be like a huge hammock," while another wants an awning system that covers the entire deck and still folds away hydraulically.

The ideas flow faster and farther out: a hot tub on deck for a dozen guests with a hydraulic lid for weather protection, a huge lounge covered by a power-assisted all-weather bubble, an observation wing for guests to ride two stories above the water, a theater-quality disco light and sound system, a hydraulic garage and swim platform on the stern, a passerelle that doubles as a crane to lift a racing catamaran onto backstay cradles, a spacious dining room that has an oversized opening skylight for alfresco meals, and—well, that gives you an idea of the "blue-skying" that must have gone into the planning sessions.

And yet, as startling as it all seems, Omega not only succeeded in designing, prototyping, and building all these unusual systems, but each works flawlessly. If, like many boat owners, you are a connoisseur of fine metalwork, you will delight in what Omega calls "boat jewelry." Blocks, stanchions, anchor rollers, and most of the deck gear have been crafted of mirror-finished stainless steel, with invisible welds and a style that jeweler Harry Winston could appreciate.

So where do you start a tour of *Andromeda*? Without a doubt, the unusual features that nearly every visitor wants to experience are the mast elevators. Each mast has a two-person hydraulic elevator that I was surprised to find are as smooth as the ones in office buildings. Once at the top of either mast, you can settle into a two-person lounge seat complete with reclining back, foam upholstery, bimini top, and, of course, a safety belt. You can also disembark from the elevator at either the upper or lower spreaders, which have non-slip surfaces and integral safety harnesses and lifelines.

That brings us to the "sky net," actually four acrobatic safety nets that can be mounted between either the upper or lower spreaders on each mast. Secured by safety pennants and body harnesses, guests can get the thrill of their life in this huge hammock as the yacht heels over under sail and the "sky riders" are suspended over the water.

But it's back on deck where Omega principal Paul Nettinga and Carl Rochte, who served as the inspiration for much of the project, point to the midship deck as the "centerpiece" of *Andromeda*. Unusual in the sense that the deck area of most large yachts is taken up either by the cabin house or by cockpit seating, the open mid-deck on *Andromeda* underlines the entertainment side of this yacht. Designed from the outset to be a social center for the yacht both at anchor and underway, the area from the foremast aft to the pilothouse is perfectly suited for parties. The area is large enough to carry an array of water toys and tenders, including up to a 22ft launch, a pair of

★ ANDROMEDA 53

Right ★ One of the two amidships staterooms that features pillow-top mattresses, and full sound and thermal insulation.

Below ★ All of the bathrooms are finished in black and gray Avonite, with whirlpool tubs and Grohe 24kt gold fixtures.

Opp. top right ★ Beyond the granite bar is the navigation station, with full electronics and communications systems.

Opp. middle ★ The compact pilothouse is straight from Star Trek, with panels for electrical systems, hydraulic systems, and a computer screen to monitor ships systems.

personal watercraft, and a compact inflatable. But once the twin knuckle cranes to port and starboard have launched the fleet, the area can be used as a dance floor, an outdoor dining area, or just for sunning. A large lounge is at the base of the mainmast and a removable 4ft-by-7ft hospitality table has integral deck mountings for alfresco dinners or entertaining.

But there's more to the midship deck than meets the eye during the day, and night brings out the party animal side of *Andromeda*. Surrounded by professional quality JBL studio speakers, the midship deck can become the centerpoint of a light show from four computer-driven High End track spotlights suspended under the spreaders that are identical to the "smart" lights used in theatrical productions. "This isn't just an 'imitation disco' as on most yachts," says Nettinga, pointing out that a medium-size disco would use only two of the High End spots, while there are four aboard *Andromeda*. Tivoli lighting encircles the deck with chase patterns to add sparkle, mast uplights accent the elevators, and 13 starburst aviation strobe lights are located on the mastheads, spreaders, and each end of the yacht to create brilliant random patterns of light. With everything lit, there would be no mistaking *Andromeda* in any anchorage.

Day or night, the deck can easily be covered by a scalloped sun awning fitted to the integral arms and supports that slide into place, allowing the deck to be covered from bow to stern in just minutes.

At the base of the foremast is a futuristic superstructure that incorporates a 10ft octagonal Jacuzzi™ spa discreetly hidden behind one-way black safety glass. Fingertip controls elevate the aerodynamic cover and, once inside, guests can close the cover for privacy that allows them to see out without anyone seeing in.

Aft of the pilothouse, a protected wraparound lounge area has been created for open-air dining, with twin gimbaled marble tables that are hydraulically linked to allow comfortable dining at any angle of heel. Nearby is a built-in barbecue which, with a powerful exhaust fan, is able to use mesquite or hickory charcoal to season the food.

Aft, the "bubble lounge" is another of the unique features that mark *Andromeda*. A king-size lounge upholstered in soft black glove leather, it can be covered by a molded black Plexiglas dome, allowing the occupants to enjoy the passing scenery or simply watch the wake, regardless of wind or weather. Inside, music controls, personal lighting, and a telephone are close at hand.

Rather than having a conventional swim platform aft, *Andromeda* sports a tubular stainless steel frame stretched with netting, which submerges well into the water to provide easy access for swimmers. *Andromeda* is fitted with commercial quality diving equipment with the capacity to refill 12 scuba tanks per hour, and two "hooka" systems provide non-scuba guests with adventure. The hydraulic transom passerelle not only serves as access to the swimming platform under the counter, but can also extend astern and up to 90° to port for boarding from shore.

The builders have found that the flybridge is a point where guests congregate while sailing, and three recliner seats that adapt to any angle of heel are atop the pilothouse roof, where a special set of arms can be hydraulically deployed to extend a sun awning over the helm and flybridge seating. The helm seat provides room for the skipper and a guest, with banks of switches surrounding the helm to control sail trim and a host of systems.

The roller furling rig was designed by Frank Maclear using custom furlers built by Nissan Pacific, and the sails can be completely furled or unfurled in less than five minutes. The more than 5300 sqft of North sails, plus a 3000 sqft gennaker, are trimmed by sheet winches custom-built by Nissan Pacific. The rig is supported by galvanized shrouds coated in a mil-spec preservative and covered with Type 316 stainless steel tubing sheaths.

Belowdecks *Andromeda* is just as unusual, although there are fewer gadgets and more systems (which control the on-deck gadgets). The pilothouse is compact, with a helm to starboard that is ready for Captain Kirk and the Star Trek crew. Custom electrical and hydraulic panels take up every inch of space around the skipper's seat, and a computer screen monitors a host of systems.

To port is a bar that would do justice to a Michelin restaurant, with racks for 30 bottles in three tiers, an overhead wine rack for another 15 bottles, and stemware storage for 60 glasses. The granite bullnosed counter seats three on custom stools, and guests have a joystick to control the view from the masthead video cameras. An adjoining navigation area has a granite chart table, comprehensive electronics, and communication systems.

The saloon is forward at the end of a short passageway, with a lounge area to port and a formal dining area for eight. The lounge area can be fitted with a cocktail table, and has a clear view of the television to starboard. The dining table, of Corinthian burled elm with ebony inlays, stands on two pillars of mirror-polished stainless steel and can be turned and expanded to a length of 11ft so that the entire saloon becomes a dining area, since the lounge seats were made at the right height for table seating.

Outboard to starboard is a granite-topped service cabinet with an undercounter beverage cooler, and deep drawers custom-fitted to hold the flatware and dinnerware. Two different table services are included, with Pickard china for the formal settings (complete with platinum chargers) and flatware from Christofle Hotel of France. Tablecloths and linens are from Rivolta Carmignani of Italy.

The accommodation deck has four relatively equal staterooms, and a fifth cabin is located on a lower level. Aft of the pilothouse, a pair of identical staterooms are arranged to provide matched accommodations for an

Left   Ensconced in the net slung between the masts, guests enjoy hanging far over the water as *Andromeda* heels.

Below right   The "cocoon" near the stern is an all-weather lounge covered by a power-assisted Plexiglas bubble, complete with stereo, personal lighting, and a telephone.

Bottom left   The Jacuzzi™ spa not only holds ten guests, but has a hydraulically activated lid for all-weather protection.

Bottom right   Underway, guests have a choice of several on-deck lounges or the observation wing on the foremast.

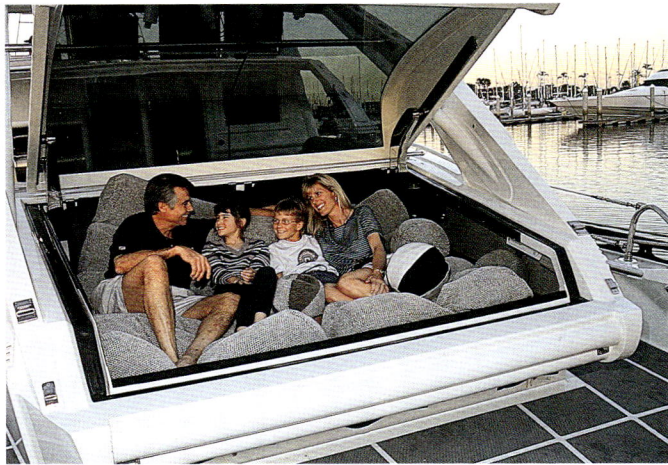

owner and his wife, with each using one stateroom as a personal dressing area and lounge. Each suite has a queen-size berth, and the en suite bathrooms are finished in black and gray Avonite, with black porcelain washbasins and whirlpool tubs set with 24kt gold Grohe fixtures. Two more staterooms are located amidships, with twin berths and en suite heads with whirlpool baths. A fifth double stateroom is located on a lower level, as well as a head with shower.

All of the staterooms feature specially made pillow-top mattresses, television and entertainment centers, and complete thermal and acoustic insulation to provide both

SPECIFICATIONS

Length	115ft (35m)
Length Waterline	83ft (25.3m)
Beam	22ft (6.7m)
Draft	13ft 5in (4.1m)
Displacement	180 tons
Ballast	35 tons lead
Construction	Steel hull, aluminum superstructure
Rig	Schooner
Designer	Omega Marine Developers
Interior Layout	Sciomachen Yacht Design
Rig	Frank Maclear
Exterior Profile	Nissan Design Group
Interior Design	Brindan Byrne Design
Builder/Year	Omega Marine Developers/1997

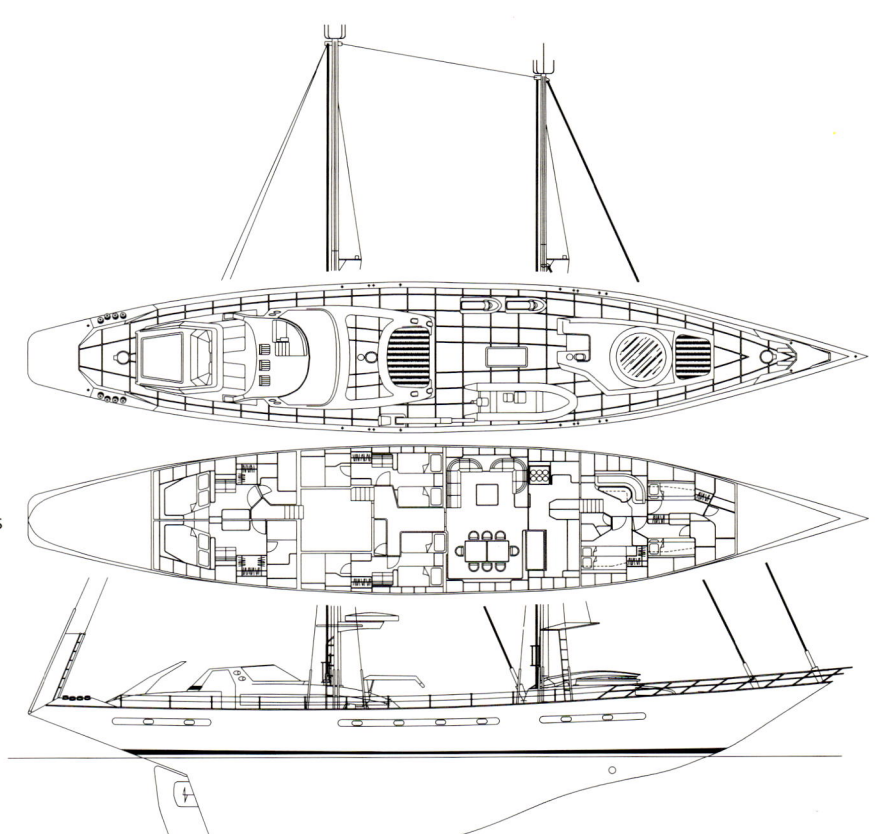

silence and optimal temperature control. The staterooms also use architectural light painting fixtures that provide an ever-changing variety of lighting moods as the programmable timer continually cycles the system.

The galley is forward of the saloon, with a complete inventory of utensils with carefully designed nesting storage for each. Designed and outfitted on a commercial scale, the galley has a double-wide and extra-deep Volrath refrigerator/freezer with a set of custom roller bearing drawers that roll completely out and then return to lock in place. Other appliances include a Toastmaster six-burner stove/oven, stainless steel Panasonic commercial microwave, Robo Coupe food processor, Waring blender, stainless steel dishwasher, deep fryer, trash compactor, and garbage disposal. On the deck below the galley are two additional custom-built deep freeze boxes.

Crew quarters are forward, with two double bunk cabins and a captain's single berth cabin, all with heads and showers. A crew lounge is opposite the galley, and a private entry is through an electric gullwing door in the superstructure surrounding the Jacuzzi™.

Décor throughout the yacht was done by Brindan Byrne Design, using an Imron finish of heather, accented by beige carpeting, bulkheads, and overheads of ultrasuede, and polished stainless steel accents. Carrying out the ancient Greek motif of the yacht are sand-carved glass panels in everything from shower doors to locker panels bearing either Greek artwork or the *Andromeda* constellation of stars.

As you might expect from the array of hydraulic gadgets, a sophisticated 2500 PSI hydraulic power system is distributed throughout *Andromeda*, with electrically driven main and back-up pumps, and a third PTO pump off the main engine. Power for the yacht is a 3406B turbocharged and aftercooled Caterpillar diesel, and the yacht has three generators: a 60kW Lima and a 20kW Lima, both with John Deere diesel power, and a 10kW night generator mounted in the bow with Kubota diesel power.

Andromeda is remarkably equipped with everything from twin 80 hp. bow thrusters to two watermakers (1800/gpd total), twin hydraulic anchor windlasses, an arc and heli-arc welder, and even a commercial icemaker that produces 100 pounds per day.

Keeping track of the systems aboard is a 3.1 gigabyte Pentium computer that includes a 19-volume operating manual, a comprehensive maintenance manual, full ship's drawings, a 19-volume component list, and a ship's storage and inventory.

Aside from the unusual design and the array of gadgets, *Andromeda* is notable for superlative construction. The watermakers, for example, roll out on a stainless steel chassis for servicing, and beautifully crafted stainless steel drip pans hold any condensation from the air handlers. In the pilothouse, a display has LED lights to show the open or closed status of any porthole on the entire yacht.

Love her or hate her, there will probably never be another yacht like *Andromeda*. And her builders could not have chosen a better way to show off their design abilities and construction talents.

★ ANDROMEDA

Dare to Dream

115-foot Crescent Motoryacht

No single moment crystallizes the complex process of building a custom, luxury vessel more than its launch. And surely no action supersedes the juxtaposition of function and form as the vessel is finally eased into the water for the very first time. That much anticipated encounter came last fall for *Dare to Dream*, a new 115-footer from the Pacific Northwest's Crescent Custom Yachts.

Dare to Dream's precise passage down the narrow ramp to the marina was carefully navigated by a giant tractor and hydraulic dollies that eased her with inches to spare past the yacht club's deck. For a short time, those who had come to watch were treated to an unimpeded vision of her substantial, gleaming white hull and rugged working side. Once safely in the water, however, the sleekness of this vessel quickly became apparent. Her exterior, styled by Jack W. Sarin Naval Architects, is defined by the suggestion of a seamless wedge that dives from stern to prow, accentuated by a single line of smoked glass from the spacious aft cockpit to the aggressively raked wedge nose. Above, the pilothouse, extended flybridge, and raked arch mast accentuate the main deck's streamlined form.

The look is minimalist and functional but also paradoxical, for *Dare to Dream* is a vessel whose simple, streamlined exterior belies a wealth of interior detail and sophisticated luxury, not to mention an immense personal statement. The new vessel represents some 110,000 hours of custom work, a fact that reflects supreme interest and attention on the part of the owner, who worked closely with Tom Horvath of Richard Bertram Yacht Sales. Horvath, who was involved in the building on a daily basis, says Crescent was selected for its ability to create a custom layout in almost any way desired within the Sarin-designed, soft-riding Westport hull. The owner's previous vessel — a 110ft Broward — also served as a solid foundation on which to build, as well as providing inspiration for the unprecedented modifications which achieve a quintessential balance of style and substance on board *Dare to Dream*.

Crescent says its usual estimate to complete a yacht of this size would be around 80 to 85,000 hours. However, the extensive use of hand-selected and custom-bleached wood and other fine materials, orchestrated by Patrick Knowles Design Group, along with the often highly ingenious departures from conventional design, required considerable effort. "To achieve quality like this takes time and patience. There are no short cuts," says Crescent's Greg Tiemann. He suggests that, in terms of interior design, *Dare to Dream* is one of the most sophisticated vessels the company has created to date. Yet despite its blend of technology and detail-driven design, this is also a vessel that exudes an easy warmth and comfortable familiarity.

Upon entering the main saloon through an electric sliding glass door aft, the eye is immediately drawn to the height and ornate design of a vaulted ceiling above the dining saloon, which presents an unusual added dimension to an already spacious and well-appointed room. On the instruction of the owner, who felt the space could be put to more imaginative use than was stipulated in the original plans, the normal height of around 7ft was increased to an impressive 9ft 3in, according to Patrick Knowles. The void had initially been earmarked for specifics such as wiring and ducts, but all were relocated

Porthole ★ Designed for informal family gatherings and surrounded by windows, an open lounge was created on the main deck forward of the galley.

Above ★ The distinctive wedge shape is virtually seamless from foredeck to cockpit, creating the effect of motion, even at rest.

Left ★ The flybridge is a continuation of the overall informal atmosphere, with twin settees and tables for entertaining and a spa aft.

★ Dare to Dream 59

or redirected to gain the desired height. Once structurally organized, the raised ceiling and inclined Majilite side panels were finished with mappa burl and plexi mirror inlays, while the central panel is highlighted in gold leaf. The ceiling treatment is only a small element of the detail that sets this area apart. The dining table, made of clear tempered glass with maple and mappa burl inlays and which can comfortably accommodate 12, is directly centered beneath the raised ceiling. Here again, the owner requested a one-of-a-kind design, with a glass and wood bullnose, but no height differential, between the materials. Challenging in its construction, the table's glass had to be laminated in a dado profile and rabbeted with a little step to give the same profile to the corresponding perimeter frame.

Maple cabinetry dividing the dining saloon from the main saloon employs curved glass and interior accent lighting over a granite base. Fine china and glassware is cosseted from breakage by formed Divinycell throughout the dining and saloon area—another example of the owner's fastidious attention to detail, and understanding of the need for well-executed storage.

Working technology is rarely far beneath *Dare to Dream*'s carefully detailed surface. Against the forward bulkhead, and complementing the entire setting, a maple sideboard contains one of myriad components that make

Main Picture ✳ The saloon is spacious, spanning the length of the full beam. The 7ft headroom draws attention to the maple and mappa burl paneling.

Left ✳ The ornate vaulted ceiling over the dining saloon soars over 9ft, presenting an added dimension to a well-appointed room.

up a sophisticated home entertainment system. At the touch of a button, a projector and platform lowers from behind a ceiling panel, while its screen is concealed above the sideboard, and flanked by maple-encased speakers worked into the cabinet. This is a vessel full of such subtle touches and discrete surprises. The speakers are an adjunct to the main system, which features a flat-screen 4-inch plasma television with full audio, video, and full sound components housed in the port aft bulkhead, all enclosed in a 6ft-tall maple-paneled cabinet. The system has to sound as good as it looks, no matter where you're sitting. Hence, a flick of a hidden switch reverses the surround-sound speaker system, depending on which component is in use—another innovation accredited to the owner.

An oval bar with sunken floor behind allows the bartender to be at eye level with guests seated on swivel chairs. Smoked windows on three sides wrap the room, whose spaciousness is accentuated by its full-beam width and the absence of any external walkway obstructing the view. The exclusion of the walkway, explains Horvath, permitted a full beam of 24ft, which in turn allows a main saloon of proportions normally found on a 150ft yacht.

The craftsmanship that elevates the main saloon is echoed throughout the vessel, but particularly in the forward port spiral stairwell that descends to the master stateroom and guest accommodations. Here a symphony of cleverly contrasting lines and seamless panels come together in elegant symbiosis, as gently curving stairs reach the lower foyer, dominated by a compass rose design on a Crema Marfil field and Uba Tuba inlays. The stairwell's height required ingenious blending of horizontal veneer seams with a mappa burl inlay that coils around the interior spiral. Below, a maple console combines the foyer's elements with mappa burl in its bow-front panels and Uba Tuba inlays below a gilt-framed mirror. Mappa-inlaid double maple doors open to the full-beam master stateroom, with mappa burl and inlaid plexi mirror-ceiling detail that conforms to the proportions of the queen-size bed. Forward of the stateroom, his and hers en suites are well appointed (with over-sized shower and Jacuzzi™ respectively), reached by separate doors on either side. All closets are full-length and cedar-lined. Aft of the master stateroom and foyer—beyond a concealed washer and dryer unit and behind doors with bird's-eye maple inlay—are twin guest staterooms, each with private shower rooms. Reached by a forward stairwell are a full-beam VIP stateroom with maple trim accentuated by natural light from a skylight, and an en suite shower room, as well as adjacent guest staterooms and concealed washer and dryer. The crew's quarters are found between the aft cockpit and the engine room, with its 1,800hp MTU 16v 2000 twin diesels, firefighting and emergency bilge pump systems, day tanks, and fuel storage all organized for easy access.

A principal requirement of the owner's brief was that *Dare to Dream* be, above all, a family vessel with plenty of room for informal gatherings. To that end, forward on the main deck, a full wraparound dinette with glass on both sides provides the perfect venue for spontaneous get-togethers. As elsewhere, no space is left unused: the forward, full-width bulkhead mirror panel conceals a four-cubic-foot freezer. The owner's propensity for practicality had an intended pantry just aft of the spacious galley—with granite surfaces and expansive maple cabinetry—converted into what he describes as the "brains of the boat." The standing-room space has been re-allocated to house the vessel's entire electrical and computer systems, all arranged for ease of access under the starboard stairwell to the pilothouse. In fact, throughout the vessel, no void that offers any storage potential has survived such keen scrutiny.

If the brains are in the kitchen, the heart of *Dare to Dream*'s operations is found in the pilothouse, reached by asymmetric port and starboard stairwells, each meticulously crafted. Full instrumentation incorporating all navigation and security systems—cameras are subtly concealed throughout the vessel's exterior—are wrapped in teak. Here again is a surprisingly intimate, well-planned

Opp. top ★ A wide galley counter faces out onto the casual lounge area that fills the forward area of the main deck.

Above ★ The detail around the mirrored ceiling and nightstand in the master suite incorporates the same mappa burl that is used throughout the interior.

Left ★ The master suite is entered via double doors from a foyer that features a maple console that has Uba Tuba inlays under a gilt mirror.

★ DARE TO DREAM 63

Right ★ Heading out beyond the Golden Gate Bridge, *Dare to Dream* shows off her speed as she sets out on a voyage.

Below ★ The pilothouse was carefully owner-engineered to include a full-sized chart table and a lounge area for guests while underway.

Opp. bottom left ★ The flybridge helm is superbly equipped with duplicate electronics, and a pair of wing controls simplifies docking.

space that bears the owner's stamp. A full-sized chart table and drawer at working height cleverly slides away under the outside roof line. The warmth and intimacy of the room is further enhanced by teak flooring, while a raised aft platform and cozy booth offer guests a good view of activities. A short stairwell leads up to the flybridge deck.

There is evidence all around that this is a craft intended for fun and easy socializing. Twin settees and facing tables that accommodate 12 are just aft of the three-seat helm and controls in a convivial arrangement that includes an eight-person Jacuzzi™, Marquip hoist, 17ft Novurania runabout, and a pair of Seadoos. The sloping nose hinges up to reveal an immense storage area, big enough to house a new VW Beetle, says Horvath, but more likely to accommodate the vessel's twin Honda scooters and other toys. Aft, a simple spiral staircase descends to a full transom cockpit, desired as a safety consideration for grandchildren, but also to keep following seas from rolling in during rough water. Here, below a canopy — which also houses life jackets — is a sheltered dining area. Again the owner's ingenious solutions to save space allows a 250lb table to roll effortlessly into place across from a bench that backs onto the aft bulkhead. The unit slides on tracks concealed in the decking and stores flush to the engine room bulkhead when not in use. The final exterior touch — and another inspiration of the owner — is a nighttime, kaleidoscopic fiber optics package that channels variable colors along the vessel's distinctive line beneath the pilothouse. The effect is one more piece of evidence that fittingly named *Dare to Dream* is a statement of fantasy turned to reality — where the owner's wishes have materialized quite literally at every glance.

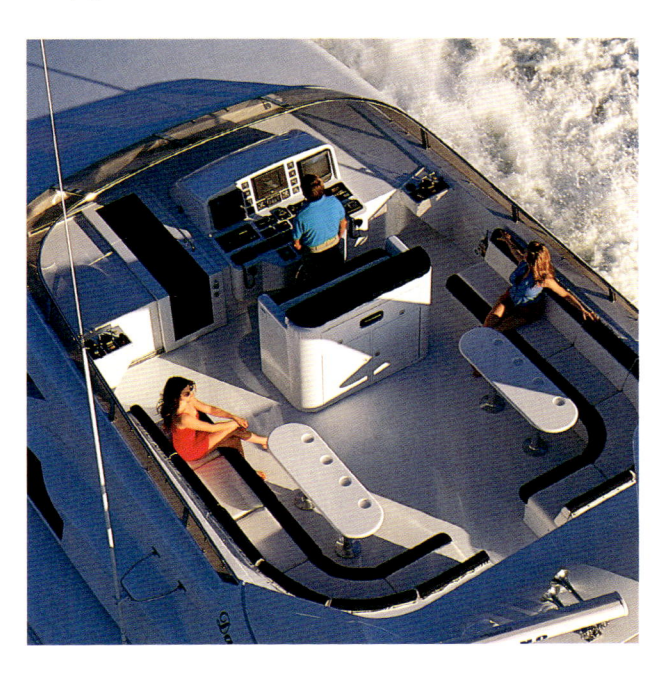

SPECIFICATIONS

LOA	115ft (35.05m)
Beam	24ft (7.32m)
Draft	6ft 6in (2m)
Displacement	156 tons
Engines	Twin 1,800hp 16v 2000 MTU/DDC
Gearboxes	ZF Gearboxes
Speed (max/cruise)	23/19 Knots
Fuel capacity	6,200 gallons
Generators	2 x 55kW Northern Lights
Bowthruster	American Bow Thruster
Stabilizers	Naiad
Interior design	Knowles Design Group
Naval architect/ Exterior styling	Jack W Sarin Naval Architects
Builder/Year	Crescent Custom Yachts/1998

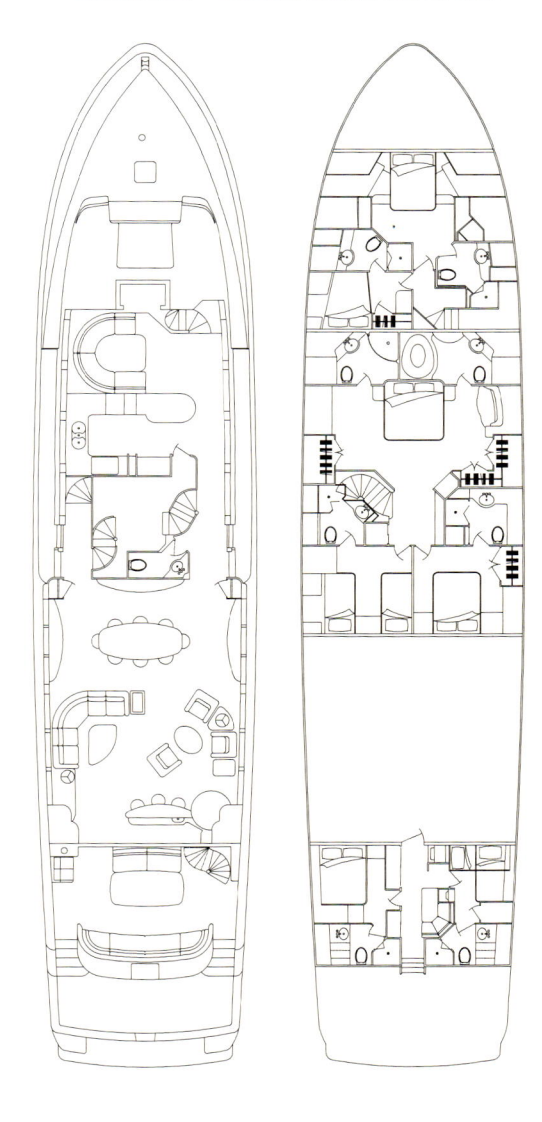

★ Dare to Dream

DISCOVERY

100-foot Romsdal Trawler

Prominently hung over the mantelpiece in the main saloon of the *M/V Discovery* is an oil painting of the *T/S Veendam* off the Battery in New York, on a June day in 1952. The artist, Captain Stephen Card, is meticulous about chronological accuracy, so the steam tug, the Staten Island ferry, and the Whitehall buildings are exactly as they would have looked that day. Next to the oil is a framed photo of John Treffers and his family, arriving from the Netherlands to begin a new life. John was 12 at the time.

Since then his life has taken many an interesting turn, and now it seems to be circling back to seaward; the family, the voyage, this time back to Holland and beyond. This is the story of the derelict Nordic vessel he found for the voyage and its exceptional rebuild.

Docked in Lake Union in the vicinity of the NOAA research vessels, the *MV Discovery* could possibly pass for one of that fleet. With the lines, the stack, and the fortitude of a small ship, her fair blue hull seems destined for discovery. She was a research vessel once, in the 60's, in an earlier incarnation, and her substantial navigation and operating systems could support some serious work aboard. But owners John and Sandi Treffers would not call their creation an expedition yacht. They simply want to cruise and live aboard, comfortably and securely; to entertain friends and family, but with no pretense of expedition. They wish to have the option of running it themselves, so the code of the vessel is safe, strong and informal, with lots of mechanical backups.

John is recently retired from a precision manufacturing enterprise in Arizona, and he enjoys the challenge of a complex undertaking. He had owned several vessels before, power and sail, but never built one. When he saw a photo of the 100ft steel trawler, *Syringa*, lying in Seattle, John Treffers saw the lines he desired for the boat of his vision. Built as a yacht by Romsdal in Norway in the 60's, it had the lines of a fishing trawler—a canoe stern, graceful sheer and low freeboard amidships, with a whaleback style foredeck. It had served several masters in its time but, when he found it, the *Syringa* had been neglected in a Lake Union dry dock for 15 years.

Commissioning this custom yacht rebuild, his vision carried him far into the domain of boat design, since building on the original steel hull structure was much more complex than starting from scratch. He couldn't find the perfect yard to undertake the project, so he contracted it himself. He hired designer Jonathan Quinn Barnett and an exceptional crew of individual craftsmen from the Seattle area to implement that dream. Three years later the result is a triumph of form meeting function. The yacht is beautifully and solidly built, full of character and light.

The original boatdeck amidships is an unusual yacht feature, and some might have elected to change it. This owner and designer recognized its utility and have handily incorporated it into use as the quayside boarding area. To port and starboard, a section of bulwark folds down flat amidships as a gangway, and where access is needed to the ship's boat or a swim ladder, a hydraulic stairway extends from its aft end. The teak planked deck is broad and danceable, and visually enhanced by an appealing curved stairway up to the foredeck. The owners foresee the boat deck canopied for open air dining, using an efficient small bar and service galley installed just inside the portside entry to the forecastle.

Porthole ✦ The cheerful Dutch tiles in the galley reflect the owner's heritage.

Above ✦ The very essence of rugged seaworthiness, *Discovery* is ready for new adventures, thanks to a thoughtful and thorough rebuild.

Left ✦ The boat deck, perfect for outdoor entertaining, is the main boarding area via fold-out bulwarks that become gangways.

★ DISCOVERY 67

Right ★ The saloon is compact, with fireplace, davenport, and easy chairs.

Below ★ Cast glass panels enclose sweeping stairs leading down to the master stateroom directly below the saloon.

Opposite ★ The galley combines hand-painted tiles with granite counters and a commercial stainless-steel range.

The forecastle cabin is secured by a watertight submarine-style door when underway. The stateroom can serve as crew cabin when more guests are aboard: it has a full bath, two berths, settee, entertainment and vessel monitoring systems, and a large window on the gangway, which allows in a lot of light and a preview of all visitors. There is also a stairway down to the guest quarters and engine room.

Down in the lower forecastle is a gear locker carrying the hydraulics and other systems equipment. Following the corridor aft are two large walk-in fridge freezers and to starboard a broad Corian counter with upper and lower cabinets; this crew staging area is a thoughtful platform for repairs and ease in handling quantities of provisions for a voyage. The passage opens up to a generous landing at the foot of the galley stairs, giving access down to the engine room and to two guest staterooms on the port side. This space is graced by a handsome carved cabinet with a bronze sculpture, just adjacent to a cabinet with guest fridge for drinks. To starboard a day head is located as well

68 THE MEGAYACHTS USA ★ 2000

as laundry and storage behind louvered doors.

The engine room is large and sophisticated, with control panels and monitors mindful of a larger ship. The yacht is powered by a huge Enterprise diesel, 400 horsepower and 400 rpm, rebuilt from a Canadian tug. It drives a slow turning, quiet, variable pitch propeller, and the exhaust goes up the stack. There are three generators, a watermaker, bow and stern thrusters, and much more. The owner's experience in aeronautics, and with the normal unforeseen boat problems, led him to install many backup systems into this vessel, including even an extra engine, in case of emergency.

To port of the landing, the VIP cabin has a light tone in décor. The double berth and vanity are trimmed in the signature scrollwork of mahogany and madrona burl, the linens in a lovely pale brocade. The other twin cabin is equipped with generous upper and lower berths and nautical light fixtures. Both have wardrobes and their own bathrooms en suite, all finished with cashew rose Spanish marble. Traffic for this lower level can move via the galley or the forward stairway.

The galley proper is just aft of the boat deck, reached via an entry foyer in jade and calcutta white marble. This entry from the starboard deck also serves the pilothouse and the owner's suite. Inspired by a Dutch country kitchen, the U-shaped galley gleams with promise from its appealing surfaces. Around a large central Miele cooking range, the walls are adorned with hand-painted Dutch tiles of a seafaring theme in tones of blue. Counter surfaces are clad in silver black granite with stunning flecks of royal blue, and the window curtains are Dutch lace. A large commercial fridge is along the back wall and a pantry just behind that under the stairs to the bridge, facing an exit to the port deck. Formal dining is in the main saloon, with attractive options on the deck amidships or above on the bridge.

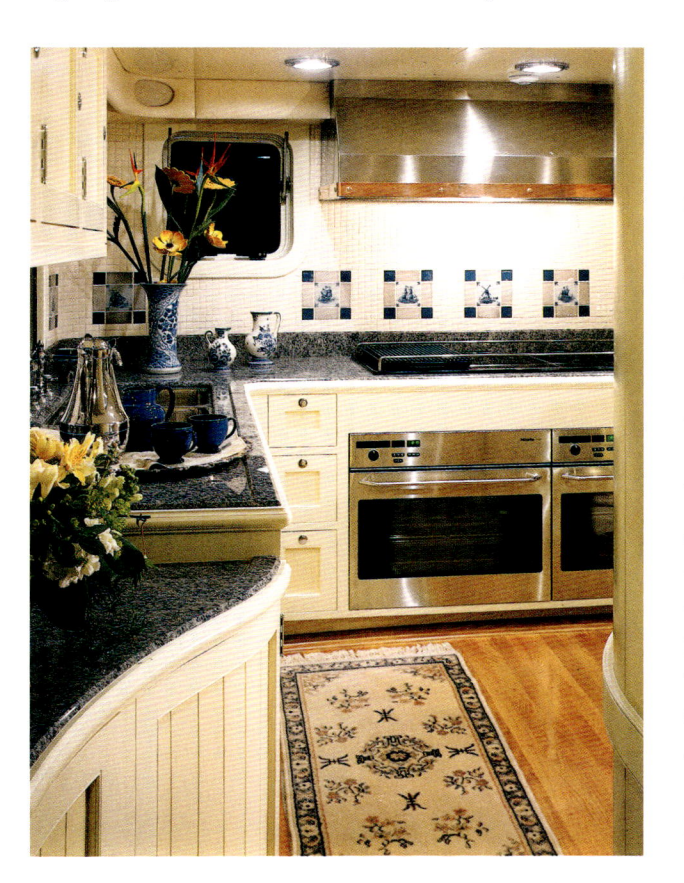

It is clear to see that this small ship was planned around the joy of travel. The wheelhouse is the heart and control center of this vessel, ably accommodating a high performance array of electronics as well as ingenious seating areas for lounging, dining, and taking in the voyage. A freestanding curved console holds the navigational equipment, radar and sonar, GPS, weather data and electronic charts, plus an innovative software program for vessel monitoring and security. Owner John Treffers wanted to be able to monitor engine trends over time to compare data, so performance information for the main engines, generators, watermakers, and hydraulics are all recorded with real time scrolling charts. A video card enables security cameras to keep an eye on all systems, as well as entry and egress on board. The implementation of this electronics package is another instance of John's vision and delegating, this time to MonArk Vessel Monitoring Systems, using Windows 95. A chart table to port completes the navigation equipment.

The wheelhouse size suggests that of a much larger ship, and its outstanding feature is the placement of the console and its seating. Forward of this grouping is an ample walkway behind the large bank of windows, with two comfortable leather seats to port and starboard. Cabinet doors on the console allow easy service access to the panoply of electronics inside. Aft of the helm, curving around the starboard corner formed by the companionway, is a commodious settee and dining area in dark blue leather. The exquisite marquetry in mahogany and madrona burl gives the impression that this living, working heart of the vessel is set in a fine and comfortable wood sculpture.

All the confluence areas and deck passages on this boat feel ample and efficient, which is a triumph in 100ft. Aft of the companionway stairs is a comfortable captain's den and day berth. There is a good-sized bathroom en suite finished in rose marble. The port side corridor leads past a quiet lounge facing aft onto the afterdeck, where the Zodiac tender and crane are positioned. From there steps lead up to a private skydeck, alongside the bright stainless-steel stack.

A great deal of living potential has been designed into just 100ft of yacht, but the layout of *M/V Discovery* is

Above ✭ Aft in the master stateroom is a comfortable library and retreat, with an office tucked under the floating stairs.

Right ✭ The central king-size bed under a matching ceiling treatment is flanked by his-and-hers baths.

Opposite ✭ The pilothouse has a walkaround area in front of the helm console, as well as comfortable seating for guests.

unusual in the sense that everything on the main and lower decks under the main superstructure, including the saloon, is considered to be part of the "owner's suite."

The traditional saloon in the aft section of the main deck, with its exceptional woodwork, is a showpiece for the solid, gracious nature of this boat. Entry is through cast-glass French doors, and the eye first falls on a lovely carved chest of rosewood and walnut burl, with ebonized strips inlaid and flush key faces. To port, a comfortable davenport, coffee table and chairs are around the fireplace. The fabric treatments are in cool cream and tans, and the overall impression is of masculine serenity.

In the aft starboard quarter of the saloon, a solid round dining table and chairs rest against the elegantly curved balustrade of madrona and mahogany marquetry and cast glass. At the far end, a symphony of harmonious

70 THE MEGAYACHTS USA ✭ 2000

SPECIFICATIONS

LOA	100ft (30.48m)
Draft	11ft (3.35m)
Beam	21ft (6.40m)
Cruise Speed	9.5 knots
Fuel Capacity	12,000 gallons
Fresh Water Capacity	2,000 gallons
Material	Steel/aluminum
Engine	Enterprise DMG 6 400hp 400 rpm
Exterior Styling/ Interior Designer	Jonathan Quinn Barnett Ltd.
Soft Furnishings & Fabrics	Lucy Design
Builder/Year	Romsdal/1962
Rebuild/Year	Discovery Shipbuilders/1999

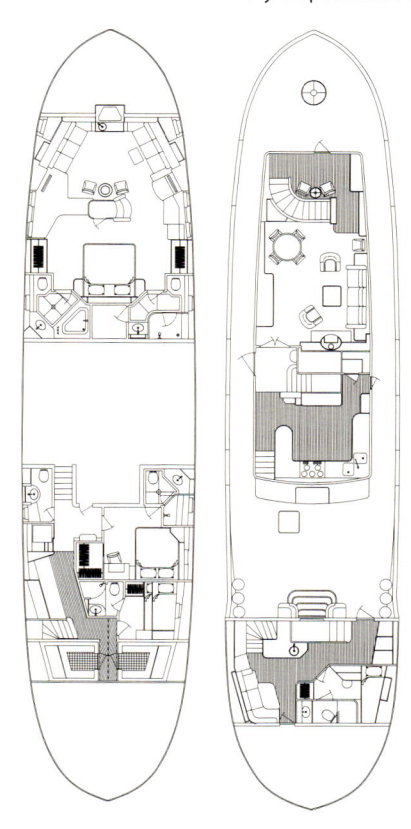

curves in jade and mahogany leads out to the intimate covered afterdeck and the chambers below. (The curved cabinets are actually storage for the buffet dining supplies, audio speakers and an air conditioning unit).

The stairs, which lead down to the owner's suite from the main saloon, are a stunning piece of architecture and a triumph of engineering. Railing, cast glass, and a mosaic of dark and light woods—mahogany, madrona burl, and ebony—lead naturally around a curve and down with the stair treads on such a gradual rise-to-run ratio that they seem to float on air. This was achieved by first creating a curving steel arc in box section and cushioning it on either end with anti-vibration rubber mounting. Then the steel and mahogany stair treads were welded in, fitted, and carpeted in short loop Karastan pile carpeting. It all began because the owners wanted an open stairway without all the spindles and balusters obstructing their view.

A very pleasant view it is, too, in the owner's private sanctuary. Aft is an office and library with golden tan couches—in a custom-woven chenille fabric—and an array of audio visual entertainment possibilities. Here in the library, on-screen repeaters bring up the navionics display from the bridge. To starboard forward lies an immense island of a bed with an ocean scene above it. Here again the woodwork is a masterpiece of artful joinery, and warm neutral colors convey a mood of peace.

The bed enclosure is flanked by a pair of outstanding full bathrooms. Her bath contains a solid mahogany two-person soaking tub, and is finished in green jade with white marble surround. His bath features a glass shower, and the floor is a stunning mosaic of jade, calcutta white marble, and gold plated inlay. A linen closet and wardrobe running athwartships is accessible through a small door at the forward end of his portside bathroom.

Flowing interior lines, thoughtful design and superior joinery distinguish this boat from stem to stern. It abounds with comfortable living spaces on deck and inside. The power plant and systems are substantial and, with a cruising range in excess of 6,000 nm and a reasonably shallow draft (11ft), she should perform well on her proposed maiden voyage to Alaska, or wherever she goes. Questions of nomenclature aside, the *M/V Discovery* seems destined for expeditions.

John Treffers ably undertook to rebuild this vessel on his own, in and outside of unnamed boatsheds on Seattle's backwaters. He succeeded so well that he just may do it again. One wonders, was it the yacht or the challenge this man was after?

Hyperion

155-foot Royal Huisman Sloop

It is always refreshing when monitoring the superyacht building scene to be brought up short by a blip in the continuous line graph, a blip representing the fortuitous meeting of an owner, designer, and builder, each dedicated to the evolution of yachting, and each willing to explore new avenues in furthering the art of sailing.

And it is also always true that once one has looked beyond the obvious and immediate impact of a new yacht that expands the boundaries of accepted practice, there is more, far more, to the aggregate total of countless details than can be easily explained away as simply a technological and technical tour de force. Technical virtuosity for its own sake is like yesterday's champagne, the taste is there but it has gone flat; intelligently applied technology is what makes sense and excites the tastebuds of the mind.

If I may be allowed to indulge in that analogy one moment further, *Hyperion*, Jim Clark's new 155ft sloop, is like a freshly opened Methuselah of vintage champagne. She simply bursts at the seams with new technology, sporting the tallest (192ft) carbon fiber mast ever built, Spectra/carbon sails especially developed for her by North Sails, and load cells and telemetry devices incorporated in all her sheet and halyard winches. Consider details such as UV-coated ports and deadlights to keep woodwork and furniture fabric from fading in the sunlight, limit switches on the digital piano cover panels, hydraulic reef point locks—the list is truly endless—and one begins to appreciate the breadth of innovation that *Hyperion* represents. To be fair, some of these features have been used on other yachts; what makes *Hyperion* so unusual is the extent to which available technology has been combined with innovative hardware and software to achieve an integrated yacht management system.

A great deal of hype has been written concerning her much-publicized computer installation. In point of fact, it will not sail the boat unaided, nor will it allow her owner to sail her from his office, as has been suggested. What is unique is the sophistication of the system, and the role it plays in the operation of the yacht. Its purpose is to control myriad shipboard functions—lights, sheet winches, night-vision camera, engine, generators, and numerous other apparatuses—rationally and efficiently, and to do so from a centralized command source. The magnitude of the installation should come as no surprise once one is aware of the quantity and variety of operations it is required to perform.

A brief example of its systems control function occurs around the electrical system. A light switch is typically wired directly to the light it controls, which is in turn

Porthole ★ The navigation station serves as the ship's office, with both computerized and hard copy manuals for all systems.

Above ★ Under sail, *Hyperion* is so well proportioned that it's hard to determine her size from a distance—although in the photograph people on deck provide a scale.

Left ★ The bridgehouse contains twin control stations, dual radar screens, and three touch screens to monitor and man the yacht.

Above ✶ The saloon has the ambience of a country home, with many thoughtful details creating a look of casual elegance.

Left ✶ The formal dining area seats up to 10 people, with side ports that open electrically for fresh air.

Opposite ✶ The articulated passageway to the guest cabins provides ample display areas for both statuary and fine art.

wired to a circuit breaker panel, which in its turn is wired to a source of energy, such as a bank of batteries. On *Hyperion* the electrical power to the light is routed through a computer controlled relay switch, and so a light switch, whose power is also routed through the computer, is assigned to the light by accessing the software program designed for the electrical system. That same light switch can be assigned through the computer system to control the owner's stateroom hairdryer or the food processor in the galley. The same basic principle applies to the entire ship. When one considers the complexity inherent in building modern superyachts such as *Hyperion*, the advantages of this approach immediately become obvious. By routing all function controls through a centralized computer system, an uncommon degree of flexibility becomes available, and the diagnostic process required by possible malfunctions is greatly simplified. The activation of the individual functions is performed by dedicated programmable logic controllers (PLCs), which will not crash (they are similar to the computers which run machines in factories), and which are in turn controlled by a Silicon Graphics Unix System via two store forward units (one a backup), activated by any of the 24 touch screens distributed throughout the boat. To avoid conflict, access to all sensitive functions such as engine starting, various machinery controls, and power distribution is achieved by punching in a discrete code assigned to responsible crew members.

A secondary function of the system is to monitor and record the performance of all machinery and, through an array of load cells installed at all load points of both standing and running rigging, the stresses incurred while sailing. As all winches include line counters as well as load cells, optimal trim and load settings for any given set of conditions can be recorded and the winches programmed to duplicate them from tack to tack, or for future use in similar conditions. Given the prodigious loads to which a rig like *Hyperion*'s is subjected, and the difficulty in predicting them, the availability of such information is priceless.

It seems to me important, at this point, to re-establish a sense of perspective. *Hyperion* is, first and foremost, a sailing yacht, and if one element of her appeal to aficionados does indeed consist of her technological prowess, I would be doing her a disservice if I did not emphasize the exceptional quality and thoughtfulness that her designers and builder have bestowed upon her. The control system, after all, is designed to facilitate, not dominate, the joy of sailing her.

Seen in a crowded anchorage, there is no mistaking *Hyperion*'s size: her 192ft single mast towers above the fleet. Moored alone, it is more challenging to determine her scale; her length makes her appear low and aggressively sleek, a design achieved with little or no sacrifice to the accommodations. Her profile is uncompromisingly modern, though there is just enough rise to the sheer to keep it from being too severe, and her lines aft tuck in neatly under the stern — one of those elegant Frers details. I thought the twin satellite communications domes mounted on the lower spreaders added a bit of clutter to her rig, though there is no denying their necessity.

Size also plays a role in her deck layout, allowing the inclusion of all necessary facilities while avoiding clutter. The stern deck, a flat expanse of flawlessly laid teak, conceals the main tender and its dedicated hydraulic crane under flush hatches. Settees on either side lead to the twin helm stations, each with touch-screen controls and monitors, and joystick control panels for sail handling. All sheets and halyards are led below deck or into the deckhouse to concealed Rondal hydraulic captive reel winches. *Hyperion*'s cruising canvas consists of a mainsail

Right ❖ The galley has a pass-through breakfast bar to the lower saloon, and also shares space with the crew mess.

Below ❖ The port side of the lower saloon features a concealed digital piano and a breakfast bar.

Opposite ❖ The starboard side of the lower saloon includes a quiet library-like corner for relaxation or reading.

furled and reefed by a Rondal carbon fiber Rollaway boom, and a staysail and 100% jib controlled by Rondal hydraulic roller furlers. The mainsail can be hoisted or lowered with the boom eased off as much as 40 degrees from the centerline, and particularly worthy of note are the hydraulically operated reef locks which eliminate the load on the furling mandrel. Rounding out the sail inventory is an MPS, which must be a truly breathtaking sight indeed when flying.

The mast is stepped just forward of the deckhouse and, aside from its awe-inspiring proportions, is notable for the neatness of its installation. Two auxiliary winches are located nearby, the main and headsail halyards being led below decks. A noteworthy feature is the elevator/crow's nest set on the forward side of the mast. Two persons can be hoisted mechanically as far as the third set of spreaders, approximately 100 feet up. Forward of the mast is another recessed dinghy garage for the crew's tender, and ahead of that is a small crew cockpit with a companionway to the crew's quarters below. All anchor handling gear is installed under an access hatch near the bow, leaving the entire foredeck uncluttered.

I was, alas, unable to sail on *Hyperion*, although it is hard to imagine that she would not perform more than creditably. Just the fact that German Frers designed her should be a clue. And besides, consider the numbers: a canoe hull measuring 127ft on the water with a waterline beam of 29ft and a hull draft of only 6ft simply has to be fast. Her ballast bulb gives her a 30% ballast to weight ratio, not race boat territory but, together with her designed hull stability and a lightweight rig, she performs outstandingly in light and medium air conditions, usually the downfall of very large sailing yachts. Leaving nothing to chance, she even sports a dagger board which lowers through the bulb to further enhance her performance to windward.

Entering the deckhouse through the tinted glass doors, I was immediately impressed by the contrast. On deck she is all business—plain teak, stainless steel, little varnish, a lot of white paint; below one enters a world of mahogany, carpet, and muted lighting. *Hyperion*'s accommodations, while decidedly luxurious, reflect a traditional taste for visual harmony and comfort. I could have been inside a country home, with the typical ageless and casual

★ HYPERION

Above ✦ The owner's suite spans the full beam, and follows the theme that runs throughout *Hyperion* of softly rounded corners.

Left ✦ A sitting area in the owner's suite provides a private getaway.

Opp. top ✦ The owner's suite includes an office area, with a computer monitor that slides out of a hidden compartment in the wooden molding. The leaded glass cabinet contains a temperature controlled cigar humidor.

Opp. bottom ✦ The spacious marble bathroom in the owner's suite has a deep tub.

elegance one would expect there, the many thoughtful details evolved over generations.

The transition from the businesslike exterior to the actual living quarters is gracefully achieved by having to transit the bridgehouse. While it gives one a foretaste of the quality of finish one will find below, it maintains a purposeful atmosphere with its control stations port and starboard, twin radar screens, and three touch screens to monitor and man the ship. A few steps down and one enters the main saloon. In terms of design, the layout from here on is quite straightforward. The saloon consists of two facing sofas with a coffee table and casual chairs to port—there is also a large flat-screen television hidden here—and a dining area to starboard which can seat up to 10 persons. The side ports, both in the bridge deck and the main saloon, can open at the touch of a button. Incidentally, the bridge deck can be closed off from the main saloon, allowing the crew to sail the ship while the guests relax.

A few more steps lead down to a second saloon. To port is a digital piano, with a breakfast bar facing an opening to the galley. To starboard is a library-like corner, another area for conversation or quiet relaxation. Tradition is nicely observed, as the mast is stepped through at the forward bulkhead defining the guest accommodations. Forward of the mast, then, is the galley and crew mess, with the comfortable crew's quarters and laundry facility beyond.

★ HYPERION

A stairway leading aft from the main saloon provides access to the sleeping quarters. There are two guest staterooms, port and starboard, with en suite heads, and the owner's quarters take up the entire beam of the ship just aft. The recurring rounded surfaces evident throughout culminate here in the subtle compound curve of the owner's berth. Not surprisingly, a drawer in the nightstand gives Jim Clark access to a touch screen. It is tempting to simply describe this area as being conventionally laid out, but that would be doing it an injustice as the details of the layout, such as the settee and desk in the owner's cabin, or the articulated design of the passageway itself, clearly represent thoughtful reflection on the part of the designers.

At the forward end of the accommodation passageway, a few steps lead down to the ship's computer room, the nerve center of her operating system, and a separate space housing the actual PLCs as well as all other electrical functions. Just forward is the engine room, spacious and well laid out. Centrally located is the 12-cylinder MTU diesel with twin sequential turbos driving a variable pitch propeller with automatic pitch control. Naturally, in the very unlikely event of a failure of the computer control system, the engine, the three 65kW

Above The 192ft carbon fiber mast is awesome, with an elevator/crow's nest that runs more than 100 feet up the front of the mast.

Right Under sail is where *Hyperion* excels, and she can easily be handled by one or two crew from the twin-shaded cockpits.

80   THE MEGAYACHTS USA ★ 2000

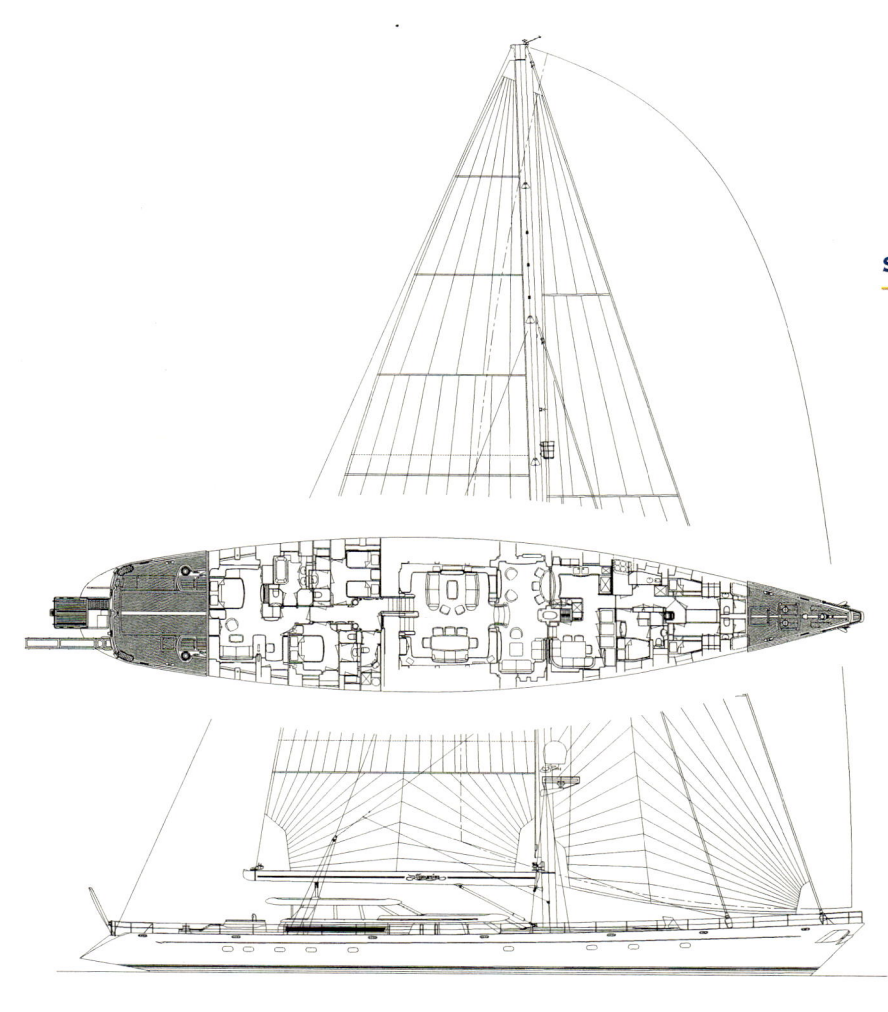

SPECIFICATIONS

LOA	155ft 7in (47.42m)
Beam	31ft 4in (9.56m)
Draft	15ft 9in (4.8m)
Displacement	285 tons
Construction	Aluminum
Engine	MTU-DDC V12-2000 1,100hp @ 2,100 RPM
Sails	North Sails
Sail Area	11,239sqft (1,064m"2")
Naval Architect	German Frers
Exterior & Interior Styling	Pieter Beeldsnijder
Builder/Year	Royal Huisman Shipyard/ 1998

generators, and all other vital ship's systems can be manually operated.

The degree and quality of the detail in the living areas, as elsewhere throughout *Hyperion*, clearly reflect Huisman's philosophy of, "the more you look the more you see." Accent lighting brings out in bolder relief the semi-detached columns integrated in the mahogany woodwork. The pattern of the texas and wenge inlay in the bulkhead panels is echoed by the custom-made solid brass doorknob and light switch plates. The sole throughout this area is carpet inset into a mahogany border; the grain of border itself radiates out perpendicularly to the vertical surfaces, following the curvature of the built-in furniture and the accent corner columns. Nowhere can even the most sensitive hand feel a seam or mismatched joint.

Indeed, if the unjust accusation leveled at Dr. Jim Clark that he loaded *Hyperion* with computer technology merely because it is available, then the craftsmen who built her interior (or, for that matter, machined her jewel-like stainless steel fittings on deck) should similarly be accused of indulging themselves in this exquisite tour de force, simply because they can do it. The Titan Hyperion, we are told, fathered Helios, Selene, and Eos, gods of the sun, moon, and dawn respectively. The yacht *Hyperion* has engendered an advance in the science and art and craft of boatbuilding. The yachting cosmos is richer for it.

JANET

92-foot Cheoy Lee Sport Motoryacht

The naysayers predicted doom and gloom for Hong Kong-based Cheoy Lee Shipyards when the British finally hauled down the Union Jack and handed the territory over to the Chinese.

"In fact, it's been just the opposite," says Bruce Majka, head of Cheoy Lee operations in North America. "Not only were we able to expand our shipyard facilities appreciably, but we now have a much larger work force from which to draw highly skilled craftsmen. It's been great."

More than a century old, this family-owned company is arguably one of the most versatile builders in the world. With a series of production motoryachts, motorsailors, and sailing yachts up to 145ft, the company can also build custom yachts in aluminum, steel, and fiberglass up to 250ft and, in addition to luxury yachts, it also builds an array of tugs, ferries, pilot boats, and patrol boats for an international market.

A force in the United States since the 1950s, Cheoy Lee introduced American buyers to Far Eastern craftsmanship with its all-teak sailboats featuring intricate hand carvings and a level of workmanship unheard of from U.S. yards, not to mention prices that undercut the competition by a sizable margin.

Today's buyers of Cheoy Lee luxury yachts are drawn by the same appealing qualities: superb workmanship at highly competitive prices. The 92ft motoryacht shown on these pages is a fine example not just of Cheoy Lee quality, but of the talents of naval architect Tom Fexas and interior stylist Melody Savio, who work as a team on many Cheoy Lee projects.

Janet particularly reflects the devotion of Cheoy Lee clients, since the owner traded up from an 81ft motoryacht and his son-in-law has a 74-footer. At 92ft, this is the upper end of the Sport Motoryacht range which uses the same 21ft beam Fexas-designed hull lines. The difference between an 81-footer and this yacht is primarily an extra eight feet in the saloon, as well as a stretched aft deck on the main deck and a full-beam VIP stateroom with en suite head on the lower deck.

Regardless of the configuration or length, all Cheoy Lee Sport Motoryachts have a composite hull and superstructure using Airex and Divinycell foam cores, with extensive use of bi-axial and multi-axial E-glass reinforcing. The interior floors are also cored with Divinycell, which not only creates a strong unibody construction but quiets the yacht as well. Each yacht is built to American Bureau of Shipping standards, and is completely finished in Awlgrip, with an International Paint anti-blister gel shield system below the waterline. Carefully engineered both for low maintenance and

Porthole   The helm console was computer designed to handle the specific electronics package chosen for *Janet*.

Opp. left   The galley is superbly finished with blue Avonite counters, wood-faced cabinets, and stainless-steel appliances.

Above   No question about it—*Janet* is a Fexas design from the mild clipper bow to the Cleopatra-eyed saloon windows to the reversed transom.

Left   The full-beam bridge is spacious, with Stidd helm chairs, dining area, and wet bar with Jennaire grill.

★ JANET

reliability, every Cheoy Lee yacht has a five-year structural and anti-blister warranty.

From the exterior, *Janet* is clearly a Fexas design, with soft lines, a reversed transom, a faint clipper bow, and Cleopatra-eyed saloon windows. What can't be seen is a very slippery underwater shape that not only gives this yacht a 27.2-knot top speed with a pair of 1,350hp Caterpillar 3412s, but a comfortable 22-knot cruising speed with full tanks and loading. A double chine provides progressive roll damping and, although the yacht has Naiad stabilizers, it also has a naturally comfortable motion at sea. Mild prop tunnels also keep the draft to just 5ft 3in, allowing the yacht access to more cruising areas than most 90+ footers.

In a word, the saloon is long, stretching unbroken for a length of more than 30ft from the sliding doors on the aft deck to the buffet separating the galley. Aft to port and

84   THE MEGAYACHTS USA ★ 2000

Main picture   Though termed a production yacht, each Cheoy Lee allows extensive owner modification which, in the case of *Janet*, meant a nearly 30ft long saloon with twin conversation areas aft.

Opp. bottom   The dining area has a lowered ceiling treatment, faux-painted to match the mahogany and sapelle wood paneling.

starboard are a pair of supple leather settees, each with a freeform gold-accented cocktail table, and an entertainment center is built into the corner. The saloon is surrounded by aircraft-style frameless windows which provide seated guests with excellent views, and the bridge deck overhangs the wide walkaround side decks to provide sun protection for the saloon. Custom carpeting is by Fabrica, and the Majilite ultrasuede headliner is on removable panels that are held in place by Velcro to provide access to the wire runs that are in the overhead rather than the bulkheads.

Superb woodwork is a trademark of Cheoy Lee and this yacht is no exception, with an interior featuring mahogany accented with sapelle pompelli, and with all the surfaces buried under syrup-smooth seven-step clear urethane finish. Even the air-conditioning ducts and soffits for the Hunter Dougless window treatments are flawlessly executed in matching woods.

It should be pointed out that while Cheoy Lee refers to the Sport Motoryacht line as "production yachts", nothing could be further from the truth. Within the boundaries of certain fixed bulkheads, almost any arrangement can be accommodated and each interior is customized to suit its owner. In this case, the spiral staircase to the bridge combines flawless wood joinery with mirror-polished stainless steel newell posts and gold accents in a swirling work of art.

The formal dining area seats eight at a custom table with gold-accented chairs and a built-in mirrored buffet against the forward bulkhead. The lowered ceiling treatment over the dining table conceals recessed lighting and, at first glance, appears to be more of the mahogany and sapelle woods — it's actually a flawlessly executed hand-painted faux treatment. A wet bar is opposite the dining area, with U-Line refrigerator/icemaker and liquor storage.

Above — The master suite has flawlessly matched mahogany and sapelle wood with the grain continuing from drawer to drawer in the built-in bureau.

Right — The three guest cabins have a separate stairwell, and the VIP suite shown here has a Jacuzzi™ tub finished in silver.

The galley is enclosed on three sides, with blue Avonite counters and backsplashes, wood-faced cabinets, and a complete array of Frigidaire Galley Professional stainless steel appliances. Opposite the galley is a day head with a Galley Maid Eurostyle head and Camden gold and crystal faucet for the sink.

The pilothouse is both comfortable and well organized, with the helm to port and a dinette covered in bright fabrics to starboard. The helm console was computer designed specifically to handle the electronic package produced by Custom Navigation South, as well as to ensure clear lines of sight for the skipper. Pantograph doors to port and starboard open onto the side decks, and the Genuwood mahogany floor makes this an all-weather area. Twin Disc Power Commander electronic controls have three plug-in remote stations so the skipper can run the yacht from either wing or stern with full controls, including bowthruster.

With a private curving stairwell from the saloon to a compact foyer (with hidden washer/dryer), the master suite takes advantage of the full beam. A king-size berth is amidships, with a seat, bureau and wardrobe to port, and a huge walk-in closet to starboard. The mahogany and sapelle pompelli woodwork is worth a closer look because not only is the grain carefully matched, but it extends over onto the top of the bureau and dresser. His and hers en suites are aft, with a shower in the port head and a Jacuzzi™ tub in the starboard side. Both have marble tiled floors, gold-lacquered cabinetry, and gold wall coverings.

The guest accommodations have a second stairwell from the saloon and *Janet* allows room for a spacious VIP suite aft of the foyer, with queen-sized berth, a large wardrobe and an amply-sized bathroom with Jacuzzi™ finished in silver Vitracore. Just forward are two more guest staterooms, with a queen-size berth in the port cabin and a pair of singles in the starboard. Both of the smaller staterooms have en suite heads with shower stalls.

Forward of the pilothouse are the crew quarters, with a lounge and office to port that can serve as an occasional crew cabin with a draw curtain, and a twin-bunk cabin with head and shower to starboard. The captain's cabin has a double berth forward and a larger private head with shower stall. The result is a seven-cabin layout in a 92ft yacht which never appears to be crowded.

Again using the full beam, the flybridge is spacious and deep, with a pair of curved lounges and a table for entertaining or dining to port. A pair of Stidd Luxury Admiral helm chairs are behind the console, and the entire area is shaded by the standard hardtop supported by a swept-forward radar arch. The boat deck easily handles the Novurania 460 tender, which is launched by a Nautical Structures davit, and a Jennaire grill and wet bar are in a console just aft of the seating area.

The aft deck is a pleasant entertaining area with protection from the overhang of the bridge and ample space for table and chairs. A pair of "garages" open onto the teak-planked swim platform, with a Yamaha Waveblaster on rollers to port and a scuba diving equipment room with shower to starboard.

The engine room is spacious, with a pair of Northern Lights generators (40kW and 30kW), a complete fuel management system for the five integral fiberglass tanks, a Horizon 1,300-gallon-per-day watermaker, Marine Air air-conditioning, power takeoffs from the generators for the Naiad bowthruster, and a carefully engineered Ansul fire system that draws on the Cheoy Lee commercial craft background. Sound insulation is equally extensive, which results in a cruise speed sound level of just 66dB in the master suite.

Having already owned an 81-footer, the owner of *Janet* knew that he would reap the benefits of a century of superb boatbuilding craftsmanship, and it's no surprise that he once again chose Cheoy Lee.

SPECIFICATIONS

LOA	92ft 5in (27.75m)
LWL	82ft 7in (24.8m)
Beam	21ft 1in (6.43m)
Draft	5ft 3in (1.6m)
Displacement	167,000lb
Engines	Twin Caterpillar 3412 TAE 1,350hp each
Speed (max/cruise)	27/22 knots
Fuel	3,000 US gallons
Generators	Twin Northern Lights (40kW & 30kW)
Stabilizers	Naiad 302
Bowthruster	Naiad 42hp
Naval architect	Tom Fexas Yacht Design
Interior designer	Savio Design
Builder/Year	Cheoy Lee Shipyards America/1998

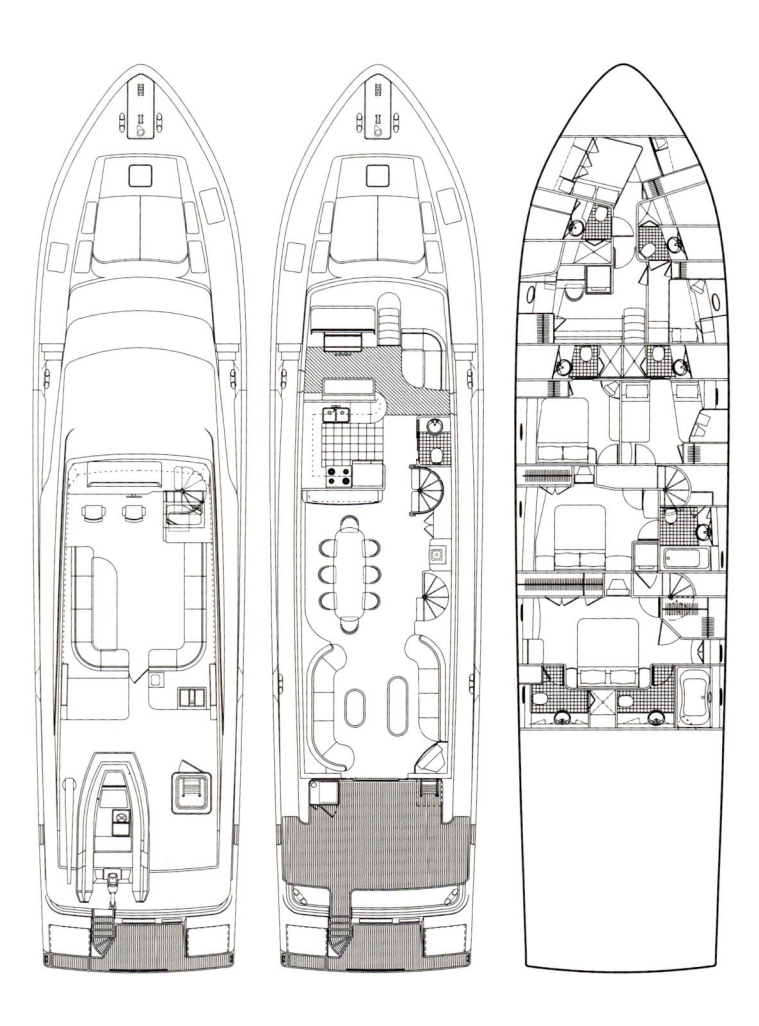

★ JANET

KATRION

158-foot Feadship Motoryacht

Threatened by the increasing popularity of superyachts with an aft engine room, the classic mid-engined, full-displacement motoryacht might have seemed to be heading towards the endangered species list, but Feadship's De Vries yard has mounted a highly promising rescue operation for the breed with the launch of the 158ft 2in (48.2m) *Katrion*. Purchased by an owner with family use in mind, *Katrion*'s novel interior layout successfully addresses the main factors that have driven owners and builders away from the central engine room, namely, that guest accommodation is usually inconveniently split by the machinery space, and that the aft guest cabins suffer from an excess of propeller noise when the yacht is under way.

This aside, any naval architect would point out that central engine rooms do have distinct advantages in that the midships section of the hull offers considerably more volume than an equivalent length in the stern, thus making a central engine room more space efficient. In addition, placing the yacht's massive weight of machinery at the center of the hull's buoyancy ensures a more seakindly motion in a seaway. In order to preserve these advantages while minimizing the disadvantages, interior designer, John Munford, worked closely with Feadship naval architect, F. de Voogt International Ship Design, to create a new and innovative accommodation layout for *Katrion*.

By careful fore and aft division of the lower deck, Munford located four sizable guest staterooms aft of the engine room, at the same time ensuring that the two aftermost ones were positioned well forward of the propellers. Then there was the question of the stairs leading down to this area. The conventional approach is to run these down from the port or starboard side of the main saloon but, in general, this has a detrimental impact on the layout of this important room. In a classic example of lateral thinking, Munford completely redesigned the conventional layout of the saloon's aft end, placing a spiral stairwell in the center of the aft bulkhead, with its semicircular volume bulging outwards—a position normally occupied by doors to the aft deck. A stunning feature was then made of the stairway by encasing it with seven full-height windows and repositioning the usually centrally-positioned door on its starboard side. With no loss of floor space in the saloon, Munford then maximized its volume by creating a token division from the dining saloon beyond with the clever use of short bookcases.

Having solved this particular layout difficulty, the remainder of the yacht follows more or less conventional lines with the master suite, located just forward of the galley and entrance lobby, filling the forward element of the main deck, while an observation lounge on the bridge deck is linked with an aft deck dedicated to alfresco dining and lounging.

Devotees of yacht interior design will doubtlessly link the name of John Munford with raised and fielded paneling and the classical influences of shape and volume which unite to form a room of ideal proportions, faithfully executed to the highest standards. *Katrion* differs from this vision only in that the Munford design office has taken this opportunity to demonstrate its talents with a modern interior that draws inspiration from the world of 1930's Art Deco. This style flows throughout the yacht, but is perhaps best seen in the main saloon, where

Porthole ★ The boat deck bar is likely to be a gathering place for guests.

Main picture ★ Withe exterior styling by Dutch designer Guido de Groot, *Katrion* has a highly distinctive aluminum superstructure.

Left ★ The raised spa on the upper deck adjoins a treadmill machine as well as a huge sunpad.

★ KATRION   89

Main picture — John Mumford's styling of the main saloon bears the stylish trademarks of the Art Deco 1930s.

Right — French doors lead from the boat deck into the comfortable lounge and bar.

Opposite — The dining area is included as a part of the saloon, creating an open atmosphere and a visually larger space.

contrasting combinations of anigré and madrona-briar veneers are molded into flowing, curvaceous cabinets, pillars, and doors with quartered chevron grain, while the Art Deco effect is enhanced by raised ceilings and subtle lighting, together with other details which exactly match the chosen period. This subtle background was the starting point for Seattle-based interior decorator, Michael McQuiston, who added custom-built furniture, along with lively yet graceful fabrics to create relaxed, eminently livable, surroundings which exactly meet the needs of the owner and his family.

Beyond the dining saloon, with its 10-seater table and fitted cabinets bursting with delightful bone china services from Hermès, Spode, and Tiffany, the yacht's starboard side entrance lobby contains an impressive flight of stairs that beckon visitors to the boat deck lounge. Softly-lit with an inverted pyramid of glass set in the ceiling, and provided with a comfortable settee, card table, and a bar topped with a glorious slab of rosa Verona marble, this is an ideal anteroom in which to gather before or after dinner-but the room's real strength is by day. Then it is brilliantly lit through tall windows and united with the bridge deck aft through wide fully-glazed sliding doors, where guests are offered a practically unbroken 300-degree vista. It is no wonder that this combination of the air-conditioned saloon with a teak deck and 12-seater table and casual seating is perhaps the most intensively used area aboard.

From this deck, stairs lead down to the main deck aft and up to the sun deck. While the former amply fills its role as a bathing center with easy access to the stern platform down a central flight of stairs, the sun deck is the only part of this otherwise superb yacht that might cause some disappointment. With the aim of clearing the aft decks of tenders, the owner's Novurania RIB is inset in the port superstructure at bridge deck level, a traditional and highly convenient location. What is more questionable is the positioning of the crew tender on the aft end of the sun deck where, in combination with its launching crane, it restricts the available deck space. With all of the remaining deck space taken up by a raised Jacuzzi™ spa pool, that adjoins a treadmill machine and a huge sun pad of equal height, it leaves only a narrow, sunken passageway between it and the built-in counter with barbecue, refrigerator and bar to starboard.

One suspects that the design of this whole area is driven not only by the demands of the tenders, but also by the need to place the yacht's air intake close to the central duct leading down to the engine room—hence the large size and awkward positioning of the sunbed. Having said

Main picture ★ The master suite is almost futuristic, with a bed that seems to "float" above the floor.

Above ★ A circular Jacuzzi™ spa bath is surrounded by blue-stained granite and bathed in soft light from a circular skylight.

this, the remaining deck areas are quite superb, while the exterior styling of the vessel by the young Dutch designer Guido de Groot, better known for his car designs, has provided *Katrion*'s aluminum superstructure with a highly distinctive appearance.

Decoratively speaking, the *pièce de résistance* of the yacht is, without doubt, its magnificent master suite. This is entered from the main deck lobby through a spacious study which, because of the semicircular design of the desk and the convenience of a connecting door to the galley, is equally suitable as a family breakfast room. Moving forward, the stateroom extends across the full beam of the yacht, and this already large space is magnified by long sight-lines extending forward into the twin dressing areas to port and starboard of the central audio-visual cabinet at the foot of the bed. Rich fabrics with colorful blue and gold highlights blend harmoniously with the surrounding anigré and madrona furniture, which includes a writing desk and dressing table to port and starboard. The bed's cantilevered plinth creates the impression that it floats magically above the floor like the overland vehicles in a Star Wars film.

Concealed behind the screen formed by the audio-visual cabinet, twin washbasins are elegantly set in a blue granite counter, but the eye moves swiftly on to the spectacular travertine-floored bathroom beyond. Here, a circular Jacuzzi™ spa bath, set centrally against the forward bulkhead and circled by more blue-stained granite, is bathed with sun or starlight from a circular skylight directly overhead. A shower and head/bidet combination is housed in separate travertine-lined compartments, one of which contains a very practical safety feature — an escape route leading to the bosun's store and foredeck beyond.

The four guest cabins, two sizable doubles with bathrooms and a pair of slightly smaller twins with shower rooms all take their decorative style from the master suite, balancing the honey tones of wood with pale silk wallcoverings and attractive pastel fabrics. Of particular note is the impeccable quality of joinery displayed in the wardrobes, where the two chevron-grained anigré doors are united by six delicate horizontal bands of darker madrona briar, like piping on a Lancer's jacket.

The crew quarters are spacious, and incorporate a highly professional galley with excellent technical spaces. A large lazarette, entered from the stern swim platform, is well fitted out for diving and there is plenty of additional space for water toys and boats equipment.

The engine room is particularly deep and immaculately laid out for easy access to the Caterpillar main engines and every ancillary component. Not only does it have neatly racked tools for every occasion, but its metalworking lathe is more than capable of turning up specialist bolts and smaller spare parts in case of emergency. Attention has also been paid to green issues. The two neatly-boxed and extremely quiet Caterpillar 156kVA generator sets have catalytic converters fitted to their exhausts, while the chlorine-based Hammen sewage treatment system discharges perfectly clear and odorless effluent when set in harbor mode.

Being a full displacement hull form, *Katrion* cruises at a steady 14.8 knots rather than the 19 to 20 knots that would be expected from a semi-displacement hull of the same proportions, but *Katrion*'s easily-driven steel hull requires far less costly 905hp engines, whose excellent economy ensures transatlantic capability at her normal cruising speed.

At the time of writing, *Katrion* had experienced a delivery passage from Holland to the Mediterranean during which she encountered Force 8 conditions with following seas, possibly the worst sea angle for any motoryacht, for a full four days. During this time her seaworthiness and performance were, reportedly, of the highest order.

Already possessing elegant exterior lines, *Katrion* is also sure to set a new trend in interior layout, while the style of her interior, in terms of both design and decoration, is certain to retain its wide appeal for a very long time. Feadship has built and launched yet another superb vessel.

SPECIFICATIONS

LOA	158ft 2in (42.2m)
LWL	136ft 1in (41.75m)
Beam	28ft 5in (8.68m)
Draft	9ft 6in (2.9m)
Fuel	12,100 gal
Range	3100nm
Engines	2 x 905hp Caterpillar 3508 DITA
Generators	2 x 156k Va Caterpillar 3306 DIT
Naval Architect	F De Voogt Intenational Ship Design
Interior Designer	John Munford Designs,
Builder/Year	Feadship/1997

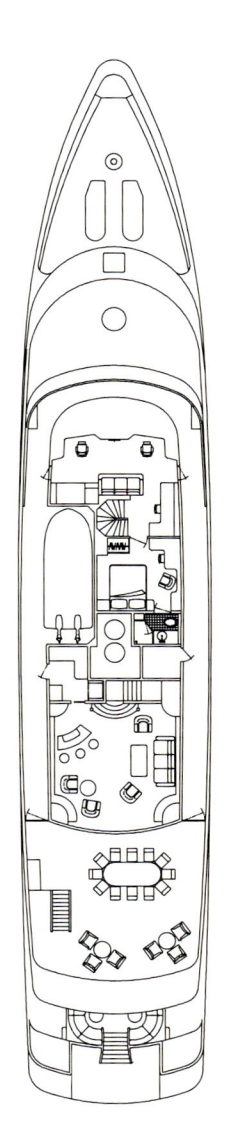

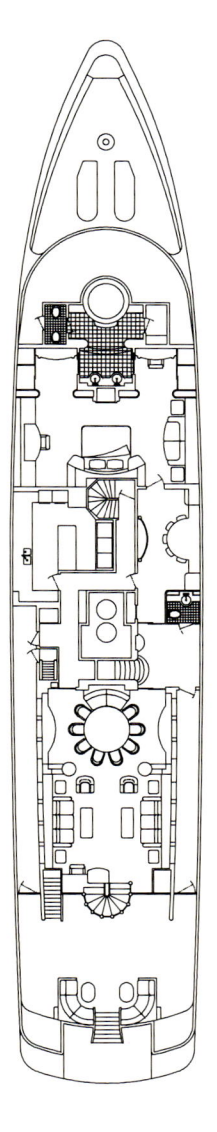

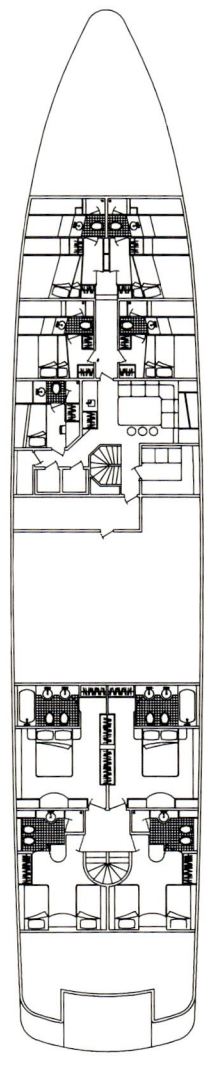

La Baronessa

195-foot Palmer Johnson Motoryacht

The shape of a yacht's hull, together with the more or less rigidly fixed positions of the engine room and bridge, severely constrain the designer when laying out an interior. Within this envelope, Western lifestyle — particularly the food and entertainment conventions — further restrict the thought processes of most designers, so it is refreshing to see a yacht conceived by a knowledgeable Oriental owner working in close cooperation with a pair of talented young European designers who are ready to cast convention aside.

Carlo Nuvolari and Dan Lenard, Venice-based stylists and interior designers, are the first to admit that *La Baronessa* is primarily the achievement of her owner. Experience with his former motoryacht, *La Baroness*, a 147-footer built by Palmer Johnson in 1994, provided him with ample opportunity to develop his requirements for this new vessel, while he found designers who were ready to listen to his ideas in the Nuvolari & Lenard partnership. Deck space was important to him, and this meant clearing the tenders from the aft decks, but the often-seen solution of an aft "garage" on the lower deck was ruled out by the need for a good diving base in this area. The location of cabins was also an issue. Although an excellent seaman himself, and never happier than on an ocean passage, concern for his wife and guests called for their accommodation to be amidships rather than forward; also, the steam and odors of Chinese cooking called for a greater than usual degree of separation between guest areas and the galley. Other needs included a gymnasium, a movie theatre, and an efficient, seaworthy hull form commensurate with a predicted annual total of 20,000 nautical miles.

Hull design was entrusted to New York naval architects, Sparkman & Stephens, who created an efficient hull with great structural integrity. Almost sailboat-like in shape, its fine, virtually hollow, entry at the bow extends to a maximum beam of 34ft 5in and a half-load draft of 11ft 5in, with her aft sections rising gently to the stern to provide a waterline length of 165ft. The underwater lines were also optimized to minimize roll when under way at low speed. The use of aluminum for her construction rather than steel realized a weight saving of some 110 tons. This permitted engines with 30 percent less power than those needed for a steel hull, saving further weight and cost, as well as increasing fuel efficiency which, together with the ability to incorporate larger fuel tanks, greatly increased her range. At her most efficient 10.5-knot

Porthole ★ The aft deck dining area is just one of many places to relax aboard *La Baronessa*.

Above ★ Arguably the most attractive motoryacht to be launched in recent years, *La Baronessa* balances proportion and function.

Left ★ The sky deck has beautiful teak steps leading to the spa pool.

Opp. left ★ A continuous side deck runs from bow to stern to allow the crew full access fore and aft without disturbing guests.

★ LA BARONESSA 95

cruising speed, *La Baronessa*'s twin 1,950hp Caterpillar diesels squeeze a remarkable 14,000nm from her 42,000 gallon tanks.

A consequence of this particular hull design is that the forward sections of the hull on the lower deck were too narrow for the crew quarters, yet Nuvolari & Lenard solved this by raising decks in the forward crew areas by half a deck, thus increasing floor area, as well as creating a useful store in the forefoot. Ultimately, after long hours of detailed consultations between designers and owner, *La Baronessa*'s styling and interior layout took shape with surprisingly few compromises.

From the outside, she is arguably the most attractive motoryacht to be launched in recent years, while her well-proportioned lines incorporate the degree of functionality demanded by her owner. The master stroke was to locate the two Zodiac tenders, 24ft and 22ft ProLuxes, forward, protecting them from breaking seas and salt spray in a sleekly-faired garage built into the forward element of the superstructure, with access through huge hydraulically-operated upwards-opening gull wing doors. This tender position permits four superb deck areas to be totally dedicated to the owner and his guests: a very private sundeck between the mast and satellite television dome; beneath this a splendid teak-laid sky deck with spa pool and casual seating located fore and aft of the gymnasium; then a deck opening aft from the upper saloon, and, one deck down, a spacious main deck aft with alfresco dining. Perhaps one should add a fifth area—the 17ft-wide teak-laid swim platform that hinges down from the attractively bustled stern. The swim platform opens directly forward to the adjacent diving room, which stores all the scuba gear, including 30 cylinders, a charging facility, and a nitrox system for longer dives, and is also linked to the aft deck with easy stairs. Although both the main deck and upper deck accommodation is, in part, built out to the full beam, a continuous side deck runs from fore to aft, broken only by a pair of stairs amidships, which gives the crew an essential route along the decks with minimal intrusion on guest areas. Five superb deck areas for the owner and his guests, garaged tenders, a dive room, and a gymnasium—not bad for a 195ft yacht!

One of the beauties of *La Baronessa*'s exterior styling is that it does not impose on the interior spaces. Portlights and windows are perfectly positioned to provide superb views and an abundance of light, while the semicircle of vertical windows that enclose the bridge provide a refreshingly reflection-free vista for the watchkeepers. Behind these windows lies an innovative interior whose volume has been thoughtfully divided to fulfill the needs of the owner's party and those of the crew.

La Baronessa is one of a very select group of custom superyachts specifically designed to suit an oriental lifestyle, and, inevitably, some of the concepts that drove her decoration, layout, and equipment might seem alien to many Western yacht owners. Primary among these is the concept that guests are invited aboard for the specific purpose of entertaining the owner, and this led to the principle that cabins are just for sleeping and waking up. Certainly, they should provide comfortable surroundings but they should not, for instance, be a place of retreat for video watching. A second concept is that the interior decoration of a yacht does not need to impress the guests—the yacht itself does that. The addition of a lavish interior would, in oriental eyes, only serve to make a guest feel relatively poor or, worse, out of place when dressed in a casual T-shirt—and this should not be the intention of a caring host.

At an early meeting to present concept drawings to the owner, Nuvolari & Lenard therefore found themselves being asked to scale down their "over-elaborate" Western

Opp. above   Cabinets, bookcases, and furnishings in the main saloon enhance the signature lacewood and ebony used throughout the yacht.

Opp. bottom left   The bar in the sky lounge sits on the herringbone sapele mahogany dance floor, and has an ultra-thin flat-screen television behind it.

Opp. bottom right   A 14-seat lacewood and ebony dining table with a lazy Susan centerpiece occupies a corner of the sky lounge.

Top   The theater has a 61-inch screen, surround-sound audio, and an abundance of comfortable seating.

Above   The smoking/games room off the sky lounge opens to the aft deck.

LA BARONESSA   97

Right ◆ The main staircase leading up to the sky lounge shows crisp and simple styling.

Opp. above ◆ Floor to ceiling oval windows line the slightly austere owner's suite on the main deck.

Opp. bottom left ◆ A simply furnished sitting area has been included in the owner's suite, further adding to the spacious feel.

Opp. bottom right ◆ Red-stained mahogany and white granite create a stunning effect in the owner's bathroom.

style. During many subsequent design meetings, they developed a cleanly executed, almost minimalist style of decoration which makes use of cream leather furniture, white granite, pale carpets, and Formica headlinings, and contrasted with just two woods in their natural form, a warm, interestingly-grained Australian lacewood and a dark, richly-colored Madagascar ebony. In its finished form, the interior is sternly rectilinear, with hardly a curve or rounded edge, but this does not mean that the result is either cheap, easy to build, or uninspiring. In fact, the result, although at first strangely empty to the western eye, is ultimately stunning.

The layout of the accommodation is also unusual. On the main deck amidships, a staircase in the lobby rises and falls to the upper and lower decks, giving access to a large day head (unusually provided with a urinal), the main deck saloon, and the master suite. The main deck saloon is primarily designed as a day area (with a collection of Italian leather settees, hi-fi, and flat-screen television), serving as an air-conditioned annex to the aft deck and swim platform, to which access is made through touch-sensitive automatic sliding doors. Forward of the lobby, entered through a comfortably-proportioned study, is the master stateroom.

This delightful full-beam room, with its six oval floor-to-ceiling windows, literally floats on the ocean, is flooded with light, and provides amazing views.

A dressing area, lit by another large porthole and lined with mirror-fronted wardrobes, fills one corner, and a king-size bed the other, but apart from a lone settee and an audio-visual unit in a sculptured display, the room is bare. That is not to say that it feels empty—just luxuriously spacious. Behind the bed, the bathroom, again spaciously bare, is astonishing in its red-stained mahogany walls. The reasoning for the owner's choice of this color is simple—a touch of red makes your skin look much better in the morning. Try it, it's true! Accordingly, the guest bathrooms and day heads are decorated in this color. On the lower deck the six guest staterooms, three doubles and three twins, follow the same scheme of decoration, but entertainment is limited to radio/CD players.

At the head of the stairs rising from the lobby, the upper saloon is the yacht's evening gathering place and entertainment heart. A huge 10ft-diameter granite-topped dining table with a central 6ft 6in stainless steel lazy Susan is surrounded by high-tech leather-covered Balleri dining chairs, the support provided by their reclining backs being controlled by the weight of the incumbent. More leather encases the bar at the aft end of the room— a center for karaoke and television as well as refreshment—from which a herring-boned tongue of sapele wood spills forward into the pale carpet to create a dance floor, flanked by two leather-upholstered seating areas and a baby grand piano. Behind the bar is a smoking room, complete with a smoke extraction system, which leads on through French doors to the open deck beyond. The adjacent video theatre, equipped with a temporary five-foot rear projection television (until plasma technology produces a wafer-thin screen of this size), and what is possibly the most comfortable viewing sofa ever designed, is popular with guests.

Forward of the saloon and theater, the deck levels are raised by half a deck and a wide passageway leads forward and down to the galley and crew quarters, while further stairs lead up to the bridge. *La Baronessa*'s captain, Alan

★ LA BARONESSA

Above ★ The gymnasium is fitted with the latest exercise equipment, including a steam room, shower, and Jacuzzi™.

Right ★ The pilothouse reflects the valuable input of the captain. It has full instrumentation and a walkaround forward of the helm console for watchkeepers, complete with a tiller for course changes.

SPECIFICATIONS

LOA	195ft (59.4m)
LWL	165ft (50.5m)
Beam	34.4ft (10.5m)
Draft 1/2 Load	11.5ft (3.5m)
Displacement 1/2 Load	1,325,000US gallons
Fuel Capacity	42,000US gallons
Water Capacity	9,200US gallons
Electrical Systems	3 X 125 kw gensets, 120/208 vac
Engines	Caterpillar 3512 B 2 x 1,950hp
Cruising Speed	16knots
Interior Design and Exterior Styling	Nuvolari & Lenard
Naval Architecture	Sparkman & Stephens
Builder/Year	Palmer Johnson/1998

Lange, was present in the Palmer Johnson yard throughout the build, and the benefit of this is clearly seen in the layout of the bridge. Every instrument and control on the huge semicircular console was individually placed by the captain, who has created a truly professional layout while at the same time displaying his clear preference for a full complement of traditional instrumentation, rather than the current trend for dials to be displayed on monitor screens. Between the front of the console and the vertical windows is a practical walkaround which enhances visibility for a watchkeeper (Interestingly, a tiller is provided in this forward passageway, making it unnecessary to return to the front of the console to change course in emergency.), as well as providing easily-accessible mounting space for sundry electronics equipment.

Stairs lead down on both sides of the raised guest settee to the side decks, those on the port side continuing to the crew quarters and galley. An advantage of this layout is that in addition to the two full-sized crew floors in the bow sections there is a laundry and store room in the narrow sections at the lowest level. Beneath the bridge is a spacious crew mess and six crew cabins, with stairs leading up to a separate crew lounge. To starboard is a sizable scullery, from which stairs rise to the galley.

This is a spacious room with a centrally positioned wooden-topped butcher block, and ample work surfaces. There is a small oven, microwave, and extensive plate warmers, but the dominant appliance is a pair of 30,000BTU gas burners specifically built for wok cookery. In full cry, they produce almost as much noise and heat as the main engines—an insulation and extraction problem efficiently solved by Palmer Johnson's designers. Up another half level on a mezzanine floor is the servery, with ample surface space on which to assemble up to 30 individual dishes that, presented simultaneously, are often the basis of a Chinese meal. How many other yachts have a galley of this size extending over three decks?

Eminently worthy of mention, the engine room is entered through the dive room, where a separate airconditioned and soundproofed control room looks out over this immaculately engineered space. The secret of its efficiency, says Palmer Johnson, is that a representation of every component was fitted into a full-scale mock-up during the design stage to ensure that accessibility, pipe runs, and wiring are all perfect.

In a period of just two years, over 250 craftsmen from Palmer Johnson, Sparkman & Stephens, and Nuvolari & Lenard, together with the world's leading manufacturers of machinery and electronics, turned lines on paper and put over 716 tons of raw materials into a yacht that is undoubtedly a market leader, both in terms of style and construction. *La Baronessa* is indeed a queen of the seas.

★ LA BARONESSA

LADY GRACE MARIE

107-foot Burger Motoryacht

Having enjoyed their previous 88ft Burger, it was no surprise that Tom and Grace Benson, owners of the New Orleans Saints football team, returned to Burger for their new yacht. The resulting 107ft *Lady Grace Marie* exemplifies its name not only with grace, but with tasteful elegance and style.

During the several years they enjoyed their previous yacht, *Lady Grace,* they made mental notes of the details they'd like on the new one. The new criteria list included a large aft deck, walk-around side decks, and an engine room located aft. Tom Benson's vision, combined with the discriminating taste of his wife, Grace, resulted in a vessel of thoughtful eloquence.

Just 18 months after construction began, *Lady Grace Marie* was delivered in the fall of 1998, a mere three weeks behind schedule, despite the elaborate artisan detailing required for her finishing touches. Jack Perkins, an 18-year veteran captain in his sixth year with the Benson family, supervised the construction at regular and frequent intervals and spent the last two months at Burger overseeing the final installations.

Douglas Richey, Burger's in-house interior designer, collaborated closely with Grace Benson on the interior design and acted as liaison between her and the Burger team of craftsmen and artisans. Aside from the design and elaborate detail, Burger built all the large furniture, and also created the hand-painted details displayed throughout the *Lady Grace Marie*.

"Mrs. Benson wanted classic, clean but elegant designs with an oriental ambience throughout," Richey says. "The Bensons' time spent in the Orient in years past embedded an appreciation and admiration of oriental style in her taste preferences. She reviewed suggestions and ideas during development, then made the definitive decisions. She knew what she wanted the interior to look like, and never swayed from her idea of a classic, yet elegant design."

Understated luxury, artistic expression, and carefully chosen furnishings are obvious, beginning with the first detail seen upon entering the main saloon. A chinoiserie-style armoire hand-painted with oriental blossoms, birds, and trees on an antique red underbase stands in the starboard corner, concealing a Sony Trinitron television and Sony stereo system. A cherry wood bookcase adorns the opposite side aft. Yet another focal point of the main saloon is an oval glass-topped coffee table supported by life-size bronze manta rays swimming peacefully side by side. Cream and taupe silk chairs and a coordinating sofa surround the table to create a relaxing and graceful seating ensemble. Chairs, sofa, and other upholstered pieces on the yacht were chosen primarily from the Baker Furniture Company collection.

Black obechee wood inlays and radiussed corners are used consistently on furniture throughout the interior, including the large round dining table. *Lady Grace Marie*'s recurring theme, however, is the Japanese "Shu" symbol, meaning "welcome." The rounded symbol, carried throughout the décor in subtle gracefulness, fits well with the vessel's overall ambient message of, "relax, unwind and enjoy." Most visitors first see the symbol as a large inlay design on the cherry and obechee dining table. Black lacquered and gold-trimmed dining chairs accented with red silk upholstered seat cushions and cream-toned tassel ties continue the classic oriental motif.

Hand-painted gold-leaf cranes adorn the ivory-based

Porthole ✶ Oriental touches throughout the yacht reflect the owners' appreciation for Far Eastern style, such as this vanity.

Above ✶ Classic, conservative, and graceful, this new 107-footer carries the "signature" Burger teak cap rail from bow to stern.

Left ✶ Protected by an aluminum top, the flybridge is fully equipped for entertaining with a wet bar, grill, and dining table.

★ LADY GRACE MARIE

sliding doors that conceal the wet bar and storage area with understated accents. The acrylic panels, also created by Burger, are purposely painted on their hidden inner side to offer protection from hands and the elements.

The carpeting and ceiling treatments of the main saloon provide the finishing touches that pull the area together in one sweeping uninterrupted flow. Blonde sculpted wool carpeting, custom woven in a swirl pattern, and padded and swirl-sculpted Ultrasuede ceiling treatments reflect the geometric shapes created by the round dining and oval coffee tables. The repetitive light touches of gold-leaf accents, soft lines, circling patterns, and naturally-finished cherry wood result in a graceful exuberance of warmth and elegance.

The elegant main deck powder room features hand-painted lacquered wallpaper in the recurring theme of flowers, birds, butterflies, and trees in tones of light and dark gold on a cinnabar base. The room's main focal point, an adaptation of a temple table, is mirrored by the open-based vanity table. Made of cherry wood by Burger craftsmen, the vanity offers upswept ends and a dark slate gray Kohler sink built into its center, appearing to be more of a lotus bowl than a basin.

Walking a few steps forward on the starboard side from the saloon, one enters the massive combination galley and casual dining area. A granite-topped center work island separates the galley from the forward dinette, yet produces an open and spacious feeling on either side. Panasonic, Gaggenau, Kitchen-Aid, Viking, and SubZero appliances were chosen as the kitchen equipment. The utilitarian aspects of the galley, however, are subdued by "golden leaf" granite countertops and backsplash, and cherry wood cabinetry hand-painted in a crackle finish with ivory and gold accents. The same treatment carries over to the cherry wood island that bonds the galley area together in a combination of graceful style and perfectly planned space.

Areas surrounding the galley dining table of cherry wood topped by Black Galaxy granite offer concealed storage areas and a convenient wine cooler behind matching cherry wood panels. Banquette-style seating upholstery displays an "astrological" motif of moons, stars, and astrologic symbols in deep reds, black and ivory. An interesting tumbled marble mosaic inlaid flooring unifies the space into a pleasant cooking and dining area.

A circular staircase with a hand-carved cherry wood railing leads from the saloon/dining area to the guest and crew accommodation below. The Shu design again meets the eye, this time as a large marble inlay on the foyer floor, and one of the Benson's personal statues offers an inviting welcome to the master and guest suites.

Oversized double doors of solid cherry with raised panels lead into the master suite, and these are matched in magnificence only by the hand-painted mural over the king-size bed. The bird design motif was adapted from a favorite photograph the Bensons took during their travels. Shoji rice paper screens concealing the portholes continue the oriental flare. They also filter strong sunlight and provide a warm-lit atmosphere. An entertainment center concealed behind cherry panels faces the bed, and just aft, the spacious cedar-lined walk-in closet offers ample wardrobe and storage space. Custom brass cabinet pulls again display the Shu symbol.

Doors on either side of the bed lead into a his-and-hers master head, meeting in the middle with a shared combination steam and shower stall. Customized cast-glass shower doors incorporate large raised Shu designs. The spacious master head has pale celery-green Corian countertops and full-width mirrored medicine cabinets.

The guest suites are identical but arranged in opposite directions, each with its own spacious en suite head and light green Corian countertops. Following the same décor as the master suite, the guest suite's focal point is the elegantly embroidered bedding, and the amenities include individual satellite television, ample storage, and cedar wardrobe closets. Also opening from the foyer opposite the master suite are a smaller guest cabin with twin berths, and a laundry room.

A staircase from the starboard passage leads to the raised pilothouse, a spacious area with a plush sofa and captain's chair, both in rich navy blue leather set against the equally rich teak and holly planked flooring. A sophisticated communications system by Electronics Unlimited of Ft. Lauderdale, FL, and an Atlas Energy Shorepower electrical system enable the yacht to cruise worldwide.

A flight of steps up to the flybridge reveals a flawlessly finished permanent aluminum top protecting this spacious area. The bridge is open and uncluttered, with seating that forms a forward-facing curve and a settee upholstered in Sunbrella navy, white, and beige striped fabric. Tom Benson's appreciation and frequent use of the flybridge made him the overseer of its mechanical and instrumentation outfitting, while Grace Benson continued with the design and décor aspects. A SubZero refrigerator

Opp. top ★ The saloon is anchored by an oval glass coffee table supported by a pair of bronze manta rays, and the bird motif on the dining area wall is one of many throughout the yacht.

Opp. bottom ★ An inlaid marble Shu design and a statue greet guests arriving at the lower foyer.

Left ★ With granite countertops and crackle-finished cherry wood cabinets, the galley is as cheerful as it is workable.

Left ✦ The master suite features a hand-painted bird mural over the king-size bed and, with Shoji screens over the ports, is distinctly Oriental in style.

Below ✦ The day head has an open-based temple-style vanity of cherry wood, as well as hand-lacquered wallpaper.

Opp. top right ✦ The raised pilothouse is well arranged for the captain and comfortable for guests.

and ice maker, conveniently located next to the Gaggenau grill, make outdoor cooking a fun pastime, and a teak-topped dining table comfortably accommodates eight people.

Interesting features include wing stations port and starboard for easy docking, while a treadmill used routinely by Tom Benson is at the ready behind the seating area. Aft, the 17-foot Novurania tender with 115 hp Yamaha engine is launched by the 4000 lb. Nautical Structures hydraulic crane.

The clean and uncluttered look of the boat deck is a result of Tom Benson's attitude about keeping a lot of toys and accessories on the yacht. Rather than carrying and maintaining them, he prefers to rent them when family and friends visit, leaving the work to their owners. Perkins notes that the design of *Lady Grace Marie* focused around enjoyment, leisure, and "getaway from business," meaning minimal maintenance.

Crew quarters include the captain's suite with an elevated bed atop a bureau of drawers (with steps for ease of entry), while the en suite head offers maximum privacy. Two crew cabins with two bunks each are spacious, and a nearby laundry area offers additional convenience in the crew area.

Impeccable attention to detail on the teak planked aft deck matches that of the interior. The custom-made cherry, maple, and mahogany dining table with an inlaid teak, obechee, and maple compass rose pattern on its top, seats eight people comfortably. Rattan McGuire chairs upholstered in a contemporary Sunbrella abstract pattern complete the outdoor dining area, continuing the clean, uncluttered style.

The foredeck has forward facing seating that matches the flybridge upholstery, and a large walk-in cuddy area stores deck equipment and accessories.

Lady Grace Marie's spacious walk-around engine room has twin Detroit Diesel 1800 hp 16V2000 DDC-MTU engines, a 20-ton Marine Air air conditioning system, a

SPECIFICATIONS

LOA	107ft (32.61m)
Beam	23ft 6in (7.16m)
Draft	5ft 6in (1.68m)
Max Displacement	150 L.T.
Fuel Capacity	10,000 gallons
Fresh Water Capacity	1,500 gallons
Engines	DDC/MTU 16V2000, 1800 hp @ 2300 rpm
Generators	Northern Lights 45kw
Tender	Novurania Model MX 530DL w/115 hp engine
Naval Architecture	Don O'Keeffe
Interior Design	Owner/Douglas Richey/ Burger Design Team
Exterior Styling	Don O'Keeffe/Burger Design Team
Builder/Year	Burger Boat Company/1998

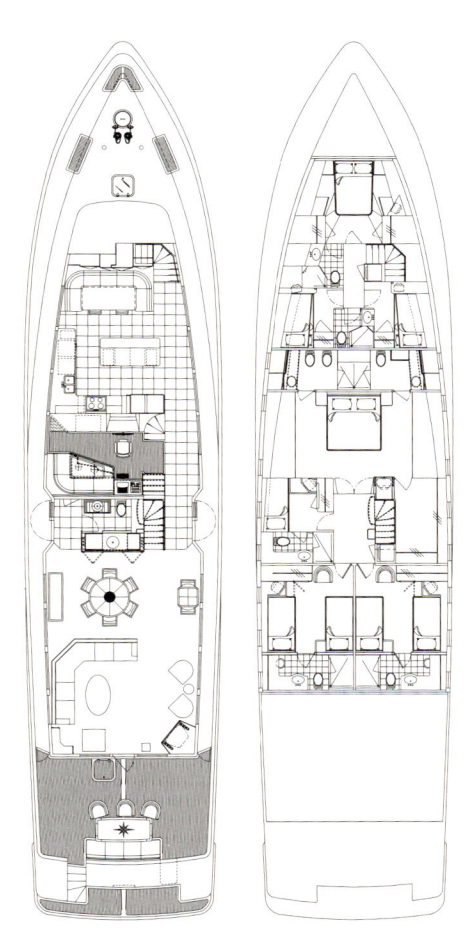

1500gpd Matrix water system and ozone generators for air purification. The adjacent sound proof generator room houses the Northern Lights 45 kW generators. The longest yacht launched by Burger since the new company formed, and the largest boat they've built in more than 22 years, *Lady Grace Marie* houses a complete waste treatment plant, Alfa Laval fuel centrifuge, and an integral fresh/waste oil system.

David Ross, president of Burger, says the idea for the *Lady Grace Marie* began some time ago: "This boat represents our first 23 1/2ft beam raised pilothouse version," he said, "as well as being the largest vessel we had built at the time. Mr. Benson provided us with the opportunity to stretch our craftsmanship abilities and technological talents to the max by making a true, world-class vessel. Not only does it have exceptional items like the hydraulic passerelle and Atlas Shorepower system, but the hydraulics and fuel oil piping throughout the boat are all stainless steel with swagelock fittings, known in engineering circles as the finest quality available. Mr. Benson was very happy to have a vessel that is a leader in its field."

Although the Burger team worked overtime to deliver the *Lady Grace Marie* in a timely manner, it wasn't a minute too soon for the Bensons. The yacht will travel from Palm Beach, FL to the Bahamas and Caribbean, but return to its home base in New Orleans, LA in ample time for football season each year. It will then travel to Rockport, TX, the family's vacation hometown, and finally on to Maine for the summer.

Whether or not there will be another yacht in the Benson future remains questionable but, if so, it will likely be another Burger. Enforcing his understanding of what being a true and loyal "fan" means, Benson repeatedly states that Burgers are like Mercedes Benz cars—they keep their proven features and place attention on continual refinements. He offers the Burger "signature" cap rail as an example, reminding us that some things are so perfect they just can't be improved upon. Richey says the teak cap rail represents a uniquely identifying Burger detail. "It accentuates the line of the sheer around the hull," he says. "It provides a sleek, elegant line to an already outstanding vessel."

★ LADY GRACE MARIE 107

Lady Linda

124-foot Delta Motoryacht

Lady Linda is a stunning example of just how far Delta Marine has changed course from its roots in commercial boatbuilding to being one of the leading yards in America building high-quality luxury yachts. The 124ft *Lady Linda* represents the sixth yacht of its size and the eighth model to emerge from Delta's mold for shallow-draft fast-cruising yachts. The owners of *Lady Linda*, in their search to find the right yard to build their dream boat, had several criteria in mind. They determined early on that they wanted the hull to be fiberglass because of what they considered to be low maintenance costs and potentially high resale value. Rugged seagoing capability combined with long-distance range were also of paramount importance. After carefully studying all the yachts from Delta's 124-foot series to refine their ideas, the owners selected Claudette Bonville of Ft. Lauderdale as the interior designer. Bonville was able to implement style, space-savings, and flair without losing sight of comfort. The combined efforts of the Delta Design Group, Claudette Bonville, and the owners resulted in a standard hull with a redefined superstructure, plus sophisticated engineering and a beautiful interior. *Lady Linda* was ready for world cruising.

The brief for *Lady Linda* centered significantly around elegant entertaining. From the custom storage for over 400 bottles of wine and 200 glasses in the entry foyer and dining saloon to the crystal chandeliers and hand-painted gold and copper-leafed ceilings, the owner's exacting and detailed requirements were achieved.

Bonville brought an element of fun to the interior design by using geometric shapes, most notably the circle as a key design technique. Her use of curves is visible in the round columns, oval seating areas, semi-circular doors, oval headliners set in domed recessed ceilings, a circular stairway, and even whirling curves etched in glass panels.

Centerline stairs sweep up from the swim platform to the spacious aft deck with its fixed oval table. From here semi-circular doors slide open to reveal a saloon that takes advantage of the full beam of the yacht. A superb hand-loomed custom carpet lends focus to the various conversation areas. Splashes of color such as vivid reds from an original painting by Orlando Aquedelo-Botero in the dining area complement the accents of red in the gold-tasseled cushions on the beige furnishings. Gold finds its way into the saloon from the gold-leaf recessed ceiling over the dining area and the hint of reddish gold in the marble and veneers.

Porthole An original painting by Aquedelo-Botero hung in the formal dining area enhances the geometric theme used throughout the yacht.

Above With a standard Delta 124ft hull, the superstructure of *Lady Linda* was redefined to fit the owner's preferences.

Opposite The spacious aft deck has a fixed oval dining table with sun protection provided by the boatdeck overhang.

Right The sundeck was designed for entertaining with a barbecue, wet bar, and outside TV. Sunpads conceal the knuckle crane for the tenders.

★ LADY LINDA

The imposing cherry columns aren't just for décor, but perform the secondary function of concealing the air ducts while the overhangs, which give the area added volume and perspective, also serve to disguise the air conditioning out-takes and the recessed lighting. Banked along the sides of the saloon are half-height cherry and maple burl cabinets with surfaces capped by pale Italian marble. *Lady Linda* is the first Delta yacht to make use of flat screen television—one actually rises from a hidden niche cut through the stone.

A predominant feature is the extensive use of marble cut with waterjets into geometric and elliptical patterns and then book-matched and hand-laid throughout the yacht. The corridor leading from the saloon forward to the main deck VIP stateroom, for example, has a flooring of Italian beige marble, Breccia Oniciata, inlaid with Botticino and Breccia Damascotta peaches and cream marble. The day bathroom to port continues the theme, adding galaxy black granite set off by hand-painted gold-leaf walls. The corridor forward has been customized with cabinets to hold the enormous selection of china and glassware aboard *Lady Linda*, and custom locks were designed to protect the fragile champagne glass stems from snapping when the yacht is underway.

Main picture The imposing cherry columns in the full-beam saloon conceal the engine air ducts, and the hand-loomed custom carpet separates the conversation areas.

Above The recessed ceiling over the dining saloon is gold-leafed, and cherry and maple-burl cabinets surround the area.

The VIP suite is a handsome stateroom of rich, red cherry with a maple burl inlay in the facades, and has a king-size bed facing forward that can be converted into a pair of twins. Panels facing the bed slide back to reveal another flat screen television, and there is a copper-domed overhead. An enormous bathroom forward features a marble flower motif on the shower wall.

The crew lounge is to port off the corridor with raised banquette seating around two tables. It is separated from the galley by a floor-to-ceiling bank of rollaway cupboards and service panels for electronics. The galley, with all commercial equipment, has a central island, with Genuwood and Corian surfaces. *Lady Linda* will run with a contingent of six crew, including a superb chef because of the exceptional amount of entertaining anticipated on board.

A circular staircase of etched glass, gold plate, and polished stainless steel leads to the lower staterooms from the upper deck. The master suite is forward of the engine room and, rather than the usual arrangement which puts the bathroom aft to create a sound buffer from the engines, the owner decided to place the bed athwartships to permit a massive bathroom to port with a two-person Jacuzzi™. Semi-precious marble keystones were cut by

★ LADY LINDA

Above ★ The oversized master bathroom has beige marble cut by waterjets, hand-painted gold wallpaper, and shoji screens over the ports.

Right ★ The bed in the master suite is arranged athwartship. Silk wallcoverings and prints by Jurgen Gorg add to the elegance.

Opp. right ★ The VIP suite features cherry wood with maple burl inlays, and a copper-leaf dome over the king-size bed.

112   THE MEGAYACHTS USA   ★   2000

waterjets into the beige marble background in the bathroom, and a new method of honeycombing the back of this delicate marble helped the builder meet the weight requirements. Hand-painted gold wallpaper hangs in the master bath, and Japanese shoji screens hide the ports. In the master suite, cherry and maple burl joinerwork mixes with pale silk fabric wall coverings, and another 36in flat screen television is hidden behind veneered panels. The artwork on *Lady Linda* was selected to go with the interior design. Prints by Jurgen Gorg are on the walls in the master and guest staterooms.

Two additional queen-size guest rooms are marked by different marble treatments: lapis from South Africa in one and verde jade from Italy in the other, both against Botticino cream. The divider wall is a series of cabinets with sound insulation between them, creating more space in each stateroom. Central mirrors slide back to reveal flat screen televisions and, as in the saloon, the air conditioning outtakes are concealed by the recessed ceiling.

The lower foyer is filled with hidden caches, including a laundry facility behind a hanging picture, a bar and fridge tucked under the mantelpiece, and video storage behind a mirror.

Fiber optic and complex lighting create a delicate atmosphere; for example, crystal figurines that repose on glass shelves are backlit by pinholes of point lighting from behind the wall. The exterior nameplates for *Lady Linda* have a South Beach effect of iridescent rays beaming out of a color pinwheel behind the stainless steel plates.

The courtly look on the lower decks gives way to a deco-feel on the upper level because the owner wanted a fun, albeit naughty, atmosphere for the bridge and skylounge. An arresting combination of dusty peach lacquered cabinets and matching Dakota mahogany granite with blue and sand fabrics is used extensively. Speckled peach plastic laminate walls are an unusual innovation in the pilothouse, where a raised oval seating area has a clear view over the helm station.

The sky lounge features an enormous circular seating area facing aft that creates, when the elliptical deck doors are open, a vast extension of the outside entertaining area. This seating area is mirrored overhead by a circular ceiling recess and, as in the saloon, there is a hidden television screen in the marble counter behind the seats. The coffee table also converts into a circular bed and, with a curtain track for privacy and a head with shower adjacent, *Lady Linda* has an extra stateroom. The open sundeck was designed for entertaining, with a large barbecue grill, wet bar, and outside television. A round custom table can be relocated to the side for more room for sun lounges or parties, and fixed banquettes form a seating area in front

Above ✦ The sky lounge features an enormous circular seating area that converts to a circular bed, creating an extra stateroom.

Left ✦ The pilothouse provides a comfortable gathering place while underway.

Opposite ✦ The lower foyer is filled with hidden surprises: a fridge behind the mantel, a laundry behind a picture, and video storage behind a mirror.

SPECIFICATIONS

LOA	124ft (37.8m)
Beam	25ft 10in (7.9m)
Draft (half load)	6ft (1.8m)
Engines	2x MTU/DDEC 2000 series @ 1,800 hp each
Displacement (half load)	186 tons
Max Speed	20 knots
Cruising Speed	17 knots
Fuel Capacity	9,000 US gal (34,020 liters)
Fresh Water capacity	1,100 US gal (4,158 liters)
Generators	Twin 65 kw Northern Lights
Stabilizers	Naiad 404
Material	Molded Fiberglass
Interior Designer	Claudette Bonville
Naval Architect	Delta Design Group
Builder/Year	Delta Marine/1998

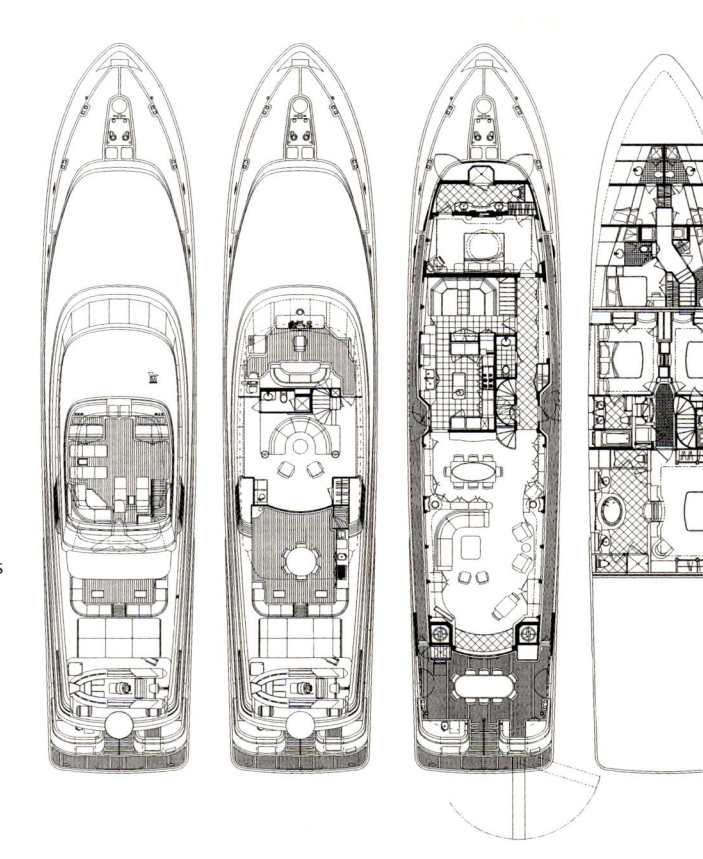

of the padded and raised sun beds. Hidden under the sun pads is a hydraulic knuckle boom crane by Nautical Structures which can launch the 16' tender aft or on either side.

A molded fiberglass bimini top protects the flybridge, and two fiberglass covers protect the two navigation stations when not in use. At anchor, parasols can be mounted on the foredeck so the guests and crew can enjoy that area as well.

This is the first Delta to use the new Detroit Diesel DDEC/MTU 2000 Series engines which, with a lower profile, adds even more space to the already large engine room. With these engines, *Lady Linda* tops out at 20 knots and cruises comfortably at 17 knots.

Other interesting features of the yacht are the sea chest in the engine room for all water inlets, and the connections for the owner's laptop computer throughout the yacht, including several exterior points, so that he has immediate access to his office and clients from anywhere on the yacht.

And, with *Lady Linda* cruising all over the world, it's obvious that she has lived up to the expectations of the owner and his wife.

★ LADY LINDA

Marlena

126-foot Trinity Sportsfisherman

I may as well confess here and now that I have always had a secret infatuation with sportfishing yachts as a genre. They exude a singleminded purposefulness, their engineering, design and styling all reflecting their one true goal— to get out there and hook a big one. All else is subordinate to that purpose. But when Sam Gershowitz commissioned *Marlena*, he understood that by building a sportfishing yacht of this size he could have all the traditional features implied by the nature of the boat, and still enjoy the comfort and spaciousness that its 126ft length affords—in short, having his nautical cake and eating it, too.

For me, the initial impression was the most memorable. I saw *Marlena* for the first time just off St Barth's, charging through a boisterous sea, shouldering aside the waves with aplomb, eventually revealing her true size when she finally came abeam of us. Our eye is trained in this age of megayachts to associate length with volume; accommodations are maximized, and the resulting profile reflects this emphasis. Compared to other motoryachts of her size, *Marlena* seems, well, endless. She has the sportfisherman's low, uncluttered profile, and her length allows her to keep her superstructure proportionately lower, thus seeming even sleeker and having to resort to none of the eyefooling design tricks to visually reduce her bulk.

Her profile is classic: the sheer sweeps aft from the bow in a graceful extended reverse curve to a subtle break by the aft end of the superstructure, continuing in a straight low line to the transom. The forward third of her length is a vast, uncluttered deck revealing practical details such as opening hatches and light prisms, features seldom seen on large motoryachts—tender storage on chocks and anchor windlasses. In keeping with her practical nature, safety rails and stanchions are painted white; no teak to varnish or stainless steel to polish. The cockpit is all business. Clad in flawlessly laid natural teak, it reflects Gershowitz's fishing style: a small central table converts to a fishing rod holder, and fish are fought standing, a preference no doubt facilitated by the size and stability of *Marlena* herself. Under the cockpit sole are two

Porthole ★ The curved staircase would be remarkable on any large yacht, let alone one dedicated to sportfishing.

Opp. left ★ With three decks of living space plus a flybridge, *Marlena* doesn't need a tuna tower for her crew to spot fish!

Above ★ *Marlena* is so well-proportioned in the sportfisherman category that her true size isn't apparent until you are close.

Right ★ The pilothouse is all business, with an unobstructed view forward, wing controls, and a Portuguese bridge.

★ MARLENA 117

large refrigerated fish boxes; a central ice-maker blows ice in either or both as needed. The bait well is set into the transom, with an aquarium-style clear face. The insistence on simplicity and practicality is also evident in details like the shock cord checking the cockpit scupper lids—nothing fancy, it just works. Needless to say, the entire cockpit coaming is entirely smooth, free of anything that could snag a fishing line. Finally, one of six steering and control stations is located here.

Five steps lead up to a small aft deck overlooking the cockpit, a thoughtfully provided area from which to observe the fishing action. A table and L-shaped settee are located to port, and a day head is to starboard. The upper deck and flying bridge are accessed via a ladder adjacent to the day head.

Upon reaching the flying bridge, the working station most logically related to the cockpit, two things become quickly evident. First, *Marlena*'s true size is revealed by the unobstructed view fore and aft. Second, Gershowitz's choice of omitting a tuna tower becomes obvious: the flying bridge is already as high as any tuna tower would be on a smaller boat. Like the cockpit, the flying bridge is all business: an L-shaped settee takes up the port side, and a comprehensive set of controls and instruments faces forward. Just in front of the helm station is another settee.

A ladder leads down to the pilothouse and upper deck, and it is here that *Marlena*'s alternative nature begins to manifest itself. The aft section of this level is devoted to an open teak deck, with a small settee to port, and a set of steering and engine controls facing aft, overlooking the cockpit. The upper lounge, just forward of the open deck, is simply and tastefully decorated in muted colors, the woodwork a combination of straight grain and bird's eye maple, bleached and lightly stained. The Gershowitzes approached the interior design and décor challenge in a sensible and straightforward way: they knew what they wanted and so decided that they might as well do it themselves. Working with designer Dee Robinson,

Opp. left ★ The main saloon, with a view of the fishing action aft, combines areas for entertaining and relaxing.

Left ★ With Lucite balusters and a graceful curve, the staircase aboard *Marlena* is functional as well as being a work of art.

Below ★ The formal dining area forward of the saloon can seat as many as 12 when fully extended, and the buffet hides a wet bar and wine chillers.

Marlena Gershowitz has crafted accommodations which reflect their preference for understated elegance and an informal lifestyle.

The lounge itself features a settee and coffee table to port, a small table with four chairs to starboard and, on the partition between the lounge and pilothouse, a wet bar and television. Together with the open upper deck, it becomes an alternate area for quiet relaxation. Forward of the lounge is the pilothouse. A centrally located helm seat allows access to all controls and instruments, as well as an unobstructed view over the foredeck. On either side just aft of the helm seat are two small settees. Side doors port and starboard lead to auxiliary docking controls and a Portuguese bridge wrapping around the steeply raked windscreen.

A curving stairway to starboard of the upper lounge leads to the main deck. Entering (or stepping down to) the open-plan main lounge and dining area can make one forget that this is a sportfisherman. As the Gershowitzes are quick to point out, they sacrificed nothing when they built *Marlena*. The pale bird's eye maple and soft, muted fabrics are a theme carried throughout the boat, and the sense of relaxation offered by furniture is sensory as well as visual: the color theme is relaxing, but the style makes no concession to their insistence on comfort. Three furniture clusters give a variety of grouping options, including entertainment by a large-screen television. Underfoot is a carpeted sole with marble borders.

The dining area, just forward of the main lounge, reveals the same décor scheme. The table can seat as many as 12 when fully extended, and a counter on the starboard side includes a wet bar and temperature and humidity controlled wine lockers. A bulkhead separates this space from the galley, with access via an open passageway to starboard. Incorporated in the bulkhead

★ MARLENA 119

Right ★ The his-and-hers bathrooms in the master suite that share a central shower have ornate touches such as wall sconces and decorative inset sinks.

Below ★ The full-width master suite, with a settee and built-in bureaus, is serene and comfortable.

120   THE MEGAYACHTS USA   ★   2000

SPECIFICATIONS

LOA	126ft (38.4m)
LWL	112ft 2in (34.2m)
Beam (max)	26ft (7.9m)
Draft (full load)	6ft 1in (1.8m)
Displacement (light)	235,200lbs
Fuel capacity	10,000 gallons
Range at 25 knots	1,200nm
Speed (max/cruise)	33/28 knots
Main engines	2 Paxman 12V185 diesels, each 3,500hp @ 1,950rpm
Generators	2 X 65kW Northern Lights
Anchor windlasses	Maxwell
Naval architect	Trinity Yachts
Exterior styling	Sharp Design
Interior design	Dee Robinson/Marlena Gershowitz
Builder/Year	Trinity Yachts/1998

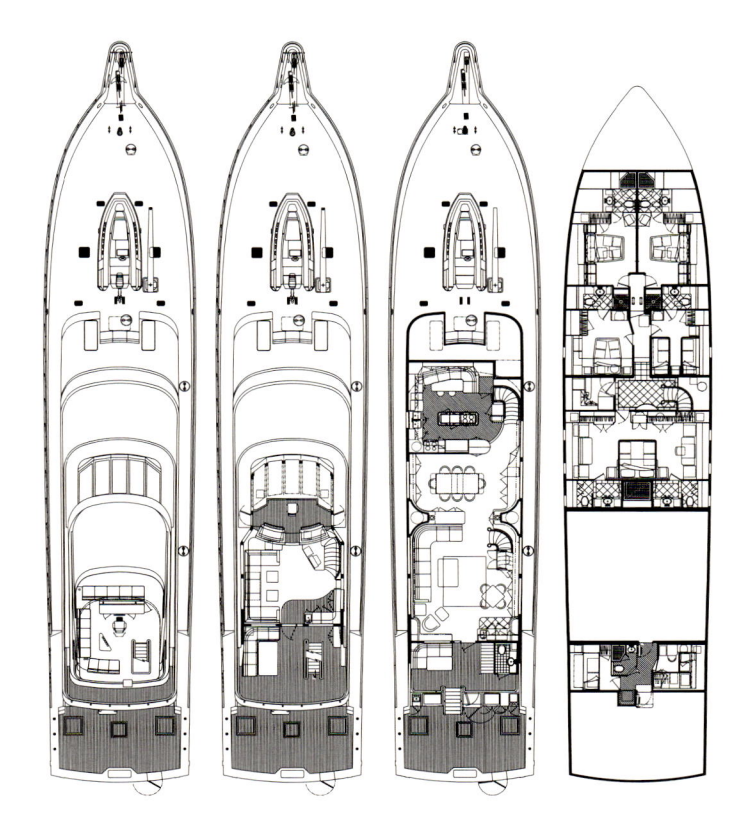

are dish and glassware lockers. At first glance the galley seems somewhat modest for a yacht this size, but I was quickly set straight by both owner and captain. They do all the cooking, and what they wanted was a well-equipped functional galley; no need for fancy professional equipment to satisfy a professional chef. There are ample storage lockers, Corian countertops, and a full range of appliances; in short, everything one would want in a good home kitchen.

The passage leading to the galley also includes a curved staircase to the accommodations below decks. At the bottom of the steps is a small foyer, clad with mirrors on all sides and overhead. An original detail is the framed mirror hung on the mirrored bulkhead. The mirrors relieve the closed-in feeling inherent in what would otherwise be a small, dark space, and the eye is easily led forward to the passageway to the four guest staterooms. Overhead hatches provide illumination, and rising steps and an offset floor plan relieve this access space of excessive linear feeling. The staterooms themselves reflect the same taste and underlying philosophy as the rest of the accommodations: elegant, discreet design and color schemes flawlessly executed. All have en suite heads, three offer queen-size berths, one has twins with an additional fold-down occasional berth. The two forward staterooms cleverly create space by having the berths set athwartships. All four staterooms also feature cedar-lined hanging lockers and, an often overlooked detail, ample storage space for empty bags and suitcases.

Directly aft of the mirrored foyer is the master stateroom. Calling it spacious would be an understatement, as it takes up the entire 26ft beam, yet there is no feeling of using space for the sake of it; the space is there, and it is well utilized to achieve a comfortable, peaceful feeling, enhanced also by the décor scheme carried throughout *Marlena*. His and hers heads just aft share a central shower, and also provide an additional sound barrier from mechanical noise, as the engine room is just aft of the owners' suite.

Access to the crew quarters and engine room is from an entry centrally located at the forward end of the main cockpit. The crew is well taken care of, with a captain's cabin and separate crew cabin, and a shared head compartment. Adjacent to the engine room entrance is a fishing rod storage space. The engine room itself reflects accepted practice in safe and efficient machinery installation, notable also for the amount of space available to the engineer, the rational layout of all ancillary systems, and thoughtful safety details such as stainless steel rails around the Paxman main engines themselves. An underwater exhaust system practically eliminates noise and fumes in the cockpit, clearly a desideratum in a sportfishing yacht.

After owning a 95ft sportfisherman, Sam and Marlena Gershowitz built *Marlena* in order to fit their growing family. Her larger size enabled them and designer Doug Sharp to pen a dramatic iteration of the sportfisherman breed, built to a scale uncommon in this type of yacht. Her practical and informal yet uncompromisingly comfortable character fits in perfectly with their lifestyle. She also brings in the big ones.

MIA ELISE

136-foot Intermarine Trideck Motoryacht

There are few lasting secrets in the marine industry other than those that apply to design and technological innovations, and a good many of these—the innovations, not the secrets—ultimately fail to pass the quality test over the long haul. In broader terms, the existence of a shipyard supported by massive resources and a proven record in the design and construction of military and private vessels exceeding 85ft can hardly be described as a secret. Yet this is a fair characterization of Intermarine Yachting, which occupies a 21-acre, fully-equipped construction and refit site on the Savannah River, and which launched the 136ft trideck motoryacht *Mia Elise*.

A virtual unknown by comparison with older established rivals, Intermarine was formed in 1986 (as Intermarine USA) to design and build GRP minehunters for the US Navy, launching nine of these 190-footers during the following decade, thereby accumulating a formidable and perhaps unparalleled expertise in large vessel GRP multi-classification conformance.

Mia Elise, hull number two since the company moved into the private yacht sector in the mid 1990s, is an exemplary beneficiary of this experience. Built to ABS standards, her preliminary hull drawings came from the design firm of Paragon, while naval architect Luiz de Basto, who has some 200 designs and refits in his portfolio, completed the hull design and was also sole designer of the yacht's superstructure.

The result is a highly pleasing exterior profile that reflects the de Basto flair for expressing elegance and harmony in the convergence of straight and curved lines—an effect that often escapes other architects whose passion for radical lines can produce an aesthetic mismatch that only the designer and the vessel's owner will truly love. In yacht design, as elsewhere, restraint has its virtues.

The interior décor on board *Mia Elise* was undertaken by Marc Michaels. For wood, the firm chose fluted, along with sliced and Honduras, mahogany, and eucalyptus burl; all of these handsomely-grained woods are either naturally dark or stained to provide contrast to Philippe Starck's stainless steel accents, which are found throughout the main public areas and guest accommodations.

Raw silk wall coverings, coffered overheads, and a floor of red onyx tile bordered by orange onyx (with tiger's eyes marking intersections) lend grace and substance to the interior design. Where used, carpeting is mainly neutral in shade except in those areas featuring a custom carpet rich in color and pattern.

The total interior effect in the yacht's public areas is notably masculine—black granite countertops in the sky lounge, for example, Majilite (faux) ostrich skin walls and raw silk panels and overheads, recessed paneling in eucalyptus burl and embossed leather, highly polished stainless steel thresholds on all exterior doors, venetian blinds, bar chairs in leather, and elsewhere, an assortment of teak and rattan easy chairs among heavy wool-upholstered or leather couches.

Our detailed review of *Mia Elise* starts at the lower deck forward where the crew quarters incorporate a spacious crew galley and lounge with ample seating for eight around a table of Tanganyika walnut. Three adjacent cabins, each with head and shower, provide berths for five crew, while the captain and engineer have separate cabins elsewhere. All the accommodations are above the waterline and thus are fitted with opening portholes or windows.

Porthole The combination of mahogany and eucalyptus burl contributes to the masculine décor of *Mia Elise*.

Above The classic styling by Luiz de Basto is best seen with *Mia Elise* underway at displacement speeds.

Right The bridge deck has a partially covered dining table that provides alfresco dining for a dozen guests.

★ MIA ELISE 123

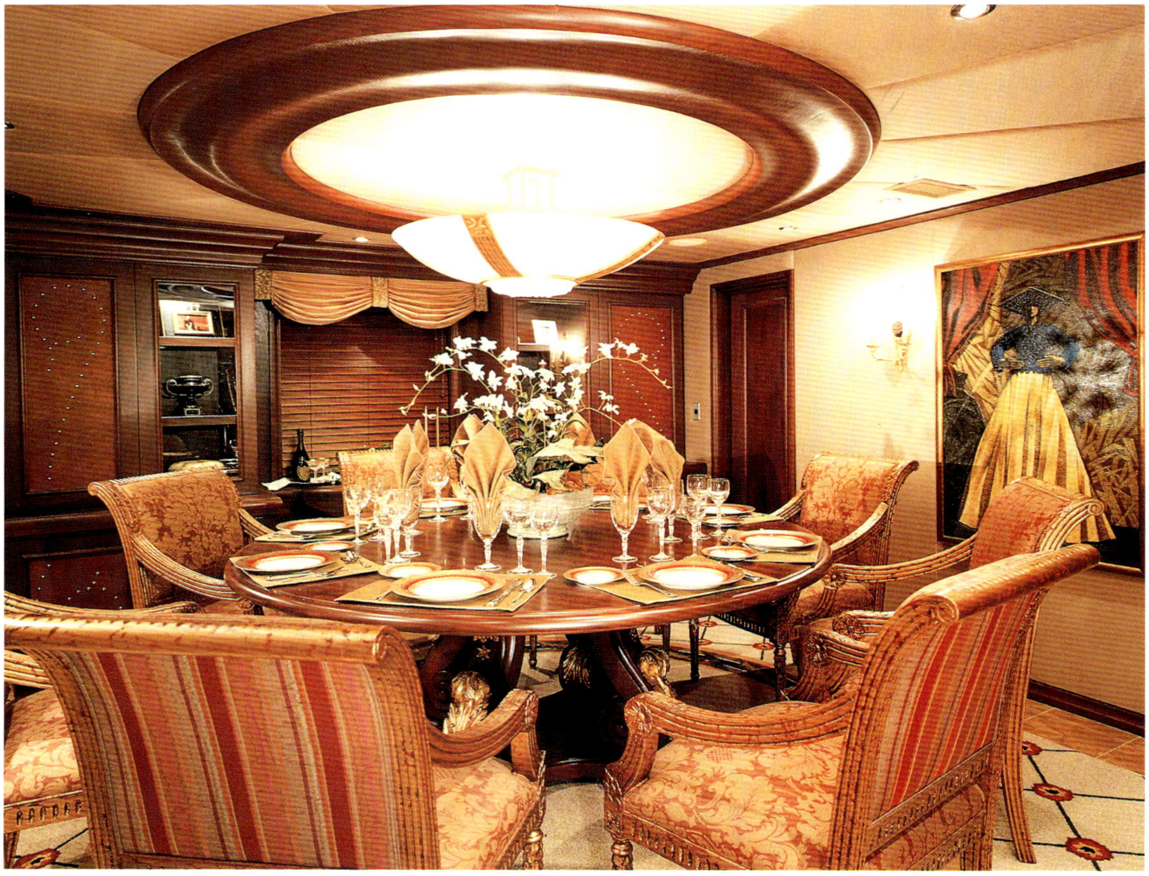

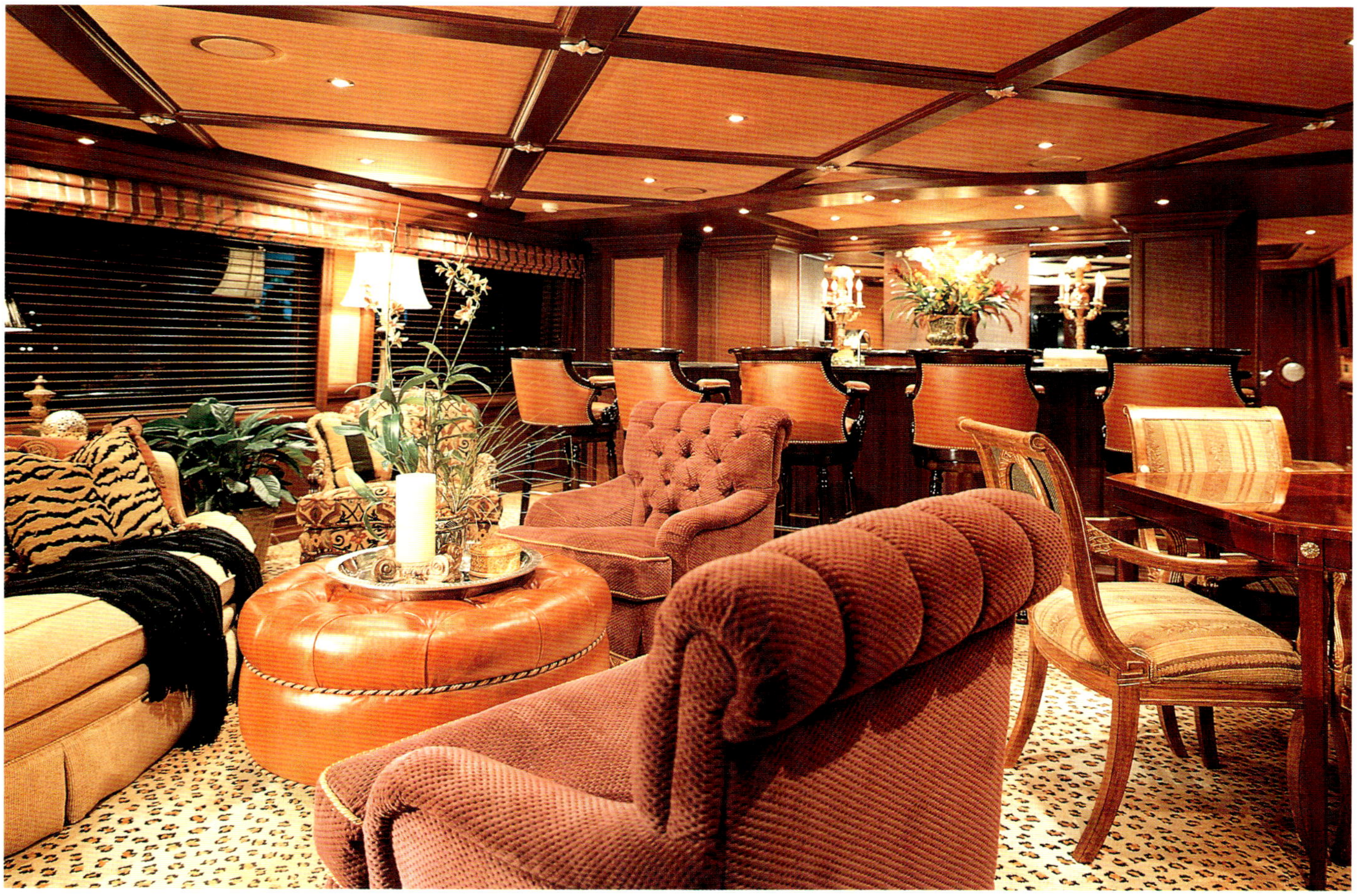

The pantry and laundry room are located aft of the crew space, which ends at the after bulkhead. Beyond this are four double staterooms grouped around the lower deck foyer.

The largest of these staterooms is the VIP suite which, like all the guest accommodations, is set away from outboard walls to minimize vibration while underway. Each stateroom offers variations on the yacht's unifying details of fluted mahogany and Majilite ostrich overheads, although all are furnished with nightstands, mirrored vanities, aromatic red-cedar closets, and wardrobes. In the VIP suite the distinctions include leather-embossed panels, headboards of fine-grained mahogany, and a bathroom flooring of Giallo Royale marble with contrasting countertops in a rich antique verde marble.

Of the three remaining guest staterooms, two are doubles, each with its own distinctive marble flooring, countertops, and walls in the bathrooms, while the third is presently used by the owner's two small children. It has full-size twin berths with polished mahogany leeboards. A bulkhead finished with a raffia overlay contrasts with the backlit ricepaper *shoji* panels that form the outboard wall of this ocean-going rumpus room. A gymnasium and steam room are located off the lower deck foyer and are notable for the plasma-screen door which may be electronically "fogged" for privacy while working out, or left clear to optimize the foyer's visual space. Vertical oval mirrors are fitted to sliding doors inside the gym, which, along with the usual equipment, has a television and audio system.

From here a spiral stairway ascends to the main deck entry hall, a magnificent and welcoming space made all the more imposing by its flamboyant design and floor of orange and red onyx. An adjacent powder room is paneled in burl eucalyptus with a bold pattern of broad nailheads at the intersections, each finished in gold leaf to match the golden overhead. This resplendent space is further distinguished by a blue marble countertop around a crystal glass sink, lit from beneath to dramatize the engraving incised in the glass. The owner's suite is forward of the foyer and occupies almost half of the main deck interior. Double doors lead to a study *cum* den to starboard, while to port a spacious wardrobe has convex doors which display another unifying detail found everywhere on *Mia Elise*—a pattern of X-shaped figures. Here they are formed of brushed stainless steel inlays, elsewhere they appear on carpeting and paneling.

The suite's main furnishings—apart from mirrored vanity and cabinetry of mahogany and burl eucalyptus over cedar interiors—include a plasma-screen television and entertainment center. As in the powder room off the main deck foyer, the focus in the owner's bathroom is on visual distinctiveness: a gold-leaf barrel vault overhead by Breccia Van Domme, onyx flooring, a large ovaloid Jacuzzi™, and separate compartments for shower, head and bidet, with a profusion of exotic marbles for the countertops.

A second entryway from the galley is a Micro Eye sliding door leading to the main deck dining room and activated by a wave of the hand for the convenience of servers. Inside the dining room, which is paneled in fluted mahogany, is a circular table of stained cherry burl standing on a richly-patterned custom carpet bordered by onyx tiling. Seating is for eight in gilded upholstered banquet chairs designed on a scale to match the heavily-built gold-leaf table base.

Opp. top ★ The dining room features a circular table of stained-cherry burl standing on a richly-patterned custom carpet bordered by onyx tiles, with seating for eight in gilded banquet chairs.

Opp. bottom ★ The sky lounge, with faux leopard-skin carpeting, a black granite bar with leather chairs, a game table, and a coffered ceiling, is striking.

Right ★ Guests staying in the four double staterooms, each with mahogany paneling, faux ostrich overheads, and marble baths, will have no complaints.

Right • The master suite, with a sculptured mahogany and leather headboard, study/den, and walk-in closet, fills half of the main deck forward.

Below • The owner's bathroom has a gold-leaf vault overhead, onyx flooring, and a profusion of marble surfaces.

A curtained entryway leads from the dining room to the capacious main saloon. Here, natural light from large windows looking out over the side decks highlights the yacht's principal décor of mahogany paneling, onyx and carpeted flooring. There is a handsome table finished in gold leaf, and abundant seating in the form of couches and easy chairs arranged around side and coffee tables. A vividly colored oil painting on the aft bulkhead slides into a recess below to reveal a large plasma-screen television.

In the main saloon, as elsewhere on *Mia Elise*, air-conditioning handlers are concealed in cabinets built to match the yacht's principal woods of choice. There are two tenders cradled on the open deck aft of the saloon, a Novurania rigid inflatable with a 130hp outboard and a Donzi speedboat (MerCruiser 280hp), each served by Marquipt telescoping cranes concealed in the overhead. Open stairways lead from here down to the swimming platform and engine room stern entry on the lower deck, and up to the bridge deck. Enclosed stairways centrally located inside the yacht connect the three guest decks.

The bridge deck is the site of the sky lounge, which has the most visually striking interior décor on *Mia Elise*. Its carpet is faux leopard skin bordered by onyx flooring with

SPECIFICATIONS

LOA	136ft (41.45m)
Beam	28ft (8.53m)
Draft	6ft (1.83m)
Displacement	253 tons
Speed (max/cruise)	20/18 knots
Range	3,500nm @ displacement speed
Engines	Twin MTU 12V396TE94
Generators	Twin Northern Lights M668T 80kW
Fuel capacity	11,500 gallons
Naval architect	Intermarine
Interior designer	Marc Michaels Interior Design
Exterior styling	Paragon/Luiz de Basto
Builder/Year	Intermarine Yachting/1998

the tiger's eye motif. There are black granite countertops forming a spacious bar, high-backed bar seats upholstered in leather, large gilded mirrors on the facing bulkhead, and a diagonally-beamed coffered ceiling.

Slatted venetian-style window shades, paneling of fluted mahogany, and a gaming table topped with burl eucalyptus complete the effect—in sum, part gentleman's club, part safari lodge with the emphasis on comfort and visual distinction. Two large windows flank each outboard wall, with sliding glass doors leading aft giving additional light—but not too much. To minimize glare, exterior glass on the vessel is half-inch-thick solar gray.

An alfresco dining table with seating for a dozen is situated aft on the bridge deck, and well forward on this deck is the captain's stateroom. This double-bedded cabin with its own bathroom lies forward and connects to the navigation station and wheelhouse, which features an instrument display set against Macassar Ebony and a chart table in the same lustrous wood. The flooring is Mayan Cherry parquet. A black leather bench facing the controls provides seating and excellent forward and side visibility for the watch crew. (It may be worth noting, for those who wonder about megayacht prices, that the narrow, curved windows at each corner of the wheelhouse cost $8,000 each.)

The flybridge (or uppermost deck) on *Mia Elise* is entirely uncovered except for the shade provided by the antenna mast. Here, there are sun pads, ample seating, and lounging space in the form of cushioned white benches; a couple of shapely tables made in Corian, a circular Jacuzzi™ of impressive size, and a wet bar with plush white stools lure guests outside. A dumbwaiter runs from here to the sky lounge bar one deck below.

There is another interior on *Mia Elise* which, for the technically minded at least, deserves special mention—and that is her engine room. This can only be described as an engineer's fantasy: brilliantly lit, with high ceilings, generous access to equipment and fixtures, a separate glass-faced monitoring station, and enough floor space for a tango contest. With the engineer's cabin, storage and equipment lockers, it takes up more than a third of the lower deck and was clearly designed for comfort rather than as a necessary but burdensome intrusion into leisurely life at sea.

Mia Elise has twin MTU 396 Series engines, giving a range of 3,500nm at displacement speed, two 80kW Northern Light generators, and stabilizers and bow-thruster by Vosper.

The minor fact that the engine room soundproofing came from Van Cappellan—a major supplier to Feadship—indicates that Intermarine is not cutting corners in its venture into the megayacht industry, and is likely to prove a mettlesome contender on both sides of the Atlantic.

★ MIA ELISE

Montana

94-foot Ferretti Motoryacht

Over two years ago, Italian motoryacht builder Ferretti announced that it was forming a new company to develop a range of larger yachts. The result was Ferretti Custom Line SpA, which has produced a variety of designs from 91ft (28m) to 111ft (34m), with the first of these making an eagerly awaited public appearance at the Cannes Boat Show.

Ferretti has set the pace in expanding the technical side of motoryacht design in recent years. It has its own Engineering Division that uses complex computer systems to find new solutions to enhance the yacht's performance. The evolution of the Ferretti style and the quality developed for the standard Ferretti range can be clearly seen in *Montana,* the new Custom Line 94. On this design, as on others, the company has worked closely with Zuccon International Project Studio to advance both the technology and styling of the boat.

Montana's profile is aesthetically pleasing, with the flowing lines emphasized by the window shapes. A molded contour above the lower windows acts as a link, bringing together the components of the superstructure and terminating in the cleanly integrated arch mast. There is a businesslike air about the half-height wheelhouse that sits on top of the main body of the superstructure, creating a base for the flybridge above. Combined with the powerful hull lines, there is an exuberance about the style, giving the 94 a youthful, exciting appearance, which is a distinct break away from the conventional Ferretti.

The sleek hull is molded from composites and has a chine line which rises in a smooth curve to merge with the bow close to deck level. Half-height bulwarks in the forward section, topped by stainless steel rails, then become full height towards the stern. There is an incline in the bulwark line to match the flow of the saloon windows and the deck level here drops down a couple of steps. At the stern the curved transom descends to the narrow swim platform in a distinct line which matches that of the aft end of the flybridge.

The hull sides are clean except for the line of oval ports, air intakes, and the slim fender line. Below the waterline it has the surprisingly deep deadrise of 15

Porthole Guest cabins feature cherrywood paneling and silk wall coverings, lending a faintly oriental style.

Above There's no question that *Montana* is pure Ferretti, yet the half-raised pilothouse and notched sheerline are breaks with tradition.

Left The cockpit has an inlaid teak table with a curved settee, and the saloon is reached through curving glass and stainless steel doors.

Opposite The flybridge controls duplicate those in the pilothouse, and the electronics panel lowers electrically when not in use.

★ MONTANA

degrees which contributes to the smooth running of the yacht. At the stern the propellers are in semi-tunnels; it's the first time Ferretti has used this concept, which makes the propellers more efficient and reduces the draft. It is a hull form which promises excellent seaworthiness and also helps to give the 94 a very sporty appearance.

The detailed engineering work of this design is particularly apparent in the rear garage. The large hinged transom door opens under hydraulic power to reveal the twin level storage for the tenders. The upper tender rolls out on rails ready to be launched by the flybridge mounted crane. The lower tender can then be deployed and there is further storage for a Jet Ski on the flybridge. The passerelle deploys from a cover on the port side, while a matching molded cover to starboard hinges out and down to reveal the swim platform steps.

A door from inside the garage leads into the engine room utility area and there is also deck access from a side door under the flybridge ladder. This utility room houses most of the auxiliaries, including the generator, so that the sound is kept well away from the accommodation. A door leads forward from here to the main engine room where there is an air of almost surgical cleanliness. Here sit the twin V-16 Detroit-MTU Series 2000 diesels with the fuel tanks which supply them on either side. The four exhausts are clad in stainless steel and are led to underwater exits designed to keep the noise and exhaust gases firmly under control. The 1,800hp of each engine is taken through the ZF gearboxes and the lowered shaft line then continues directly to the propellers.

Montana has a layout with the lounge and dining area combined in a large saloon, allowing space for the master cabin at main deck level forward. However, if this main cabin is located below, then there is space for a separate lounge and dining room with the galley in between. In this latter version the crew accommodation is much more compact.

Access to the lounge is through the beautiful curve of the stainless steel framed doors. The interior invites you in, the wide sweep of the cream leather settee being the focus of the seating area, with a bar opposite on the starboard side. The Ferretti trademark, a highly lacquered cherrywood finish, is very much in evidence, particularly in the dining area, which is adorned with full-height

Opposite ★ The saloon, with leather settee and forward dining area, is finished in highly-lacquered cherrywood, a Ferretti trademark.

Top ★ The master suite reflects the curve of the forward superstructure around the headboard, and features a spacious marble-lined bathroom.

Above left ★ Each guest cabin has a spacious bathroom, as well as a combination desk/vanity/entertainment center.

Above right ★ The twin guest cabins have walk-in closets behind shoji-style doors, as well as en suite bathrooms.

Above In the pilothouse, a leather captain's chair faces the leather-lined dashboard offering an array of electronic choices. Easy access is provided to the forward deck through a pantograph door beneath the electrical panel to starboard.

Opp. top The transom folds down hydraulically to create an extra-wide teak swim platform, as well as to provide access to the cleverly-engineered double-decker tender storage that holds two tenders, launched by the flybridge crane.

wood paneling. Here mirrors help to enhance the space and the large windows, which have unique horizontal fabric blinds, allowing natural light to permeate.

The dining table is an engraved glass oval unit with eight cream leather chairs to match. A sideboard is set into the forward bulkhead and a door on the port side opens directly into the superbly equipped galley, which has adequate space for a small dinette for the crew. An outside door gives deck access from the galley and another one inside to starboard leads to a vestibule which houses the stairs to the staterooms below, as well as those up to the pilothouse, and also includes the stairway (via a door) to the crew accommodation forward, a day head, and finally, access to the master cabin.

This is a delightful cabin, with the curve of the forward superstructure styled to frame the mirrored glass behind the bed. Finished in cherrywood paneling, there is a settee and a vanity unit as well as hanging closets and drawers in the entrance passageway. The bathroom is stunning, with a full-size bath, twin basins, and a head and bidet set off with large mirrors, contrasting with the hand-selected green marble tops and deck.

Down below there are two mirror-image twins, both with en suite bathrooms and huge walk-in closets. Silk paneling separated by horizontal wooden strips gives a faintly oriental ambience. The VIP cabin aft follows a similar theme, but with more emphasis on wood paneling. Here, doors on each side of the bed give access to the closet to port and the bathroom to starboard. The walk-in closet has access to a separate head. A settee and vanity unit complete the picture of this full-width cabin, which rivals the master in terms of style. Throughout the staterooms, the high quality of craftsmanship is evident.

The pilothouse features a black leather captain's chair facing an array of electronic screens. Black leather is also used to provide contrast to the polished wood around and over the dash. Above on the flybridge are matching instruments in an electronics panel, which can be lowered when not in use. There are twin seats on both sides in a very professional-looking layout while behind are all the leisure facilities—bar, barbecue, sunbed, settee, and table. A fold-down Bimini top can be erected to give shade.

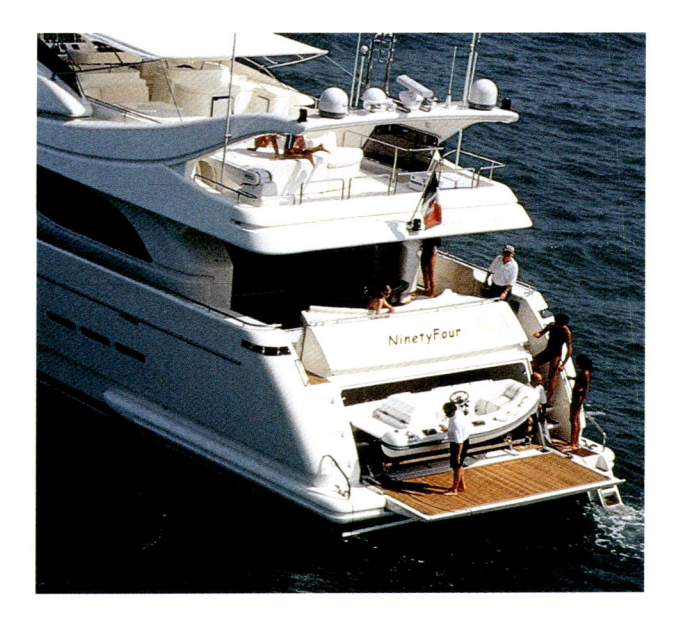

The cockpit is equally well-equipped for leisure use, with a beautiful inlaid oval teak table and a matching settee against the transom. The mooring facilities on each side are covered over, sadly hiding the stainless steel fittings which are in themselves a work of art. Forward there are matching fixtures and good anchors, while the sunbed on the far end of the superstructure lifts under hydraulic power to reveal a second garage capable of housing a couple of jet skis, complete with launching crane.

It all adds up to a wonderful motoryacht which also performs impeccably. In sea conditions, which were stirred up by the remains of a Mistral, the ride was smooth and very controllable and the benefits of the deep deadrise hull were very evident. Upwind or downwind, it was comfortable, and even at slow speed there was good stability. Thrusters were very helpful for harbor maneuvering, enabling the 94 to perform well even in prevailing strong winds and crowded waters. The top speed is 28 knots with the 1,800hp engines, but larger engines can be installed to increase this to 30 knots.

Taking *Montana* into Monte Carlo harbor seemed to be just the right setting for this magnificent addition to the Ferretti fleet. It is not always easy to make a successful move up the size scale, but Ferretti's experience, backed by superb engineering, has once again proved just what a successful combination this can be. The Custom Line 94 sets the scene for a whole new generation of Ferretti motoryachts.

SPECIFICATIONS

LOA	94ft 6in (28.8m)
LWL	78ft 9in (24m)
Beam	23ft 3in (7.08m)
Draft	5ft 9in (1.75m)
Displacement	98 tons
Engines	2 x 1,800hp MTU 16V 2000 M 90
Speed–Max/Cruise	28/26 knots
Fuel Capacity	2376 gal
Water Capacity	792 gal
Design	Ferretti Engineering and Zuccon International
Builder/Year	Ferretti Custom Line SpA/1998

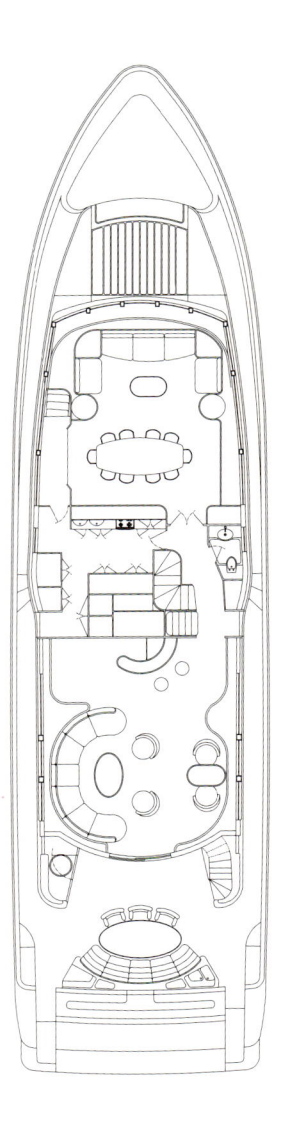

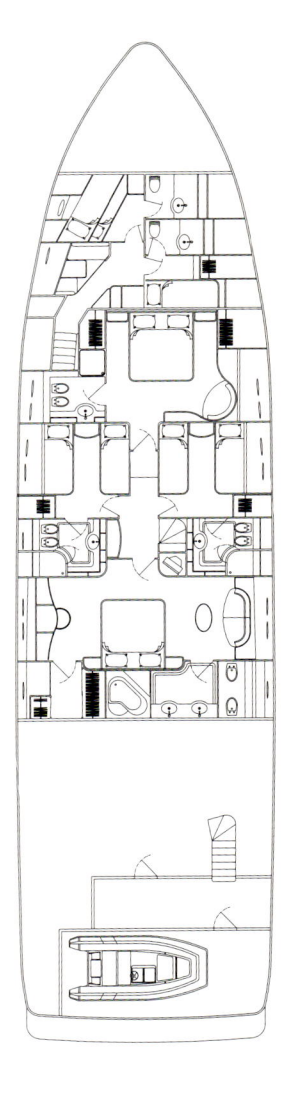

SAVANNAH

90-foot David Pedrick/ Concordia Sloop

There has been, in the past several years, a quiet revolution in the world of sailing, a trend which is sparking a heartfelt response among lovers of traditional yachts. Joining the fleet of modern large sailing craft, built to maximize interior volume with their uncompromisingly straight sheer and high freeboard, is a small but growing number of lovely anachronisms — of long, low, narrow boats, with long overhangs and lofty spars.

One of the most recent creations to join this exclusive fleet is *Savannah*, a 90ft tour de force of single-minded aesthetic purity made possible by the intelligent application of modern boatbuilding technology. Her owner, Randolph Watkins, himself a naval architect, had always desired a classic, but was unwilling to accept the maintenance requirements inherent in old wooden boats. He had some reservations about their performance as well: he wanted to blend the style of the vintage classics with today's America's Cup technology.

After poring over hundreds of traditional large yacht designs and boarding dozens of the surviving classics, Watkins developed an intensely focused understanding of what he wanted, and defined an exhaustive and detailed set of parameters which his dream boat had to satisfy. Watkins worked with Dave Pedrick of Pedrick Yacht Designs, Newport, RI, who became the principal designer and engineer of the project. A great deal of research went into engineering a yacht that, as Pedrick put it, "would last 100 years." The old great yachts we love so much survived because they were well made — engineering to the desired proportions became a very real challenge." Nigel Ingram of Marine Construction Management, joined the team as project manager to coordinate what would undoubtedly be an intricate process. John Munford Design was retained to refine and detail the interior arrangement.

My eye had to readjust when I first saw *Savannah*; she has absurdly long ends, an outrageously narrow beam. Her LWL is 59ft, her beam is 17ft, for an overall length of 90ft. Her sloop rig towers 100ft over a deck swept by a 34ft boom. I looked again and it all made perfect sense, the sailor's atavistic self reawakened to the realization that this is indeed the way proper yachts were designed. The common pitfall of modern "replicas" is that they all too frequently become an amalgam of features lifted from many sources, and so lack aesthetic cohesion. Not so *Savannah*: Watkins and Pedrick distilled their research

Porthole ✶ The cast iron woodstove was designed especially for *Savannah* by Vermont Castings.

Opp. left ✶ The teak deck of *Savannah* is the epitome of the "uncluttered look," with no house to break the expanse of planking and no deck gear to fall over.

Above ✶ Underway, *Savannah* harkens back to a former era of graceful sailing yachts, unmarred by lifelines and uncluttered by deck hardware.

Left ✶ Though small, the steering cockpit continues the classic look of *Savannah* with bronze Lewmar hydraulic sheet winches.

✶ SAVANNAH

into a truly harmonious totality—one can take her or leave her, but there is no arguing with her integrity. Look carefully at her stern: the transom achieves that elusive elegance so often unsuccessfully attempted in recent years—the "wine glass" shape that only works aesthetically when the transom is steeply raked with a long overhang. The latter is here exquisitely detailed with a subtle crease running down the centerline. The overall design is so well proportioned that it plays tricks on the eye as well. Moored or docked near other boats her size is evident, but when I circled her by dinghy while sailing off Mount Desert Island I lost my sense of scale. She could have been 50ft or 100ft, an 8-meter or a J-boat.

Stepping on board requires a partial surrender of cherished beliefs and prejudices. *Savannah* is the most paradoxical yacht I have seen in a good long time, the paradox stemming from her owner's uncompromising prerequisites and the compromises these criteria demand from those sailing her. "The driving force [for the project] was purely aesthetic, unhampered by convenience,"

Main picture   The saloon takes full advantage of the 17-foot beam to create a traditional looking, yet high-tech, interior. Though the wood-burning stove is cast iron, the "vintage" deck beams are actually carbon fiber box sections bonded to the deck for strength and the vent grills are laser-cut aluminum made to look like ornamental ironwork.

Above   The longitudinal galley is narrow enough to provide bracing for the cook while underway, but fully equipped with every possible amenity.

remembers Nigel Ingram. The sweep of her teak deck gives new meaning to the adjective "uncluttered." There are no lifelines, dorade boxes, padeyes, chocks—all the paraphernalia we are so accustomed to tripping over on most boats. The clean sweep is carried right to the bow, as there is no anchor gear on deck. A small section of the stem opens to reveal a roller; the end of the anchor chain must be brought up on deck through this opening and attached to the anchor (normally stowed under the foredeck locker hatch) in order to moor. Given the size of the boat, this can be a bit of exercise for the crew, but it satisfies the desire for clean decks. Seven feet aft of the bow, the Rekmann hydraulic jib furler is recessed below deck level, accessible for servicing from the forepeak locker. One mooring cleat, a capstan, the hatch giving access to the crew's quarters, and the Kevlar inner forestay are the only other elements forward of the mast.

Sailors alarmed by the fact that there are no lifelines should rest easy. For offshore sailing, titanium stanchions can be fitted to the flush carbon fiber receptacles along

★ SAVANNAH   137

the varnished margin board. Aft of her carbon fiber mast the deck is equally clear. The only features are two Fife-inspired skylights exquisitely detailed with fluted Lexan panels; the main companionway, which incorporates vent boxes for the engine room; and the small oval cockpit, with its companionway to the owner's cabin aft. Further aft is the Vectran permament backstay, set well inboard and led below decks to a hydraulic adjustment, a mooring cleat, and the removable radar mast. The only other hardware items noticeable are custom bronze Harken blocks and bronze Lewmar hydraulic winches. The standard Lewmar foot switches were rejected as too clumsy, and custom-designed unobtrusive carbon fiber switches were substituted. Even the ensign staff socket is recessed.

Below decks, *Savannah* changes personality. One steps back into a "between-the-wars" ambiance, a perfectly crafted, traditional but not opulent, interior. Raised paneling enhances the mahogany bulkheads, the deck beams have delicately chamfered edges, and the fine seams of the overhead run fore and aft to tie the interior together visually. With muted fabrics, glass front lockers in the main saloon, and ornamental ironwork vent outlets, the interior seems lifted directly out of a traditional yacht and reassembled here. In point of fact, *Savannah*'s

Opp. top ✶ The dining area adjoins the saloon and, with raised-panel bulkheads and a varnished teak sole, continues the classic décor.

Opp. below ✶ The navigation area is a private compartment off the main passageway, and has a full complement of electronics.

Left ✶ The owner's cabin has direct access to the steering cockpit, and is furnished with a settee to starboard, and a double berth to port.

Below ✶ The owner's head has what appears to be a traditional claw-footed cast-iron tub, but is actually a composite replica.

accommodations are a showcase of technology at the service of aesthetics. The deck beams are carbon fiber box sections, bonded to the deck to create an immensely strong unit. The vent grills are black anodized aluminum, laser cut to a pattern computer-scanned from original wrought iron units. And, for the final tour de force, the bathtub in the owner's head, while looking for all the world like a traditional claw-footed cast iron tub, is a composite replica. A further touch of authenticity is lent by the occasional exposed backing plates and bolt ends for the deck hardware. Classic yachts rarely bothered to hide them, as is so often the practice these days.

The layout is straightforward, in keeping with *Savannah*'s heritage. The narrow beam and short waterline give her the usable interior volume of a modern 65-footer, a concession to aesthetics Watkins deems more than acceptable. Starting aft, the owner's cabin features a double berth to port, with access to the head immediately forward. To starboard past the centerline vanity is a console, settee, and hanging lockers.

The quality of the joinerwork and finish is immediately apparent, as is the meticulous attention to every detail. Indeed, some of the lockers do not have proper catches because Watkins has yet to find what he considers satisfactory ones! Entering the head, one's attention is immediately drawn to the previously mentioned composite tub; the head

Above   Savannah has traditionally long overhangs and such perfect proportions that, from a distance, she could be 50ft or 100ft, an 8-meter or a J-boat.

compartment is otherwise in keeping with the rest of the boat—functional, well laid out, and with excellent quality German-made fixtures. Moving forward, one enters a passageway with engine room to port and navigation station to starboard. Needless to say, the boat has a full complement of electronics. I thought the navigation station a bit too remote from the helm for easy communication with the watch on deck, though its location makes sense in terms of the overall layout. The engine room, to port of the passageway, is small but well laid out, with reasonable access to the engine, generator, and various other mechanicals for servicing.

The main companionway and skylight create a saloon that is light, airy and spacious, unusual for deep, narrow boats. Muted fabrics on the settees complement the varnished mahogany finish, with additional accents provided by the cast iron wood stove and the polished sterling silver displayed in the glass-fronted lockers. Eschewing the now ubiquitous teak-and-holly, plain varnished teak was chosen for the sole. Again, the feeling is of classic elegance, with no jarring overstatements. Continuing forward, a guest cabin with a private head is to starboard, while a linear galley is to port. Ventilators and classic Camper & Nicholson round deck prisms add light and air. The narrow galley is well laid out for cooking under way, as the longitudinal bulkhead of the guest cabin acts

SPECIFICATIONS

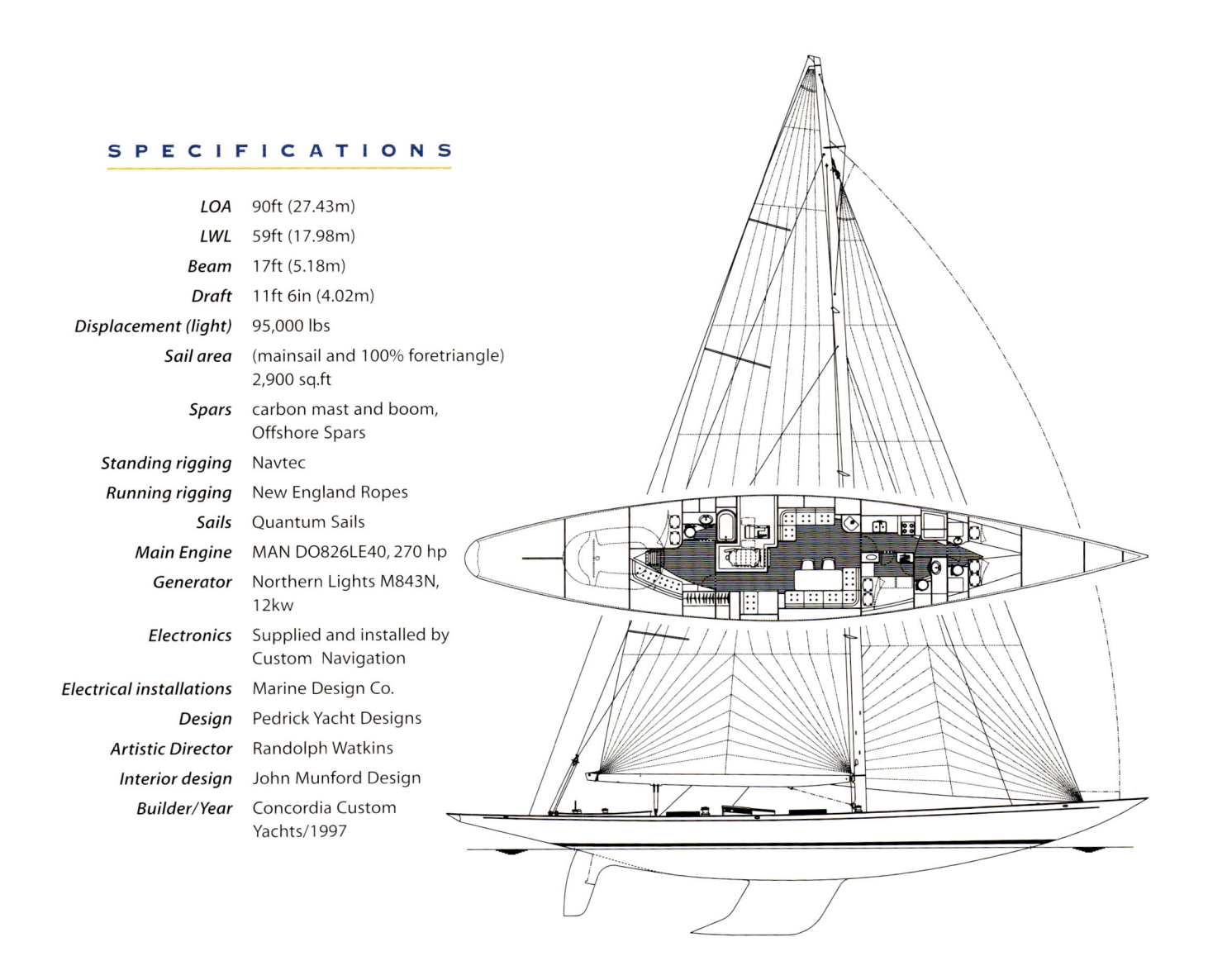

LOA	90ft (27.43m)
LWL	59ft (17.98m)
Beam	17ft (5.18m)
Draft	11ft 6in (4.02m)
Displacement (light)	95,000 lbs
Sail area	(mainsail and 100% foretriangle) 2,900 sq.ft
Spars	carbon mast and boom, Offshore Spars
Standing rigging	Navtec
Running rigging	New England Ropes
Sails	Quantum Sails
Main Engine	MAN DO826LE40, 270 hp
Generator	Northern Lights M843N, 12kw
Electronics	Supplied and installed by Custom Navigation
Electrical installations	Marine Design Co.
Design	Pedrick Yacht Designs
Artistic Director	Randolph Watkins
Interior design	John Munford Design
Builder/Year	Concordia Custom Yachts/1997

as a restraint for the cook. The countertops are granite over honeycomb veneer. Nestled into the counter is a custom flush-top stove surrounded by stainless sea rails to deflect the heat. Forward again is a double cabin and head for the crew, spartan but comfortable.

All those hours spent studying classic yacht designs more than paid off when one considers *Savannah*'s accommodations. Watkins, Pedrick, Munford, and Ingram have achieved a near-perfect synthesis of tradition, function, and hidden technology.

The traditional aspects of *Savannah* were wisely left out when it came to her underbody design and her construction. Built by Concordia Custom Yachts of carbon fiber and kevlar composites, she is a very strong boat. She has a modern underbody with a blended bulb keel and a balanced rudder. The configuration, together with the rigorous weight control Pedrick insisted on, gives her a ballast/weight ration of 50%. Her short waterline means that she responds to steering inputs like a 65-footer, which can become quite exhilarating in a 90ft yacht.

I had the opportunity to sail her on a very light day, and her responsiveness and speed, even in those circumstances, were noteworthy. *Savannah* accelerated quickly and proved sensitive to small adjustments in sail trim. It was impressive to watch her bow change course as I turned the steering wheel, with virtually no time lag. In three knots of true wind there was never any fear of getting caught in irons! She was truly a delight to sail. The only reservations I would mention are the very low height of the boom over the deck (approximately 5ft), and the somewhat restricted amount of room in the steering cockpit. The boom height was a deliberate choice Watkins made in the interest of aesthetics, and an alert crew should have no problem with it; it certainly makes furling the main an easier task.

I left her by dinghy, looking back as she ghosted along, a lovely, daring, yet most successful expression of one man's ideal; and a remarkable illustration of the use of modern materials and systems to recapture an elegance which can no longer be improved upon.

★ SAVANNAH

SHERIFF

92-ft Hatteras Cockpit Motoryacht

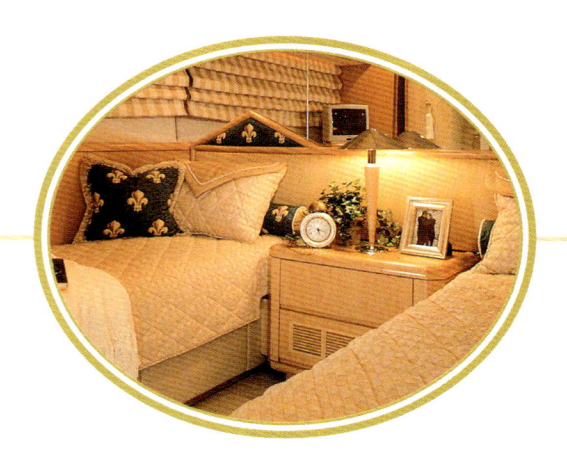

The recipe is ideal for creating an exceptional yacht: Take one owner, a man both extremely charming and extremely experienced with yachts. Stir in a quality boatbuilder who is willing to work closely with a client to customize a yacht. Allow to simmer for about three years. And, voila! Serve up a superlative yacht.

"It was a win-win situation," the owner of *Sheriff* said with a grin, "Both for Hatteras and for me." He was right: both builder and owner benefited from the collaboration that produced the first of the Hatteras Elite Series 92-foot Cockpit Motor Yachts.

When the client, a knowledgeable Jamaican who had owned six Hatteras yachts previously, decided to move up from a Hatteras 70, he considered the 105, but saw drawbacks for his planned use that led him to look at the 92. "With a 105-footer, you can't go alongside a lot of docks in the Bahamas, and I might not always want to anchor out. With the 92, I can slide right in." That is just a sample of the thoughtful planning that is incorporated into *Sheriff*.

When it came to laying out the flybridge, for example, the owner requested a port wing station, but not on the usual free-standing tripod. He wanted the station right on the inside edge of the flybridge to give him a perfect view and, since he only tied up on the port side, he didn't need wing controls to starboard. But, indicative of the careful planning that went into *Sheriff*, was his order for the davits to be placed to starboard so that, even while tied to a dock on the port side, he could still launch his fleet of water toys.

Walk through *Sheriff* and you can find literally hundreds of changes, from something as simple as putting a storage locker into dead space to a transformation as complex as turning the usual crew quarters forward into an apartment for children and creating space aft for new crew cabins.

"When we first started this project, all Hatteras had was a side profile," the owner explained. "I said to them, 'Let's take our time and not rush, so we both get what we want.'" Over a gestation period of about three years, both owner and builder got exactly that.

Intended as a family boat for enjoying the Caribbean, the cockpit styling was necessary for swimming, snorkeling, and other water sports. But the owner chose to

Porthole One of the guest cabins has a pull-apart queen-size berth that converts easily to a pair of singles separated by a nightstand.

Opp. left The flybridge is designed for tropical entertaining, with a central bar, wraparound seating, a well-supported Bimini top, plus room for water toys.

Above Though retaining the basic Hatteras 92 lines, Sheriff has a restyled forward house that incorporates a foredeck settee for guests.

Right The aft deck was reconfigured to add L-shaped lounges on both sides, as well as a bar, built-in barbecue, and, in the lower cockpit, a bait prep area for fishing.

rearrange the raised aft deck by eliminating the planned curved stairs to the cockpit in favor of straight stairs that not only allowed L-shaped lounges to port and starboard, but a place for cockpit controls, a bait prep area for fishing, and a built-in barbecue.

The saloon is the living room of this very comfortable yacht and the owner designed a pair of comfortable couches that are wide enough for naps and have hidden storage areas underneath. The 40-inch television built into the forward bulkhead can be seen from the entire saloon, which has a curved bar with a pass-through to the aft deck, where another bar with icemaker keeps guests from tracking into the saloon for more ice.

Forward on the main deck is the country kitchen-style galley adjoining the dining room. Open and cheery, it fits the owner's needs for casual family gatherings, and a built-in counter was enlarged for use as a buffet.

The three guest cabins on the lower deck are grouped around a foyer that also hides a washer/dryer relocated from the upper level ("Who wants to carry dirty clothes all over the boat?" asks the owner). The master stateroom is forward and since the owner wanted French doors leading into the stateroom, he had the forward bulkhead moved 12 inches, resulting in a spacious feeling, with huge walk-in closets to port and starboard as well as a pair of comfortable settees. The his-and-hers head has marble floors and wall panels and a large Jacuzzi™ tub with sliding doors for use as a shower.

Main picture   The full-beam saloon has comfortable seating to port and starboard, a centerline television visible throughout the area, and a bar with a pass-through to the aft deck.

Opp. top   The dining area has been kept casual since it adjoins the galley, but it has a separate table rather than the usual dinette.

Opp. bottom   The country-kitchen style galley has an extra-wide counter for use as a serving buffet during meals. The area is perfect for casual family gatherings.

Right   The pilothouse was planned by an experienced yachtsman, and the instrumentation is identical to that on the flybridge to ensure continuity at both stations.

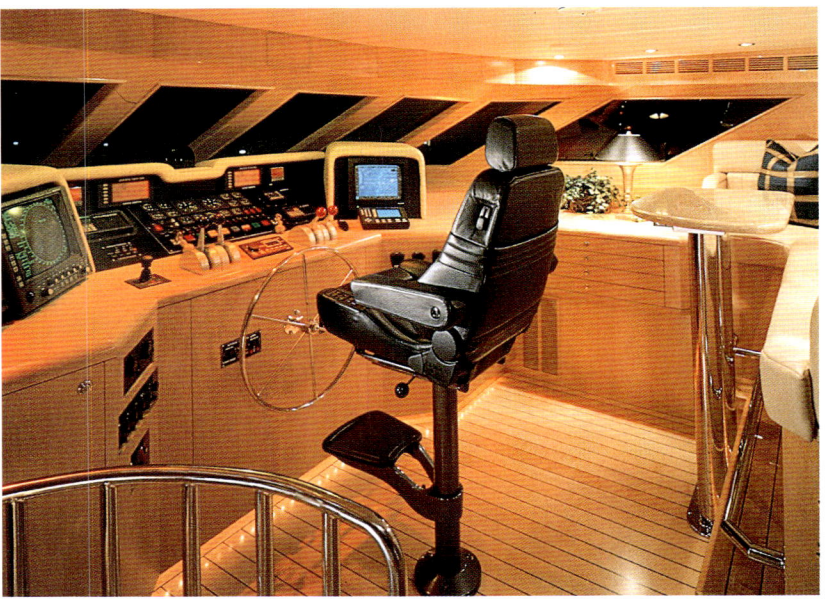

SHERIFF 145

Top ✦ The master suite was enlarged to include oversize walk-in closets as well as a pair of comfortable settees.

Bottom left ✦ The marble-lined his-and-hers bath in the master suite has a large Jacuzzi™ tub with sliding panels for use as a shower.

Bottom right ✦ This port guest cabin has a queen-size berth that pulls apart to create two singles separated by a nightstand.

The two guest cabins aft are similarly sized, although the port cabin has a queen-size berth that pulls apart to create two singles separated by a nightstand ("It's good for kids when they have friends staying on board.") and the other cabin has a permanent queen. Both have en suite bathrooms with tubs.

"I wanted a separate area for the kids so they could play their stereo, watch TV, and be away from the adults when they want," says the owner, and that's what he achieved by converting the forward crew quarters into a pair of comfortable staterooms (one with a twin bed and the other with bunks) that share a head with shower. In addition, he added a lounge area with settee, television, stereo, microwave, and refrigerator. He also added another washer-dryer ("That way, the kids' clothes won't get tracked all through the boat.").

To replace the crew quarters, the owner converted an equipment area aft of the engine room into two staterooms, each with a private head and shower and yet another washer/dryer.

The pilothouse also benefited from the owner's ideas, with an enlarged chart table, and a curved settee moved back to allow a table that serves as a gathering place while underway. On the bridge, the arrangement of instruments and electronics is not just duplicated, but exactly the same to create a continuity at both stations. Aft of the helm is a full bar, and two curved lounges have a walk-through to the boat deck with Novurania tender and twin personal watercraft.

With a civil engineering background, the owner was able to study the plans for the 92 as she was being built, and his changes resulted in a user-friendly and personalized yacht. An access ladder from the boat deck to the aft deck was added so crew didn't have to pass through the yacht, and the boat deck was extended for more space as well as sun protection.

In the saloon, the air handlers were moved from fore and aft positions so the air conditioning enters from the sides inwards to create a tumbling airflow that "eliminates cold air blowing in your face and dead spots." The same system was used in all the guest cabins, too.

In the engine room, the pair of Detroit 16V92TA DDEC diesels were customized by moving all filters to the centerline walkway, while all plumbing, hydraulics, and electrical systems were arrayed neatly on the forward bulkhead. The Onan generators were upgraded from 35kW to 45kW, and one provides power for the bow thruster.

At the bow, the house was changed to incorporate a lounge seat, and Hatteras engineers eliminated the usual anchor hawse pipes on each side and designed a system for a single anchor directly through the stem, which is

SPECIFICATIONS

Length	92ft 10in (28.29m)
Beam	22ft 6in (6.85)
Draft	6ft 6in (1.97m)
Displacement	232,300 lbs
Engines	Twin Detroit 16V92TA DOEC Diesels
Generators	Onan 45kW
Fuel	4975 gallons
Water	800 gallons
Builder/Year	Hatteras Custom Yacht Sales/1997

more usable in shallow Bahamas anchorages. The windlass was also upgraded to a Maxwell 4500 according to the owner, because, "We use it so much!"

With a comfortable cruising speed of 19 knots (top speed 21 knots) and more than 5000 gallons of fuel, *Sheriff* has the long-legged range to explore the Caribbean.

Best of all, everyone is happy. The owner got exactly the yacht he wanted, and Hatteras has another stylish yacht in their growing fleet.

★ SHERIFF

Tigress

93-foot McQueen's Sportfisherman

For many yachts, the christening party, with champagne corks popping and flags flying, is the high point of a career which then slides into months of idleness. Moored to a pier, the yacht may occasionally be used for the odd overnight cruise or cocktail party on board. But for *Tigress*, a new 93-footer from McQueen's Boat Works in British Columbia, the christening was just the beginning. As you read these words, this sportfishing motoryacht might be stalking marlin off Cabo San Lucas, or perhaps cruising along the jungle coastline of Costa Rica. Wherever she may go, the owners of *Tigress* conceived and built her with ambitious plans that don't include spending much time in one place.

"For many years, I had a strong desire to build my own boat which would be able to travel and fish almost anywhere," says Gary Whitener, the owner of *Tigress*. At the time, Gary had a Bertram 54 convertible which, although a legendary sportfishing yacht, wasn't nearly large enough to match the plans of Gary and his wife Sueannah.

As the collection of sketches and drawings grew, the Whiteners started looking for a builder in the Pacific Northwest—an area which has become a hotbed of custom yacht construction. After seeing *Illusion*, the 108ft yachtfisher from the McQueen's yard, the die was cast and the Whitener's project began in April of 1995.

To reach the McQueen's yard on Canada's fabled Fraser River, you first drive through an industrial area past mountains of sawdust destined to become wedding announcements or Visa bills. Arriving at an unprepossessing building, you walk along a slightly shaky pier which, like a dark tunnel leading to the golden Tut chamber in a pyramid, delivers you to a gem of a yacht at the end.

Similar to several other builders, McQueen's started with an Ed Monk, Jr. designed hull built in Airex-cored fiberglass by Nordlund Boat Co. in Tacoma, WA. Again drawing on Monk for the lines of the house, McQueen's then built the superstructure using one-off molds and Klegecell coring. Tim Nolan Marine Design of Port Townsend, WA, did the structural engineering, and the interior is by Pokela Designs of Tacoma.

The result is a yacht which is comfortable and well-suited to its purpose. One look at the interior woodwork and it's easy to see why McQueen's was chosen, although its fiberglass craftsmanship is hidden by a glossy layer of Imron. The light and airy interior combines birdseye and solid maple with quarter sawn sycamore, and the joinerwork is exemplary. The theme throughout the yacht underlines the *Tigress* name, from the bronze tiger statue in the saloon to upholstery in tiger fabrics.

The focal point of the yacht—as well as the reason for its existence—is the fishing cockpit, which is a model of efficiency. A Rybovich fighting chair is stored on the boat deck and lowered into place by the tender crane, which leaves the cockpit open for stand-up fishing or entertaining. Teak floored, the cockpit boasts twin 200-gallon bait wells, a complete tackle and bait prep area, a Gaggenau grill/barbecue, and even a flash freezer under the sole.

Steps to port and starboard lead to the "California deck," a raised deck tucked under the bridge overhang that allows guests to enjoy the fishing action without getting in the way. A fold-out sleeper sofa and wet bar are aft, and a U-shaped dinette allows anglers to lounge while watching their bait. To starboard, a compact day head with shower keeps fishermen from tracking through the saloon.

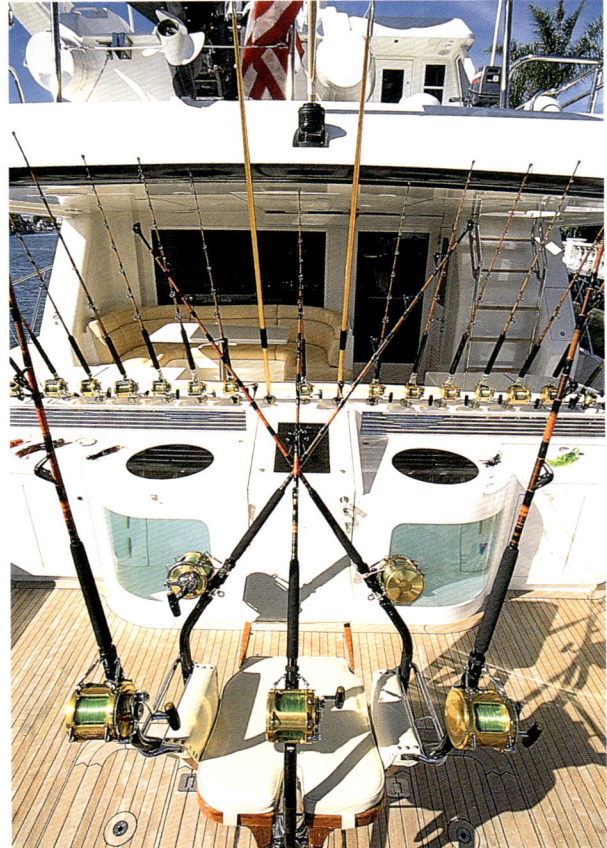

Porthole   The purpose of *Tigress'* existence is apparent in the rows of fishing rods, the array of lures, and the spacious cockpit: this is a sportfishing yacht.

Above   The lines of *Tigress* reflect her long-range cruising itinerary.

Left   A pair of 200-gallon bait tanks and a Rybovich chair that stores on the upper deck are two of the features that make *Tigress* a world-class sport fisherman.

★ TIGRESS   149

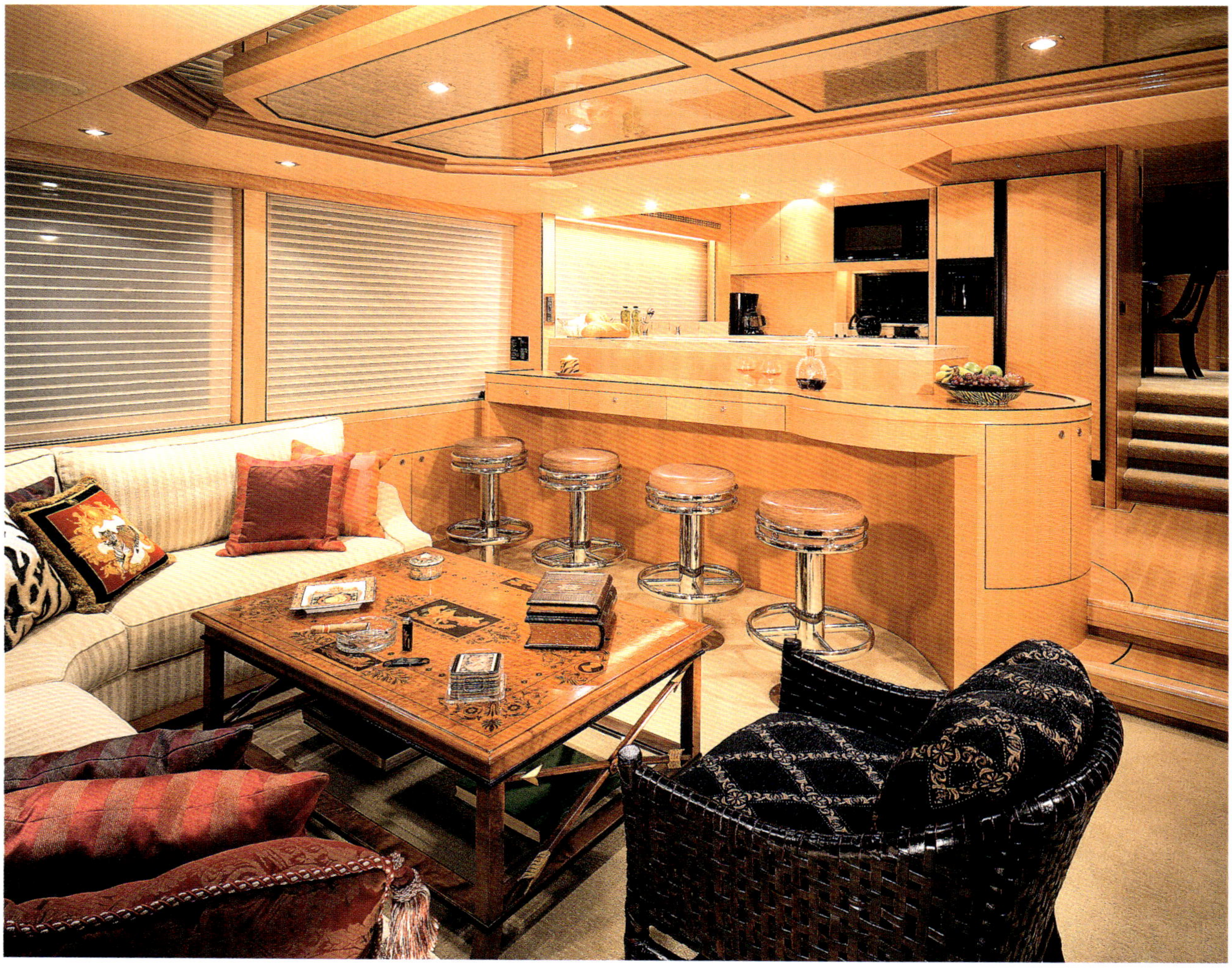

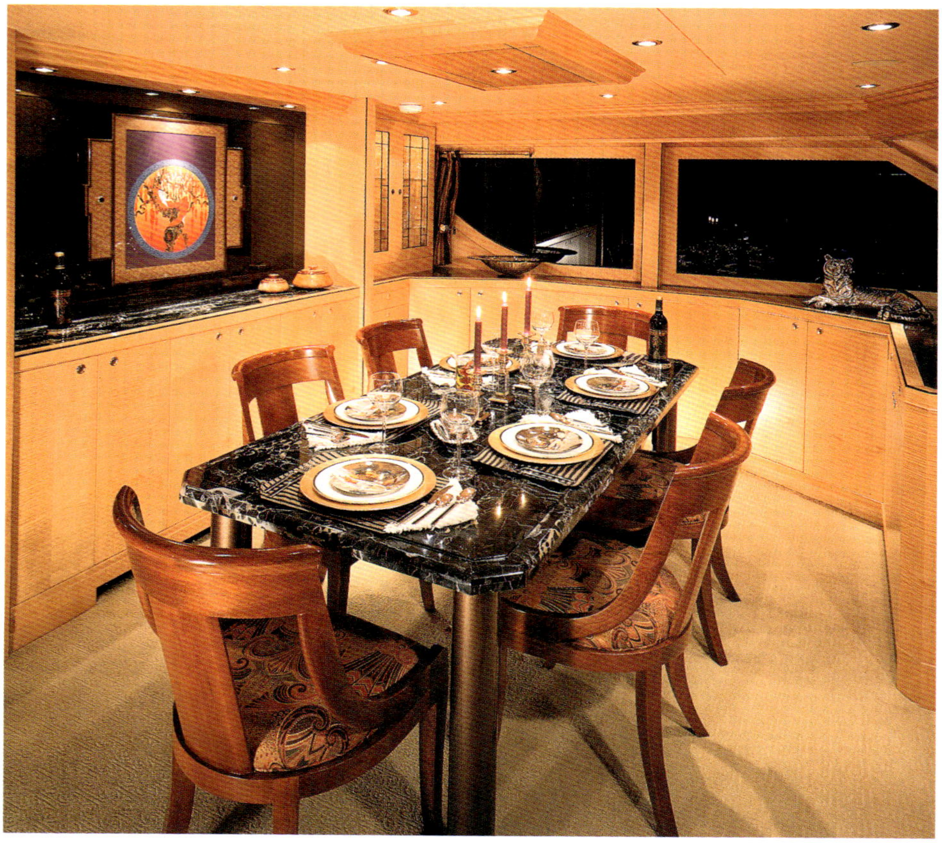

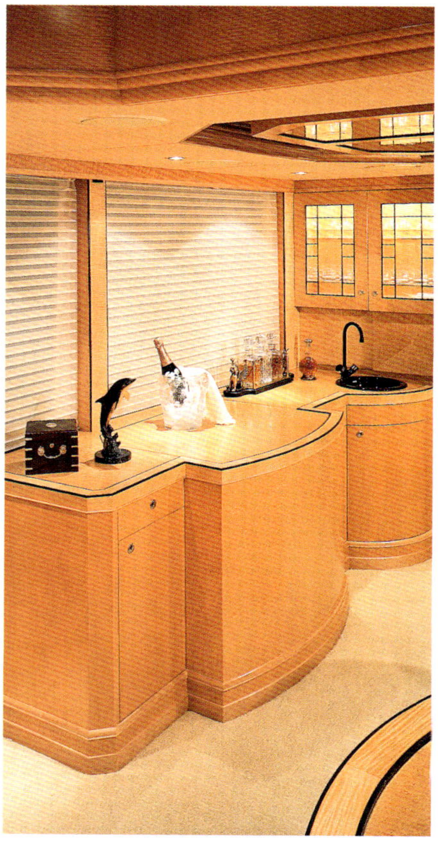

Opp. top ★ The saloon is compact because space has been devoted to the cockpit area, but it is comfortably arranged for lounging or watching the fishing action in the cockpit.

Opp. bottom left ★ A marble table, Erté serigraph, and surrounding maple buffets are distinctive features of the dining room located in the forward cabin area..

Opp. bottom right ★ Hidden inside this buffet in the dining area is a pair of wine chillers, and the leaded glass cabinets hold crystal glassware.

Right ★ The galley, with faux marble counters and large windows, is compact and functional.

Since the cockpit and California deck have taken up a sizable amount of space, the saloon is petite by yacht standards, with a functional L-shaped couch to port and an entertainment center with a pop-up 32-inch television to starboard. The galley, forward, is separated by a breakfast bar with four permanent stools and, like the saloon, has large windows giving good views whether standing or seated — a necessary consideration as Gary Whitener is 6ft 4in tall. The U-shaped galley is workmanlike rather than luxurious, with Avonite faux marble counters, G.E. side-by-side refrigerator-freezer, Gaggenau electric stove, hidden spice area, and twin pantry closets.

Forward and up four steps is the formal dining area, with a solid marble table surrounded by six cherrywood chairs. With large windows, the view is panoramic, and maple buffets surround the area, while an Erte' serigraph is spotlighted on the aft bulkhead. To starboard, a pair of temperature-controlled wine chillers, with a capacity for 50 bottles, are stocked with *Tigress* private-label wines.

A stairway opposite the galley leads to the master suite past a utility room, a spare refrigerator/freezer, full-sized stacked washer/dryer, work bench, and engine room access. The full-width master stateroom combines black counters and wall treatments with bronze mirrors, maple woodwork, black tile, and ornate reading lights. Twin Karadon night stands flank the king-size bed, a love seat is to starboard, and a large vanity with sink is to port. The master head is compact, with maple flooring and an unusual sunken shower two steps down.

Two mirrored guest staterooms forward are reached by a funnel-shaped companionway from the dining area. Each stateroom has a queen-size bed, Karadon headboard, and an entertainment center, as well as a cedar-lined hanging locker and maple vanities with tiger-upholstered stools. The twin guest en suites feature Karadon sinks and lighted showers behind bronze glass doors.

The spacious captain and crew quarters are forward, with an overlapped full bed above a settee bed, an entertainment center, desk area, and head with shower.

Considering the extensive cruising planned for *Tigress*, the enclosed pilothouse is likely to be the living area while underway and has been outfitted as such with a coffee-maker and microwave. The electronics are built into the raised dash, with twin Furuno radar and twin Northstar GPS linked to an IBM Pentium II computer using Nobletec plotting software and actual NOAA charts stored on CD-ROM. On the communications side, Furuno single sideband provides 6,000nm coverage, backed up by a Furuno VHF radio and a Westinghouse Wave Talk satellite telephone system. The Simrad/Robertson AP-9 autopilot has been linked to a custom seven-station Mathers Clear Command system and integrated to the bowthruster, which allows course correction with the thruster controls even when the boat is not moving. Since fishing is the focus, a Furuno 360-degree searchlight 1kW sonar has automatic target tracking for fish schools, and a Furuno video sounder provides a 10-inch high-resolution color display. For weather information, a satellite receiver displays and analyzes computer weather, and a complete CCTV security and monitoring system can be accessed from any of the televisions on board.

Right ★ Guest cabins are identical, with queen-size berths, Karadon headboards, and maple vanities with tiger-upholstered stools.

Below ★ The master suite combines black counters, bronze mirrors, and an ornate love seat with Karadon nightstands and a spacious vanity.

Opp. top ★ The enclosed pilothouse, with large chart table and amenities such as a microwave and coffeemaker, is intended for making passages.

A pair of Stidd helm chairs are behind the dash, a day head is aft to starboard, and a sleeper settee and table is elevated to port. Backing up the computer charting system is a unique drop-down chart table aft and drawers for paper charts.

A walk-around Portuguese bridge has wing engine and bowthruster controls on both sides, and another set on the boat deck aft. Also on the boat deck are a pair of Nautica tenders: a 15-footer with 75hp Yamaha and a 9ft with 8hp Yamaha, as well as an 8-man survival raft. A 2,000lb hydraulic crane by Steelhead Marine handles the tenders as well as the fighting chair storage. Power for *Tigress* is a pair of Caterpillar 3408 diesels rated at 800hp each, with underwater exhausts and ZF transmissions. With a fuel capacity of 4,500 gallons in three aluminum tanks, *Tigress* has a comfortable cruising range of 2,500nm at 10 knots, although the normal cruise speed is 15 knots, and she tops out at 19.5 knots with full fuel. A pair of 40kW Northern Lights generators provide the daytime power, and an 8kW Northern Lights is hidden in the lazarette for nighttime use with minimum noise. The spool anchoring system reflects the commercial fishing heritage of the Northwest, using a Harrison Robbins winch with 400ft of 5/8-inch cable and another 100ft of 1/2-inch chain. The yacht also has complete firefighting capabilities, including three Halon systems and fire hoses fore and aft. Rounding out the complement of equipment are Naiad stabilizers, twin Vantage Marine watermakers with a capacity of 1,200 gallons per day, and a KVH TracVision stabilized satellite television system.

Launched in April 1998, *Tigress* immediately headed north for a three-month cruise to Alaska, and in November set out on an ambitious two-year fishing adventure. From Mexico and Costa Rica, she will transit the Panama Canal, fish the Caribbean and around Florida, and then head north to Nova Scotia before reversing course for California.

Considering her itinerary, it looks like *Tigress* won't be using the hydraulic mast needed to reach her dock in front of the Whitener's California home until well into the next millennium.

SPECIFICATIONS

LOA	93ft (28.3m)
LOD	86ft (26.2m)
LWL	76ft 4in (23.2m)
Beam	21ft (6.4m)
Draft	5ft (1.5m)
Speed (max/cruise)	19.5/15 knots
Range	2,500nm @10 knots
Engines	3408 Caterpillar, 800bhp @2,300rpm
Generators	Northern Lights
Fuel	4,500 gallons
Interior designer	Pokela Designs
Hull design	Nordlund Boat Company
Structural engineer	Tim Nolan Marine Design
Naval architect	Ed Monk & Sons
Builder/Year	McQueen's Boat Works/1998

★ **TIGRESS**

Ubiquitous

112-foot Westport Pilothouse Motoryacht

It's difficult to believe that a yard building composite motoryachts over 92 feet in length can be a production builder, but that is exactly how Randy Rust, the eminently likable chairman of Westport Shipyard, sees his company.

Founded in 1964, Westport drew on the latest technology from nearby aerospace giants in Washington to pioneer the introduction of composite technology to its range of sturdy offshore trawlers, but a declining market during the 1970s prompted a successful transition to yacht building. In the early years the yard was a custom builder, but since 1987, it has actively discouraged requests for customization.

Randy Rust is confident that Westport can create a superior product in a shorter time at a very competitive price, the proof of which is simply that for the last ten years his yard has been working flat out, selling everything it has built. But while some 54 hulls have popped from its variable dimension mold that adjusts from 90ft to 120ft in length and from 22ft to 25ft in beam, not all have ended up as off-the-peg production yachts. Westport Shipyard is at the forefront of composite boatbuilding in the Pacific Northwest, supplying economically-priced bare hulls, together with highly valued advice, to at least six other yards in the area for custom completion. It is an ideal business: while Westport focuses its unblinking concentration on the improvement of building techniques and the development of an ideal production yacht, the other yards satisfy the custom market, building their own superstructures and working with a wide range of designers to develop their clients' wishes.

The Westport 112 is the latest phase in the yard's policy of continuous improvement in its production series. Visually, there is little difference from the previous 108ft model—a marginally deeper swim platform and the almost imperceptible addition of a further 2 feet to both the aft deck and boat deck above—but this extra 4 feet in overall length, together with a whole range of other modifications, has constituted yet another notable leap forward for the product. As the main thrust of these improvements has been to the stern of the yacht, it is appropriate to begin our tour here.

For some time now Westport has positioned its crew quarters aft of the engine room, rather than in the bow area that seems to be favored by most designers, builders, and indeed, owners. Such positioning makes excellent sense, particularly in a yacht of this size. With access from the swim platform or the aft deck, the crew live in an area of the yacht which is appropriately close to the yacht's systems, and one which offers comfort in a seaway, while the owner and guests are provided with a higher degree of privacy. But there are problems that must be overcome, including the suppression of noise and heat in the yacht's stern sections. Aboard *Ubiquitous*, this is achieved in part by the inherent noise-dampening properties of a GRP hull made from a five-layer sandwich incorporating two layers of Airex core material, and also by careful design and routing of the main engine exhaust system to minimize both heat and noise from that source. Apart from its permanently open eight-inch bypass, *Ubiquitous'* exhaust system has its main outlets underwater. Following tank tests to ensure that gas would not be drawn into the propeller tunnels, these are precisely positioned relatively

Porthole ★ A peek into the formal dining area.

Main picture ★ At speed, *Ubiquitous* shows the straight clean lines and low profile of a yacht that will remain contemporary for many years.

Left ★ As you would expect from a yacht born and bred in the Pacific Northwest, the forward flare of the Westport makes her ideal for rough seas.

★ UBIQUITOUS

Left In addition to the upper helm with wing controls, the spacious flybridge is equipped with a bar, lounge and dining area, spa, and sunbeds.

Below The fully covered aft deck allows for alfresco dining in pleasant weather, but can be enclosed for all-season use.

Far right The raised pilothouse gives excellent visibility over the deckhouse and allows for separation of crew and guests.

well forward on the chine, and faired to create a lower back pressure than on a conventional exhaust when the yacht is running in semi-displacement mode. Noise is also generated by the propellers, but this has been reduced by using highly skewed, 5-blade Teignbridge propellers which are sunk into hull tunnels. While the main object of these tunnels is to reduce draft and shaft angle, they also minimize noise as the blade tips remain at a constant distance from the circumference of the tunnel.

In contrast to the Westport 108, the 112 has an extra 2ft6in in length together with some rearrangement, permitting an additional single crew cabin which shares a head and shower with the double-bunked cabin to provide a greater degree of crewing flexibility, as well as a further utility compartment with twin washer/dryers and a chest freezer. The design of the crew mess has also been improved with the addition of a microwave-based galley with sink and refrigerator.

Opening forward from the crew mess, the engine room contains what is the yacht's major innovation — a pair of the new MTU-DDC 16V2000 diesels which represents the first fruits of the design and marketing agreement between the German diesel giant MTU and the Detroit Diesel Corporation. Randy Rust is euphoric about these new 1,800hp 16-cylinder Friedrichshaven-manufactured, Detroit-assembled units, particularly their high power, low noise, ease of installation, reliability, and low heat output. This new design makes use of sequential turbocharging, using a single blower at low revolutions before pulling in a second as the speed increases, at the same time incorporating a waste gate to allow the escape of any excess pressure. The benefits are extra power at low revolutions, together with excellent acceleration. Randy quotes a figure of 13 seconds from idle to maximum revolutions.

For much the same weight of engine, this extra power, combined to a small degree with the additional waterline length, has provided a two-knot increase in speed over the 1,525hp 8-cylinder units used in the Westport 108, while their lower heat output has also meant that single Delta-T intake and exhaust fans are able to supply air to the engines and cool their operating environment.

Traditionally, a yacht's engines are positioned in the early part of the build to allow for the completion of the superstructure and commencement of interior work. This approach did not make sense to Westport as it meant buying the engines almost a year before they were needed. The 112 was therefore designed with sufficiently strong main deck beams so as to avoid having deckhead-supporting stanchions in the engine room. This meant that a large hatch could be incorporated in the floor of the main saloon, through which the engines could be set in position in the last 10 weeks of build. The result — clean engines and less investment.

Sea trials on the completed yacht showed responsive handling and a top speed of 28 knots at light load; while fully loaded she still provided a maximum speed of 26 knots and a continuous cruising speed of 24 knots. As soon as the first Westport 112 was completed, she left the yard on a 5,000nm voyage south along the Pacific Coast, through the Panama Canal and on through the Caribbean to Fort Lauderdale, a passage that was completed without trouble in 13 days at sea in a wide range of conditions and temperatures. Few production vessels get such intensive testing trials in the hands of their builders.

The interior division and decoration for any production yacht must appeal to the largest number of potential clients, and Westport has taken great pains to get both of these right. In essence, the Westport 112 is a raised pilothouse configuration — a two-deck yacht with the central pilothouse by-passed by passageways on either side and raised some 4ft from the main deck to provide optimum

Below ✭ The forward portion of the main saloon is set aside as a formal dining area, with seating for six under recessed lighting that reflects the shape of the glass table.

Opp. right ✭ Forward of the raised pilothouse is the country galley with a dinette for casual dining.

visibility over the forward part of the superstructure. Aft of the pilothouse is a large saloon/dining saloon opening to an aft deck shaded by the boat deck above, while the forward element of the superstructure is filled by an open-plan "country kitchen" that combines an attractive galley with a comfortably casual dining table. A stairway leads forward and down from this area to a VIP cabin in the bow, while the full-beam master stateroom and two further guest cabins, accessed by stairs to port of the pilothouse, fill the central element of the lower deck forward of the engine room.

The pilothouse, entered up short flights of stairs from port or starboard, is comprehensively equipped with the triple necessities of control, navigation, and communication equipment, and is provided with a guest seating area. From the pilothouse, stairs lead up through a sliding stainless door to a huge sun deck with flying bridge controls and a pair of wing control stations, as well as a bar, sitting/dining area, spa pool, and sunbeds.

All of the yacht's rooms and deck spaces are so beautifully proportioned and practical in their use that it would be hard to improve on *Ubiquitous*'s layout within the confines of this hull. Decoratively, the yacht was the responsibility of Sheryl McLaughlin who, aiming for approval from the widest possible client base, created an inviting yet stylish interior of very high quality, using a pleasing combination of honeyed colors, warm fabrics, and rich marble, together with a mix of loose and built-in furniture.

The saloon, for instance, has a background of ash wood, hand-blocked silk wall coverings, and a custom woven carpet which, together with the extensive windows, ensures a welcoming sense of light and space. Add to this a fully-equipped bar, topped with handsome speckled beige-brown Giallo St Venezia marble, a seductively comfortable settee upholstered in chenille, a coffee table and ottoman stool, and a carefully chosen selection of lamps and accessories, and this is a space that anyone would be proud to call their own.

The dining room in the forward part of the saloon is equally carefully outfitted with a custom-built circular glass-topped table and boldly patterned balloon-backed chairs from furniture maker Donghia, but, as in the rest of the yacht, some of the vessel's more important assets are not immediately obvious. Concealed in custom-built racks within the three marble-topped buffet cupboards that surround the table is a complete set of Tiffany china, hand-cut crystal, and Christofle cutlery, all of which is included in the price of this fully outfitted "turnkey" yacht. Any new owner merely has to step aboard with his suitcases of clothes, ask the chef to fill the fridges, and tell the captain where he wants to go!

No review of this yacht would be complete without a mention of what is perhaps her star feature: the master bathroom. Positioned across the yacht's full beam behind the California king-size bed, this his-and-hers bathroom is comparable with those found aboard the most luxurious superyachts afloat. Encrusted with Summer Peach marble containing the fossils of nautilus shells, the room is laid out with a head and wash basin on either side of a central block containing a spa bath and huge shower, the former large enough for two, and the latter a veritable human car wash with twin shower units and multiple spray heads. If anyone was wavering over signing a contract, this room alone should clinch the deal!

The Westport 112 is a well designed, sturdily built, low-maintenance vessel with an attractive appearance and an easy decorative style that offers a swift route to large yacht ownership without the personal involvment and additional cost of custom design. Priced at around $7.35 million, this yacht is worthy of attention from any buyer considering entry to this area of the market.

★ UBIQUITOUS

SPECIFICATIONS

LOA	112ft (34.13m)
Beam	23ft 9in (7.24m)
Draft (half load)	5ft 6in (1.68m)
Displacement (light ship)	196,000lbs (88,906 tonnes)
Engines	2 x 1,800hp MTU-DDC 16V2000 diesels
Propellers	Teignbridge high skew Nibral 5-blade
Speed (max/cruise)	28/24 knots
Fuel Capacity	4,580 gallons
Range at 12 knots	2,500nm
Electricity Generation	1 x 65kW & 1 x 50 kW Northern Lights
Interior Design	Sheryl McLaughlin, Pacific Custom Interiors
Exterior Styling & Naval Architecture	Jack W Sarin, Bainbridge Island, WA
Builder/Year	Westport Shipyard/1998

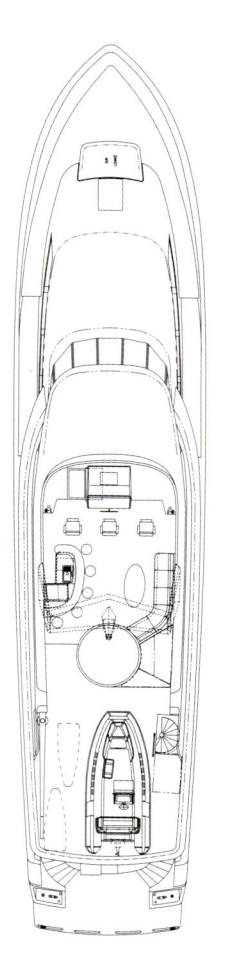

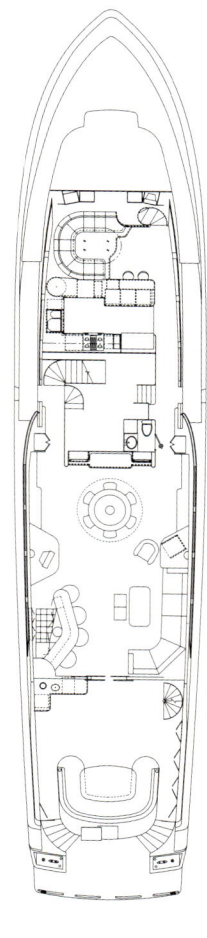

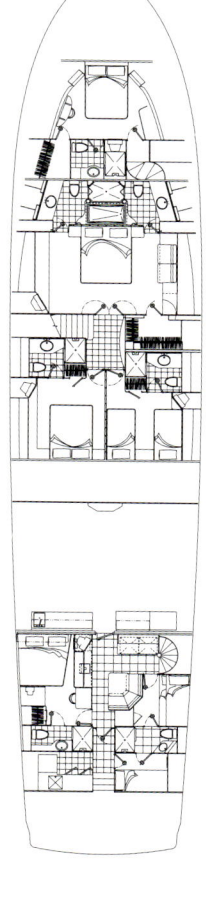

Main picture Spanning the full beam, the homey saloon has a bar, formal dining area, and comfortable seating.

Opp. below The large master suite has a California king-size bed, settee, desk, and full-beam his-and-hers bathrooms.

160 THE MegaYachts USA ★ 2000

★ UBIQUITOUS 161

Varsity Jacket

111-foot Broward Raised Pilothouse Cockpit Motoryacht

Perfection is a familiar term in the yachting industry, but combining a fiftieth anniversary creation by Broward Marine, a highly detail-oriented captain, and an owner with a "nirvana" attitude, the result is a 111ft raised pilothouse cockpit motoryacht that offers new meaning to "customized for enjoyment." Launched in August 1998, *Varsity Jacket* was a labor of love for Captain Paul Giusti. Hired at the initial stages of design work, he spent every working hour during the 60,000 total man hours it took to build the yacht at the Broward Marine boatyard, overseeing details and specifications. Besides having a bird's-eye view of every item as it went on the vessel, Giusti collaborated with every company whose products were utilized, from the first screw to the very specialized finishing accents.

Varsity Jacket's name is appropriate. The owner is the CEO of a major national sports apparel company specializing in varsity jackets, caps, clothing, and nearly anything else one might find adorning high school, college or university athletes and fans. *Varsity Jacket* is his third yacht, each increasing in size. Although he's sure there will be others—probably larger yachts—in the future, for now he's spending every possible moment doing exactly what he wanted to do with his time—enjoying himself. "It was meant to be, and is, the perfect playboat," Giusti says. "Every detail that went into this yacht is intended for the owner and his guests to enjoy themselves."

"Play," according to Giusti, means cruising, diving, jet skiing, motorbiking, entertaining, and just about everything else imaginable that means "fun." "Our stewardess holds dive-training instructor certification, so we can offer guests scuba training and certification while they're on board," Giusti says. "*Varsity Jacket* is fully equipped with eight dive tanks and a remote fill tank that refills four tanks in 20 minutes." Other "toys" include four Nautico underwater motor scooters, a Novurania tender, two Jet Skis, four motor bikes and a diving platform. "We say it gives new meaning to walking the plank," Giusti continues. "It is a custom-built aluminum plank that bolts into the floor of the flybridge. It's a long jump—about 20 feet—but it's a tremendous amount of fun for the more adventuresome." Because too much fun can sometimes mean problems, the crew, including Giusti and two mates, hold CPR certifications. "We carry a mini-hospital of emergency equipment on board in case of illness or accident," Giusti adds.

Setting out to build a "yacht to be used" didn't mean lack of style or class in this case. Elegant and stylish decor was created by the prestigious Merritt-Knowles Design Group in Ft. Lauderdale, Florida who closely collaborated

Porthole This desk was designed and built with extraordinary detail. It was outfitted for the owner's laptop, which links into the large plasma television screen.

Above *Varsity Jacket* displays lean lines. She has a unique notched bulwark with *Varsity Jacket* initials in the boarding door (shown opposite).

Left The innovative Pipewelders aluminum flybridge hardtop has a hydraulically-operated ten-by-ten foot opening "sunroof" over the spa and lounge areas.

★ VARSITY JACKET

with the owner and Giusti. Patrick Knowles and Ruth Merritt, partners in the firm, delved deeply into their client's personal style, enabling them to approach each project with a precise understanding of their assignment goals. In this case, understanding the owner's cosmopolitan style and demand for unaffected and comfortable living was imperative. Merritt-Knowles' tasteful use of furnishings, colors, and space resulted in uncompromising comfort and pleasure for the owners. Fit for down-to-earth casual video viewing for two, or elegant parties for 50, it's easy to visualize the vessel's interior lending itself to virtually any situation. Upon entering the aft deck, one faces the main saloon's focal point: a bird's-eye, straight grain maple desk with fluted legs and applied molding. The desk's Olympic design molding, uba tuba granite top, fluted legs and pyramid dies blend perfectly with the accompanying crackled-finish desk chair. The ensemble is perfectly positioned as a room divider, partitioning the saloon into cozy groupings. "The owner saw a desk he felt was perfect for the décor, but it was too large for the space," Knowles said. "Rather than copying the desk, we designed one with the style in mind, but with extraordinary detail, and had it built by Broward's craftsmen." Knowles says the desk was outfitted for the owner's laptop

Above ★ Facing aft, the main saloon is marked by separate seating areas, a game table on the right, and large windows that provide excellent visibility when seated.

Opposite ★ The focal point of the saloon is the granite-topped desk from which the owner, using his laptop computer, can turn the hidden plasma television screen into a monitor.

THE MEGAYACHTS USA ★ 2000

computer. "It links into the large plasma television in the saloon, thereby converting the television screen into a computer monitor," he explained.

Abutting the desk is a custom chenille-upholstered sofa, two chairs and a three-foot ottoman that converts into a cocktail table and storage compartment. Aft to port is a maple and mahogany game table with *Varsity Jacket* inlaid into its top around the circumference. A custom-dyed long leather sofa with hand-painted throw pillows, painted by artisans at Starshine Studios in Hollywood, FL, completes the room's seating. Situated to starboard, two bird's-eye maple and granite tables hold an inlaid center X pattern — the predominate theme throughout the yacht — and antique style lamps. Knowles says the X theme was originally developed by following the wood grain pattern when building all the cabinetry units. A stunning Lucite sculpture of three women's faces titled *Dream Fragment # 3* sits on a side table aft and is illuminated from behind. The saloon also features light bird's-eye maple, verde crown molding, hand-painted silk and wood lambrequins, and hand-painted fabric inserts. Remote-controlled duet blinds and a lacquered soffit overhead in the center of the room create an open and airy space. The bulkhead entertainment unit is designed to extend over the stairwell leading to the master stateroom and guest cabins. Built of maple with ebony inlays, the wood-grained panels form the X pattern and camouflage the 42in flat screen plasma television, full entertainment unit and adjacent wet bar. The television pulls out so space normally wasted behind is divided into a battery of storage cubicles for videos and CDs. The owner's dignified yet "down-earthing" of the *Varsity Jacket* extends into the combination galley/dining area that is separated by a granite-topped center island. Giusti says rather than taking up valuable space for a "pompous" dining area, the user-friendly country-style galley and eat-in area allows dining comfort and a casual atmosphere. Five beveled mirror doors with decorative gold-leaf wood frames mask storage areas above the teal leather contoured seating area. Light-colored planked flooring and custom-made wood blinds add additional warmth. The galley's green granite countertops and back splash are scored sections (one full, uncut and seamless granite slab), with outlets for electrical appliances installed underneath the upper cabinets so the granite line is undisturbed. SubZero refrigerator/freezer and General Electric appliances, according to Giusti, mean they can be serviced anywhere the vessel docks without the concern of finding parts or service companies qualified for repairs. "Deep thought and consideration was given to every detail of what went into the interior," he says. "The owner wanted elegance, but without avoidable maintenance problems."

The on-deck powder room continues the gold detail with accented gold sink and fixtures, gold-leaf wall covering, bird's-eye maple and ebony flooring, speckled marble vanity, and gold-leaf framed mirror. Every inner door of the *Varsity Jacket* is radius framed, and unique shelving systems contour to the bow flare. The curved staircase (accessed from the galley) features a gold-leaf sphere topping a grooved colonnade stairwell.

The VIP stateroom, positioned forward, offers occupants a spacious area with built-in desk/vanity. The queen-size island platform bed with storage drawers underneath has a fabric-covered headboard and bountiful coordinating throw pillows. A television is concealed in the cabinetry and the bed is flanked by marble-topped nightstands. The master suite features an elegant combination of craftsmanship and sophistication, but again offering unpretentious functionality. Light maple and ebony-trimmed cabinetry surround the room and the familiar X design patterns adorn both sides of the bed. His-and-hers master bathrooms are situated on opposite sides of the 14in-deep bed that is covered with copious pillows and custom Nomi fabric treatments. The bathrooms connect in the middle with a shared shower and marble steam room. For added privacy, melted-glass pattern doors with the X etched in their front were used to create privacy and separation. Gold plumbing accessories add the final shower accent. Custom Surface tonal wall coverings and Creama Marfil floors with uba tuba inlays and borders complement the double bullnose uba tuba granite countertops. The cabinetry has black reveals and bombe fronts, and there is a giant wood-framed three-panel mirror/medicine cabinet.

Two matching but opposite aligned guest staterooms comprise a double bed on the outside of the wall and a twin, inward, aligned bed in the opposite direction. The rooms continue the yacht's interior theme with light woods, subtle green, beige and gold tones, rounded doors, and molding. Each offers cedar-lined closets, television, stereo, telephone/intercoms, Tempwise 2000 temperature controls, Vantage lighting systems, and adjoining spacious heads.

Access to the expansive flybridge is via the custom-tailored circular staircase on the aft deck or from the pilothouse. A first-of-its-kind Pipewelder's 27ft hardtop with ten-by-ten foot hydraulic opening sunroof provides superior sun protection when necessary, or the option of open-air day or night. The hardtop is inlaid with fiber optic lighting on a custom color wheel so colors can be

Opposite ★ The dining area just forward of the galley is casual and comfortable, with mirrors hiding large storage areas.

Above ★ The master suite continues the theme of maple and ebony cabinets with X patterns on each side of the island berth.

Right ★ The VIP stateroom forward has a private stairway and built-in desk and vanity in the foreground.

Above ✦ The flybridge bar, with grill and margarita machine, has an etched stainless-steel mural by Kertz Man.

Opposite ✦ The boat deck is cantilevered so there are no support pillars to mar the view from the seating area and alfresco table on the aft deck.

varied to meet the mood of the moment. The helm station is centered, and port and starboard wing stations are each outfitted with Crown Marine helm chairs. The pivotal feature of the flybridge is the walk-behind bar faced with an etched stainless steel mural. The artist, Kertz Man, was located after an aggressive search by Merritt-Knowles. "The owner had seen a piece by the same artist displayed at the Oceanographic Institute in Bermuda, and fell in love with it," Knowles said. "He asked us to find the artist, and although it took us three months of tenacious research, we tracked him down in Canada, contacted his representative, and commissioned this piece. The brief called for an underwater reef scene with a lot of marine life. The stainless steel was templated and pre-formed at the shipyard, shipped to Canada where Man etched it, then shipped back for installation."

Adjacent to the bar is a Jenn-Air grill and "margarita machine." The opposite side of the flybridge houses a settee and adjustable cocktail-to-dinner height table. Aft of the bar and settee is a grand-size six-plus person Jacuzzi™ that fills in 12 minutes. Tender, twin Jet Skis, underwater scooters, motorbikes, dive platform and bicycles round out the "toy" selection on *Varsity Jacket*'s flybridge. Equal attention was paid to the cockpit and swim platform as in other areas of the vessel. It offers a hot and cold shower system, fresh-water wash down, and remote air fill with hose to connect to the dive tanks. Two Glendinning shore cable retrieve systems; two 1200 gallon per day reverse osmosis watermakers; a 600 pound-per-day Eskimo ice chipper with a hose to fill ice chests aboard the tender; two electric underwater spotlights with close-off valves and electric alarms (operated from the helm); two electric capstans; cutting station; chipped ice cooler; and large

SPECIFICATIONS

LOA	111ft (33.8m)
Beam	20ft (6.1m)
Minimum Draft	5ft 8in (1.7m)
Maximum Draft	6ft 4in (1.9m)
Displacement	105 tons
Fuel	7,800 gallons
Water	1000 gallons
Engines	2 x 1850 HP diesels Detroit Diesel/Allison 16V2000DDEC
Range	2400 nm
Maximum Speed	24 K @ 2350 rpm 195gals/hr
Cruise Speed	21 K @ 2150 rpm 160gals/hr
Hull	Aluminum
Builder/Year	Broward/1998

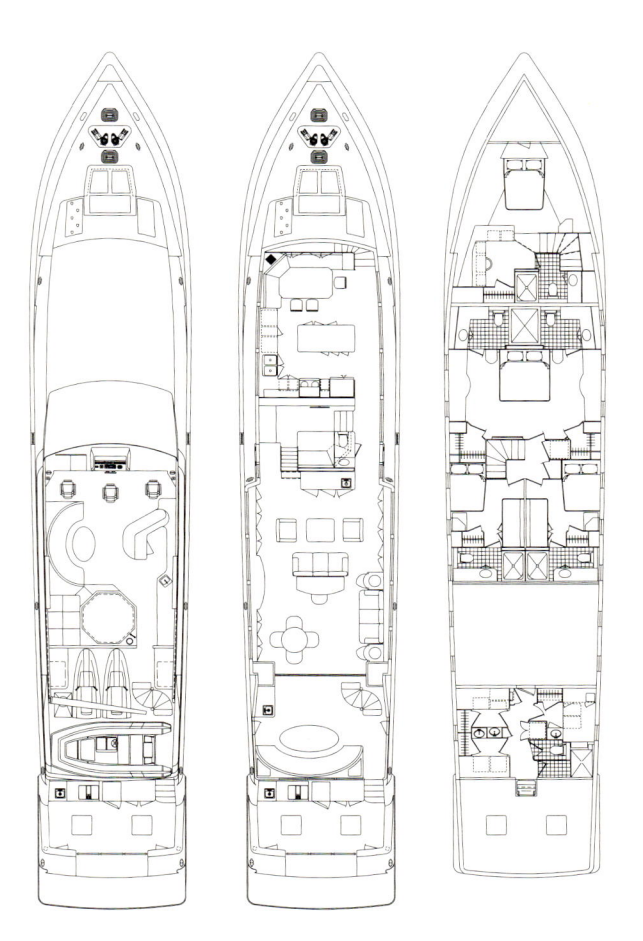

freezer complete the list of accessories. Insuring comfort, security, and technological ease of use, as well as the continuing theme of enjoyment, the *Varsity Jacket* is outfitted with the latest Toshiba intercom, security cameras and monitors in every room, SEA CB radio, B & G speed indicator, Detroit tachometer, tide data programmer, Furuno weatherfax, digital chart library laser plot and chart navigation, chronometer, two SEA hailers, Microphone, Simrad Anritsu electronic rangefinder, and telephone jacks to service the onboard computer, Internet and fax systems. *Varsity Jacket*'s owner insured the comfort of his crew with three spacious rooms, each with vanity, separate head and shower. Carrying a range of technology, with engine and electrical detail at least equal, if not superior, to any yacht today, and a full and varied range of "toys," it appears as though the *Varsity Jacket* is the epitome of pleasure. Knowles, however, says there is something else one can't appreciate until they've walked onto the yacht on a beautiful sunlit day on open water, "With the blinds in the main saloon drawn, and the blue of the water shimmering through her windows and reflecting on the beautiful wood grain and natural buff colors, she is truly 'one with the water.' It's a cool, comfortable, elegant yet happy vessel that reflects a part of the sea."

★ VARSITY JACKET

Wehr Nuts

124-foot Christensen Raised Pilothouse Motoryacht

Some yachts are designed for cruising, others strictly for entertaining, and some serve only as a weekend retreat for their owners. *Wehr Nuts*, a new 124-footer from Christensen Shipyards, is a fine example of a truly multipurpose yacht that combines all of the attributes of each category, along with an attention to design and detail rare even among megayachts.

The owner, an extremely experienced yachtsman who has several other boats ranging from a 42ft Cigarette and a 47ft Fountain to a 52ft Hatteras, had moved progressively upwards through a 70ft Hatteras to a 112ft Broward. So when he and Capt. Raymond Young sat down to plan a larger yacht, there was a wealth of experience brought to bear on the design.

With an eye for clean lines, the owner didn't want a tri-deck motoryacht that would be, in his words, "too stumpy." And, with a Florida homeport and long range plans for cruising the warm areas of the world, the yacht would need ample outdoor space and a big flying bridge.

The result is a raised pilothouse motoryacht with contemporary lines and a pleasing appearance that will remain in vogue long after the trendy Euro-styling has been forgotten. The Christensen yard was chosen not just because they would build in the low maintenance fiberglass that the owner had grown to appreciate in his other yachts, but because of their reputation for superlative woodwork and joinery.

The starting point for *Wehr Nuts* was the Christensen 28ft beam hull mold and, at 124ft, the yacht would fall in the middle of the 100ft to 155ft range for that versatile design. Hull, deck, and superstructure were all cored with foam and the fiberglass tankage was molded with the hull, resulting in a yacht that is at the upper end of the strength scale, yet at the lower end of the upkeep range.

One advantage of the nearly 28ft beam is that it allows *Wehr Nuts* to have full walkaround side decks, yet there is none of the constriction usually found in a saloon that doesn't push out to the full beam. The crew benefits from an easy passage from bow to stern for line handling, and the arrangement also allows the owner and his guests to enjoy the saloon without having crew members constantly passing through the area.

While *Wehr Nuts* has a low profile even for a raised pilothouse yacht, her lines cleverly conceal the outdoor areas required by the owner. The usual transom platform has been expanded into what Christensen terms a "sport deck," yet, from the side, the extended topsides hide that extra-wide platform with the appearance of a reversed transom. Those extensions also provide wind protection for this area, turning it into an onboard "beach" for swimming and a base for scuba diving, with hinged concealed quartz lights for night use. The aft deck sits atop a huge lazarette that not only stores the scuba gear and water toys, but thoughtfully also includes a full head for use by swimmers or by mechanics servicing the engines. Hidden in the transom platform (and isolated from the main hull) is a 300-gallon fuel tank to simplify refueling the tender and watertoys.

Twin curved stairways lead from the stern to the aft deck, which has been designed for entertaining rather than simply left as the open area found on many yachts. Protected from the sun by the overhang of the boat deck and from the wind by the superstructure, this teak-planked area serves as a gracious entry to the saloon as

Porthole ★ The railing sculpted out of stainless steel sweeps from pilothouse to lower deck.

Above ★ Wehr Nuts is a Raised Pilothouse motoryacht with clean lines and a low profile.

Left ★ The flybridge is the fair-weather entertainment center, with a large Jacuzzi™ spa, dining area, and built-in bar with a high-tech infrared grill and a slush machine for making lethal "Rum Runner" punch.

★ WEHR NUTS

well as an ideal place for alfresco entertaining. A Corian-topped bar is offset to port with Timeless stools, and a beautifully inlaid table by A.J. Originals reflects the curve of a settee inset into the transom.

Interestingly enough, the usual sliding doors into the saloon have been replaced by a single entry door and, again, it shows the thought that went into this design. The single door combined with large aft windows provides a conversation area with comfortable chairs in what would have been a useless wasteland if sliding doors had been chosen, yet there is no loss of accessibility or view.

The saloon is cool and elegant, with anigre combined with mapa burl for a light and open décor. The Christensen talent with wood is evident throughout, and everything from the intricate crown molding to the unusual toe-kick moldings are flawlessly executed. To add to the visual space (and to accommodate a tall owner), headroom throughout *Wehr Nuts* is a minimum of 7ft 2in.

What appears to be a large cabinet aft to starboard is the entertainment center, and its bulk merges into a sunken bar area with a black granite counter and a pair of comfortable chairs. The cabinet, which actually conceals

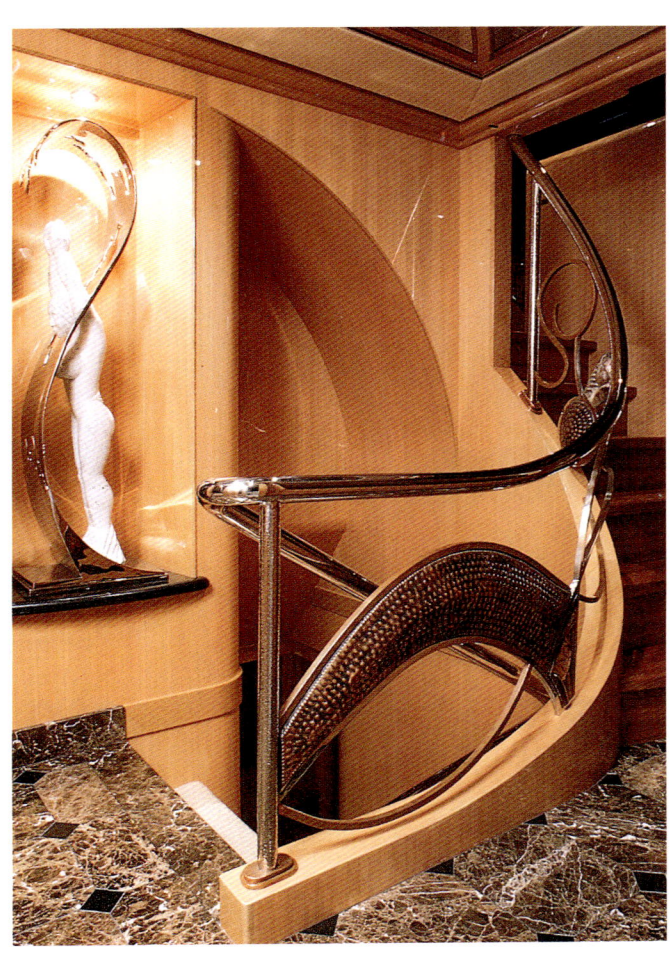

Opp. top ★ The saloon is comfortably furnished with a loose-pillowed sofa under a waterfall ceiling treatment.

Opp. bottom ★ A recurring column theme and a hand-painted mural of a mountain scene are special features in the lower foyer.

Left ★ With the artistic rail, inset marble, stainless steel sculpture in the alcove, and marble floor tiles, the entry foyer is truly spectacular.

Below ★ Since *Wehr Nuts* does not have sliding doors aft, the area usually devoted to entry space can be used for a seating arrangement, and the large cabinet conceals not only the entertainment center but the outside bridge stairs.

★ WEHR NUTS

outside stairs both to the bridge and the engine room, holds a 48in Mitsubishi television with full digital video equipment, a 1700 watt (!) sound system and, since the owner is a cigar fancier, a large humidor.

The saloon is divided into areas, with the primary seating being a loose-pillowed sofa that curves out from the port side. To further delineate the area, interior designer Robin Rose added a waterfall ceiling treatment with mirrors and recessed lighting.

If the windows surrounding the saloon seem overly large, it's probably the result of another thoughtful touch: mirrored frames. By installing Mitsubishi mirrors in the window surrounds, the usual blank look created by the frames is eliminated.

Another feature of the walkaround side decks is that the overhang from the bridge also holds the air handlers for the air conditioning, so there will never be any condensation drips in the saloon and the ducting can easily be cleaned from outside via hinged drop-down panels.

The formal dining area, also with a waterfall effect overhead, is forward with a glass-topped table for six. An oversized buffet, accented by mapa burl and black granite, is forward, low cabinets to port have been carefully router-notched to hold the glassware, and a pair of chairs with a small table are opposite.

Another example of thoughtful planning is something missing aboard *Wehr Nuts:* visible electrical or system outlets. All wall plugs, including those for telephones, are hidden so there is nothing to mar the décor.

The galley is fully enclosed, in part to keep guests arriving at the entry foyer or on their way to the day head from getting an insider's look at the food preparation. The pocket door for the galley, which opens onto the entry foyer, has a proximity switch so that the crew can open and close the door even when using both hands to carry the meal service.

The galley is comprehensively equipped with everything from an oversized wine chiller to a six-burner Gaggenau electric cook top, and all the cabinet doors have touch latches for a clean look that is easy to use. The informality of *Wehr Nuts* is evident since the galley has a dinette tucked in one corner, facing a spacious L-shaped Corian counter with brushed stainless steel backsplashes. An outside door allows the crew to enter the yacht via the galley (the crew quarters are forward), and it also allows meal service to the aft deck without passing through the saloon. Accessed from the galley is a huge pantry and storage area under the raised pilothouse, which also contains many of the electronic systems for easy maintenance and servicing.

Forward along the starboard passage is the master suite and, once again, the decisions made in the layout reflect the experience of the owner. Since he and his wife will often be aboard the yacht without guests, having the master suite on the main deck not only provides a spacious retreat, but puts them close to the living areas without having to ascend and descend to a lower accommodation level.

Anigre pillars accented by braided leather ropes frame the mirrored headboard, while a built-in bureau of mapa burl is to port along with a large walk-in closet. To starboard is a retro-style couch and the aft bulkhead, with inlaid diamond panels, hides the television behind electric sliding doors.

Forward, the his-and-hers bathroom spans the width of the house, with a centerline curved glass shower stall (lined with book-matched marble) and a Jacuzzi™ tub set in black Emperador marble dividing the two areas. Both sides have a toilet, and the "her" side to starboard incorporates a vanity into the marble counter. The floor is intricately patterned marble, and anigre columns beside the tub continue the theme.

Opp. top ★ The master suite features anigre columns flanking a mirrored headboard, built-in cabinets, and a retro couch.

Opp. bottom ★ The his-and-hers master bathroom has a centerline Jacuzzi™ spa set in black Emperador marble.

Below left ★ The two VIP staterooms have built-in cabinets, bookshelves and desk, as well as queen-size berths.

Below right ★ The guest heads feature the pale anigre paneling that has been painstakingly stained in either a checkerboard or art deco pattern.

The curving staircase leading down to the four guest staterooms is also a work of art. Carved from hammered stainless steel, a reclining mermaid is designed into the middle, beneath the peened copper railing. The stairwell also showcases a stainless steel and marble statue and, with a mirrored ceiling and a skylit effect from the pilothouse windows, provides a spectacular entry to the yacht.

The lower foyer hides a refrigerator for the use of guests, and has a full-height hand-painted mural of a mountain scene on the aft bulkhead. The two aft cabins mirror each other, with queen-size berths amid the theme of anigre pillars and diamond-patterned bulkheads. Shoji screens over each bed provide both privacy and light from the ports and, to reduce sound levels, the cabin doors are solid wood and the Edwin Fields wool berber carpet has lead foam underneath. Each of the cabins has a stylish head with shower, with a decor of detailed mahogany staining on the anigre paneling in either checkerboard or deco-style. The forward two guest cabins are smaller, with a double to starboard and twins to port, both with built-in bureaus and spacious heads. In all of the cabins, Rose has used the fabric of the bedspread to create the matching padded panels beneath the beds, the wall sconces are unique to each cabin, and the hand-blown glass drawer pulls are exquisite details.

The pilothouse is up a wide teak stairway from the starboard passage and, here again, the benefit of experience has resulted in a professional and seamanlike design. Mechanical engine gauges in an overhead panel serve as a backup to the Detroit Diesel DDEC digital gauges set in the black and copper Magilite dashboard. An L-shaped settee with an inlaid table is raised to overlook the helm area and offer a full view forward.

Another easy stairway leads from the pilothouse to the bridge, which spans the full beam and stretches from forward of amidships to the transom. Across the forward end of the cockpit behind a low windscreen and under a soft Bimini top is the helm with three Crown Ltd. pedestal seats and wing controls to port and starboard. Just aft of the divider behind the helm is an L-shaped settee and triangular table, providing ample space for outdoor dining or a buffet spread.

To starboard is a large bar area with six Timeless fixed stools in a semicircle. In addition to the expected bar amenities, there is a TEC grill that uses infrared 1600° burners to serve up perfect barbecues. Even better, there is a *petite sorbetière*—better known to Americans as a slush machine—that can make and hold up to eight gallons of Rum Runner punch, a potent mixture whose ingredients are jealously guarded by the owner and crew of *Wehr Nuts*.

Twin sunpads aft flank a large centerline Jacuzzi™ spa, and the sunpads hinge up to reveal cavernous storage for chairs, cushions and other deck gear. Aft, a 22ft Novurania RIB tender with a Yamaha 225 hp outboard nests with a trio of SeaDoo GTX personal watercraft. All are launched by the Christensen-built 4500lb crane and, when the tenders and toys are launched, the chocks are removable to open the area for entertaining.

The crew quarters are forward, reinforcing the American notion that the crew are part of the "family" with far more comfortable cabins than usually found on European yachts. The captain has a private double cabin to port, while two upper-lower bunk cabins are forward, all with private heads and stall showers. A crew lounge has seating and all the necessities from separate DSS satellite television reception to a compact galley, and there is a housekeeping area with a trio of stacked washer-dryers. The primary entry to the crew quarters is via portside stairs to the side deck but, in bad weather, the crew can also reach the main accommodations through a door in the lower foyer.

The ship's systems are no less thoughtfully arranged and chosen than the accommodations, starting with the equipment room/lazarette that provides access to the engineroom from the transom platform. With a complete Christensen Exclusive All Voltage 50/60 Hertz shore power system, *Wehr Nuts* is equipped to cruise worldwide. The engine room was built to MCA standards (the yacht is also classed ABS ✠ 1-AMS), with a pair of 1800hp. DDC-MTU 16V2000 sequentially turbocharged

Opposite ✦ The pilothouse is a model of nautical design and full redundancy, with analog gauges overhead to back up the digital instruments in the dashboard.

Left ✦ The engine room is spacious and, except for a few hoses, entirely hard-plumbed with pipe.

SPECIFICATIONS

LOA	124ft (37.8m)
Beam	27ft 6in (8.4m)
Draft	6ft 6in (2.0m)
Displacement (half load)	383,219 lbs.
Fuel	8000 gal.
Water	1850 gal.
Power	2x1800hp DDC-MTU 16V2000
Interior Design	Robin Rose Assoc.
Builder/Year	Christensen Shipyards Ltd./1999

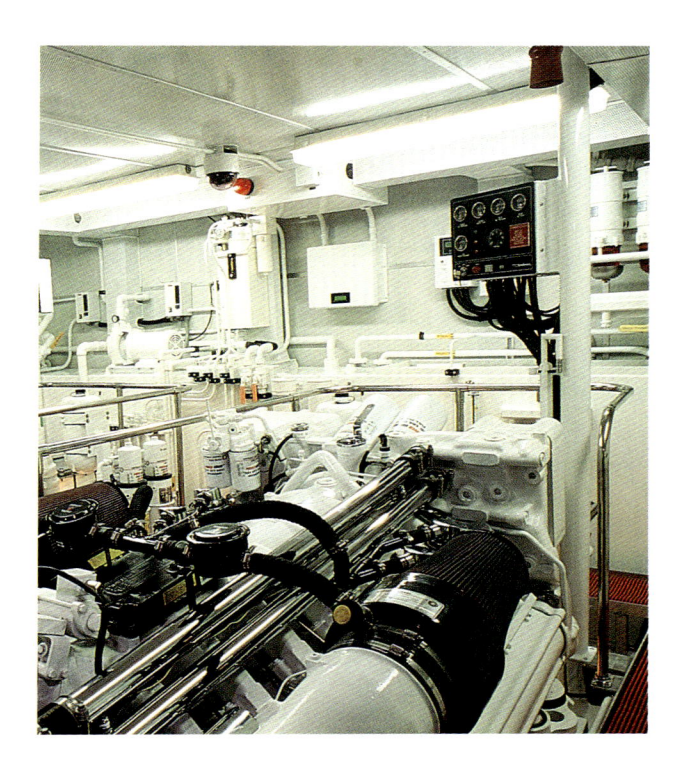

diesels with access on all sides. A pair of Northern Lights 65kW generators provide power, and there is exceptional redundancy including dual freshwater pumps, dual air compressors, dual raw water pumps for the air conditioning, and even dual steering systems. To simplify engine replacement far in the future, the saloon sole and boat deck have hatches that can easily be lifted so that the engines can be removed using a crane. A look around the sparkling engine room shows that everything is hard-plumbed: from the engines to the deck drains, there are no hoses to be found on the *Wehr Nuts*. Extensive sound-proofing (specified by Van Capellan of Holland and E.A.R.) is evident, and even the Aqua Air air conditioning is cosseted in a sound box to eliminate the usual whine. An Envirovac waste water system like that on cruise ships eliminates the need to penetrate bulkheads and has suction toilets using only one pint per flush.

On the foredeck, the anchor windlass is on a raised pedestal putting it at the right height for use and, to maintain the clean profile, the hand rails around the deck are tucked inside the bulwarks. Even the fire hoses have been recessed into the house to keep the passages clear.

Shortly after launching, *Wehr Nuts* cruised the West Coast and transited the Panama Canal en route to her Florida homeport, but it's likely that she'll be a regular visitor along the Eastern seaboard and to both Caribbean and Mediterranean ports.

Carefully conceived to meet one owner's needs but embodying the sort of thoughtful design that will make this yacht desirable to a wide range of tastes, *Wehr Nuts* is the offspring of a fine marriage between experienced owner and talented boatbuilder.

WEHR NUTS

Wild Horses

76-foot W-Class Sloop

To talk about *Wild Horses*, the first of the W-Class sloops to be launched, is to talk about a concept, a vision, more than a specific boat. *Wild Horses* is the inspiration of a romantic muse, the realization of a dream of reviving the big boat level racing of the "'tween the wars" era, when J-boats, M-boats, 23-meters and 12-meters, and New York 50s and 70s, were considered day racers. The concept belongs to yachtsman Donald Tofias who, after years of researching that glorious era of yachting, decided that the time is ripe for a renewal of level racing in large, lovely, traditional yachts. He is the driving force behind the W-Class, and has dedicated his time and resources to make his dream come alive.

Traditional design and construction can present a challenging, delicate dilemma in this day and age, with the appeal of true traditional construction weighed against the variety of modern technology available to the boatbuilder, technology that will usually produce boats that are safer and stronger than their original counterparts. Tofias approached the late Joel White, naval architect of Brooklin, Maine, with the problem—the W-Class is White's last design, a fitting closure to a career devoted to classic boat designs imaginatively realized with modern woodworking techniques.

Stepping aboard modern "classics," I always feel a brief initial moment of disorientation: the eye sees the sweep of the traditional lines, the crafting of the numerous details of the shipwright's art, yet is also drawn to hydraulics, cross-linked pedestal winches, and touches of Vectran and carbon fiber. *Wild Horses* is straightforward in this regard, making no bones about her contemporary engineering, and within minutes I was seduced by the promise of performance and security owed to this canny blend of tradition and technology. She is also uncompromising about her purpose, her layout on deck and below reflecting the exigencies of competitive sailing.

Her accommodations, considering her intended use as a day racer, are adequate in scope, and impeccable in execution. The large forepeak is devoted to sail and gear

Porthole   The galley is finished in Herreshoff style, with white panels and varnished cherrywood trim.

Opp. left   The clean lines of the teak-planked foredeck are clearly visible below *Wild Horses* battle flag.

Above   Underway with the crew settled on the weather rail, *Wild Horses* displays the classic lines that were inspired by big boat level racing from the "'tween the wars" era.

Left   The traditional gold-leafed cove stripe ends in a stylish script "W" aft. Even the bulwarks are detailed with a graceful recess.

★ WILD HORSES   179

storage bins, chain locker, and ample space for any additional equipment requiring safe storage. Chocks for the 110-pound anchor are provided to keep the weight off the bow when racing. Two pipe berths to accommodate crew overflow are also located here. Next aft is a full-width crew cabin, with lower and upper berths port and starboard, small storage lockers outboard of the berths, and a wash basin. A passageway to starboard, with access to a crew head, leads to the main saloon. The forward part of this space is taken up by another full head to starboard, and a U-shaped galley to port.

The main part of the saloon features a well-equipped navigation station just forward of a large hanging locker to starboard, and an L-shaped settee to port, with a pilot berth outboard. *Wild Horses* has a wooden picnic table that seats eight and stows flat on the engine room bulkhead. The main saloon, as is the rest of the interior, is finished Herreshoff style—bulkheads and flat vertical surfaces painted white with varnished American cherry trim everywhere. Overhead, the laminated deck beams are varnished, the traditional fore and aft spruce deck planks with chamfered edges are painted white. Strategically placed handrails are hung from the deck beams. The cabin sole throughout is teak mounted on core plywood, finished with a light oil, with

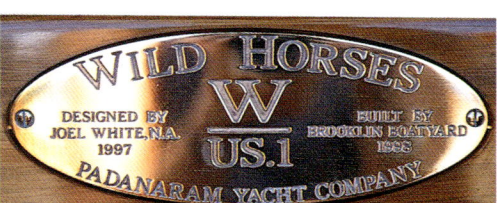

180   THE MEGAYACHTS USA ★ 2000

bright varnish accents. A small door on the aft bulkhead provides access to the vast open space under the cockpit, mostly empty except for the main engine in a soundproofed box, steering gear, watermaker, and storage.

The gains in simplicity afforded by *Wild Horses'* primary mission as a day racer are evident on deck. Her abbreviated cabin trunk, a low box with rectangular deadlights, a tip of the hat to the old New York 50s and M-boats, leaves most of her deck length available for sail handling. The cockpit is huge, dominated by a large-diameter laminated teak steering wheel which is a work of art in itself. The three-speed Harken grinder system can be cross-linked in any combination; two winch pedestals take up the center, and the flat coaming top sports four winch drums. To ease crew functions, the outboard part of the cockpit sole is sloped approximately 20 degrees. Located just aft of the helm station are the main sheet and main traveler winches, as well as the hydraulic control panel for the vang, permanent backstay, and outhaul. The running backstay winches are further aft, adjacent to two hatches which provide access to storage space below deck and double as individual cockpits for the runner trimmers. A neat detail here is the padding on the underside of the hatches, which when open allow a comfortable seat for the trimmers throughout a long race. A small detail I would criticize—admittedly nit-picking—is the location of the fuel fills on the bridge deck next to the companionway. As spills are inevitable, they would be better located closer to the deck scuppers.

The foredeck hands are also well provided for. A cluster of five winches around the mast base is dedicated to halyards and reef lines, with a rope tail box integrated into the forward side of the cabin trunk. The main halyard winch is electric. Forward of the mast is an uncluttered expanse of teak deck, interrupted only by a large hatch for sail handling, the anchor windlass, and two mooring cleats. A low bulwark with a varnished teak cap rail sweeps aft and additional security is provided by double lifelines.

Opp. above ★ The saloon reflects the day racer simplicity of *Wild Horses*, with the U-shaped galley forward to port and a wraparound settee aft. When needed, a folding dining table can seat eight.

Right ★ The well-equipped navigation station is in the saloon, with everything needed for both closed course racing and passagemaking.

The rig on *Wild Horses* is consistent with her character: a carbon fiber mast and boom, stayed with stainless steel rod rigging—the spinnaker pole is carbon as well—supports a $7/8$ths double-head rig. The combination of forestaysail and Yankee, while undoubtedly aesthetically pleasing to traditionalists, seems unnecessarily complicated in this era of powerful winches and rugged rigging; my guess is that the forestaysail will be used mostly in heavy weather and passage-making, and the preponderance of sailing, and certainly racing, will be with the 100 percent blade jib or 140 percent genoa alone.

A note about *Wild Horses'* construction is in order at this point. Several experiments with different West epoxy lamination schedules resulted in a laminate consisting of a fore and aft tongue-and-groove Douglas fir inner skin, three layers of diagonal cedar veneers, and a final layer of fore and aft cedar planking. Each skin is applied with plastic staples and vacuum bagged for curing. The plastic staples are a particularly clever touch; the hull can be faired

★ WILD HORSES

Right ★ The long foredeck is broken only by the inner forestay and a trio of hatches, leaving ample space for the carbon fiber spinnaker pole, with added security from the permanent double lifelines.

Inset ★ A detail of the spectacular helm.

Bottom ★ The huge cockpit is dominated by the teak steering wheel and the twin Harken three-speed coffee grinders which can be cross-linked to any of the winch drums on the wide coamings. The outboard portion of the cockpit sole slopes upward to improve crew footing when *Wild Horses* is heeled.

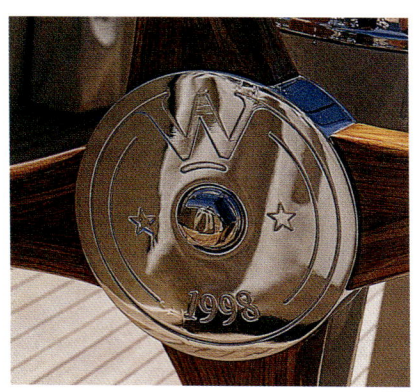

with power tools without worry about blades, thus no time need be wasted removing metal fasteners after each skin is applied. A final thin layer of fiberglass is applied, mostly to protect the relatively soft cedar topsides from dings and scratches. As the hull is built, a massive framework of bronze stringers and floors is installed to support the keel stresses and mast compression loads. The deck is supported by laminated spruce beams, and consists of fore and aft cedar planks overlaid with plywood, then finished with traditional teak planking bonded to the plywood. With the exception of highly sophisticated and expensive composite structures, this type of wood construction results in an exceptionally light, strong, rigid hull. A glance at her specifications reveals a ballast-to-weight ratio of 50 percent, with a remarkably light overall weight.

What does it all translate into? I had a chance to sail her, in one of those "picture postcard" Maine days, with a fresh breeze to help show off her pace. And it is sailing that truly brings together the diverse components which make up *Wild Horses*. Hanking on the jib is a bit of nostalgic flashback, although her sails are made of soft Vectran cloth from Hood Sailmakers and notably easy to handle. Once the sails are set, she simply takes off. She is stiff, her high ballast to weight ratio ensuring that puffs are converted into acceleration, exhilarating on any point of sail, she tracks well and has a sweet, light touch to the helm. The impressive rigidity and strength of her structure can be felt when strapping down sheets for windward work in a breeze, a procedure which usually elicits "complaints" from inferior boats. Sitting at the helm working her to windward, I started fantasizing about sailing in a fleet of sisterships racing to the weather mark. Perhaps not such a fantasy after all: the second W-class boat, *White Wings*, was launched in late September 1998, and a match racing schedule has been ongoing.

We headed for shore all too soon, *Wild Horses* ending the day with a demonstration of her maneuverability under power as well, spinning around in less than her own length and coming to rest.

From the dock, more details become apparent. Her waterlines forward reveal a subtle, Herreshoffian hollow under the compound curve of her flare, decidedly a designer's virtuoso employ of ducks and splines. Her sheer shows a sure sweep, sufficient to give her profile power and grace but not so much that it weakens her lines. The gold-leaf cove echoes that sweep, ending in a stylized, flowing "W" aft, and the bulwarks are detailed with a classic recess. All the lines are brought together convincingly at the transom, a perfect wineglass shape, the sheer tucked in with just the right amount of tumblehome under the cap rail.

But mainly, *Wild Horses* is not about superlatives, and definitely not about showing off. She is the most honest large yacht I have sailed in a long time, a tribute to her builders, Steve White of Brooklin Boatyard and Taylor Allen of Rockport Marine, brothers-in-law, both dedicated to the tradition of wooden boatbuilding. The meticulous craftsmanship evidenced by her many details is there because that is how proper yachts are built, and to the seasoned eye it does not conceal the simplicity and "rightness" of the design. Just like the New York 50s.

SPECIFICATIONS

LOA	76ft 4in (23.5m)
LWL	53ft 11in (17.07m)
Beam	16ft 1in (4.95m)
Draft	11ft (3.35m)
Displacement	52,900 lbs.
Ballast	25,000 lbs.
Sail Area	(100% fore triangle) 2,239 sqft
Main Engine	170 hp. turbocharged diesel
Naval Architect	Joel White
Contact	Padanaram Yacht Company
Builders/Year	Brooklin Boatyard and Rockport Marine/1998

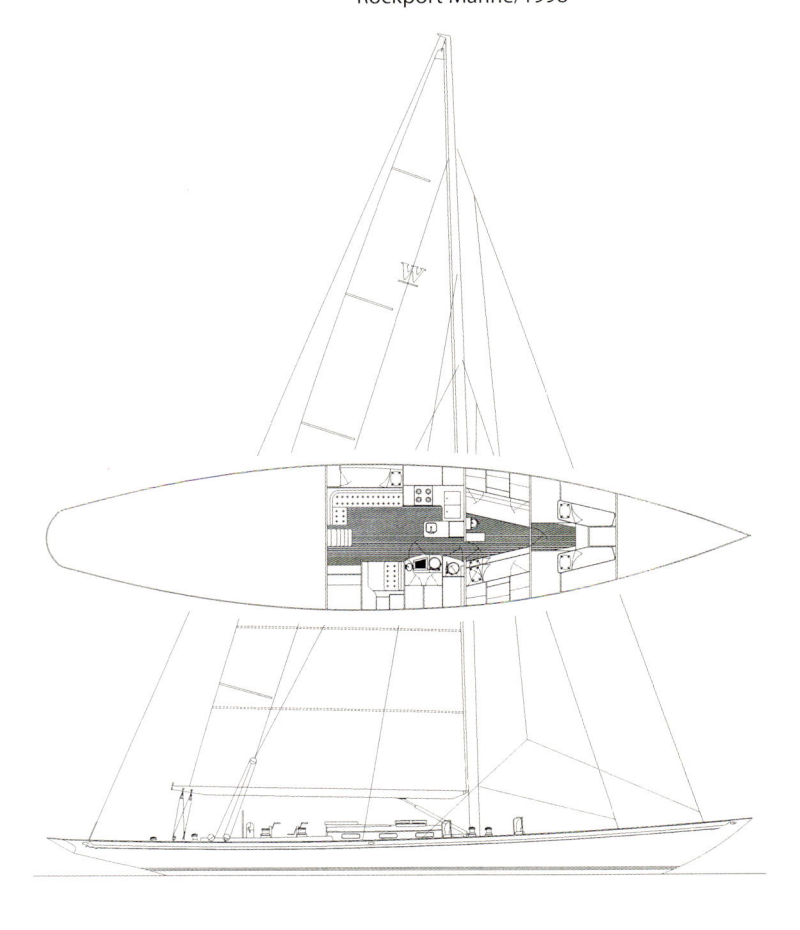

CREATIVITY AND EXCELLENCE IN YACHT DESIGN

LUIZ DE BASTO
D E S I G N S
444 Brickell Ave. Suite 828 Miami, FL
33131 (305) 373-1500 Fax 377-0900
Email: luizbasto@aol.com
www.luizdebasto.com

W-Class

BIG BOAT RACING IS BACK

Designed by Joel White, N. A.
Masterfully built in Maine of cold-molded wood by Brooklin Boat Yard and Rockport Marine
LOA 76' 4" • LWL 53' 11"
Beam 16' 1" • Draft 11'
Displacement 52,900 lbs.
95' carbon-fiber mast and spars by Hall
Hood Vectran® sails (2,239 sq. ft.)
Harken hardware

Aspire to greatness. Contact us today.

PADANARAM YACHT COMPANY, LLC
Reservoir Place • 1601 Trapelo Road • Waltham, Massachusetts 02451
781-890-5511 • fax 781-890-1512
email: info@w-class.com • www.w-class.com

The Spirit of the Future . . . The Soul of the Past

GTH DESIGN TECHNIQUES
OFFERS A *FULL* DESIGN SERVICE

- Space Planning
- Interior and Exterior Styling
- Joiner Detailing
- Color and material specs
- Lighting Design
- Systems Integration
- Pilothouse Console and Electronics layout

Also, custom furniture, china & crystal, metal and glass sculpture, and other yacht accessories. Embroidered accents and crew clothing

GTH DESIGN is a full service interior design firm serving the marine industry and owners of fine yachts. We design unique, dynamic, functional, and cost effective solutions to suit your needs. If you are considering the design of a new vessel or the refit of an existing one, we would be happy to assist you.

Please visit our website for extensive photos and details of a number of our projects:
www.gthdesign.com

Tom and Patty Henderson

TEL 360.779.1909
FAX 360.779.6133
17791 Fjord Drive NE, Suite Z
Poulsbo, Washington 98370

Web Address: www.gthdesign.com
Email: gth@tscnet.com

Northern Pacific 64

San Juan 38

GREGORY C MARSHALL NAVAL ARCHITECT LTD.

1009 Langley Street,
Victoria,
British Columbia
V8W 1V7
Canada

Phone: +1 (250) 388 9995
Fax: +1 (250) 388 4260

email: gcm@pacificcoast.net

TRICONFORT
FURNITURE OF DISTINCTION

For more information, call
(001) 704 875 8787
or (33) 04 76 53 30 00
email: Triconfort@aol.com

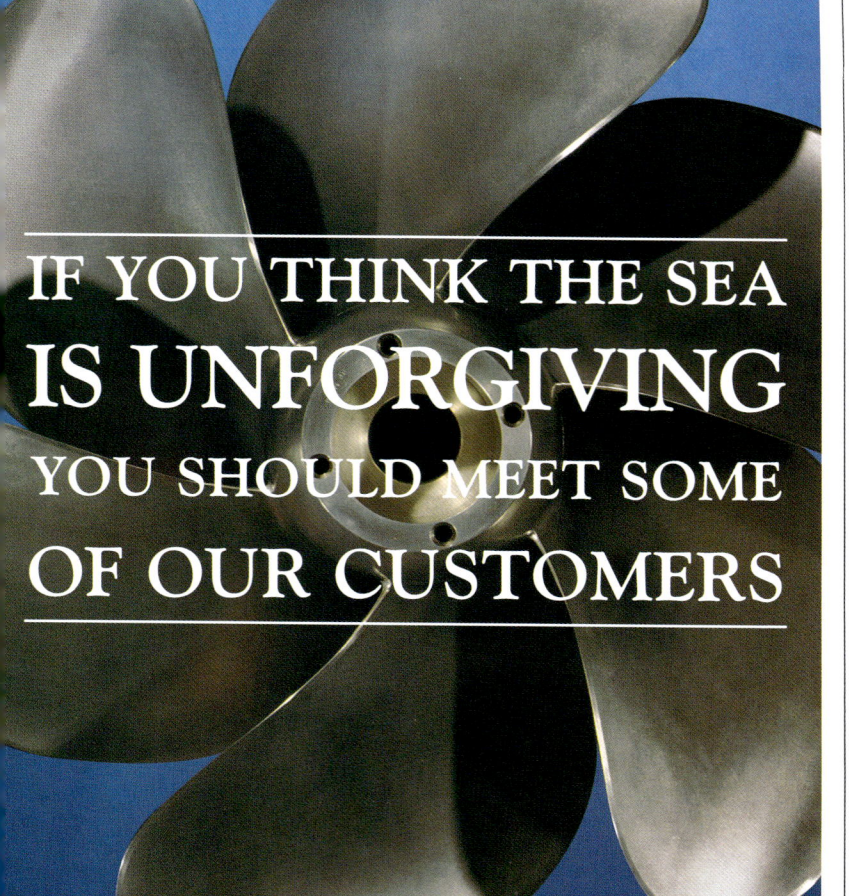

IF YOU THINK THE SEA IS UNFORGIVING YOU SHOULD MEET SOME OF OUR CUSTOMERS

From the US Navy to Superyacht owners, the people and organisations that use our propellers won't tolerate second best. We understand their sentiments precisely. Brunton's propellers are custom designed to suit the boat. This gives you:

First time fit ● *Lower noise and vibration* ● *Faster, smoother running*

● *Minimum cavitation* ● *Maximum performance*

To complement our propellers, we supply a full range of propulsion related equipment, including:

Shafting ● *Sterngear* ● *Bearings* ● *Struts* ● *Seals*

In addition, all our products (including our famous Autoprop automatic variable pitch propellers) are supported by a worldwide service and repair network.

So to take advantage of our service and unmatched CNC machine shops, take a tip from the world's most uncompromising sailors - and contact your nearest Brunton's office.

BRUNTON'S PROPELLERS
Part of the Langham Industries Group

1999

BRUNTON'S PROPELLERS LTD PO BOX 4074, Clacton-on-Sea, Essex, CO15 4TQ, England
Tel: +44(0)1255 420005 Fax: +44(0)1255 427775 E-mail: sales@bruntons-propellers.com www.bruntons-propellers.com
BRUNTON'S PROPELLERS USA PO BOX 607, Newport, RI 02840, USA
Tel: (401) 847 7960 Fax: (401) 849 0631 E-mail: sales@autoprop.com

---

Thruster Technology into the 21st Century

advanced propulsion and thruster systems for the superyacht

- Standard Hydraulic Bow Thrusters available up to 150 HP
- Electric Thrusters designed for 'Silent' operation, complete with E-motor and variable frequency drives
- BowJets and Azimuthing PumpJets rated form 25 to 200 HP
- Retractable and Swing type thrusters - Retracable 'Legg' propulsion drives
- Rotatable Propeller Drives - up to 6,000HP
- Electric Azipod Drives - up to 2,500HP

DynaSea International Inc.
511 Rutile Drive
Ponte Vedra, Fl 32082
Tel 904 356 0604
Fax 904 543 0836

PokelaDesign+

International Yacht Interior Design

4015 Ruston Way
Tacoma, Washington 98402, USA
206/752-9704 ◆ Fax 206/752-9704

Our background creates our future

exterior styling
general concept & layout
naval architecture
interior design & decoration
project management

for

CRN - FERRETTI GROUP
PERINI NAVI
RODRIGUEZ GROUP
CANTIERI DI SARNICO
ASTONDOA
GEMINI YACHTS
PALMER JOHNSON

tel: +39 041 45 72 72
fax: +39 041 45 73 93
e-mail: nlyachts@mpbnet.it

www.nuvolari-lenard.com

NUVOLARI ⬦ LENARD™
naval design Venezia Italia

Pacific Custom Interiors, Inc.
2601 West Marina Place, Suite P
Seattle, Washington 98199
(206) 282-5540 Phone
(206) 282-2803 Fax

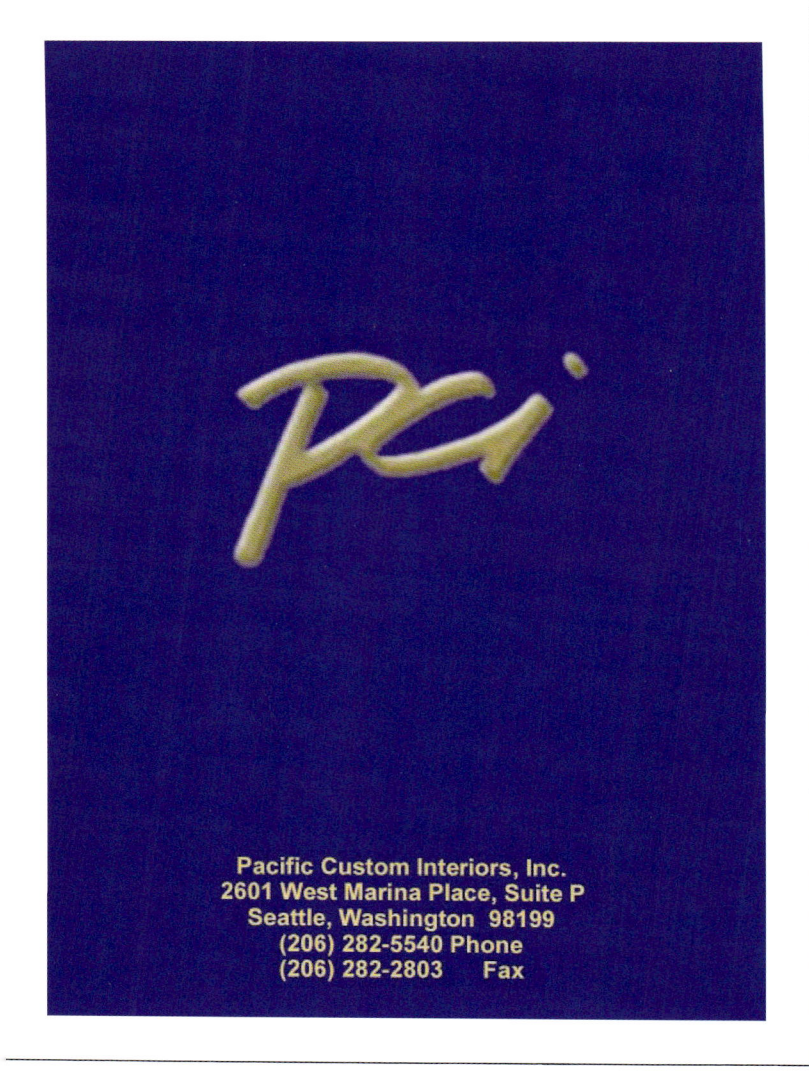

Delta Marine International, Inc.

1700 NW 65th Avenue, Suite 8 • Fort Lauderdale, Florida 33313
Phone. (954) 791 0909 • Fax. 321 8145
http//www.deltamarineozone.com

Designers and Manufacturers of Chem-Free™
OZONE TECHNOLOGIES FOR MARINE APPLICATIONS

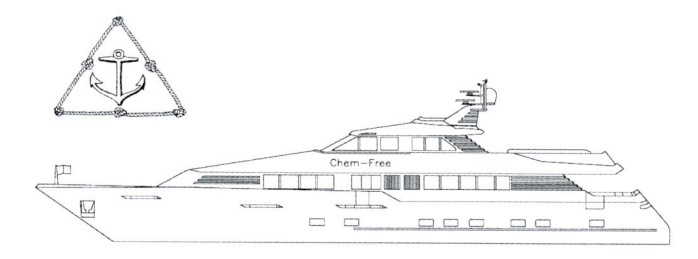

Ozone systems from stem to stern. If it doesn't have the Chem-Free™ label, it's not from Delta Marine International

- **Potable water purification and quality assurance**
- **Indoor air quality and odor control**
- **Black water holding tank and vent line odor control**
- **Gray water holding tank and vent line odor control**
- **Diesel fuel odor control**
- **Bilge odor control**

Guido de Groot design

Interior and exterior design for luxury yachts
Hogewoerd 122 • 2311 HT Leiden • Holland
Telephone: +31 (0)71 - 566 30 40 • Telefax: +31 (0)71 - 566 30 39

www.yachtworld.com/degroot

Tradition, moving fast

Sapphire

Best elapsed time - Antiqua Classic Yacht Regatta May 1999.

Creating and refitting yachts of distinction, builders of Truly Classics and Lemsteraak yachts.

Meet us at:

MONACO YACHT SHOW
22 - 25 sept. 1999
Berth P11

FORT LAUDERDALE
28 okt. - 01 nov. 1999
Dutch Pavilion Nr. 722

HOLLAND JACHTBOUW BV

VREDEWEG 32 B, 1505 HH ZAANDAM, TEL. +31 (0)75-614.91.33, FAX +31 (0)75-614.91.35
HOMEPAGE: www.hollandjachtbouw.nl   E-MAIL: hjb@hollandjachtbouw.nl

70' Hatteras "Sentry" – American Custom Yachts, Stuart, FL

Interlux

A WORK *of Art* or a **PAINT JOB?**

When you pay thousands to have your yacht professionally polyurethaned, you want a Work of Art. Not a paint job. Of course, how it's applied, and who does the application has a lot to do with it. But the depth of gloss, the durability and the repairability of the finish will ultimately be determined by the choice of primer, filler, fairing compound and, above all, by the topcoat. Interspray has the complete system. Everything from start to glorious finish – developed by Interlux, the largest, most technologically advanced marine coatings company in the world. Why would you trust your yacht to anything less? Talk to your local Michelangelo.

INTERSPRAY
FINISHES

Interlux Yacht Finishes, 2270 Morris Ave., Union, NJ 07083 • Technical Service Help Line, 908-964-2360
Internet, http://www.INTERLUX.com

HELIYACHTS

32 m ketch launched in 1998

YACHTS
REFITS
REPAIRS

| **HELI YACHTS INTERNATIONAL SA**
OFFICE: VIA TESERETE 67
6942 LUGANO /SAVOSA · SWITZERLAND | PHONE: +41-91 961 80 30
FAX: +41-91 961 80 39
GSM: +41-792 87 92 93 | **HELI D.D.**
SHIPYARD: SV. POLIKARPA 8
52100 PULA/ISTRIA · CROATIA | PHONE +385-52-21 66 33
FAX +385-52-21 66 34
HELI@PU.TEL.HR |

Design Alliance

YACHT DESIGN & INTERIORS

*Exterior and Interior Design
Construction Consultation
Concept Development*

3911 Southridge Ave.
West Vancouver, B.C.
Canada V7V 3H9

604 926-9408 Tel
604 926-9405 Fax
designalliance@home.com

SYLVIA BOLTON DESIGN

Sea Your Dreams...

1818 Westlake Ave North, Suite 203, Seattle, WA 98109, USA
Tel: +1 (206) 217-0863 • www.SBDdesign.com • Fax: +1 (206) 286 7633

Interior Design for Yachts

MARBLE CRAFTSMANSHIP

The art of stone has been with us for most of man's civilized history. Over the past century it has made its way into the maritime industry from the elegant Luxury liners of days past to the private yachts and cruise ships of today. Over the past decade, technological advances have made the possibilities endless. The introduction of natural stone composite products has changed the face of the industry. Marbles and semi precious stones, once impossible to work, are now available cut as thin as 4mm.

Proprietary techniques in the impregnation of marble blocks, (Epoxy) has allowed 100% yield of block of raw stone. It can then be cut in various thicknesses. Thin material (4mm) for veneers, walls floors and cladding. With matching thick material for use as sea rails, tub decks, jambs, columns, sinks and more. This allows a marble mason to emulate a monolithic look, yet at a fraction of the overall weight.

Autocad and water jet technology has also made an impact. Once laborious expensive inlay work has become relatively affordable, curved cutting, some of which is impossible by any other means is now an everyday occurrence. Computerized saws now allow a project to be cut directly from a designers drawings. Semi precious stones, mother of pearl, abalone, gold, stainless steel, bronze, and various other materials are now being inlaid along with marble using these techniques. Mosaics that were once difficult to accomplish are now more easily achieved with today's technology.

While all of today's technologies have enhanced our ability to accomplish a task, there will always be a need for an artisans hand work. The idea, sketch, design, block selection, layout and sculpture of a project will never be replaced by a machine. The placement of each individual stone will always be in the hands of one of these master craftsmen.

With each launch, the yachting world continues to raise the standard of magnificence and design, and in doing so, has created new challenges for the marble industry throughout the world.

J · HOMCHICK
CLASSIC STONEWORK

1605 South 93rd Bldg. E, Unit P Seattle, Washington 98108 Phone: 206.762.3933 Fax: 206.762.3974 Cell: 206.947.9756

To Arrange The Perfect Crewed Charter, We Need To Know Your Preferences.

Sail Or Power? Caribbean Or Med? French Or California?

The yacht and destination are only the beginning. A truly memorable crewed charter vacation must exceed your expectations on every level. We've been serving the worldwide chartering needs of discriminating clients since 1968. So we know the yachts, the crews and, most importantly, the right questions to ask. If you are considering a luxury yachting vacation, please call 800-223-2050.

THE FINEST CREWED CHARTERS IN THE WORLD.

Lynn Jachney Charters, Inc.

Lynn Jachney Charters, PO Box 302, Marblehead, MA 01945
Fax: 781-639-0216   e-mail: ljc@boston.sisna.com

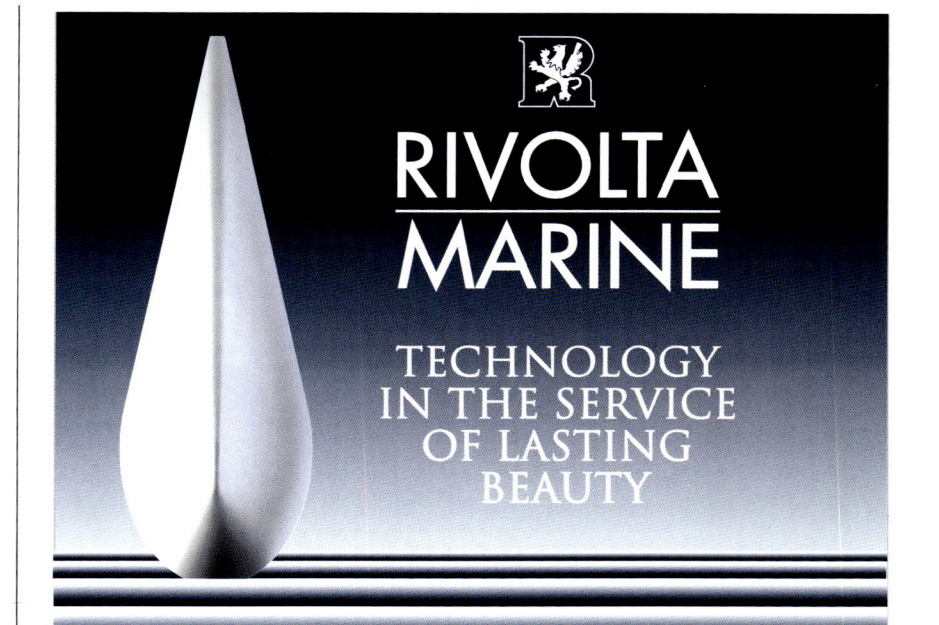

RIVOLTA MARINE

TECHNOLOGY IN THE SERVICE OF LASTING BEAUTY

The RIVOLTA 90 redefines high-speed, comfortable sailing for our time.

A unique combination of high-technology and tradition, the RIVOLTA 90 features a retracting keel and twin rudders, simple to sail, easy to maintain.

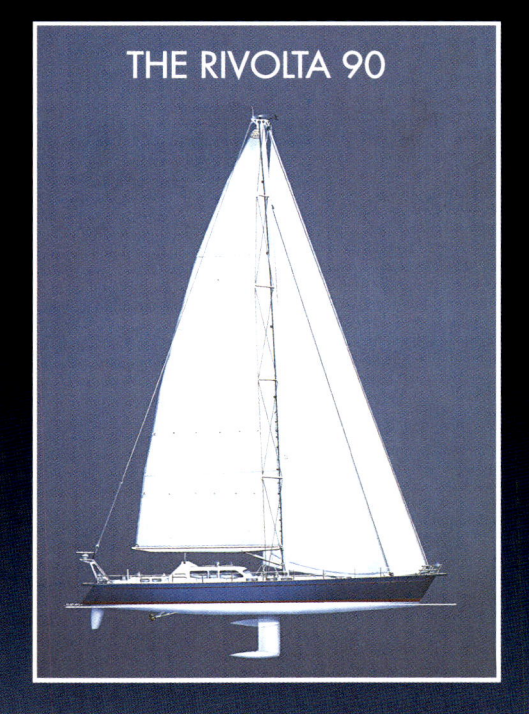

THE RIVOLTA 90

THE JET SETTER

THE RIVOLTA JET SETTER 38 perfect for a weekend getaway or a simple evening sortie.

Combining the classic lines of a traditional coastal cruiser with the latest in efficient hull design and jet power, the JET SETTER is ready for everything from dining to diving.

RIVOLTA GROUP • 1741 MAIN STREET • SUITE 101
SARASOTA, FLORIDA 34236-5812 USA
TEL (941)954-0355 • FAX (941)954-0111
WWW.RIVOLTA.COM • EMAIL: rrivolta@gte.net

extravagance you can enjoy.

Or the simplicity.

Freedom of choice for the discerning few on the world's finest luxury yachts. For two decades the Crestar approach to private yacht charter has become synonymous with a service that is second to none ~ an exclusive charter formula tailored for those who demand excellence.

CRESTAR
YACHT CHARTERS

COLETTE COURT 125 SLOANE STREET LONDON SW1X 9AU, ENGLAND.
Tel: +44(0)171 730 2299   Toll Free from USA: 1 800 222 9985   Fax: +44 (0) 171 824 8691   E-mail: crestaryachts@mail.com

CRESTAR YACHTS...DEDICATED TO EXCELLENCE

DESTINATIONS

ARCTIC PASSAGE

S/Y Shaman *in Spitsbergen*

ROB JOHNSON

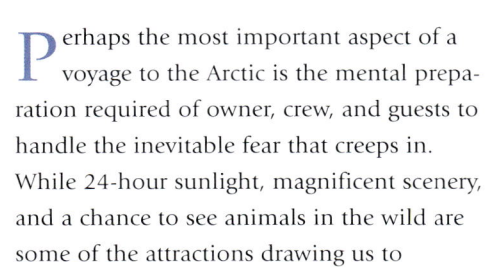

Perhaps the most important aspect of a voyage to the Arctic is the mental preparation required of owner, crew, and guests to handle the inevitable fear that creeps in. While 24-hour sunlight, magnificent scenery, and a chance to see animals in the wild are some of the attractions drawing us to Spitsbergen, we learned that fear can act like a gatekeeper, prohibiting us from entering the richness of experience that lies within. The fear is not irrational, for there is very real danger and risk in a place such as Spitsbergen. It is unsettling to sail amid ice flows; water less than 30 degrees Fahrenheit is threatening to anyone overboard; there is a fear that the vessel could be trapped in ice; and the existence of polar bears on shore is a real hazard.

For my part there are three key ingredients that an owner can insist upon to make an expedition of this kind go smoothly. First, one cannot be in a hurry. Second, one cannot cut corners on expenses—the crew needs to know that you will be doing everything in your power to create a safe and successful voyage. Third, and perhaps most importantly, one should enlist the services of an experienced guide.

We were very fortunate that Captain Steve Branagh found Per-Magnus Sander to act as our liaison with the government of Norway on Svalbard. He gave us direction regarding every aspect of preparation for the voyage, then made the delivery with the crew from mainland Norway across to Spitsbergen.

Per-Magnus is a historian and a geologist, and he is familiar with the animal life of the region. Whether alleviating anxiety, spotting a polar bear in the distance, or illuminating the sights, Per-Magnus was a godsend.

Logistically there were many requirements. We were required to post a rescue bond of approximately $20,000 with the Svalbard government as a precondition for travel there. Logistic procurement included 10 survival suits (one for each person aboard); two high caliber rifles with at least two trained riflemen were a required precaution when walking ashore in the event one crossed paths with an angry polar bear. Hunting polar bear is strictly forbidden and the government has been known to dole out heavy fines to those deemed to have killed a polar bear without clearly establishing that they were defending themselves.

Spitsbergen is navigable for a brief period each year primarily because the Gulf Stream currents move North and thaw the ice between Greenland and the western shore of the island. Rarely does it thaw to the east and south, allowing one to circumnavigate the island.

As my wife, children, and I were on our way to Svalbard via Oslo, we began to sense something extraordinary while changing planes at the Oslo airport. The walls were covered with photographs of Spitsbergen. It is clear the Norwegians view this place as a national treasure and a feeling of excitement was tangible among the passengers as we boarded our flight. The ticket-taker at the gate told my 10-year-old son, "You are so lucky to be going to Spitsbergen, it is wonderful."

When we descended over Spitsbergen we saw a very stark landscape and glacial ice rivers traversing the region. As the plane landed at the airport in Longyearbyen, the doors swung open and we got a blast of polar July air at 39 degrees Fahrenheit!

Disembarking, we saw signs in the airport warning of the danger of polar bear attacks. Inside we were met by Steve, Kate, and Per-Magnus who had been there exploring for a few days following the delivery trip. I saw in their eyes a look that was recorded on everyone's face for the next month—awe.

Longyearbyen is a small town centered around coal mining and, for a brief window each year, tourism. It has basic shops for clothing and provisions and a very fine restaurant featuring an extraordinary wine list and elegant local cuisine.

In the afternoon we went to Barentsburg about 30 miles west and saw the Russian settlement. Rumor has it that this coal mining town also functioned as a strategic outpost during the Cold War. We visited the coal mine, the local museum, the sports complex—which included a gym, pool, and weight-training area—the livestock barn, and an adjacent greenhouse.

At 3 a.m., in broad daylight, we departed to the north along the west coast of Spitsbergen to Ny Alesund, a town which houses a scientific research center sitting across a bay from a glacier. It is the site where Amundson took off on his dirigible voyage toward the North Pole. The mast for anchoring the dirigible is still standing beside a monument built in Amundson's honor. Also in Ny Alesund is the northernmost post office on earth—some 650 miles from the North Pole.

Perhaps the most notable memory we have of Ny Alesund is of the little dive-bombing birds called terns that swoop down and peck you on the head. From the moment you walk onto the shore, signs warn that you have to hold a four-foot-long

★ ARCTIC PASSAGE   *199*

Previous pages: middle inset ★ The polar July air temperature was 39° Fahrenheit.

Righthand page ★ Navigating through floating ice required slow going and a lookout on the bow.

Main picture and opposite top right ★ The reflections in a calm sea combine with cloud patterns to create a breathtaking landscape.

Right ★ A fine specimen of a polar bear skull was discovered.

stick above your head to keep the birds from attacking your scalp.

The following morning we moved north at 13 knots under main and genoa and winged-out jib under clear skies. We arrived at Magdalenefjord to see its spectacular glacier with large blocks of ice calving off and plunging into the water below. The only drawback was that we had to stand watch at anchor to fend off the ice blocks with large barge poles.

We went for a hike around the area with our two marksmen, Steve and Adam, donning rifles and walking on high ground where we were on the lookout for polar bears. We hiked every day for two to four hours at a time. Continuous daylight permits visibility at all times and the rule was "go when the going is good and sleep whenever".

The next afternoon we motored north to Smeerburgfjorden and the sun came out to illuminate a magnificent series of glaciers in front of mountains that reminded us of the Sawtooth Range near Stanley, Idaho. We continued on north and around to the east to our spectacular anchorage at Raudfjorden. Kate prepared a marvelous barbecue of salmon, reindeer, and vegetable shish kababs followed by toasted marshmallows. We hiked a little way up the beach and found a grave with an ominous human skull and remains which guidebooks suggest are those of a trapper who died in 1922. Per-Magnus reminded me that "remains" only see the light of day (and night) for about 50 days each year and are otherwise well preserved in ice. Furthermore, the all-time maximum recorded temperature in Spitsbergen is 50 degrees Fahrenheit! Shades of Woody Allen's comedy film, *Sleeper*.

The next morning we set out north from the land toward the polar ice pack. We arrived there and pulled the boat up to dock against the ice before wandering on the pack ice 588 miles from the North Pole. We then reboarded and set sail to the southeast toward Moffen Island, along the way noting several walruses sunbathing on the ice.

As we approached Moffen Island, staying about half a mile offshore per government regulation, we saw 20 to 30 walruses sleeping on the beach. Using binoculars, we could see that four or five were in the water keeping guard. Perhaps you can guess the classic Beatles song blaring from the stereo.

From Moffen Island we sailed south into Moussa-

ARCTIC PASSAGE

Bratka Bay near the northeast corner of Spitsbergen. Tilman spoke of sailing here. We spotted a polar bear and two cubs on the shore and went off in the dinghy with Adam and Per to follow them for about five miles along the coast. At one point they broke into a run and we saw them chasing reindeer up the beach. Our first sighting of polar bear was very exciting. Pulses raced as we moved the dinghy as close as we safely could to watch these dangerously gorgeous animals loping along the coast.

We returned to *Shaman* for dinner where the entire group remained spellbound. My son and Per-Magnus led the toasts over a fine chicken dinner. Van Morrison's *I've Seen Days Like This* played in the background. In one day we had crossed 80 degrees north latitude, climbed on the polar pack ice, saw walruses and chased polar bear along the coast. As baseball great Yogi Berra might say, "Whadda day, all 24 hours of it."

The next morning, or at least the next time we arose from sleeping, be it night or day, we went for a walk and saw three reindeer scampering around. We found the bones of a walrus, whale vertebrae, and numerous reindeer antlers before heading back to the boat for the move on to Leiffjorden.

In the afternoon we saw two more polar bears near the shoreline: a mother and her cub. We saw whales out at sea, a school of seals swimming alongside the boat and, as we approached our anchorage, a bearded seal on the rocks let us come within 17 feet. The frequency of sighting of animal life at this northeast corner near Leiffjorden is stunning. At the same time it is increasingly eerie to walk on land wondering if polar bear are near. I've never listened so attentively while walking.

As we returned to *Shaman* after hiking, the governor's police rangers were out in their boat and radioed that they had seen a polar bear on the banks on the opposite side of the glacier from where we were hiking. We refueled the dinghy and went out to find a male bear alone on the beach. The water was deep and Adam drove to within 25 feet of the shore and 80 feet from a bear that we estimate stood about 11 feet tall.

We received one other call from the governor's rangers a day or so later. They had sighted another bear, this time eating a seal on the beach near their cabin in Moushamma. We traveled about 30 miles to get there and anchored a quarter of a mile from the bear which was lying down on the seal. We went ashore to meet with Bjorn and Peter, the men posted at Norway's most northern outpost. We walked 30 minutes from the anchorage to their hut and shared a beer and tall tales with them as the sun reached the low point, about 20 degrees above the horizon, before rising again. They told us stories of being confined to their cabin as a bear hovered outside their door for several days. We were able to walk back to *Shaman* and the dinghy at 1:30 a.m. after several hours of good cheer. When we arrived the bear was tearing at the seal and we sat in the dinghy for a couple of hours to watch him eat. A white Arctic fox and a seagull were waiting in the wings for the bits of flesh that the bear tore from the seal carcass.

The next morning, out to sea again, we headed up over 80 degrees north and saw that the pack ice lay six miles north of the entrance of Hinlopen Strait running down the east side of Spitsbergen. Very few circumnavigations of Spitsbergen have been accomplished. Tilman did it in 1974 in a fashion no mariner would want to emulate. To see the regions we aspired to explore, we had to re-emerge around the north coast and travel home down the west coast of Spitsbergen again. With only six miles between the pack ice, we were acutely aware of how fragile is the window we crawled through to continue our expedition. This was an anxiety we could not dismiss.

As we headed south there was no sign of civilization past or present. We saw no planes overhead and no other boats. There are no governor's cabins here. This place makes loners lonely. It is like a frozen nautical desert. We spent a night at anchor in Murchisenfjord where it was bitter cold and windy. Our morning walk revealed a fox jaw, reindeer vertebrae, and a bear skull. It was a scene like the desert footage in the film, *The English Patient*.

We resumed our voyage south stopping at Von Otter Oya. Fog moved in as we anchored at 10 p.m., then I walked along the shore with Onne and his camera bag until 2 a.m. We wondered aloud how many people had walked these beaches since World War II. We found many reindeer antlers, a bear skull with all its teeth, and a beautiful wild flower. The geology here is like the rocky coast of Maine near Mistake Island. Captain Steve found an entire whale skeleton lying in the mud with all its elements.

We were 120 miles south of Hinlopen Strait — 14 hours at full throttle to reach our escape point — though the wind was

Opposite below ★ A cross made of driftwood marks a human grave.

Above right ★ In Raudfjorden, the adventurers traveled for six miles to see the sun shine on this glacier at 3:00 a.m.

Right ★ Birds abound in this bleak and beautiful environment.

★ ARCTIC PASSAGE   203

still out of the south holding the pack ice back. After a brief sleep we were off toward Austfonna glacier to the east—our ultimate objective. A glacial coastline of nearly 100 miles, it is the largest continuous seafront glacier in the Arctic, reported to be 115 feet high in places.

We passed Franzhoya and the ice pieces grew larger and larger. When we were 20 miles out the fog descended and the ice was too dense to continue; the wind from the south forced the ice north and it bunched tighter and tighter. We reversed our course and raised sails after the fog lifted.

In the morning we decided, with continuing fog, that we had better not press lady luck any further. Austfanna would remain the temptress to bring us back for a future voyage.

We proceeded north to Lomfjord. On our walk we found reindeer, a little trapping hut clawed apart by a bear, an overturned rowboat and a most beautiful coastline that reminded me of the terrain near the Ghost Ranch in Abiqui, New Mexico. An arctic Georgia O'Keefe landscape and geologists' paradise—it was painful to leave this place, perhaps the most beautiful of all the varied landscape that Spitsbergen revealed to us.

We moved to the north again the following day and reached an old battle site called Sorjafjord on our way out of Hinlopen Strait. Our walk on the beach and ride through the bay in the dinghy revealed many birds but little animal life. Our minds were focused on the pack ice to the north and our escape from Hinlopen Strait the following day.

In the morning we made our run, and with wind up to 30 knots behind us, we put up our new orange storm trysail to have a look, then made our run out of Hinlopen Strait. There was substantial floating ice all around and we had to proceed slowly but we were not hemmed in by the pack ice. We motored around to Mousshamma to pick up my parents and their friends, Barbara and Rich Reynolds, from a helicopter. The chopper pilot was a delightful man named Snorja who had previously worked with law enforcement in Washington DC, and obviously loved his work.

With our new guests we went out to see Moffen. We came back into Raudfjord, the site of the human grave, and drank champagne to celebrate Kate and Steve's third wedding anniver-

Opposite top   A glimpse of *Shaman* through the ice bergs.

Opposite below   Investigating a walrus skull and other found objects.

Top   *Shaman* sailing off Von Otteroya to the south of Hinlopen Strait.

Above   Navigating an 88ft sailboat in the Arctic with drifting glaciers can be quite hazardous.

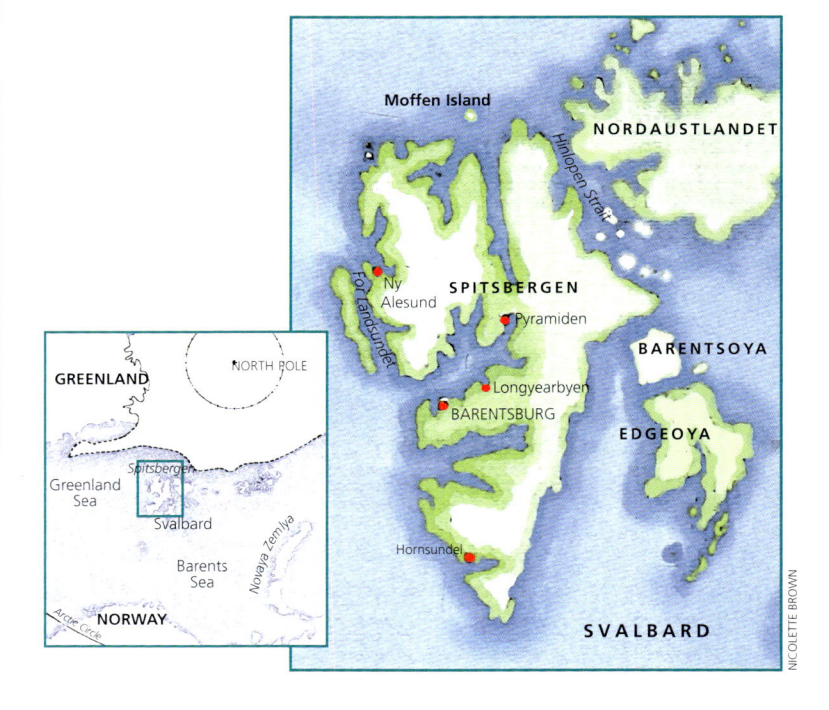

★ ARCTIC PASSAGE   205

Main picture ✶ There appeared to be no sign of civilization, past or present.
Opp. left ✶ A polar bear in the wild is a sight to behold!
Opp. right ✶ " I recall being overcome with a feeling of humbleness before the power of nature over and over again," said writer Rob Johnson.

sary in the midnight sun. I watched as my parents and their friends developed that same awe-struck look that we had acquired during our stay here.

We followed our route back through Smeerburgfjorden, Magdalenefjord, and Ny Alesund before finishing the trip with a wonderful multi-course celebration meal.

In the aftermath of the voyage, I often wonder why this barren island, so cold in the summer, is the most magnificent place I have ever visited. The geology, the animal life, and the glaciers are certainly a part. The anxiety of the ever-present prospect of polar bear attack may add to the romance. Then there is the camaraderie with others when nature compels you to work together at the edge of survival—getting beyond the barrier of fear. But analysis after a point loses value. It becomes hollow and always falls short of the poetry of the experience. I think my son's 10-year-old fresh-eyed wisdom and humor conveys it best when he says, "Dad, this is the coolest place I have ever been, it is the coolest thing I've ever done."

TRAVELER'S GUIDE ★

READING
Triumph and Tribulation and *Voyage of the Reindeer* by HW Tilman in The Eight Sailing/Mountain-Exploration Books. Diadem Books, 1987.
Includes vivid description of Tilman's 1974 circumnavigation of Spitsbergen.

YACHT
Shaman: 88ft sloop designed by Tripp Design and built by Derecktor Shipyard and Green Marine. Interior by Andrew Winch Design.

GUIDE SERVICE
Polar Quest
Per-Magnus Sander
Stockholmsgatan 42 s
S-41669 GOTEBORG, Sweden
TEL: +46 707-50-18-81   FAX: +46 31-19-82-97
E-MAIL: pmsander@hotmail.com

LOGISTIC SUPPORT
Marine Construction Management (MCM)
Thames Street, Newport RI 02840
TEL: (401) 849-3387

If you would like to contact the crew or owner of *Shaman* for assistance in planning a voyage to Spitsbergen, please address all inquiries to MCM.

★ ARCTIC PASSAGE

CRUISING THE TURKISH AEGEAN

On board M/Y Turquoise

ROGER LEAN-VERCOE

The ramshackle taxi tore up the steep winding road, driven, apparently, by the local chairman of the Formula 1 fan club, who blindly took the fastest line at every corner, quite oblivious to the possibility of oncoming traffic. Outwardly calm, but inwardly recalling every detail of our travel insurance policy, it was time to apply the antidote which had been given to us by a Turkish friend, who confided, "You are certain to need it." "Yavash, Yavash," we insisted to the driver over the roar of the engine. He turned. "Slow?" he inquired incredulously, lifting his foot a fraction as we reached the top of the pass. In fact, the downward journey to our destination, the village of Göcek, was no less fast but our thoughts of danger were distracted by the occasional glimpses of an astounding vista.

Göcek is Turkey's fledgling St Tropez, a village of great charm that, thankfully, lacks the huge hotel developments that have swamped much of this coast in a flood of low-cost tourism. Göcek's source of income is yachting. Its sheltered inlet boasts two marinas capable of servicing the largest yachts, together with a newly constructed quayside and restaurant-fringed promenade that provides a charter base for local *gulets* (the ubiquitous Turkish motor sailers), a Sunsail fleet, and a sprinkling of private yachts.

Our home for the next ten days, the 164ft motoryacht *Turquoise*, on her first return visit to her country of build after a highly successful 60,000 mile, four-year world cruise, was not in the marina, but her tender was at the dock ready to whisk us out to the clear blue sea we had seen from the road. Speeding through the sheltered waters of the Skopea Liman it was easy to see the appeal of Göcek. Not only is it close to Dalaman Airport with its very frequent services to Istanbul, but it offers a compact cruising area with a myriad of serene anchorages protected by its off-lying islands. Everywhere, cruising yachts were moored close to the rugged shoreline, their stern lines attached to pine trees and bow anchors dropped into the warm and deep, crystal-clear water.

Despite the numbers of *gulets* and yachts tucked into the coves there was, quite amazingly, no impression of overcrowding as the scene was dominated by the stunningly beautiful and mountainous backdrop which receded in ever-decreasing tones to high mountain ranges inland. Rounding a headland, we discovered *Turquoise* in the company of several other large superyachts, including the classic C&N *Marala*, the Lürssen *Be Mine* and the recently launched Heesen, *New Century*, all basking in the scent of pine, sage, and thyme that flowed from the hillside.

Turquoise, having previously cruised the Greek islands, was now headed into Göcek's Skopea Marina to stock up with supplies, giving her guests a chance to explore the village as well as the larger town of Fethiye, some 20 miles away across the bay. In contrast to Fethiye, a big and brash tourist center with bustling meat, fish, and vegetable markets that more than satisfied the yacht's needs, little Göcek was a one-street charmer. Lifted perhaps by its yachting scene, it had the classiest selection of carpet, antiques, and souvenir shops that we were to see outside Istanbul, and although we did not know it at the time, the shopkeepers were certainly less pushy than in our other ports of call.

Steaming out through the delightful scenery of the Skopea Liman that afternoon, we resolved that Göcek is a place that demands more than one visit. We were headed west out of the

Gulf of Fethiye around Cape Kurtoglu towards Marmaris, the region's largest tourism and yachting center, but our immediate aim was sporting. Just round the headland a sandy beach at Sarigerme provided the venue for a game of baseball for crew and guests alike to work up enthusiasm for dinner—one needs a good appetite to appreciate the excellent cuisine aboard *Turquoise*.

Once a sleepy fishing village, the fact that Marmaris is now a tourist Mecca was quite evident as, just after dusk, we passed beneath the walls of the little Ottoman Castle to be welcomed by a wall of flashing neon and an insistent disco beat. The old town, just across from our berth, was a hubbub of noise and a blaze of color, packed with visitors still shopping within the maze of the covered bazaar or dining alfresco at the many restaurants alongside the quay wall. Past midnight, the bazaar closes and the focus turns to nightclubs, most of which seem to be concentrated cheek-to-jowl in Haci Mustafa Sokak, a single narrow alley where the conflicting over-amplified beat is enough to fell an ox.

By day the bazaar was calmer and the morning was spent shopping for trinkets. No one can leave Turkey without a selection of the blue and white glass pendants that protect against the "evil eye," or a selection of culinary spices. Carpet shops are everywhere, their persuasive owners offering carpets at prices

★ TURKISH AEGEAN

Previous pages: middle inset ★ An ancient relic at Ephesus.
Righthand page ★ The sun sets over the port of Bodrum

Above ★ The magnificent crusader castle at Bodrum.
Right ★ A vendor proudly displays his wide array of produce to be sold at market.
Opposite ★ Once a sleepy fishing village, Marmaris has developed into a very popular yachting center over the past ten years.

210   THE MEGAYACHTS USA ★ 2000

between US$300 and $25,000. (If these attract you be sure to look around and gain some knowledge before purchasing.) An afternoon expedition took *Turquoise* to a nearby beach in Kumlu Bay to sharpen up our volleyball and water polo skills before we returned to Marmaris Marina for dinner, leaving the crew to represent us in the local nightclubs.

Through the yacht's agents, Gino Yachting, a tour to ancient Kaunos had been arranged for the next day. *Turquoise* kept a rendezvous with a *gulet* at the mouth of the Dalyan river, 20 miles eastwards. As the beamy wooden craft slipped over the sandbar, we were pumped up with information by our guide. Loggerhead turtles, the Mediterranean's last surviving colony, lay their eggs on a protected beach to port, sensibly avoiding the golden sands of the packed tourist beach to starboard. Beyond the beaches a huge sea of reeds was pierced by a maze of narrow and shallow channels through which an armada of *gulets* ferried eager tourists to the ruins. Kaunos had been a successful Carian city-state at its peak in 400BC, but its success was self-defeating. Upstream, a necessary expansion of agriculture to feed an increasing number of citizens and slaves caused severe soil erosion which silted the once-deep inlet, creating the sand bar and marsh we see today. Unable to take large ships, the city's trade declined; the final blow was struck by marsh-dwelling mosquitoes that brought malaria, making the inhabitants famous for their yellow complexions, and eventually causing the abandonment of the site.

Our next port of call was Bodrum where we arrived after midnight, having dined at sea on *Turquoise*'s warm decks. With its magnificent crusader castle romantically floodlit, this must surely be the best way to see it for the first time. Bodrum is ancient Halicarnassus, the seat of King Mausolus (376-353BC), who was immortalized by his self-designed white-marble tomb, a wonder of the ancient world, the Mausoleum. Partially ruined by an earthquake and buried for centuries, its destruction was sadly completed by the Knights Hospitaller who, after rediscovering it, stole its stones in 1581 to strengthen their castle against attack from the Turks. Still, the crusader castle itself remains intact and, although it is over-commercialized in some areas, it is certainly worth a visit just to see its massive construction and ancient graffiti. The local bazaar, with narrow streets and distinctive wafting aromas, so evocative of the Middle East, is worth a stroll, but it has little to compare with the better shops of Göcek or even Marmaris.

That afternoon our sport was scuba diving, an activity that must be arranged through a local company as a guide is a legal requirement, as they safeguard underwater antiquities. The visibility was particularly good and we saw a few broken amphorae, the ancient world's pottery shipping containers, but they had

★ TURKISH AEGEAN

Main picture ★ Yachts anchored in the Gulf of Fethiye are surrounded by mountains.

Below ★ The mouth of the Dalyon River is too shallow for large boats so access to the ruins at Kaunos is only with local *gulets*.

Bottom ★ The ruins cut into the sheer rock face at the ancient city of Kaunos.

every appearance of being planted for the tourists. The rest of the seabed was, disappointingly, little more than a desert.

Next day we sailed to Türkbükü, only ten miles or so from Bodrum but for *Turquoise*, a lengthy journey around the peninsula. The attraction was a full-moon party at a restaurant whose dining deck extended out over the sheltered water of the bay, to which the whole yacht's complement (barring one unlucky duty officer) was invited. "Ship Ahoy" might be a corny name for a restaurant, but the evening, having started with cocktails during which the full moon rose majestically over the silhouette of *Turquoise* at anchor in the bay, and continuing with a true banquet of Turkish specialities, was certainly memorable. The white goat cheese—*beyas peynir*—and watercress with a yogurt sauce—*yogurtlu semizotu*—stood out among a host of starters before the arrival of the grilled fish main course, while the baklava honey-sweet pastries were a dream for anyone with a sweet tooth. All this was illuminated by soft moonlight and surrounded by shoals of fish writhing in the jetty's footlights—incredible!

Reluctantly, we left just after midnight with the party in full swing, but the silver lining was that after an overnight northwards passage along the coast to Kusadasi we were due for the major treat of the cruise—a visit to Ephesus. Next morning, stern to the quay with a half dozen other superyachts, our breakfast was interrupted by an agitated Turkish guide who had been hired through Gino Yachting. Yes, he had said we would start at 9:30, but the *Grand Princess*, the world's largest cruise ship, had arrived and she alone had booked 70 large coaches, not to mention Club Med and another nondescript Greek cruise liner. Unless we got to Ephesus before them, all we would see would be peoples' posteriors. Faced with this dire threat, we hurried to board our own mini-coach where, en route, we were well briefed by our entertaining guide. Famous as the best preserved classical city in the Mediterranean, Ephesus had, it seemed, suffered the same fate as Kaunos, but much later in history, as this was still a thriving city in New Testament days when it was a major missionary target for St Paul. To walk its stone-flagged streets, some still showing ruts from ancient cart wheels, was an experience not to be missed, especially as our guide explained the significance and former use of the buildings. The huge façade of the library was amazing, and the men's public conveniences an interesting insight into communal life of the time, as was the huge theatre and the pictogram inscription cut into the flagstones guiding merchant sailors of the period to the local brothel. The heat was intense and so we decided that this is a place worthy of a more leisurely visit in a cooler time of the year, May or October, perhaps.

Setting off that afternoon, we embarked on the final leg of our journey, a 30-hour cruise northwards and then eastwards through the narrows of the Dardanelles and across the sea of Marmara to Istanbul. For the rest of the day, the sun deck really came into its own as we wound a sinuous passage between Turkish mainland and Greek islands, the sea so calm that the Jacuzzi™ pool hardly wetted the deck.

By daybreak we were at Gallipoli, the entrance to the Dardanelles, taking in the history of ancient Troy. The distant sight of two low mounds on the eastern side of these straits that divide Europe from Asia caught our eye. They mark the burial places of Achilles and Patrocles, as recorded in Homer's *Odyssey*: "In this your white bones lie, my lord Achilles, over them all, we the soldiers of the Argive force build up a great and glorious mound so that it may be seen by sailors of today and future ages." Little could Homer have guessed that 3,000 years later, in 1916, the other side of this much disputed strait would be the scene of nine months of bloody fighting during the First World War — 100,000 wasted lives memorialized by two rather more prominent and certainly more evocative modern monuments, together with 31 separate war cemeteries.

Our cruising bible, Rod Heikel's *Turkish Waters* and *Cyprus Pilot* had been infallible so far, but it embarrassed us slightly as we approached the Dardanelles' Mehmetcik control station: "Why did you not call in two hours before your arrival requesting clearance as the regulations require?" was the curt response to our VHF call. The answer was simple: Heikel's pilot book, geared primarily to smaller yachts, had not mentioned this as a necessity. But some grovelling from the captain soon smoothed

Opp. top left ★ The spectacular ruins at Ephesus.

Top left ★ An ampitheater and ancient ruins at Ephesus.

Bottom left ★ *Turquoise* noses her way into Bodrum.

Above ★ The library is one of many monuments to be seen at Ephesus.

★ TURKISH AEGEAN

things over and we proceeded on our way, having signed a form agreeing to pay the dues, but dispensing with the services of a pilot. By now the sun was illuminating the green fields and forests on either side as we navigated through the 4204ft-wide, strongly fortified narrows at Canakkale, before breaking out into the Sea of Marmara. Marmara translates as "Marble," and the sea is so called because it was once the prime source of marble for the classical world. The quarries on the Marmara Islands are still being worked today, a fact that was clearly visible from the rising clouds of dust as we passed, as well as from the more solid evidence of the elegant, grey-flecked white marble that adorns the bathrooms aboard *Turquoise*.

As we eased into the mouth of the Bosporus, the rouge of sunset was already outlining the pencil-thin minarets of the Blue Mosque, the early 16th century triumph of Sultan Ahmet I, as well as those on the nearby Aya Sofya, in pre-Muslim times the Byzantine Church of Divine Wisdom, which was completed almost a thousand years earlier in 548AD. Then the liner-like funnels of the vast kitchens of the Topkapi Palace, the Ottoman Sultans' court from 1453 to 1856, paraded past us as the waters of the Golden Horn, truly glinting gold at this time of day, outlined the northern limit of the old walled city of Constantinople. North of the Horn, *Turquoise* motored past the ornate façade of the Dolmabahçe Palace to which the Ottoman Sultans moved in 1856 in a belated attempt to Europeanize their living style, and then on to the Çiragan Palace, the slightly more modern, but equally grand residence of Sultan Abdülaziz (1861-76), where we were to berth. It is difficult to imagine a more splendid mooring anywhere in the world, especially when the reception organized to welcome *Turquoise* back to her birthplace got underway later that evening, a grand affair attended by the dignitaries of the city.

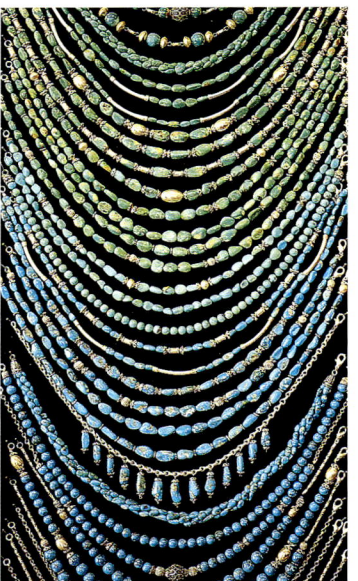

Time passes much too quickly in Istanbul, a city which can keep any sightseer amused for a week. Our two days were totally insufficient — fleeting visits to the Blue Mosque and Topkapi Palace were enough to whet one's appetite for another time, while a few hundred yards away the Grand Bazaar was a magnet for shoppers like no other. These narrow, dimly-lit mysterious alleys, their shops brimming with an incredible selection of Turkish arts, crafts, and antiques, are heaven for shopaholics.

Cruising the Bosporus the next day, the two vast modern bridges that cross the Bosporus to unite Europe with Asia appeared to us to be a living symbol of Turkey — a nation with its long and historic past in the east and a bright new future in the west, the two united by an uncertain present. This history, together with its beauty and its current intriguing position in the world, make it a fascinating place to visit — again and again. Everyone returns to Turkey, for as long as they survive the taxis.

Opp. top ★ *Turquoise* moored at Çiragan Palace in Istanbul.

Opp. middle ★ At Istanbul's Grand Bazaar, beaded necklaces reflect the colors of the sea.

Above and right ★ A maze of covered alleyways lures visitors to the Grand Bazaar.

Below ★ A bird's-eye view of the red-tiled roofs of Istanbul, as seen from from Galata Tower.

★ TURKISH AEGEAN   217

Below left ★ The striking domed ceiling of the Blue Mosque in Istanbul.

Right ★ The entrance to Topkapi Palace.

Bottom ★ *Turquoise* cruises past the Hagia Sophia in Istanbul.

TRAVELER'S GUIDE ★

HISTORICAL

As a major interface between Europe and Asia, Turkey's history covers a 10,000 year span. Hittites, Phrygians, Mysians, Urartians, Lydians, Ionians, Dorians and Persians, Celts, Greeks, and Romans are but a few of the peoples who marched into the area from east and west to create a confusing jumble of ancient culture and religions that were finally supplanted by Islam (669–678 A.D.) and the coming of the Seljuks (1037–1109). The Roman Empire's capital of Constantinople, built on the remains of Hellenic Byzantium, was dedicated by Constantine in 330 A.D. and toppled first by the rag-tag western European army that comprised the fourth Crusade (1202–1204). It finally fell to the warrior Turks in 1453 when, renamed Istanbul, it became the capital of the powerful Ottoman Empire, which later extended to the gates of Vienna. After a long and enlightened period of Ottoman rule noted for its religious tolerance and decorative art, 19th century ethnic nationalism led to dissatisfaction and steady decline which reached its nadir after the empire's alliance with Germany. Their subsequent defeat in World War I led to its dismemberment at the hands of the allied powers. Shortly after this, a successful revolution (1920–1922), led by General Mustafa Kemal, established the Turkish Republic, a secular state within Turkey's present boundaries. Hugely popular, Kemal was renamed Kemal Atatürk (Father Turk), and introduced a written constitution, together with wide-ranging reforms which Europeanized many aspects of the country. These included the introduction of a Latin alphabet, and the adoption of western-style laws. After Atatürk's death in 1938, Turkey remained neutral in the Second World War and staggered towards democracy in the politically unstable post-war years. Today, after turbulent periods in the 70's and 80's when the military regained control, true democracy is once again in place (challenged to a degree by Islamic fundamentalism) and the country shows increasing signs of prosperity, despite serious monetary inflation and Kurdish terrorism in the extreme east. It remains strongly allied to the West and is seeking full membership in the European Community.

CLIMATE

The Mediterranean coast of Turkey lies around latitude 35 degrees North. The best times to visit are Spring (April/May) and Autumn (September/October) when temperatures are in the high 60s Fahrenheit. Summer temperatures on the coast are between 80 and 90 but can top 110 degrees. In winter the climate is pleasantly mild, but expect heavy rains.

GETTING THERE

Regular air services fly to Istanbul's Attatürk airport from all major European cities, as well as frequent services direct from North America. Within Turkey, domestic air services connect all major cities and resorts. Those arriving in Istanbul on international flights must change to the domestic terminal for onward travel to Dalaman, the airport serving Göcek.

MONETARY

All first-time visitors are confused by Turkish currency which, through rampant inflation, requires very large amounts of Lira for trivial purchases. Current exchange rate is approximately Turkish Lire (TL) 400,000 to $1.00 U.S.

CRUISING

Foreign yachts must arrive at an entry port such as Antalya, Bodrum, Fethiye, Kas, or Kusadasi, where they must clear in with the local authorities and purchase a 'transit log' which is valid for three months. This is used to log passages between Turkish ports and is surrendered when leaving Turkish waters. It should be noted that while snorkelling is permitted, scuba diving may only be carried out in the presence of a licensed Turkish guide. The removal of any antiquities from the sea bed is absolutely prohibited. Violators risk confiscation of their yacht.

YACHT CHARTER

Several local charter agencies are in operation.
CONTACT: Gino Group Netsel Marina, Marmaris 48700, Turkey
TEL: + 90 252 412 0676
FAX: +90 252 412 2066

FURTHER INFORMATION

CONTACT: The Turkish Tourist Board
821 United Nations Plaza, 4th floor
New York, NY 10017
TEL: (212) 687-2194

★ TURKISH AEGEAN

MARINE MEDICAL INTERNATIONAL

DEFIBRILLATORS • CLASS 4 MCA
24-HR TELEMEDICINE • CREW TRAINING
MEDICAL KITS • PHARMACEUTICALS
HYPERBARIC CHAMBERS

+1.954.523.1404 • +33.493.33.26.28
W W W . M A R M E D . C O M

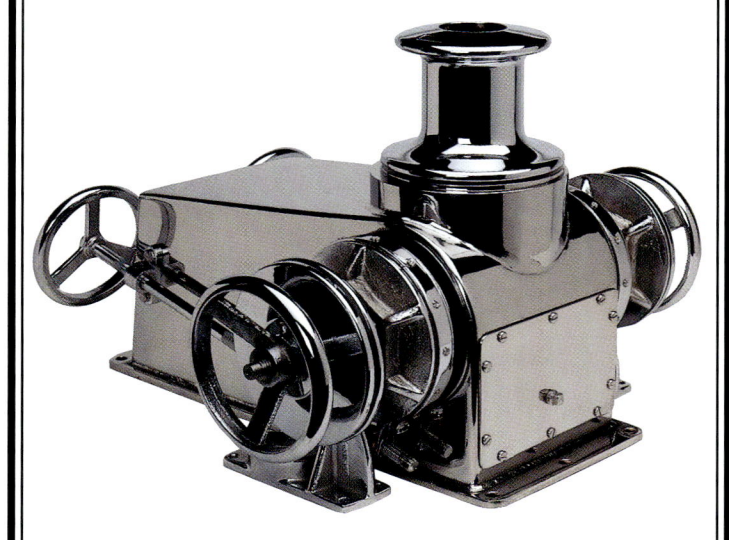

DataStar* MARINE PRODUCTS INC.
V-MAC 5500

Integrated
Vessel
Monitoring,
Alarm &
Control
System

Yacht Smart — Tug Tough

The Smart-looking, Hard working DataStar *V-Mac 5500*. The most fully-featured Vessel Monitoring and Control System in the world! Check this out...

DataStar Marine Products Inc.
Tel: (604) 990-6900
Fax: (604) 990-6890
e-mail: info@datastarmarine.com
http://www.datastarmarine.com

- Supervises all onboard alarm conditions:
  - Fire, Flood, Intrusion (security), Nav Lamp fail, Fumes, etc.
- Monitors engines, gensets, power, pumps and tanks
- Logs all events
- Accepts any sensor type
  - Up to **248 Input Zones**
- Completely **programmable**
- Extremely **affordable**
- **Available now!**

Who do you call when "off the shelf" won't do?

Every installation planned with extraordinary attention to detail.

Every windlass hand crafted to your specifications for that custom "fit".

**The Ideal Windlass Company
Custom Division**

Ideal Windlass Company * PO Box 430 * E. Greenwich, RI 02818 USA
401-884-2550 * FAX 401-884-1260 * e-mail IDLWINDLAS@aol.com

ROBINSON HALLÉN-BERG
Custom Yacht Interiors and Styling

CHRISTINE HALLÉN-BERG A.S.I.D
2894 South Coast Highway
Laguna Beach
California 92651
Telephone: 949·494·9951
Fax: 949·494·6281
Voicemail: 949·494·6184
Email: CHallenber@aol.com

MANAGEMENT · CHARTER · SALES · NEW

koch, newton &partners
LÜRSSEN YACHTS

More and more owners of large yachts choose Koch, Newton and partners.

Our success is measured by proven results – following are some of our most significant sales

108' Tauro · Almaviva · 108' Iliki III · 112' Renalo · 112' Aschanti · 115' Basil's · 118' Blue Attraction · 118' Maalana S · 121' Extasea A · 131' Be Mine · 135' Zew · 138' Limitless · 138' Dariana · 141' Still Shark · 141' Renegade · 148' Bengal · 151' Victory Lane · 154' Maalana · 154' Azzurra · 171' A+R · 174' Lady Azteca · 180' Tits · 180' Oceanfast · 194' Sakura

U.S.A. Ph.: (+1)954/525-7080 · Fax: (+1)954/525-7095 · E-mail: yachts@kochnewton.com
Europe Ph.: (+34)971/700- 445 · Fax: (+34)971/700-551 · E-mail: info@kochnewtonandpartners.com
www.kochnewtonandpartners.com

EXPECTATIONS

Meeting yours means holding ours at the highest possible level. We know. We have done it successfully with clients from around the globe for over twenty-five years.

Compromise should play no role in building a custom motoryacht. Instead, the final result should be a vessel constructed to suit the owner's specific operational and styling requirements. In other words, built to individual order. We think that innovation, experience and attention to the smallest detail are the hallmarks to getting this done.

Launched August 1999

THE FUTURE

Yours and ours. We would like to earn an opportunity to become partners with you in your next custom yacht building project. And we would like to tell you how our involvement in Shipyard 21 — a project to develop the shipyard of the future — should make your decision a bit easier.

swiftships inc.

Represented in Fort Lauderdale by International Yacht Collection
1515 S-E -17th Street, Suite 125 Fort Lauderdale, FL 33316
Tel (954) 522 -2323 – Fax (954) 522-2333

For more information, please contact Swiftships
1105 Levee Road, P.O. Box 1908, Morgan City, LA 70381
Telephone (504) 384-1700 — Fax (504) 384-0914

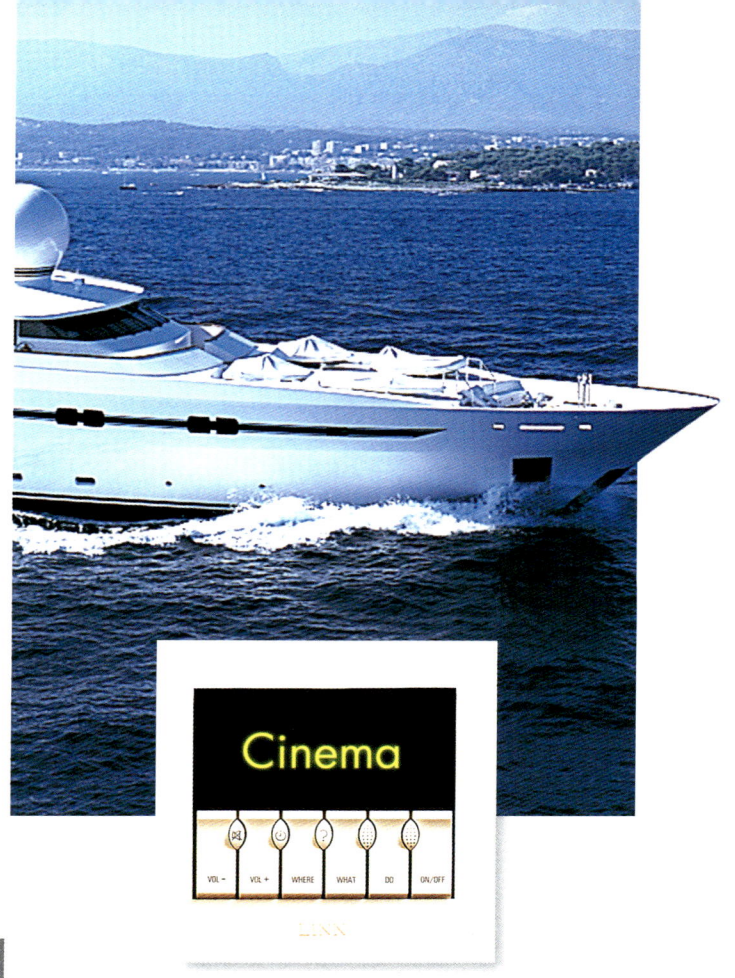

total
entertainment for
visionaries

To hear and see exactly what you are looking for, contact Linn

LINN
*total entertainment
for superyachts*

UK Tel: **(141) 307 7777**   UK Fax: **(141) 644 4262**
USA Tel: **(904) 645 5242**   USA Fax: **(904) 645 7275**
e-mail: **helpline@linn.co.uk** or **linnincorporated@compuserve.com**
internet: **www.linn.co.uk** or **www.linninc.com**

Photograph: Bill Muncke

NEW CONSTRUCTION — **MANAGEMENT**

WORLD WIDE — **CENTRAL AGENTS**

CHARTER — **BROKERAGE**

Wilson Management
Charter & Brokerage, New Building Supervision & Yacht Management

MONACO & ITALY
Contact : Jacob Brown-Thomsen
Tel.: 33 (0) 492 10 79 79 - Fax.: 33 (0) 492 10 79 78

Nassau, Bahamas
yachts@wilson-management.com
www.wilson-management.com

TURKEY
Contact : Ms Aylin
Tel.: 90 256 613 2679 - Fax.: 90 256 613 2977

UNITED KINGDOM
Contact : Allan Wilson, MNI
Tel.: 44 (0) 1482 648 322 - Fax.: 44 (0) 1482 648 277

USA
Contact : Greg Smith
Tel.: 1 954 584 6187 - Fax.: 1 954 584 1014

FRANCE
Contacts : Christopher Cook - Steven Gamble
Tel.: 33 (0) 492 92 16 09 - Fax.: 33 (0) 493 75 89 69

Summit's completely storable Sun Deck Collection by the ASID award-winning designer John Munford

Antibes • Atlanta • Chicago • Dallas • Dubai • Fort Lauderdale • Houston • Los Angeles
New York • Paris • Philadelphia • Phoenix • San Francisco • Seattle • Toronto • Vancouver

SUMMIT

Summit Furniture, Inc.
5 Harris Court, Monterey, CA 93940
Telephone: 831.375.7811   *Facsimile:* 831.375.0940

Summit Furniture (Europe) Ltd.
198 Ebury Street, Orange Sq., London SW1W 8UN
Telephone: 207.259.9244   *Facsimile:* 207.259.9246

VAN CAPPELLEN CONSULTANCY

SILENCE IS GOLDEN . . .

You really need specialized expertise before a yacht owner can enjoy the comfort of silence aboard. Don't enter into expensive experiments. Just choose for the one stop solution offered by:
VAN CAPPELLEN CONSULTANCY.

The clear facts:
- more than 15 years experience in providing custom designed noise control solutions
- refit projects as well as newbuilding, no matter in steel, aluminium or composite
- noise level prediction and structural analysis with special computer programs (S.E.A.)
- finite element method for ship response, shaft bending and other structural calculations
- 2D/3D CAD stations see to meticulously engineered, detailed insulation systems

A few well-known names amongst the many success stories:
Juliette, Double Haven, Shanakee, Lady Marina, Cyrano de Bergerac, Rasselass, Talitha G, Borkumriff III.

Van Cappellen
Consultancy
[Noise and Vibration Control]

1535 SE 17th Street, Suite 107
Fort Lauderdale, FL 33316
United States of America
Telephone (954) 524 2662
Telefax   (954) 524 5662
e-mail: vancappellen-usa@prodigy.net

"Het Vierde Kwartier"
de Wederik 12
3355 SK Papendrecht
The Netherlands
Telephone (31) 78 641 10 22
Telefax   (31) 78 615 53 49
e-mail: capnoise@wxs.nl
Website: www.vancappellen.org

At *Nordlund*... Custom is taken to a new Dimension.

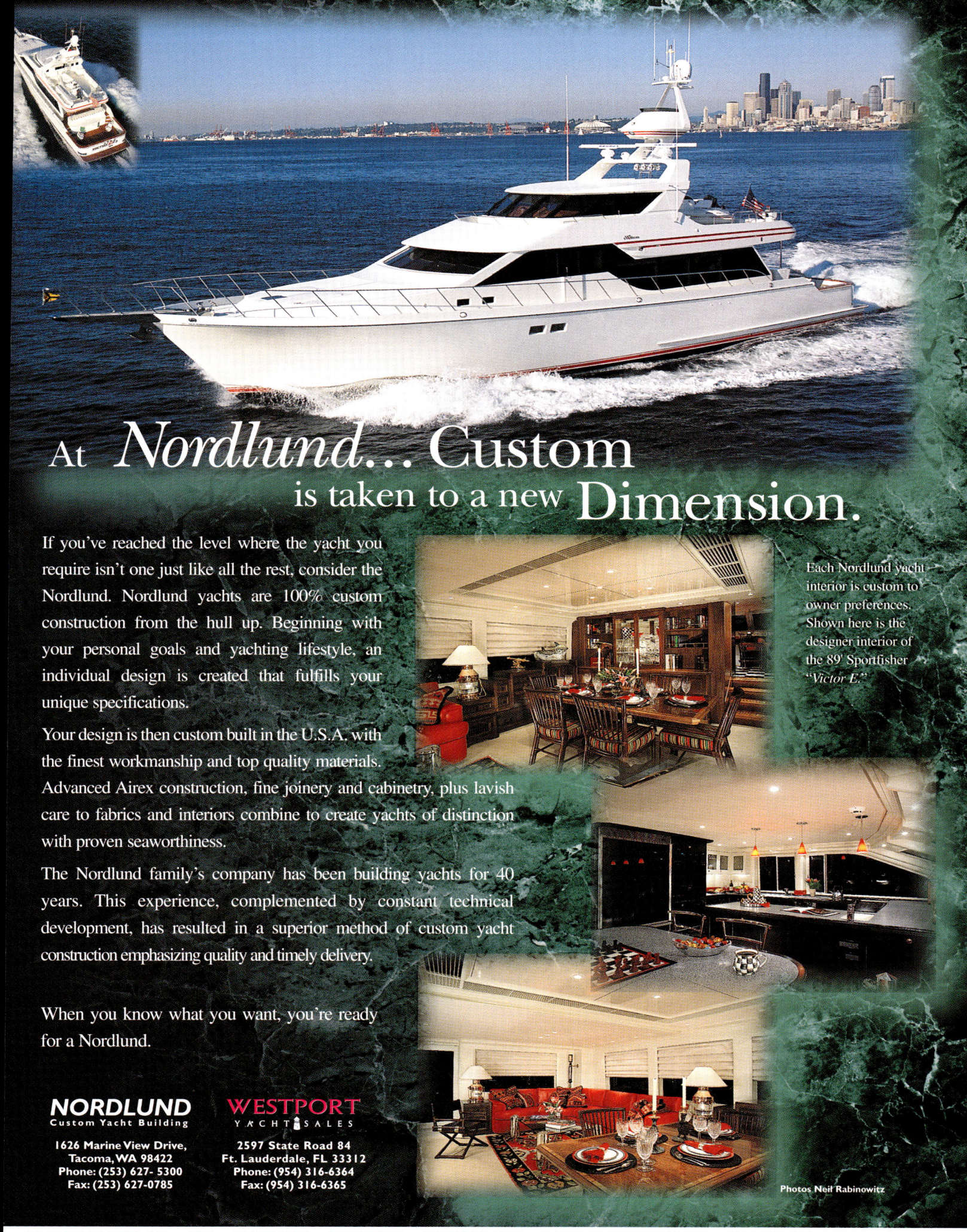

If you've reached the level where the yacht you require isn't one just like all the rest, consider the Nordlund. Nordlund yachts are 100% custom construction from the hull up. Beginning with your personal goals and yachting lifestyle, an individual design is created that fulfills your unique specifications.

Your design is then custom built in the U.S.A. with the finest workmanship and top quality materials. Advanced Airex construction, fine joinery and cabinetry, plus lavish care to fabrics and interiors combine to create yachts of distinction with proven seaworthiness.

The Nordlund family's company has been building yachts for 40 years. This experience, complemented by constant technical development, has resulted in a superior method of custom yacht construction emphasizing quality and timely delivery.

When you know what you want, you're ready for a Nordlund.

Each Nordlund yacht interior is custom to owner preferences. Shown here is the designer interior of the 89' Sportfisher *"Victor E."*

NORDLUND
Custom Yacht Building

1626 Marine View Drive,
Tacoma, WA 98422
Phone: (253) 627-5200
Fax: (253) 627-0785

WESTPORT
YACHT SALES

2597 State Road 84
Ft. Lauderdale, FL 33312
Phone: (954) 316-6364
Fax: (954) 316-6365

Photos Neil Rabinowitz

CUSTOM YACHTS 60' - 106' • SPORTFISH • YACHTFISH • MOTORYACHTS • COCKPIT MOTORYACHTS • PILOTHOUSE MOTORYACHTS

When style and versatility combine
to inspire your...

Emotions

- L.O.A. 100' X 24' X 5' 6" Tri-Level
- 1200 NM Range @ 18 Knots
- 5 Guest Staterooms Plus Crew
- Master Stateroom On Deck
- Full Beam VI Plus 3 Staterooms Below
- Jon Overing Design to ABS Class

Adventure

- L.O.A. 83' X 22' X 6'8"
- Steel Hull, Aluminum Superstructure
- 2X Caterpillar 3406 Main Engines
- Master, 2 Guest Staterooms Plus Crew
- 4000 NM Range @ 10 Knots
- Designs to 130' Available

Individuality

Interior design with assistance of Michael Kirschstein Design

Inace Shipyard in harmony with your desires!

FRASER YACHTS WORLDWIDE
www.fraseryachts.com

Please contact:
Central Agent: John S. DeCaro • Fraser Yachts
2230 SE 17th St. • Ft. Lauderdale, FL 33316
PH: 954-463-0600 • Fax: 954-763-1053
E-mail: johnd@fraserfl.com

Inace Shipyard — 30 Years
AV Presidente Kennedy,
100-Praia de Iracema
Fortaleza Brasil CP:60.060.610
PH: 55-85-254-4806 • www.inace.com.br

TILSE Industrie- und Schiffstechnik GmbH

PROJEKTIERUNG • PLANUNG
TECHNISCHE VERTRETUNGEN • EXPORT UND IMPORT

Our homepage:
http://www.tilse.de
or
http://www.tilse.com

We specialize in supplying our customers with all sorts of technical equipment and know-how.

SY "HYPERION"
ROYAL HUISMAN SHIPYARD

All windows on the bridge are bent *and* heated operated by our microprocessor based controller *TIMON 500* online with the board computer systems.

For the yacht industry we especially deliver:

FORMGLAS Spezial
Formed compound security glass
- Various colours and qualities
- perfect fulfilment of optical demands
- highest dimensional accuracy

MARELCO
Anti-marine growth and corrosion system
- for seachest and pipes
- extroded anodes
- without chemicals, operating on cathodic principals
- environmental friendly

Latest Ships equipped with FORMGLAS or MARELCO

SY "Teel"	Trident Shipyard / USA
MY "Leander"	Peene Werft / Germany
MY "Astarte II"	Blohm & Voss AG / Germany
MY "Golden Odyssee"	Blohm & Voss AG / Germany
SY "Aquel II"	Sensation Yachts / New Zealand
MY "Siran"	de Vries / Netherlands
MY "Stefaren"	Brooke Yachts / England
SY "Anakena"	Royal Huisman / Netherlands
SY "Surama"	Royal Huisman / Netherlands
SY "Hyperion"	Royal Huisman / Netherlands
SY "Wal"	Dübbel & Jesse / Germany
SY "Mari Cha III"	Sensation Yachts / New Zealand
MY "Galactica Plus" ex "Goldeneye"	PRmarine / Germany
MY "La Masquerade"	van Lent / Netherlands
MY "El Bravo"	Retrofit in Spain
SY "Phocea"	Lürssen Werft / Germany
MY "Thunder A"	Oceanfast / Australia
SY "Aphrodite II"	Vitters Shipyard / Netherlands

TILSE Industrie- und Schiffstechnik GmbH
Sottorfallee 12 • D-22529 Hamburg • Tel.: +49 40 56 10 14 • Fax: +49 40 56 34 17 • e-mail: tilse@t-online.de

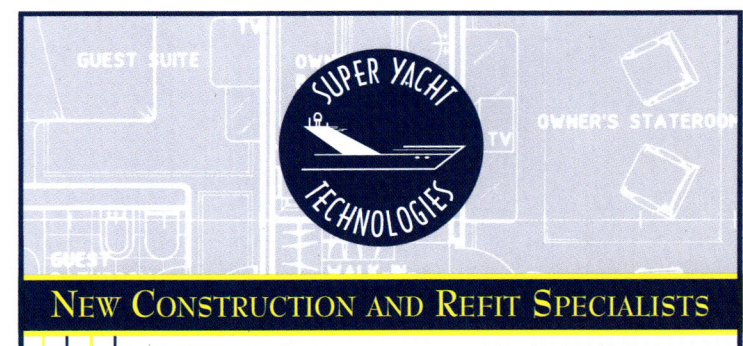

OVERING YACHT DESIGNS
998 Robinson Avenue • Ocean Springs, MS 39 564 • USA
Tel: + 1 228 872 1881 • Fax: + 1 228 875 2862
Email: overing@datasync.com

100' ALUMINIUM TRI-LEVEL MOTORYACHT
ABS, AI, AMS CLASSIFICATION

112' ALUMINIUM COCKPIT MOTORYACHT

122' ALUMINIUM TRI-LEVEL MOTORYACHT

166' STEEL AND ALUMINIUM TRI-LEVEL MOTORYACHT ABS, AI, AMS CLASSIFICATION PRESENTLY UNDER CONSTRUCTION AT SENSATION YACHTS LTD, AUCKLAND NEW ZEALAND

For the past 10 years OVERING YACHT DESIGNS has built a reputation of quality and integrity. We specialize in the complete design and engineering of ocean going motoryachts constructed in aluminium and steel.

SUPER YACHT TECHNOLOGIES

NEW CONSTRUCTION AND REFIT SPECIALISTS

We serve the Owners, Designers, Brokers and Captains of the SuperYacht Industry

It is SuperYacht Technologies approach that makes us one of the world's most progressive project management teams available today......

Our speciality is overseeing the construction and refitting of luxurious yachts in any location throughout the world

Tel in the UK: (0) 181 477 5990 • Fax in the US: 954 761 3192
E-mail: superyot@aol.com

We Monitor, Advise and Act on your behalf
Assuring your vessel is delivered to your satisfaction

www.super-yachts.com

DERECKTOR SHIPYARDS
Since 1947

Your Dream Builder

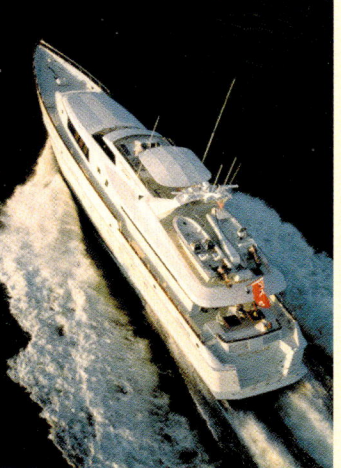

That's right, this is our business – giving body and shape to the boat of your dreams. From America's Cup winners to Superyachts and Super High Speed Ferries. For fifty years Derecktor has been redefining its leadership in the industry with innovative design, superior craftsmanship and uncompromising dedication to quality. Why not tell us today about your dream?

www.derecktor.com

311 East Boston Post Road, Mamaroneck, New York 10543 USA
Voice: ++1-914-698-5020 Fax: ++1-914-698-6596 Toll free: 800-691-2100

The
LUXURY
YACHT MARKET

The Luxury Yacht Market

Builders

ABEKING & RASMUSSEN

Dating back to the beginning of the century, this German yard has built more than 6000 yachts and commercial or military vessels. Building in both steel and aluminum, the largest yacht built was the 188ft (57m) *Ultima III* launched in 1998, although the company has built commercial vessels to 262ft (80m).

ADMIRAL MARINE WORKS

Best known for the 161ft (49m) all-fiberglass *Evviva* and the cold-molded 71ft (21m) *Plum Duff*, this builder was recently acquired by Queenship Yachts of Canada and will continue as a separate operation to build custom yachts as well as handle refits. Just launched is a Pedrick-designed 75ft (23m) raised saloon sailing yacht with an elegant interior, and a 70ft (21m) Berretta-series motoryacht from Queenship is being finished for delivery in 2000. In addition, the yard has several refitting projects underway.

ALPHA MARINE

At press time, Alpha Marine is in the process of a name change to Yukon Trawler. Taking over the Northrop Pacific facility and crew, this builder is represented by Fraser Yachts and, with experience building yachts and commercial vessels over 200ft (61m), the company is presently finishing a 100ft (30m) long range motoryacht on spec. Other yacht projects are being negotiated.

BAGLIETTO

This Italian builder is very busy, and the first yacht to be completed under new management was launched in 1999. Of steel and aluminum construction and named *Blue Ice*, the 135-footer (41m) was shown at the 1999 Ft. Lauderdale Boatshow. A sistership, named *Benedetta II*, was also launched in 1999, and a 150ft (45m) trideck is under construction.

BENETTI

This builder, now under the Azimut umbrella, specializes in custom yachts with steel hulls and aluminum superstructures. A semi-custom line of 115ft (35m) fiberglass "Classic" yachts have proven popular, with four delivered already and three more for delivery in 2000. Four different engine options and several layouts offer either three or four stateroom layouts plus an owner's suite on the main or upper deck. The company recently launched *Felicity*, a 230ft (70m) seven deck yacht, with one deck set aside for owner and family only. To take on the project, Benetti enlarged their shipyard. Also under construction for mid 2000 delivery are a pair of 166ft (50m) motoryachts: *The Dreamer* and *Golden Bay IV*. *The Dreamer* is a full displacement development of the original Golden Bay and, with a larger hull, there will be a sub-deck that allows the crew to reach their quarters via the engine room.

BROWARD MARINE

Established in 1948, this aluminum builder was acquired in 1999 by new owners, who plan to revitalize the company. The largest yacht built to date is the 156ft (47m) *Bubba Too*, and the company specializes in yachts from 80ft (24m) to 150ft (45m).

BURGER BOAT CO.

Much like the mythical phoenix, Burger has a renewed life. Founded in the 1800s, the Manitowoc, WI company earned a reputation for old-world craftsmanship but, in the mid 1980s, the company passed through the hands of several owners and was shut down. In 1993, new owners reopened the yard and were able to bring back nearly all of the longtime craftsmen. Burger has five yachts under construction ranging from 85ft to 118ft, and a 21,000 sq. ft. building specifically for mechanical and joiner work represents the second phase of a five phase renovation of the Burger yard. Recent launchings include *Lad*, a 103ft (30m) motoryacht and *Simaron*, a 118ft (36m) flush deck motoryacht. Under construction for 2000 delivery are *Seaquester*, an 85ft (26m) raised pilothouse; *Jubilee*, an 83ft (25m) flush deck; *Fae Lon*, a 118ft (36m) raised pilothouse; and *Serenity*, a 105ft (32m) raised pilothouse. *Dynasty*, an 81ft (24m) raised pilothouse is slated for 2001 delivery.

CBI NAVI

Located in Viareggio, Italy, this company is a full-service builder including engineering, design, construction and service on yachts from 80ft (24m) to 147ft (45m) in steel and aluminum. Recent launchings include the 105ft (32m) *Nirvana*, the 135ft (41m) *Sophie Blue*, and the 78ft (24m) *Wolf Two*. Under construction is a 100ft (30m) motoryacht, an 85ft (26m) trideck displacement expedition trawler, a 105ft (32m) yacht with a split-level master suite on the main deck, and a 105-footer due for mid-2000. A trio of Luca Dini-styled raised pilothouse motoryachts are under construction, including a pair of 92-footers (28m) and a 105ft (32m) with main deck master suite and skylounge.

CNB

This French builder, Construction Navale Bordeaux, is the custom yacht and workboat division of the Beneteau Group, specializing in aluminum and composite yachts from 70ft (21m) to 150ft (45m). The company also builds passenger ferries and fishing boats as well as large catamarans. Due to launch in early 2000 is a Briand-designed CNB 70 sloop, followed by *Virgo II*, a 93ft (28m) motoryacht to a Cabon design.

CANTIERI DI PISA

This company builds the Akhir series of composite Euro-styled motoryachts from 110ft (33m) to 140ft (42m). Designed by Luca Dini, two yachts are destined for the US: a 110ft (33m) raised pilothouse motoryacht and a 140ft (42m) trideck on spec. Also under construction at the yard are 95ft (29m) and 105ft (32m) motoryachts for mid-2000.

CHEOY LEE SHIPYARDS

This Hong Kong builder is more than a century old and, in addition to production and custom yachts in fiberglass, it builds commercial vessels and yachts in both aluminum and steel. A number of yachts are under construction for the US market in both conventional motoryacht and expedition yacht styling. Just delivered is the first 65ft (20m) Sport Motoryacht with a master suite using the full 20ft (6m) beam. The Sport Motoryacht series will range from 65ft to 92ft (28m). Next to launch and likely to debut at the Ft. Lauderdale Boatshow is an 88ft (26m) expedition yacht designed by Tom Fexas with a Savio interior. Featuring "wide body" styling and a beam over

★ BUILDERS 233

CHRISTENSEN 150ft

21ft (6m), it has semi-displacement lines, a top speed of 14 plus knots, a Portuguese bridge, and a forward welldeck for carrying tenders. Following that will be an unusual 92ft (27m) yachtfisher with an enclosed bridge and a completely open transom. A 66ft (20m) Long Range Cruiser will be delivered in 2000 with a canoe stern, followed by a 100ft (30m) Mulder-designed Global-series yacht with a sport deck transom. A full custom design, it will have a top speed of 27 knots and transatlantic range at 17 knots. In the design stages are a 125ft (38m) Global motoryacht for 2001 and a 66ft (20m) expedition yacht, both by Mulder. Cheoy Lee recently added a new 15-acre yard in China, which will handle the large motoryachts and the Global series.

CHRISTENSEN SHIPYARDS

The builder of more composite megayachts over 120ft (36m) than any other shipyard in the world, Christensen builds the entire yacht on site in a state-of-the-art plant to assure high standards in every component. Recent launchings have included *Wehr Nuts*, a 124ft (37m) raised pilothouse motoryacht and *Big Bad John*, a 140ft (42m) motoryacht. The 25th Christensen, the 145ft (44m) *Primadonna*, started construction in mid-1999, and five other yachts are also being built, including a pair of 150-footers (45m), a 135ft (41m), a 155ft (47m), and a 140ft (42m).

CODECASA

Specializing in aluminum, steel and composite construction up to 295ft (90m), the usual size of yachts from this Italian builder is in the 150ft (45m) and larger range but the recently launched *Antares Star* was a mini-ship at 110ft (33.5m). Also under construction are a 165ft (50m) motoryacht for an American client, and the company has recently started construction on another 165ft (50m) motoryacht on spec.

GUY COUACH

This French builder specializes in fast cruisers and luxury yachts up to 130ft (40m), and has wide experience in military and commercial craft such as patrol boats and customs vessels. Newly launched in the first in their Open series, a 92ft (28m) Kevlar-hulled yacht capable of speeds to 45 knots. Another recent launching was a 100ft (30m) raised pilothouse motoryacht built on a semi-displacement tunneled hull also used for military craft. This yacht featured a flybridge protected by a hardtop with hydraulic sunroof, and a circular Jacuzzi™. Under construction is a 112ft (33m) trideck for early 2000 delivery, and a 120ft (36m) trideck built on a high performance military hull. Several other projects over 110ft (33m) are in design stages.

CRESCENT CUSTOM YACHTS

This Canadian builder specializes in custom fiberglass raised pilothouse motoryachts using hulls designed by naval architect Jack Sarin. The company prides itself on the high quality of both the mechanical systems and the level of the finish for both interior and exterior, and offers a range from 95ft (29m) up to more than 145ft (44m). Recently launched was *Dare To Dream*, a 115ft (35m) motoryacht and *Escape*, a 120ft (36m) raised pilothouse design styled by Bill Scales on a Westport hull with a dark wood interior. Under construction is *Crescent Lady*, a 104ft (31m) raised pilothouse spec motoryacht by Jack Sarin, and *Nectar of the Gods*, a Sarin-designed 121-footer (36m) that will be the first Crescent trideck in six years. The company has just moved into a new 42,000 sq. ft. facility with a 220-ton TraveLift, giving the ability to build and refit yachts to 150ft (45m).

DELTA MARINE

This company transitioned from building rugged commercial vessels to seaworthy luxury yachts in fiberglass from 100ft

DELTA 147ft Gran Finale

(30m) to 200 (61m) in length. Two styles include an expedition yacht capable of cruising worldwide and a contemporary motoryacht. Recently launched is the 151ft (46m) *Affinity* which is also the first composite motoryacht by sailing yacht designer Ron Holland, who collaborated with the Delta in-house design team and Ardeo Design. Owned by a racing yachtsman, the yacht will make the 7000nm voyage to New Zealand for the America's Cup and then will serve as the "mother ship" for his worldwide racing program. Due to launch in 2001 is *Gran Finale*, a 147ft (45m) Espinosa-styled motoryacht notable for a skylounge with 360-degree view and a raised bar overlooking the bridge. A floating staircase topped by a skylight will connect all decks, and the owner's stateroom and bathroom will both have atriums. A gold-leafed coffered ceiling will stretch from the formal dining saloon to a sunken bar aft with a view of the sea. Delta is also due to launch *Gallant Lady* in 2000.

DERECKTOR SHIPYARDS

Founded more than fifty years ago, Derecktor Shipyards has a reputation for high quality in an eclectic range of aluminum yachts. The company built America's Cup winner *Stars & Stripes '87* among many other projects. Recent construction has included a 95ft (28m) sailing yacht, a 114ft (34m) motoryacht, and a 74ft (22m) aluminum and composite motoryacht. Current projects include a 112ft (34m) S&S performance cruising sloop for a South American client and *Star Light*, a 102ft (31m) Hunt-designed motoryacht.

DESTINY YACHTS

A new Florida yard, Destiny Yachts is building a series of fiberglass yachts from 94ft (28m) to 120ft (36m) designed by naval architect Giovanni Arrabito and designer Evan K. Marshall. The fiberglass hulls and superstructures will be built in Italy and completed in Florida. First of the series is a 94ft (28m) motoryacht with a bi-level master suite on the main deck and three guest staterooms on the lower level. Future projects include a 100ft (30m) cockpit motoryacht and a 120ft (36m) motoryacht.

DIASHIP

The brand name for yachts built at the Heesen Shipyard in Holland, this company specializes in high speed, luxurious aluminum motoryachts, and the company has built some of the fastest megayachts, including the 132ft (40m) 60mph *Octopussy* and the fastest megasportfisher *Obsessions*. Under construction for delivery in 2000 are *Alumercia*, a 122ft (37m) Vripack expedition yacht, a 115ft (35m) Cichero/Acubens design, and a pair of 100ft (30m) motoryachts by the in-house Diaship design team.

FEADSHIP

Celebrating their 50th anniversary and a benchmark worldwide for the highest quality megayachts, Feadship is a three-member Dutch consortium combining two shipyards (De Vries Scheepsbouw and Van Lent & Zonen) and a naval architecture firm (Frits De Voogt). Most of their yachts are built in steel with a few in aluminum, and half of all their yachts are sold to American owners. Recent launchings have included the 164ft (50m) *Iroquois*, the 171ft (52m) *Solemates*, the 200ft (61m) *Meduse*, and

★ **BUILDERS** 235

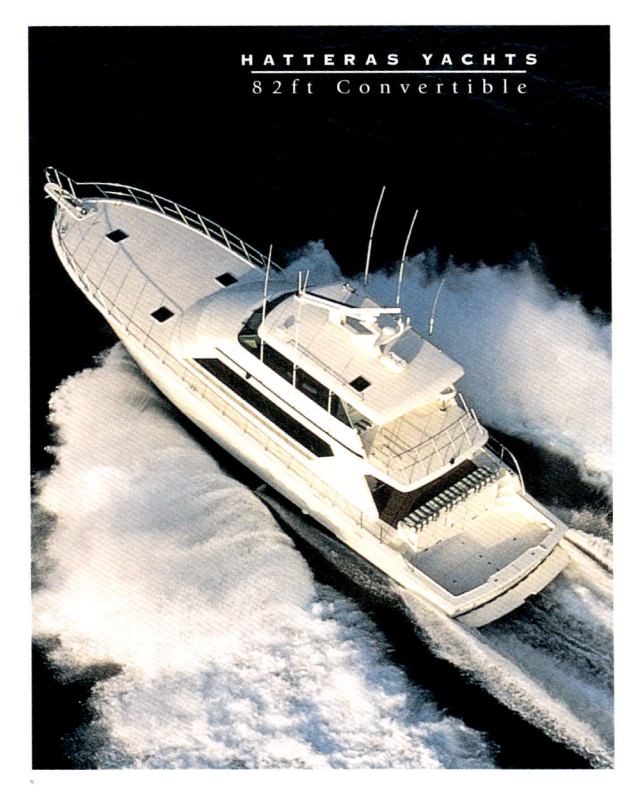

HATTERAS YACHTS
82ft Convertible

the 159ft (48m) *Katrion*. Under construction for American owners are five yachts ranging from 150ft (45m) to 204ft (62m). These include the 156ft (47m) *Excellence II*, the 165ft (50m) *Blue Moon*, the 171ft (52m) *Kisses*, the 204ft (62m) *Cakewalk*, and the 150ft (48m) *Detroit Eagle*. Feadship has recently acquired the yard of one of its hull and superstructure subcontractors, which now opens the way to build yachts up to nearly 500ft (150m), and the consortium is now in negotiations with two clients interested in yachts over 328ft (100m). The longest Feadship built to date was the 212ft (64m) *Al Riyadh* in 1978. Since 1970, Feadship estimates that they have delivered a total 2.1 miles (3.5km) of superyachts.

FERRETTI GROUP

Italy's Ferretti Group has been aggressively buying companies to broaden their portfolio of yacht offerings. The mother company is Ferretti S.p.A, which builds a line of luxurious motoryachts from 39ft (12m) to 82ft (25m) in fiberglass, with glossy joinerwork and sleek Euro styling. The company has also purchased Bertram Yachts, the US builder of convertible sportfishers from 36ft (11m) to 72ft (22m); Pershing Yachts, which builds a line of sporty express yachts from 39ft (12m) to 82ft (25m); as well as Resin Systems, which manufactures the fiberglass for the Ferretti boats. A recent expansion is Custom Line S.p.A, an extension of the original Ferretti line into custom yachts from 92ft (28m) to 164ft (50m). Three basic models comprise the Custom Line: 95ft (29m), 105ft (32m), and 115ft (35m). The most recent Ferretti acquisition is CRN Ancona, a builder of steel and aluminum custom motoryachts well over 200ft (61m).

FRANCK'S BOAT COMPANY

This family owned company is in its eighth decade and third generation, specializing in wood and fiberglass yachts. A recent launch is the Sarin-designed *Sinbad*, a 90ft (27m) motoryacht. Due to launch in early 2000 is *Que Linda*, a 55ft (17m) expedition-style yacht designed by Steve Seaton for world cruising. Also in the negotiating stages is a 75ft (23m) heavy displacement cruising motoryacht.

GREENBAY MARINE

This Singapore builder of expedition-style yachts is presently working on a Setzer-designed 98ft (29m) expedition yacht.

HALTER

Under the umbrella of Halter Marine, this is a sister company to Trinity Yachts, but specializing in expedition-style yachts with easily maintained exteriors to commercial standards and yacht interiors. Recently launched was the 94ft (28m) *Maloekoe*, the first in a series, and that yacht has already cruised on its own bottom to Indonesia. With the looks of a coastal freighter and the interior of a luxury yacht, the 94's have a welldeck for tender storage and a Portuguese bridge. At 185ft (56m), *Samantha Lin* is a fine example of a modern expedition yacht, with four decks including one just for the owner, and an array of tenders and toys including a 35ft Predator, a 26ft Shamrock, a 20ft Novurania, and a three-man submarine capable of submerging to 1000ft. Due in late 2000 is *Whale Song*, second in the 94ft (28m) series.

HATTERAS YACHTS

Hatteras Yachts builds twenty models of sportfishing convertibles, motoryachts and custom luxury yachts to 130ft (39m) as a member of the Genmar Yacht Group. The company launched their 25th large yacht with *Sheriff*, a 92ft (28m) motoryacht that was the first of the Hatteras Elite

HALTER MARINE
94ft *Maloekoe*

LAZZARA 94ft *Legacy*

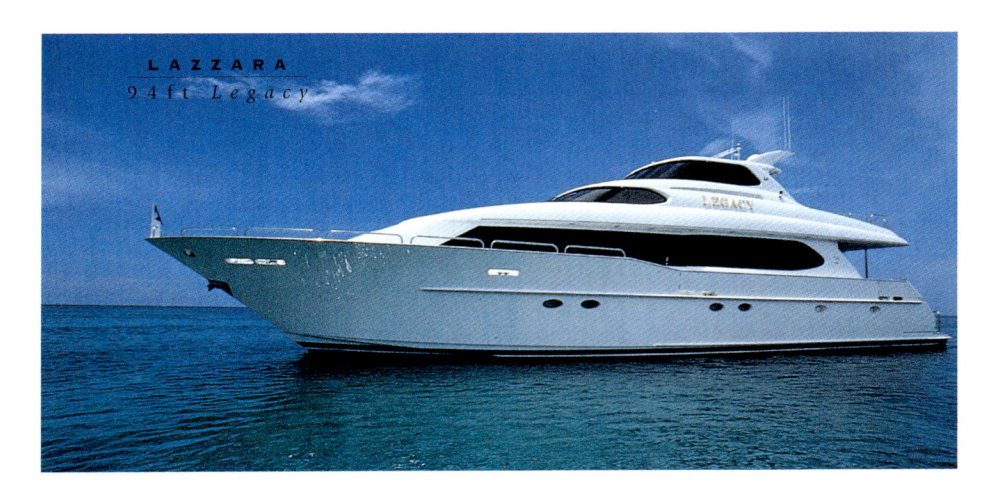

Series powered by Detroit Diesel 2000 Series engines. Motoryachts presently under construction include three 92-footers and a 100ft (30m) due to launch in 2001. Hatteras has also expanded their sportfisher line, with a pair of 82-footers (25m), an 86ft (26m) and a 90ft (27m) under construction.

HODGDON YACHTS

Just launched is *Antonisa*, a 124ft (34m) flushdecked sloop by Bruce King that has carbon fiber spars, the largest furling boom ever made, and a pipe organ in the main saloon. Under construction is a King-designed 151ft (46m) ketch for delivery in 2002.

HUCKINS YACHT CORPORATION

While the Huckins reputation was built in wooden yachts and the famous PT boats, they now produce semi-custom and custom composite yachts. Under construction is a 60ft (18m) motoryacht along with a pair of 44 footers (13m).

INACE

This Brazilian builder, represented by Fraser Yachts, specializes in steel and aluminum construction. The company builds from 70ft (21m) to 130ft (39m) in motoryachts, expedition yachts, and NATO patrol boats. Recently launched was *Belleza*, an 83ft (25m) expedition vessel that features a rugged hull and a yacht interior designed by Michael Kirschstein, who used Brazilian marble and local hardwoods for durability. An 89ft (27m) version is under construction with an enlarged superstructure and skylounge, as well as a 76ft (23m) flushdeck motoryacht. Plans are on the boards for a 128ft (39m) Explorer with exterior and interior styling by Kirschstein.

INTERMARINE YACHTING

A new player on the luxury yacht scene is Intermarine Yachting, which was recently purchased by a group of investors. Recently launched was *Mia Elise*, a 136ft (41m) motoryacht. Raised pilothouse yachts under construction are a 95ft (29m), the 105ft (32m) *Aquasition*, and *Savannah*, a DeBasto 116-footer (35m). Tridecks being built include a 120ft (36m) and 142ft (43m). The shipyard covers 21 acres and can haul and refit any size yacht.

LAZZARA YACHTS

Combining a family legacy of boatbuilding with sophisticated design and construction technology, this company builds a series of semi-custom composite luxury yachts. Recent launchings in their 76-80ft (23-24m) series include a 76ft Skylounge and an 80ft Cabriolet featuring an enclosed bridge with electric windows. Just launched is *Legacy*, the first of the 94ft (29m) raised pilothouse motoryachts, with an oversized skylounge. The 94-footer is unique since four different options are available for the aft 14ft of the yacht: twin jetski pods, a tender garage, a combination of pods and garage, or an aft crew cabin. The 94 also has several different bridge options including cabriolet, flybridge, and skylounge, allowing buyers to customize each yacht. Six of the 76/80-footers and four of the 94s are scheduled for construction in 2000.

LECLERCQ MARINE CONSTRUCTION

Founded in the early 1970s, the company originally built for the fishing industry but, in the mid-'90s, LeClercq converted an 85ft yacht (25m) into a 100-footer (30m) that proved an entree into yacht construction and refits up to 130ft (40m). Recently launched was *Encore*, a 70ft (21m) raised pilothouse motoryacht. Under construction are a pair of 76ft

★ **BUILDERS**

(23m) Espinosa/Sarin trideck, a 60ft (18m) raised pilothouse motoryacht on spec, and *Anita*, an 88ft (26m) motoryacht. The company is in demand for refits, and a 73ft (22m) Maiora is being "LeClercq-ized" with a new interior and stretched cockpit, while a 107ft (32m) motoryacht is getting a new interior.

LEGENDARY YACHTS

This builder is committed to bringing back designs from the golden age of yachting, but with modern materials and techniques. Their first yacht was *Radiance*, a replica of L. Francis Herreshoff's 72ft (22m) ketch *Ticonderoga* and the company has continued with Herreshoff designs since then. A replica of the 57ft (17m) ketch *Bounty* was built on spec and is available, as is the 56ft (17m) schooner *Marco Polo*. Under construction is *Araminta*, a 33ft (10m) Herreshoff ketch, and construction has also started on *Mistral*, a 63ft (19m) schooner.

LITTLE HOQUIAM SHIPYARD

This family-run shipyard, represented by Fraser Yachts, has built more than 250 vessels over 27 years, and offers custom yachts to 150ft (45m). Launching early in 2000 is a 100ft (30m) Sarin-designed cockpit motoryacht with a raised pilothouse, twin Cat power, and a Jonathan Quinn Barnett interior that has been stunningly executed. From a flexible beam mold that can produce hulls from 85ft (26m) to 110ft (33m) and beams up to 24ft (7.3m), the company has two trideck motoryachts under construction for the charter market at lengths of 85ft (26m) and 90ft (28m).

LURSSEN YACHTS

A total facility shipbuilder, this German company specializes in steel or aluminum yachts at the upper range of the scale, with the 316ft (96m) *Limitless* as an example of a recently launched project and a hush-hush 426-footer (130m) under construction.

MAIORA YACHTS

This Italian builder originally supplied composite hulls to other yards but now builds their own line of yachts from 70ft (21m) to 136ft (41m). A pair of molds in 28ft (8.5m) and 30ft (9.1m) beams offer flexibility, and a 102ft (31m) raised pilothouse motoryacht is under construction as a spec boat for the US.

McQUEEN'S BOATWORKS

Founded in 1952 to build wooden yachts, the company has been devoted to composite construction since 1984, sharing 21ft (6.4m) and 23ft (7m) beam hull molds with Nordlund Yachts and also using Westport hulls in 22ft (6.7m) and 24ft (7.3m) beams, which can stretch to 115ft (35m). Recent launchings include *Tigress*, a 93ft (28m) sportfisher. Under construction are an 88ft (27m) motoryacht with trans-oceanic range, a 78ft (24m) Ed Monk trideck with a cockpit and offshore capabilities, and an 86ft (26m) Monk widebody motoryacht with European styling.

MONTE FINO CUSTOM YACHTS

This builder specializes in fiberglass motoryachts that can be customized for each owner, while still maintaining the cost effectiveness of production yachts. A pair of new 80-footers serve as a perfect example of this ability to build to the requirements of each buyer: the 82ft (25m) *Vanguard* has a cockpit and a casual interior, while the 81ft (25m) *With Interest* has a skylounge and an aft master suite which required moving the engine room forward.

NAUTOR SWAN

This Finnish company builds the famous Swan line of fiberglass sailing yachts, and has expanded their series upwards to include the Swan Plus, a 112ft (34m) sloop launched in late 1999. All Swans are designed by German Frers, and the layouts are flexible on the larger yachts. A recent launching was an 80ft (24m) sloop.

NORDLUND BOAT COMPANY

Founded in 1958, the company focus shifted exclusively to the yacht market in 1970. In 1976, Nordlund built their first composite yacht and recently launches include 63ft (19m) and 73ft (22m) motoryachts, and a 74ft (22m) pilothouse motoryacht. Under construction are three Ed Monk designs: a 78ft (24m) motoryacht, an 80ft (24m) enclosed bridge motoryacht, and a 105ft (32m) sportfisher. Also under construction is a pilotboat for the Puget Sound Pilots and the company added two additional bays last year to handle more projects.

NORTHCOAST YACHTS

A custom builder of motoryachts since 1980, Northcoast has two expandable hull molds for yachts from 75ft (23m) to 145ft (44m) with beams from 23ft to 28ft. Recent launches include *Regency*, a 115ft (35m) raised pilothouse, the 82ft (25m) cockpit motoryacht *North Coast Lady*, and a 118ft (36m) raised pilothouse motoryacht. Under construction for 2000 delivery are an 84ft (26m) cockpit motoryacht and an 82ft (25m) motoryacht, with a large volume 125ft trideck motoryacht due in 2001.

NORTHERN MARINE

Northern Marine has five yachts under construction, ranging from 64ft (15m) to 85ft (26m). Launched in 1998 was *Starship*, a 75-footer (22m) now on a 99,000 mile, 1000 day research voyage that underlines the company emphasis on expedition-style yachts. Just launched is *Gaarden Party*, a 75ft (23m) yacht with an arts-and-crafts interior, and a similar 75-footer was launched in late 1999. For 2000 delivery will be a 64-ft (15m) motoryacht and a pair of 85-footers. With waterfront facilities, the company is able to provide full after-market repair facilities for yachts up to 100ft.

NOTIKA TEKNIK YACHTS

A very advanced Turkish builder, this company builds both classic and contemporary designs and, with a new 20-acre facility in Antalya, can handle up to 12 yachts at a time. Seven projects are currently under construction, including a 144ft (43m) four deck motoryacht designed by Evan K. Marshall with a huge master suite linked by elevator to a private sundeck above the skylounge. Other construction includes a sleek 100ft (30m) motoryacht designed by Bill Dixon and Silkline Creations, a 136ft (41m) Bill Murray and Evan Marshall design, and a 115ft (35m) motoryacht. A 90ft (27m) open sport-styled cruiser is also on the drawing boards.

OCEANCO

This firm designs large yachts in Monaco, builds the hulls and superstructures at their yard in Durban, South Africa, and then finishes them at yards in Alblasserdam and Dreumel in Holland. Launched in the summer of 1999 was *Constellation* which, at 265ft (80m), is the largest yacht to be fitted out in Holland. Launching at press time is

OCEANCO
265' *Constellation*

PADANARAM
46-ft racing yacht

Trick One, a 311ft (95m) motoryacht, while *Stargate II*, a sistership to *Constellation*, is due in 2000. For delivery in the summer of 2000 is the 161ft (49m) *Avalon*, with an Andrew Winch mahogany and oak interior.

PADANARAM YACHT CO.

This company not only builds sailing yachts but has also created a one-design racing series for them in the tradition of J-boats and 12-Meters from years past. Spearheading the project is Donald Tofias, who commissioned Joel White to design the W-Class racing yacht-a 76ft (23m) cold-molded sailing yacht with a mast more than 100ft (30m) high. While the appearance is classic, the underbody is thoroughly modern with a fin keel and carbon fiber spade rudder. The first two yachts, *Wild Horses* and *White Wings*, are already competing on a world circuit. A smaller version at 46ft (14m) has been designed and two of these will be delivered in the summer of 2000. Also built of cold-molded wood and designed by Bob Stephens, the two will be built at Rockport Marine. Future plans beyond the W-76 and W-46 classes include W-Class yachts of 62ft, 105ft, and 130ft.

PALMER JOHNSON

Founded in 1918, this Wisconsin builder became one of the first yards in the world to convert to welded aluminum construction. They recently launched the largest aluminum yacht built in the US, the 195ft (59m) *La Baronessa*. PJ has created their 115ft (35m) Constellation series of yachts that share basic design traits while allowing each owner to fully customize the interior. A recent launching is *Twisted Pair*, a 100ft (30m) motoryacht. Due to launch in 2000 are a 123ft (37m) motoryacht, a 144ft (44m) trideck, and a 130ft (39m) motoryacht.

PERINI NAVI

This Italian builder pioneered the concept of luxurious sailing yachts that can be sailed with very small crews, using sophisticated gear to raise and trim the sails. The company will build in steel or aluminum, and recently launched the 163ft (49m) *Phryne*. A similar 163-footer, also with a forward rather than a raised pilothouse, and a 174ft (53m) sloop are also under construction. After nearly two decades of building to their own designs, Perini Navi is now bidding on projects from independent designers who can share in the company's wealth of experience in large sailing yachts. Perini Navi recently expanded with the addition of a second nearby shipyard capable of handling larger yachts.

PERINI NAVI
163ft *Phryne*

PALMER JOHNSON
115ft *Mostro*

RYBOVICH SPENCER
55ft Shibumi

PHILBROOK'S BOATYARD

This Canadian yard specializes in building, repairing and renovating motor and sailing yachts, and is able to handle yachts up to 120ft (36m) or 150 tons. Just launched is *Tango*, a composite 69ft (21m) Robert Perry-designed pilothouse sloop that has attracted considerable media attention, and a Howard Apollonio-designed 76ft (23m) motoryacht is under negotiations. The yard has a reputation for quality refits, and is presently refurbishing a 70ft (21m) Romsdal trawler and a 55ft (17m) Vitters sailing yacht.

QUEENSHIP

This Canadian company was reorganized in 1992 to focus on high quality custom and semi-custom fiberglass motoryachts ranging from 59ft (18m) to more than 100ft (30m). Three series—Admiralty, Berretta and Caribe—offer a wide variety of styles, layouts and interiors, and the company also builds custom yachts to 140ft (42m). Just launched are a pair of 70ft (21m) Admiralty series motoryachts with cockpits and Caterpillar power, along with *Oregon Mist*, the first of the 86ft (27m) Caribe raised pilothouse yachts with Detroit 12v2000s. Two full pilothouse motoryachts at 68ft (21m) and 70ft (21m) are also under construction. A pair of Caribe sportfishers are being built at 89ft (27m) and 91ft (28m), both with Detroit 16 cylinder diesels. *Souvenir*, a custom Fexas-designed 86ft (27m) raised pilothouse motoryacht due in 2000, sports a revolutionary semi-displacement planing hull design and will serve as the first of a series of 86ft to 110ft (33m) yachts. To keep up with the demand for yachts, the yard has undertaken a three-stage expansion and has just moved into a new 100,000 sq. ft. building with 1400ft of waterfront.

RAYBURN CUSTOM YACHTS

Formed when Ron Rayburn took over Forbes Cooper Yachts in 1998, this Canadian builder focuses on composite yachts between 60ft (18m) and 80ft (24m) with an emphasis on high quality custom and semi-custom designs and has a low overhead philosophy to keep the prices competitive. Just launched was *Misty One*, a 62ft (19m) Apollonio designed motor-yacht with a Portuguese bridge, and a 66ft (20m) raised pilot-house motor-yacht is due early in 2000. Under construction is a 74ft Apollonio one-off with a 21ft (6.4m) beam, and two other motoryacht projects are in the negotiating stages.

ROYAL HUISMAN SHIPYARD

This Dutch yard set a new standard for mega sailing yachts with the launching of the 155ft sloop (47m) *Hyperion*, designed by German Frers and Peter Beeldsnijder for Jim Clark. Under construction is another Frers design, the 110ft (33m) *Unfurled*, a high performance sloop for an American owner.

RYBOVICH SPENCER

Synonymous with sportfishing from the first more than 50 years ago, the profile and deep vee hull of the "Rybo" sportfisher have been legendary. Merging with the Spencer Boat Co. in 1991, Rybovich Spencer builds custom cold-molded wood sportfishers. Recently launched was *Cutting Edge*, a 72ft (22m) open flybridge and the 55ft (16m) *Shibumi*, the 100th yacht built by Rybo. Also under construction is a 60ft (18m) sportfisher, and the yard is involved in refits of a 137ft (41m) Perini Navi, a 124ft (37m) Christensen, and a 115ft (35m) wooden sailing yacht.

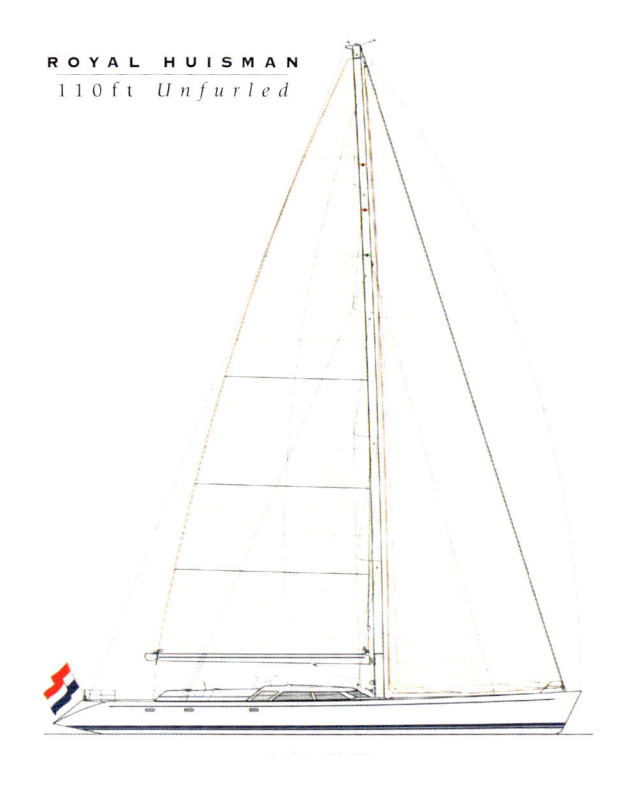

ROYAL HUISMAN
110ft Unfurled

★ BUILDERS 241

SUNSEEKER
84ft Manhattan

The company has recently expanded their 220-acre facilities, and dredged the channel to provide 14ft (4.2m) depth to a 300-ton TraveLift.

SOVEREIGN YACHTS

This Canadian company is devoted to building custom fiberglass yachts over 100ft (30m). They recently launched *Donna C III*, a 120ft (36m) raised pilothouse motoryacht as well as a sistership, the *Sovereign Lady*. Under construction are a 120ft (36m) trideck for delivery in early 2000, a 90ft (27m) raised pilothouse, and another 120ft trideck. A 138ft (42m) trideck will be completed in 2001. A recent yard expansion and the addition of a new building allows Sovereign to build four 140-footers at a time.

SWIFTSHIP
150ft *Cherosa*

SUNSEEKER

This English fiberglass builder has just announced the largest semi-custom Sunseeker, the Manhattan 101, which will debut early in 2000. Their production series has also grown with the Manhattan 84, which is a larger version of the successful Manhattan 80. Other new yachts for 2000 include the Predator 56 sport yacht, the Manhattan 64 flybridge, and the Camargue 50 with a spacious cockpit and transom tender garage. To handle this growth, Sunseeker has recently expanded into a two acre site next to their Poole headquarters.

SWIFTSHIPS

This commercial yard, the world's largest builder of aluminum boats over 100ft, entered the luxury yacht market a decade ago, and recently launched the 150ft (45m) trideck *Cherosa*. On the drawing board is a 148ft exploration motoryacht to be built to military standards with the emphasis on full autonomy for remote regions. With waterjet power to keep the draft under six feet, the yacht is designed to carry both a 41ft sportfisher as well as a medium-range helicopter.

TARRAB YACHTS

This Argentine builder of semi-custom fiberglass yachts from 60ft (18m) to 125ft (38m) combines old world craftsmanship with modern fiberglass technology. Recent launchings include *Siesser's Palace*, a 92 footer (28m) with Paola Smith interior and *Charlie's Angel*, an 86ft (26m) motoryacht.

TRINITY YACHTS

Trinity Yachts is the megayacht arm of a group of 16 shipyards owned by Halter Marine Group, a publicly traded company (the fourth largest shipbuilder in the US) with vast experience in military and commercial construction. Trinity Yachts can build up to 500ft (152m) in steel or aluminum at their 30-acre yacht facility near the center of New Orleans. Recently launched was *Marlena*, the world's largest sportfisher at 126ft (38m), *Allegra*, a 156ft (47m) motoryacht, *Nova Spirit*, a 150ft (45m) trideck intended for corporate entertaining, and *Bellini*, a

WESTSHIP
140ft Trideck

150ft trideck designed by Ward Setzer for Victory Lane. Under construction is a 135ft (41m) trideck spec boat for Victory Lane, and *Sea Hawk,* a 177ft (53m) trideck that will carry twin 26ft tenders.

WEST BAY SONSHIP

This family-owned and run Canadian builder originally specialized in commercial vessels but now builds fiberglass semi-custom motoryachts in three sizes: 58ft (17m), 75/80ft (23/24m), and 103ft (31m). Each yacht is custom-finished to the specifications of each client, with virtually everything created on site in their 230,000 sq. ft. plant. The 103ft (31m) hull is a Sarin design built by Westport. Recently launched are a 58ft (21m) raised pilothouse motoryacht and a 103ft (31m) raised pilothouse motoryacht that is the first over 100-footer built by West Bay SonShip. Also under construction are a pair of 78-footers and six 58-footers for delivery in 2000. On the drawing board from the in-house design team is a new 68ft (41m) raised pilothouse motoryacht with soft styling intended to fill the gap between the 58ft and 78ft models. The company is also planning to expand their facilities in 2000.

WESTPORT SHIPYARD

This company, which has built more composite hulls over 80ft (24m) than any other builder in the US, now has their own line of large luxury yachts. Recently launched are a pair of Jack Sarin-designed 112ft (34m) motoryachts including a spec boat that will be shown at the Ft. Lauderdale Boatshow. The company is completing a 112-footer every 3-4 months. Under construction for delivery in the fall of 2000 is a Greg Marshall-designed 128ft (39m) motoryacht, and a sistership was recently started. The company also continues to supply Sarin-designed hulls to the Sovereign, Crescent Custom and West Bay SonShip yards, and also builds commercial craft such as a recently launched high-speed 85ft (26m) patrol boat. Newly expanded facilities provide Westport with more than 190,000 sq. ft. of covered area.

WESTSHIP

This yachting firm designs, builds and markets a line of proprietary 100ft (30m) to 165ft (50m) megayacht designs which are built under the supervision of Herb Postma. Each Westship is delivered virtually "turn key" with everything from electronics to bed linens and the design is optimized for low maintenance fiberglass and small crews. Recent launchings include *Norwegian Queen*, a 132ft (40m) trideck motoryacht and *Westship One*, a 140ft (42m) trideck. Westship is negotiating at press time to take over the Trident yard, and is planning a new generation of 108ft (32m) to 112ft (34m) raised pilothouse motoryachts designed by Jack Sarin.

TRINITY
126ft Sportfisherman

★ BUILDERS

Mea Culpa, Escape, Sovereign Lady, Donna C III, Melreni, Sinbad, Barbarina, Mary Ann, North Star 92, Dare to Dream, Scorpio, Miss Iloilo, Anita, Westship One, Westport 112, Warrior, Anchor W, Loretta Anne, Krisha, Countach, La Corniche, Sea Safari, Bravo Zulu, Sojourn, Rainmaker, Primadonna, Carpe Diem, Black Sheep, Crystal, Mardiosa, Northstream, Mary J II, Norwegian Queen, Lalysos, Crescent Lady, South Beach II, Lady Dorron, La Baroness, Golden Delicious, Glory, Tahiti, Splash, Christian, Mary J, South Beach, Panasea, Peppermint, Lestralaur, Kay Jay, Numero Uno, Champagne & Roses, White Knight, Silver Eagle, Ste. Jill...

We offer the full design experience including custom hull design, engineering, interior design and décor. We stand ready to meet your needs.

JACK W. SARIN NAVAL ARCHITECTS, INC.

382 Wyatt Way N.E. ■ Bainbridge Island, Washington 98110 ■ Telephone 206.842.4651 ■ Fax 206.842.4656 ■ www.jacksarin.com

Beauty of the Beast.

Your windlass is more than a bow ornament. It's meant to provide peace of mind and security in every imaginable sea condition. That's why Maxwell windlasses and capstans are built to exacting ISO 9001 standards so you get all the performance you'll ever need. Now that's real beauty.

Ask For Performance By Name.

MAXWELL

For more information call or write:
Maxwell Winches, 1606 Babcock Street, Costa Mesa, CA 92627   phone (949) 631-2634   fax (949) 631-2846

Commitment to Quality...

- Builder of custom yachts over 100 ft
- All inhouse fiberglass construction from one-piece molds
- Covered facilities—two 140' x 80' buildings, cabinet shop and 470' of dock space

For more information:
23511 Dyke Road, Richmond
British Columbia, Canada V6V 1E3
Tel: (604) 515-0992 • Fax: (604) 515-0994
Email: info@sovereign-yachts.com

SOVEREIGN YACHTS (CANADA) INC.

Do you know what David Pedrick has under his belt?

- Two America's Cup winners – Courageous and Stars & Stripes.
- Two 1998 superyacht awards for Best Sailing Yacht – Savannah.
- Unmatched attention to detail, applied technology and client service.
- Your best yacht design team for the third millennium.

PEDRICK
YACHT · DESIGNS

Pedrick Yacht Designs • Three Ann Street • Newport, RI, USA • 401-846-8481 • pedrickyacht.com

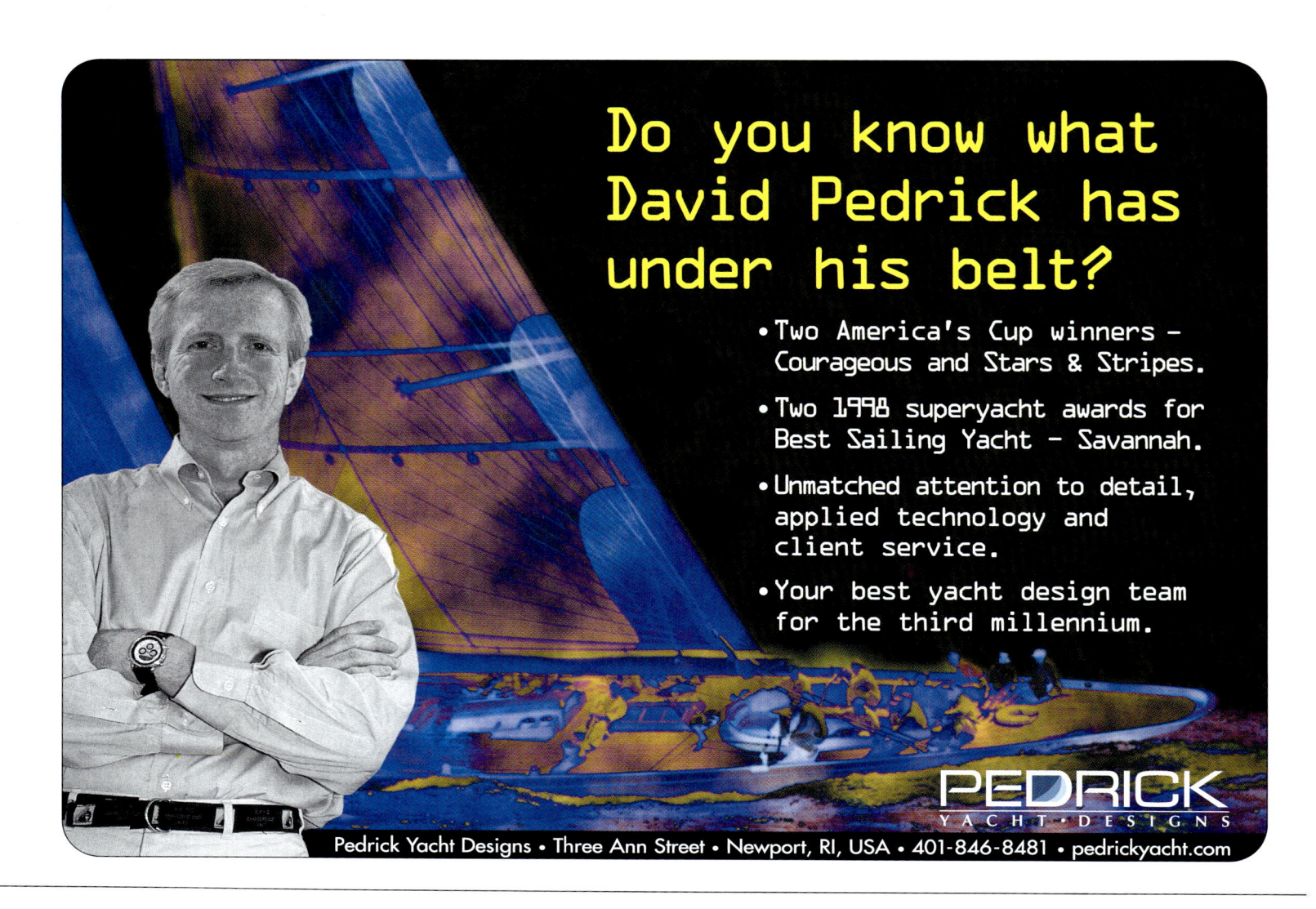

STRIDA

a whole new way to move

STRIDA 2 FEATURES

- Ultra-portable bike with leading edge design
- Lightweight - 10 kilograms
- Folding and unfolding in 7 seconds
- Can be wheeled when folded
- Rust and maintenance free
- Belt driven means no oil
- Hub brakes
- Marine grade stainless steel components

THE ULTIMATE FOLDING BIKE MADE WITH A PASSION FOR PERFECTION

Strida Limited
c/o Roland Plastics Limited
High Street, Wickham Market
Woodbridge, Suffolk IP 13 0QZ
Telephone: 01728 747 777 Fax: 01728 748 222
email: ben@rolandplastics.co.uk

Strida North America
P.O. Box 381054, Cambridge
MA 02238
Tel: 1-800-STRIDA 2
website: www.strida.com

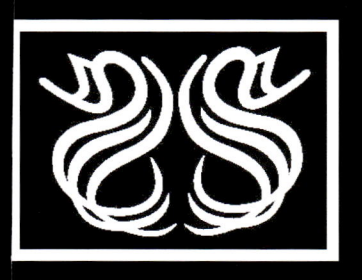

Paola D. Smith

Yacht Styling

'PDS 2002'

Interior Design

300 N.E. 3rd Avenue, Fort Lauderdale, Florida, 33301
Telephone: (954) 761-1997 • Facsimile: (954) 767-6270
E-Mail: pds@pdsdesign.net • Website: www.pdsdesign.net

Photography: Bill Muncke, Donna & Ken Chesler

M/Y *Taipan*
Refit by
Rybovich Spencer

Dana Jinkins
PHOTOGRAPHY

Specializing in Interior and Exterior
Yacht Photography

(802) 496-5580 fax (802) 496-5581
email: concepts@madriver.com

Photographed, designed, and produced 8 books
on yachts and yachting

Over 20 years experience in the field

Available for full yacht photography,
as well as design/production of yacht brochures

# Global Power Systems is The Gold Standard in Onboard Shore Power Converters Worldwide.

We invited yacht owners, designers and builders worldwide to compare all of the shore power converters on the market. They returned to Global Power Systems for superior design, construction and value, backed by the strongest performance guarantee in the industry. Discerning owners prefer Global Power Systems.

GP3000 SERIES

30 - 50kva
Size: 24"w X 30"d X 52"h
Weight: 1100 lbs.

72 - 120kva
Size: 45"w X 30"d X 39"h
Weight: 1800 lbs.

YACH T OWNERS PREFER GLOBAL FOR

1. Styling that complements their yachts' designs
2. Non-interruptible, reliable power transfer
3. Patented noise-free, distortion-free output
4. Proven state-of-the-art technology
5. Compliance with the standards, including CE
6. Demonstrated high motor-starting capability
7. Unsurpassed output efficiency
8. Compact, lightweight, and extremely rugged self-contained unit
9. The only true marinized shore power converter, built to withstand the harsh marine environment

You'll appreciate the Global Power Team's professionalism and experience. We stand ready to assist you in selecting the power sizing to meet your requirements in yachts 50- to 300-feet. We will provide electrical wiring recommendations, installation advice, on-site engineering help and complete documentation. We can assist with single- or three-phase power, 8kva to 360kva. Contact us today about the Global product for your yacht and the dealer nearest you.

GP2000 SERIES

8 - 18kva
Size: 30"w X 12"d X 22"h
Weight: 270 lbs.

24 - 40kva
Size: 14"w X 30"d X 39"h
Weight: 500 lbs.

GLOBAL POWER SYSTEMS
A Thermo Voltek Company

GLOBAL POWER'S WORLDWIDE HEADQUARTERS
Phone 206-301-0515 • Fax 206-301-0660
1500 Westlake Ave. North, Suite 4, Marina Mart Building
Seattle, Washington USA 98109

Global Power Systems is a Thermo Voltek company, a subsidiary of Thermo Electron.

Timeless elegance depends on a balance between function and style

Atlantide
Built 1930, Restored 1999

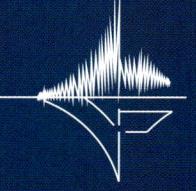

KEN FREIVOKH DESIGN
INTERIOR DESIGN AND STYLING

ASH STUDIO CROCKER HILL FAREHAM HAMPSHIRE PO17 5DP UK
TEL 44 (0) 1329 832514 FAX 44 (0) 1329 833326
EMAIL all@freivokh.com WEB www.freivokh.com

DISCOVER...*superior yacht design*

elegant

simplicity

★

enduring

style

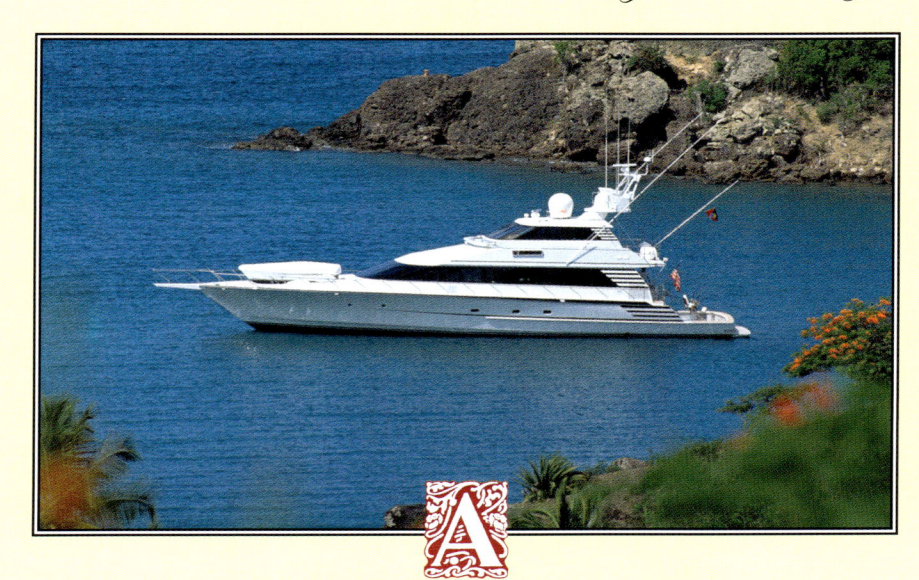

leading

performance

★

exceptional

seakindliness

APOLLONIO
NAVAL ARCHITECTURE

Contact Howard Apollonio, Naval Architect and Professional Engineer
PMB 514; 1225 E. Sunset Drive; Bellingham, Washington 98226 USA   Telephone 360 733 6859   Facsimile 360 715 9474   E-mail hapollo@az.com

Dramatic Designs...

TOM FEXAS YACHT DESIGN, INC.
naval architects · marine engineers · yacht designers · yacht surveyors & consultants since 1966
1320 South Federal Highway · Suite 104 · Stuart · Florida · 34994 · USA
Phone: (561) 287 6558 · Fax: (561) 287 6810 · Email: tfyd@aol.com

The Luxury Yacht Market

Designers

JOHN G. ALDEN NAVAL ARCHITECTS

This designer has *Borkumriff IV*, a 164ft (50m) aluminum schooner, under construction at Royal Huisman in Holland for delivery in 2002.

ANITA'S INTERIORS

Having recently completed refits on *Nina*, a 110ft (33m) Denison and the 111ft (33m) trideck *Crystal*, this interior design firm is working on a custom interior for a new 95ft (28m) Alaskan trawler, and also handles the standard interiors on production Alaskans.

APOLLONIO NAVAL ARCHITECTURE

This prolific designer's order book covers the spectrum from an elegant 74ft (45m) long-range cruising yacht to an advanced technology 45 knot gas turbine/waterjet catamaran and a small 40 knot hydrofoil. Two production series yachts in several different models are under construction at McKinna Yachts, and a 70ft (21m) 42-knot express yacht has been ordered by Sundance Yacht Sales. Apollonio continues his relationship with Queenship Yachts on the semi-custom Caribe Series with several yachts under construction. In the negotiation stage are two SWATH yachts at 120ft (36m) and 160ft (48m), a 110ft (33m) hydrofoil yacht, and two 70ft (21m) to 90ft (27m) semi-custom series for boatbuilders.

ALDEN
Borkumriff IV

ANITA'S INTERIORS
114ft *Crystal*

ARDEO
151ft *Affinity*

ARDEO DESIGN

Named for the Latin word for "passion," this team of principal Scott Cole and senior designer Marcia Collins was involved in the 151ft (46m) *Affinity*, a four-deck expedition yacht from Delta that will be used for viewing the America's Cup races in 2000. Designed to be "used hard" the interior also includes subtle details to evoke a sense of maritime tradition since the owner is a prominent yacht racer, and *Affinity* will eventually serve as the "mother ship" for his racing program. Also under construction is a 78ft (23m) composite motoryacht with both pilothouse and enclosed bridge at McQueen's Boatworks, and finishing up is the interior design on an 86ft (26m) Queenship designed by Tom Fexas.

JOE ARTESE DESIGN

Calling himself an "interior architect," Artese is known for his innovative and luxurious large yacht designs. At home in both power and sail, he has built a reputation for superb use of wood as well as "human engineering" to make yachts both comfortable and workable. Recent projects are the 100ft (30m) *Illusion* from McQueen's as well as a series of large sailing yachts including the 100ft (30m) ketch *Signe,* and 90ft (27m) sloop *Whitefin*. Under construction is a 52ft (16m) catamaran with AeroRig for Pedigree Cats, a 110ft (33m) motoryacht, and a 75ft (23m) motoryacht with an enclosed pilothouse for a Canadian client. He recently produced a design for Legendary Yachts as an update of the classic Rhodes 77 motorsailer, and continues to design the interiors for the Cabo sportfishing yachts.

BARBEITO DESIGN

This naval architecture firm has a 132ft (40m) motoryacht in the design and tank testing stages, with series production intended in composites by an undisclosed builder. Other projects on the boards are a 222ft (67m) diesel-electric motoryacht and a 110ft (33m) gas-turbine high-speed passenger ferry.

JONATHAN QUINN BARNETT

Specializing in the interior and exterior design of yachts, this Seattle company also provides design and project management for refits as well. Under construction at Delta Marine is the 124ft (37m) *Aerie,* a raised pilothouse motoryacht. At Northcoast, a 118ft motoryacht will be the second in the builder's Regency Series and, at Little Hoquiam, a 100ft (30m) Sarin design will be launched early in 2000. In the preliminary design stages for both interior and exterior styling is a 150ft (45m) motoryacht.

M. CASTEDO ARCHITECTS

This New York-based architecture and interior design firm recently completed the total retrofit of a 150ft (45m) Benetti including all new interiors and the extension of the hull to provide a 20ft (6m) cockpit for fishing.

LUIZ DeBASTO DESIGNS

A full service naval architecture and design firm, this company is presently working on a 300ft (91m) eight-deck motoryacht for an American client. The yacht will feature three elevators, a

M. CASTEDO
M/Y *Francine*

★ DESIGNERS 253

DEBASTO
101ft Sportfisherman

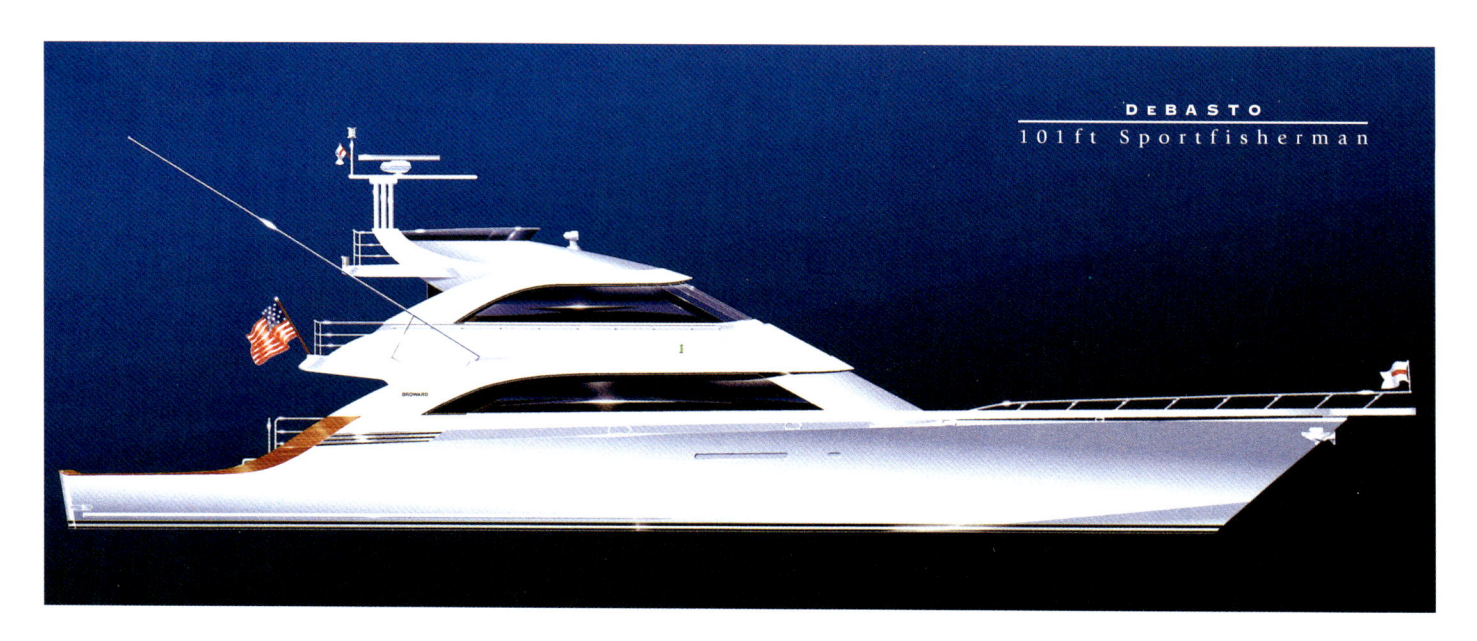

double-height main saloon with a library on the mezzanine, an upper deck pool, and one deck devoted entirely to the owner. Also in the design stage is a 150ft (45m) four-deck motoryacht for an American owner that will be challenging because it requires full wheelchair access. Under construction are a 101ft (30m) sportfisher at Broward and a 90ft (27m) high speed composite sportboat with a split level interior. At Intermarine, construction is underway on a 116ft (35m) raised pilothouse motoryacht and a 120ft (36m) trideck with DeBasto providing both the exterior lines and the interior design. Three refitting projects include the 165ft (50m) *Braveheart*, the 156ft (47m) Broward *Inspiration* (ex-*Bubba Too*), and *Magic One,* a 120ft (36m) Diaship (ex-*Bonita*) that burned in Singapore and is being rebuilt at Cable Marine.

ESPINOSA

Led by principal Juan Carlos Espinosa, this full-service interior design firm has a number of projects in the works. Recently launched are the 95ft (29m) trideck *In Full Bloom* at Premier Yachts, featuring Espinosa exterior styling as well as interiors on a Howard Apollonio hull, and an 86ft (26m) raised pilothouse Caribe model at Queenship, which will be followed by an 87ft (26m) sportfisher. *Nassa Too*, a 147ft (45m) composite trideck is under construction at Trident, and *Gran Finale*, a 147ft (45m) composite motoryacht, will be launched late in 2001 by Delta. Espinosa has just completed the first 60ft (18m) express yacht for McKinna, which also has orders for eight of a 65ft (19m) pilothouse motoryacht.

TOM FEXAS YACHT DESIGN

This prolific design firm produces many of the designs for Cheoy Lee and currently has a 122ft transatlantic expedition motoryacht under construction, a 73ft express motoryacht with a pair of 1000hp Caterpillars giving a top speed of 27 knots, and a 65ft high speed express cruiser in the style of the early Fexas Midnight Lace designs.

KEN FREIVOKH DESIGN

This multi-disciplinary team specializes in both custom and production projects. Several recent projects, including the refit/conversions of the 110ft tug *St Eval* and the icebreaker *Fredrikstad*, led to the full exterior and interior design of the 1930s sailing motoryacht *Atlantide*, which was completed in 1999 by Camper & Nicholson. Other projects under way are a 104ft semi-displacement motoryacht and the conversion of *Vega*,

HUNT
66ft Sedan M/Y

ESPINOSA
147ft Trident

254   THE MEGAYACHTS USA   ★   2000

FEXAS
122ft Expedition Motoryacht

a 145ft icebreaker/salvage vessel that will have underdeck storage for a Land Rover. Work is also progressing on *Leopard 2000*, a 90ft Reichel-Pugh sloop, and a 112ft lightweight Farr-designed ketch. As exclusive designers for Sunseeker International, KFD has recently completed new models in the 50ft to 84ft range, as well as layouts for the forthcoming 105ft, 120ft and 130ft Sunseekers.

FRYCO

Principal Edward Fry has several projects under way worldwide. An 89ft (27m) cold-molded wood sportfisher with triple props and a trio of Detroit/MTU diesels is under construction in Turkey and, also at the Dragos yard, a 78ft (23m) motoryacht for the Red Sea will feature flybridge only controls and a galley in the hull aft of the engines, allowing a full length main saloon. Fry also has three different designs from 65ft to 70ft licensed to Neptunus Yachts, with more than ten yachts under construction there.

RON HOLLAND DESIGN

This Ireland-based New Zealander has carved a reputation in the yacht racing world, and is now pioneering large sailing yachts as well as dabbling in motoryachts as well. On-going projects include designs for the Dutch yard Trintella, with the new Trintella 65 starting production this year. A new Discovery 55 will have an on-deck saloon and a Ken Freivokh interior. Recently launched at Delta Marine is the 151ft *Affinity*, a long-range motoryacht for one of Holland's racing clients. And at Perini Navi, Holland is in the design stages of a 206ft (63m) ketch/cutter to be built in Turkey/Italy.

TED HOOD DESIGN GROUP

Over four decades, this group has designed more than 2500 boats up to 220ft (67m), with an emphasis on very fast, shallow draft sailing yachts with classic American styling. Currently under construction is *Erica XII*, a 155-footer from Royal Huisman with an Andrew Winch interior, and *Pamina*, a 112ft (34m) sailing yacht.

HUNT DESIGN

This design firm, which pioneered the deep-vee hull, has several projects under way. At Palmer Johnson, an 88ft (26m) motoryacht styled by Nuvolari-Lenard is being built, along with a 110ft (33m) Med-styled motoryacht with waterjet

FREIVOKH
1930s Atlantide

★ DESIGNERS

propulsion and a similar 112ft (34m) motoryacht with props is being built on spec. At Derecktor-Goetz, a 102ft (31m) composite motoryacht is due to launch this year. The firm has also finished the latest in their Eastbay series of yachts, a 43ft Express, for American Marine.

GLADE JOHNSON
159ft *Georgia*

GLADE JOHNSON DESIGN

With a diverse interior design background that includes VIP aircraft interiors, auto styling, and yacht design, principal Glade Johnson has a 159ft (48m) sloop under construction at Alloy Yachts in New Zealand. With a 195ft (59m) carbon fiber mast, a drop keel and a fully automated sailing rig, Johnson is providing the overall concept, exterior styling and interior design and decor. Other projects include a pair of 103ft raised pilothouse motoryachts from West Bay SonShip, both launching in late 1999 or early 2000.

BRUCE KING YACHT DESIGN

This firm, with several well-known large sailing yacht designs including the 90ft (27m) sloop *Whitefin,* the 92ft (28m) ketch *Whitehawk,* and the 135ft (41m) ketch *Hetairos,* offers naval architecture, exterior and interior design services. Just launched was the 125ft (38m) sloop *Antonisa* at Hodgdon Yachts, a wood-epoxy flush-decked yacht with carbon fiber spars and a cherry interior that includes a working fireplace and a pipe organ. Soon to begin construction is *Scheherazade,* a 151ft (46m) contemporary ketch, and *Cecelia Marie,* a 128ft (39m) traditional sloop will begin construction in mid-2000 at Royal Huisman.

PATRICK KNOWLES DESIGN

Two recent launchings include the 115ft (35m) *Dare to Dream* from Crescent Custom and the 111ft (34m) Broward, *Varsity Jacket.* New projects include a 132ft (40m) trideck at Palmer Johnson with a classic interior of mahogany, and an 80ft (24m) Nordlund with a cherry interior and cherry-and-maple floors rather than the usual teak and holly. Nearly finished is a 90ft (27m) Hatteras convertible sportfisherman with a highly customized interior in maple and bird's-eye maple, including intricately patterned overhead treatments.

LANGAN DESIGN ASSOCIATES

With more than 20 years of experience as the chief designer for Sparkman & Stephens, Bill Langan founded this naval architectural firm to focus on large yachts. Off to a quick start, the company has *Breeze,* a 130ft (39m) classic ketch, under construction at Alloy Yachts in New Zealand with delivery set for late 2000. *Sagamore,* an IMS Maxi yacht, was completed and is already in the winner's circle on the racing circuits, and two large motoryachts are in preliminary design stages.

LIEBOWITZ & PRITCHARD

This design firm specializes in everything from project planning to interior and exterior design to construction management. The company has four projects on the boards, including an unusual 125ft (38m) trimaran motoryacht with surface piercing propellers. Also under design

LANGAN DESIGN
130ft *Breeze*

THE MEGAYACHTS USA ★ 2000

LIEBOWITZ & PRITCHARD
148ft Long Range M/Y

are a 150ft (45m) 500-ton ocean-going motoryacht that will feature a double-height greenhouse dining atrium; an 85ft (26m) "mini-megayacht" with classic lines; and a 96ft (28m) sailing yacht with a terraced saloon layout.

MARINE DESIGN INTERNATIONAL

Headed by naval architect and marine engineer Phil Andrawis, this company has a reputation for tackling unusual projects, and a 155ft (47m) trideck motoryacht meets that description. The yacht will have transoceanic range, classic interiors, a skylounge and four guest staterooms in addition to the owner's suite. A rotating aft lounge area is under consideration and, with bids out for construction in either steel/aluminum or composite, delivery is expected in early 2003.

RODGER MARTIN YACHT DESIGN

This designer specializes in high performance sailing yachts and his 60ft (18m) *Duracell* set an American solo circumnavigation record that still stands. A new racing project is a yacht for the BOC Around Alone Race and, on the cruising side, a 65ft (19m) shoal draft sailing yacht is in design. A pair of production sailing yachts, the Aerodyne 38 and 47, are performance cruisers for a South African builder.

LIEBOWITZ & PRITCHARD
148ft Long Range M/Y

ED MONK YACHT DESIGN

This design firm is very busy, with several yachts underway at both Nordlund and McQueen's. Working with Tim Nolan Marine Design, which specializes in engineering and structural design, this second generation designer has a reputation for seaworthy motoryachts. An 80ft (24m) Northwest-styled motoryacht with an enclosed bridge is under construction at Nordlund, along with a 78ft (23m) motoryacht. Monk recently did the lines for a new flexible hull mold at Nordlund, which can handle 85ft (26m) to 106ft (32m) lengths with beams from 22ft to 24ft. First from that mold will be a 105ft (32m) California-style sportfisher, with a second 105-footer under negotiations. At McQueen's, a stout Monk-designed 89ft (54m) offshore cruising motoryacht is being built from a hull mold that is likely to lead to a limited series of similar yachts.

PACIFIC CUSTOM INTERIORS

This firm, which began by specializing in yacht upholstery, now offers a range of interior design services. Projects

★ DESIGNERS

PAVLIK DESIGN
150ft Monitor

underway include two Westport 112ft (34m) motoryachts, a Sovereign 121-footer designed by Sarin, and several of the Pacific Mariner 65s designed by Greg Marshall. Recent projects include an Espinosa-designed 76ft (23m) motor-yacht at LeClercq and a 71-footer (22m) at Admiral.

PAVLIK DESIGN TEAM

This large company, ranked among the top five design firms in the US, has a yacht design department based in Florida but draws on specialists throughout the company. Being refitted is *Monitor*, a 150ft (45m) Bill Murray-designed motor-yacht. New construction includes a pair of Browards: *Holly Belle*, a 112ft (34m) motoryacht, and *Home James*, a 105-footer (32m). Other new construction includes a trio of Michael Peters designs: *Christina*, a 95ft (28m) motoryacht at Intermarine, a 130ft (39m) motoryacht, and a 125ft (38m) motoryacht.

PEDRICK YACHT DESIGN

While specializing in sailing yachts, this well-known designer of America's Cup yachts (he was involved in designing a challenger for Team Caribbean from the US Virgin Islands) has also applied those design concepts to motoryachts. Just launched at Admiral Marine is a 75ft (23m) raised-saloon sloop with elegant styling and decor. Pending construction is a 138ft (42m) high-tech motorsailor capable of speeds exceeding 25 knots under power. Ketch rigged, the yacht will use a swing keel to give less than seven feet of draft under power or 23ft of draft under sail, and the aluminum hull will also have a water ballast system. Two 60ft (18m) sailing yachts are also in the concept stages.

MICHAEL PETERS YACHT DESIGN

Well established as a leader in high-performance sport and raceboat design (including four World Championship victories), this company has shifted its focus to the design and engineering of large custom yachts to 160ft (48m). Currently under construction at McMullen & Wing in New Zealand are a pair of 80ft (24m) Garlington Landeweer 38 knot sportfishers: one with an enclosed flybridge and one open. A 78ft (23m) Magnum sport yacht is under construction in Italy, with twin Detroit 12V2000 diesels and a top speed of 45 knots. A pair of 95-footers are under construction at Intermarine, with the

POKELA DESIGN
250ft M/Y

MICHAEL PETERS
117ft M/Y

first due in mid-2000, and a 117ft (35m) motoryacht is building at Metalnave in Brazil. The company is also working on the preliminary design for a 114ft (34m) aluminum motoryacht.

POKELA DESIGN

Specializing in both exterior and interior styling from concept to construction, a recent launching is *Tigress*, an 86ft (26m) sportfisher from McQueen's. Under construction is *Crosser*, an 88ft (27m) long range cruiser with transoceanic capabilities at McQueen's and *Hana How*, an Ed Monk designed 85ft (26m) raised pilothouse motoryacht at Nordlund. In the design stages is the planning and interior styling of a 75ft (23m) Fleming, with delivery in 2000, and the company has recently signed to produce a 250ft (76m) cruise ship. In the process of a refit is a 65ft (20m) Garden motoryacht of the Blue Heron series.

ROBIN M. ROSE & ASSOCIATES

Specializing in project management, space planning and design, this design firm has three recent launchings. *Wehr Nuts* is a 124ft (37m) Christensen with an anigre and mappa burl interior set off by a Picasso-motif stairwell, while *White Star* is a 92ft (28m) Hatteras with a rearranged interior finished in high-gloss mahogany. *Escape* is a 120ft (36m) Crescent Custom with bubinga and ebony joinery and a unique raised cove ceiling in the saloon.

DEE ROBINSON

With full design and decor services on both new construction and refits of megayachts, recent launchings include *Bellini*, a 150ft (45m) motoryacht from Trinity and *Endless Summer*, a 124-footer (37m) refitted Lloyds Ship in Australia. Two yachts are currently being completed: *Equinoccio* is a 139ft (42m) Oceanco spec boat, while *Nova Spirit* is a 150ft (45m) Trinity with wrap-around window treatments in the 30ft wide main deck master suite.

JACK W. SARIN NAVAL ARCHITECTS

A full-service naval architectural firm that has designed more than 400 yachts and commercial vessels up to 180ft (54m), the company combines everything from naval architecture to interior styling in one source. In addition to the semi-production 112ft (34m) motoryacht hulls at Westport Shipyard and the 103ft (31m) motoryachts at West Bay SonShip, the company has a number of other projects under construction, including a 130ft (39m) yachtfisher at Sensation Yachts in New Zealand that will be the largest sportfisher in the world. Two projects are underway at Crescent Custom Yachts, with a 121ft (36m) trideck motoryacht due to launch in early 2000 that will have a pair of spacious family staterooms as well as a split-level owner's suite on the main deck. Starting construction in late 1999 was a 104ft (31m) raised pilothouse motoryacht with an arrangement similar to previous

JACK W. SARIN
Mea Culpa

★ DESIGNERS 259

PAOLA D. SMITH
158ft Baglietto

Crescent/Sarin collaborations. At Sovereign Yachts, three Sarin designs are under construction, including a 120ft (36m) trideck and two 120ft (36m) raised pilothouse motoryachts, while a 100ft (30m) yachtfisher was launched at Little Hoquiam in late 1999.

SETZER DESIGN GROUP

Prolific naval architect Ward Setzer and his team have a number of projects both under construction and in design stages. Recently launched is *Bellini*, a 150ft (45m) trideck from Trinity which is the third in the Victory Lane series, with a 118ft (35m) trideck to follow. *Surprise*, a 112ft (34m) well-deck expedition yacht is under construction at McMullen & Wing in New Zealand in steel and aluminum for world cruising, and Australia's revitalized Lloyd's Ships is building both a 96ft (29m) expedition yacht and a 94ft (28m) high speed motoryacht in fiberglass. A 98ft aft superstructure expedition yacht is under construction at Greenbay Marine of Singapore. At Lyman-Morse, a 77ft (23m) modern classic motoryacht is being built in composite for delivery in late 2000. Described as a combination of trawler and lobster boat styling, it has Down East lines and will be the first of a 48ft (14m) to 78ft (23m) production series. A 136ft (41m) trideck ultra-sleek motoryacht is also in the bidding stages.

SIEWERT DESIGN

Principal Greg Siewert has spearheaded two recent refitting projects at Palmer Johnson in Savannah. The 120ft (36m) Feadship *Allegra* (ex-*Gallant Lady*) involved major exterior cosmetic work as well as a new carbon fiber radar mast and a completely rearranged pilothouse. The 102ft (31m) motoryacht *Horizons* is a trawler-type yacht that serves as a mothership for a custom 65ft (20m) Merritt sportfisher. Refitted from keel to mast with extensive interior and exterior changes, the yacht will be fishing the Caribbean in 2000.

PAOLA D. SMITH & ASSOCIATES

One of the top interior design firms in the megayacht industry, this firm is known for technical support that provides complete interior design services as well as exterior styling and space planning for both new construction and refits, featuring marquetry detailing and luxurious fabrics. Due in early 2000 is a 158ft (48m) Baglietto that combines silk furnishings and wall coverings, an imposing staircase of steel and nickel, and both wood and marble flooring in a neo-classic design. She is also designing both exterior and interior styling for a 160ft (49m) motoryacht. Due in 2000 is *Siesser's Palace*, a 92ft (28m) Tarrab, and a 130ft (39m) motoryacht will be launched at Heesen in 2001 with an extremely sophisticated interior.

SPARKMAN & STEPHENS

Founded in 1929 and one of the most prestigious names in yacht design, S&S provides both naval architecture

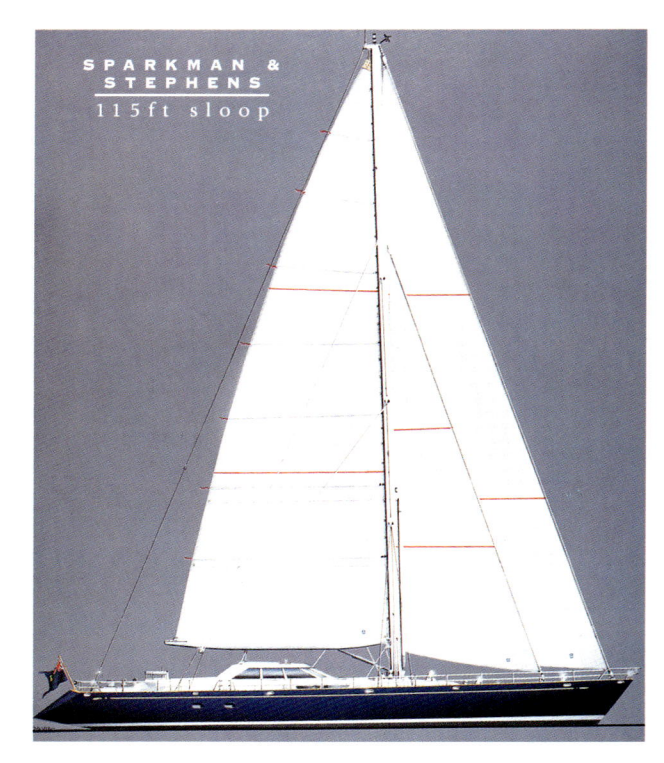

SPARKMAN & STEPHENS
115ft sloop

SPARKMAN & STEPHENS
93ft Marguerite

ZURN
50ft sport cruiser

ANDREW WINCH DESIGN

This English designer has a reputation for traditional interiors and under construction at Feadship is *Cakewalk,* a 204ft (62m) world cruiser, while Oceanco has *Avalon,* a 161ft (49m) motoryacht for delivery in mid-2000. Other projects include the 125ft (38m) Langan-designed Victoria of Strathearn ketch at Alloy Yachts and, at Royal Huisman, the 112ft (34m) Frers sloop *Unfurled* and the 153ft (46m) ketch *Erica XII* by Hood Design. Due for 2003 delivery is *Scheherazade,* a 151ft (46m) ketch by Bruce King under construction at Hodgdon Yachts.

ZURN YACHT DESIGN

Under principal Douglas Zurn, this naval architecture firm turns out both power and sailing yachts, including the Shelter Island 38ft (11m) Runabout for musician Billy Joel which, with Down East styling, has proven popular with more than 17 sold. A larger version, the Shelter Island 50, is under construction, and the Explorer series of high performance trawler yachts from 57ft (17m) to 65ft (20m) are being built in New Zealand. An 85ft (26m) pilothouse sloop for world cruising is also starting construction in 2000.

and marine engineering, with over 2600 designs to their credit including many America's Cup winners. Recently launched was the 195ft (59m) *La Baronessa* at Palmer Johnson, which was the largest aluminum yacht ever built. Under construction is a 118ft (36m) performance sloop at Derecktor, and a 93ft (28m) ketch at Vitters. In the design stages is a 150ft (46m) trideck motor-yacht to be built at Palmer Johnson.

★ DESIGNERS

Merrill-Stevens Dry Dock

Complete Repair, Maintenance and Refits...
Reverse Osmosis Watermakers, Vosper and Naiad Stabilizers,
Complete Brokerage and Charter Services

Since 1885, **Merrill-Stevens** has been recognized 'round the world as the premier yacht repair and maintenance facility.

Year after year, season after season, the world's most prestigious yachts are meticulously maintained by **Merrill-Stevens'** highly trained and dedicated shipwrights.

A few of the yachts on which we've worked:

HORIZON	SHAMWARI
HIGHLANDER	BATTERED BULL
LADY ALLISON	PARLEY FREEMAN HARRIS
GALLIANT LADYS	EMBARK
BLACKHAWK	MALANA STAR
BLUE DANUBE	KATRION
ENTERPRISE IV & V	LA APRILLIA
INTREPID	PERFECT PRESCRIPTION
LADY ADIVA	ZOPILOTE
SOUTHERLY	FORIN SEA
IL VAGABONDO	SEA CREST
BLUE ATTRACTION	MOECCA

1270 NW 11th Street, Miami, Florida 33125 Phone: (305) 324-5211 Fax: (305) 326-8911
Contact Ron Baker, Tom Dinan, or Walter Richardson

Directory

DIRECTORY

CONTACT INFORMATION

KEY TO CATEGORY SYMBOLS

B	Builder
BMA	Builder's Marketing Agent
NA	Naval Architect
YS	Yacht Services
D	Interior Designer
BR	Yacht Broker
C	Charter Broker
O	Other

TELEPHONE NUMBERS

Please note that telephone numbers are written in International Notation, with the national code number prefixed with a '+'. To call foreign numbers you must first dial your own country's International Access Code—i.e. 011 if you are in the United States, or 00 if you are in the UK—and omit any number within brackets. If the number is within your own country you should omit the number prefixed with a '+' and include the bracketed numbers.

E-mail (Em) addresses may be printed on two lines in The Directory but when used they should always be typed without breaks.

A

Abeking & Rasmussen
1600 SE 17th Street, Suite 409
Fort Lauderdale, FL 33316
Tel (954) 522-4007
Fax (954) 522-1161

Also:

Abeking & Rasmussen
Schiffs und Yachtwerft,
An der Fahre
27809 Lemwerder
Germany
Tel +49 (0) 421-6733532
Fax +49 (0) 421-6733115
Em info@abeking.com

Admiral Marine Works
2140 W.18th Street
Port Angeles, WA 98363
Tel (360) 452-5833
Fax (360) 457-9767
Em admrlde@olympus.net

Advanced Yachts
326 First Street, Suite 32
Annapolis, MD 21403
Tel (410) 626-0100
Fax (410) 626-2700
Em sales@advanced yachts.com

Advanced Yachts is the exclusive North and South American distributor for Prout catamarans from England and Venturer catamarans from Australia. Prout's magnificent Panther 64 combines revolutionary technology with unbridled luxury.
BMA, YS, BR

Alaska Diesel Electric, Inc.
PO Box 70543
4420 14th Avenue NW
Seattle, WA 98107-0543
Tel (206) 789-3880
Fax (206) 782-5455
Em ade@northern-lights.com
YS

Alden, John G., Naval Architects
89 Commercial Wharf
Boston, MA 02110
Tel (617) 227-9480
Fax (617) 523-5465
Em aldendesign@worldnet.att.net
www.aldendesigns.com

Alfa Laval
955 Mearns Road
Warminster, PA 18974
Tel (215) 443-4000
Fax (215) 957-4859
Em www.us.alfalaval.com

Alfa Laval offers the key technologies: separation, heat transfer and fluid handling as products, systems and services to customers throughout the world. With our ambition to be the world leader in our key areas, we help to make industry more efficient, to save natural resources and to protect the environment.
YS

Alliance Marine, Inc.
2608 N. Ocean Blvd.
Pompano Beach, FL 33062
Tel (954) 941-5000
Fax (954) 782-4911
www.alncmarine@aol.com
BR

Alliance Marine Risk Managers, Inc.
1400 Old Country Road, Suite 307
Westbury, NY 11590
Tel (516) 333-7000
Tel (800) 976-2676
Fax (516) 333-9529

Consultation and arrangement of insurance for large yachts worldwide.
YS

Allied Marine
Superyacht Division
1441 SE 16th Street
Fort Lauderdale, FL 33316
Tel (954) 462-7424
Fax (954) 462-0756

Alstom Engines Ltd.
Hythe Hill
Colchester, Essex
England, CO1 2HW
Tel +44 1206 795 151
Fax +44 1206 797 869

Alstom Engines is a manufacturer of a range of engines for marine duties. The Paxman VP185 range is compact, with excellent fuel economy and long service intervals—ideal for the propulsion of superyachts. The top of the range 18VP185 is rated at 4,000 kwb at 1950 r/min.
YS

American Bow Thruster
517-A Martin Avenue
Rohnert Park, CA 94928
Tel (707) 586-3155
Fax (707) 586-3159

American Marine Model Gallery
12 Derby Square
Salem, MA 01970
Tel (978) 745-5777
Fax (978) 745-5778
Em wall@shipmodel.com

The prestigious American Marine Model Gallery is appropriately located in historic Salem, Massachusetts, one of America's busiest seaports and maritime centers during the Great Age of Sail. Here, on view, is an extensive selection of one-of-a-kind ship models built by internationally acclaimed marine model artists. Custom-made models of historic ships, contemporary vessels, or modern yachts are a specialty and may be commissioned. Restorations, appraisals, display units and accessories are also available.

Anderson Fine Scale Replicas
405 Osage Drive
Derby, KS 67037
Tel (800) 314-7447
Fax (316) 788-8904
Em anderent@msn.com

Manufacturer of museum-quality custom model replicas. Your favorite yacht, boat or any marine vessel can be duplicated from photographs. Custom models can be created in any size or paint scheme.
YS

Anita's Interiors, Inc.
429 Seabreeze Blvd., Suite 217
Fort Lauderdale, FL 33316
Tel   (954) 525-3050
Fax (954) 525-3031

Specializing in interior design, interior styling, and space planning for yachts. Anita Unger, President of Anita's Interiors, Inc. has the following credentials: professional member of the International Interior Design Association, certified listing in the International Edition of Who's Who In Interior Design, licensed Interior Designer in the state of Florida, ID-0003708.
D

Antibes Yachtwear
1532 Cordova Road
Fort Lauderdale, FL 33316
Tel   (954) 761-7666
Fax (954) 779-1144
Em   info@antibesyachtwear.com

Antibes Yachtwear is an American corporation that provides uniform and logo apparel to the marine industry. Our offices and warehouse are in Fort Lauderdale, Florida, but our customers are worldwide.
YS

Apollo Lighting Studio
1635 South Miami Road, Suite 4
Fort Lauderdale, FL 33316
Tel   (954) 524-3030
Fax (954) 524-9837
Em   futuralt@icanect.net

Manufacturer and supplier of custom lighting, featuring full line of line and low voltage recessed lights, transformers, and bulbs. Also, product line includes fiber optics, led, and electroluminescent lighting.
YS

Apollonio Naval Architecture
PMB 514
1225 East Sunset Drive
Bellingham, WA 98226-3529
Tel   (360) 733-6859
Fax (360) 715-9474
Em   napollo@az.com

Leading-edge yacht and commercial craft design. Engineering, styling and space planning for a wide range of unique and advanced craft including catamarans, SWATH's, and hydrofoils. Licensed Professional Engineers. Versatile and flexible. Specialists in hull form, ride comfort, propulsion, structure, and noise control.
NA, D

Aqua Air Manufacturing
1050 East 9th Street
Hialeah, FL 33010
Tel   (305) 884-8363
Fax (305) 883-8549
Em   pt@aquaa.com

Manufacturer of chillwater systems for megayacht air-conditioning. Also walk-in coolers.
YS

Architectural Alliance
800 East Broward Blvd. #608
Fort Lauderdale, FL 33301
Tel   (954) 764-8858
Fax (954) 764-0731
Em   archall@bellsouth.net

Specialties in interior design/space planning, and finish specifications. Computer generated drawings and renderings available. Interior design development through fabrication and installation.
D

Ardell Yacht & Ship Brokers
1550 SE 17th Street
Fort Lauderdale, FL 33316
Tel   (954) 525-7637
Fax (954) 527-1292
Em   yachts@ardell-fl.com

With offices in Fort Lauderdale and Newport Beach, California, Ardell enjoys an excellent reputation of credibility in the yacht brokerage industry with 36 years of dedicated service to our clients. Ardell's first-hand knowledge of both international and domestic markets ensures your confidence in a team of brokers who work well together. Please visit our online list of yachts for sale and charter, then contact either of our offices for more information. We look forward to your inquiry.
BR, C

Also:

Ardell Yacht & Ship Brokers
2101 West Coast Highway
Newport Beach, CA 92663
Tel   (949) 642-5735
Fax (949) 642-9884
Em   yachts@ardell-ca.com

Ardeo Design, Inc.
755 Winslow Way East, Suite 303
Bainbridge Island, WA 98110
Tel   (206) 855-9027
Fax (206) 855-9028
Em   scott@ardeodesign.com
       www.ardeodesign.com

Yacht interior designer Scott Cole chose the firm's name, Ardeo Design, with his customary attention to detail. Ardeo is the Latin word for "passion," which describes this design team's commitment to excellence. This extends from the smallest detail to the most important element of a yacht's design: the client.
D

Joseph Artese Design
16003 34th Avenue NE
Seattle, WA 98155
Tel   (206) 365-4326
Fax (206) 365-7009
Em   jartesedesign@compuserve.com
D

Astondoa Americas, Ltd.
966 Fern Drive
Delray Beach, FL 33483
Tel   (561) 276-7858
Fax (561) 276-2699

Astro-Pure
3025 SW 2nd Avenue
Fort Lauderdale, FL 33315
Tel   (954) 832-0630
Fax (954) 832-0729

Manufactures complete line of water treatment equipment: purifiers, filters, decalcifiers, reverse osmosis, iron filters, chemical feed equipment, sizes for portable, point of use, central, commercial and industrial. Custom manufactures and offers private labels countertop units.
YS

Atlas Energy Systems
5101 NW 21st Avenue Suite 520
Fort Lauderdale, FL 33309
Tel   (954) 735-6767
Fax (954) 735-7676
Em   mikep@shorpower.com
       www.shorpower.com

Atlas Energy Systems manufactures and distributes one of the most complete and extensive lines of energy products worldwide. Atlas' primary products are the unique ShorPOWER Frequency and Power Conversion systems and the TecPOWER Marine Electrical Switchboards.
O

Avalon Marine Electronics
1598 Cordova Road
Fort Lauderdale, FL 33316
Tel   (954) 527-4047
Fax (954) 728-9465
Em   avalonmar@aol.com

We are authorized dealers for all major manufacturers of marine electronics, including Furuno, Raytheon, and Northstar. We offer competitive pricing, custom installations, and service. Avalon Marine Electronics has been providing sales and service since 1979.
YS

B

Baglietto, Inc.
First Union Financial Center
200 S. Biscayne Blvd. Suite 4815
Miami, FL 33131
Tel   (305) 373-7016
Fax (305) 373-7017
Em   salussolia@aol.com

Arthur M Barbeito & Associates
4967 SW 74 Court
Miami, FL 33155
Tel   (305) 669-3211
Fax (305) 669-3228

Jonathan Quinn Barnett Ltd.
3201 Fairview Avenue East
Seattle, WA 98102
Tel   (206) 322-2152
Fax (206) 322-2153
Em   jqbltd@ix.netcom.com

Bartram & Brakenhoff LLC
2 Marina Plaza
Goat Island
Newport, RI 02840
Tel (401) 846-7355
Fax (401) 847-6329
Em bartbrak@aol.com

Bartram & Brakenhoff LLC specializes in the marketing, sales, charter, and donation of high quality and high-caliber sailing, and power and luxury yachts, (new and used). Established in 1967, Bartram and Brakenhoff offers 2 locations for client convenience: Newport, Rhode Island and Fort Lauderdale, Florida. Professional & personalized service since 1967.
BMA, YS, BR, C

Beard Marine Air Conditioning and Refrigeration, Inc.
624 SW 24th Street
Fort Lauderdale, FL 33315
Tel (954) 463-2288
Fax (954) 527-0362
Em Info@beardmarine.com

Beard Marine Air Conditioning and Refrigeration, Inc. is based in Fort Lauderdale with affiliated offices in Palm Beach and Savannah. We are dedicated to designing and producing high quality air-conditioning, refrigeration, and watermaker systems for the yachting industry. Beard Marine has earned a reputation for providing superior service and customer satisfaction worldwide.
YS

Bell Design Group
2125 Western Avenue #200
Seattle, WA 98121
Tel (206) 728-9990
Fax (206) 728-9996
Em belldesign@msn.com

Bell Design Group provides comprehensive, state-of-the-art interior design services using computer images, 3D modeling, composite materials and high-tech construction techniques. It delivers beautiful design and premium value, while making customer satisfaction the top priority. Founder Judy Bell-Davis has 26 years experience as a design professional.
D

Benetti Shipyard
Via Michele Coppino, 104
Viareggio
Italy 55049
Tel +39 0584-3821
Fax +39 0584-396232
Em azimut.benetti@telcen.caen.it

Builders of luxury motoryachts from 115 to 230ft. Last launchings: Ambrosia (177ft) Queen M (164ft) Benetti Classic (115ft). Next launchings: Lionheart (164ft, June 1999), Felicity (230ft, July 1999)
B

Bennett Brothers Yachts
1701 J.E.L. Wade Drive
Wilmington, NC 28401
Tel (910) 772-9277
Fax (910) 772-1642
Em bby@wilmington.net

Bennett Brothers Yachts is located in a brand new facility, The Cape Fear Marina. We are a full-service repair yard with the same staff of skilled craftsmen who work on our custom-building projects. We offer fine yacht brokerage and specialize in selling world-class cruising boats, both power and sail.
B, YS, BR

Richard Bertram, Inc.
3660 NW 21 Street
Miami, FL 33142
Tel (305) 633-9761
Fax (305) 634-9071

Also:

Richard Bertram, Inc.
850 NE 3rd Street, Suite 206
Dania, FL 33004
Tel (954) 925-9070
Fax (954) 925-9540
Em rbi@bertramyacht.com

Also:

Richard Bertram, Inc.
801 Seabreeze Blvd.
Fort Lauderdale, FL 33316
Tel (954) 467-8405
Fax (954) 763-2675

Donald Blount and Associates, Inc.
Naval Architects/Marine Engineers
1316 Yacht Drive, Suite 305
Chesapeake, VA 23327
Tel (757) 545-3700
Fax (757) 545-8227

Sylvia Bolton Design
1220 Westlake Avenue North
Seattle, WA 98109
Tel (206) 217-0863
Fax (206) 286-7633

Boston Yacht Haven
87 Commercial Wharf
Boston, MA 02110
Tel (617) 523-7352
Fax (617) 523-2270
Em bostonyachthaven@earthlink.com
Marina, YS

Bounty International
1535 SE 17th Street, Suite 201
Fort Lauderdale, FL 33316
Tel (954) 524-9005
Fax (954) 524-7009
Em brokerage@bountyintl.com

Bounty International serves the major segments of the marine industry through its worldwide operations, with its US headquarters located in Fort Lauderdale, Florida. Staffed with specialists in each area of operations, Bounty International is dedicated to providing world-class service to its clients and customers.
BR, C

Bradford Marine, Inc.
3151 State Road 84
Fort Lauderdale, FL 33312
Tel (954) 791-3800
Fax (954) 583-9938

Philippe Briand Yacht Architecture
61 Avenue Marillac
La Ville en Bois
La Rochelle
France 17000
Tel +33 (5) 46 50 5766
Fax +33 (5) 46 50 57 94
Em 100445.1543@compuserve.com
NA

Broward Marine
750 NE 7th Avenue
Dania, FL 33004
Tel (954) 522-1701
Fax (954) 725-8777
Em browardship@aol.com

Custom aluminum yacht builder, 85ft to 155ft
B

Also:

Broward Yacht Sales
1535 SE 17th Street, Suite 202
Fort Lauderdale, FL 33316
Tel (954) 763-8201
Fax (954) 763-9079
Em browardys@aol.com

Since 1988 Broward Yacht Sales, under the direction of Ken Denison, has listed and sold 93 Broward motoryachts, more than any other worldwide brokerage firm. Broward Yacht Sales also specializes in other world-class motoryachts, including Feadship and Oceanco.
BR

Luke Brown & Associates
1500 Cordova Road #200
Fort Lauderdale, FL 33316
Tel (954) 525-6617
Fax (954) 525-6626
Em lukebrownassoc@att.net
BR, C

Burger Boat Company
1811 Spring Street
Manitowoc, WI 54220
Tel (920) 684-1600
Fax (920) 684-6555

Burger Yacht Sales
17th Street Quay
1515 SE 17th Street, Suite 129
Fort Lauderdale, FL 33316
Tel (954) 463-1400
Fax (954) 463-3100
Em toddyachts@aol.com

Nigel Burgess Ltd
Le PanoramaFL
57 Rue Grimaldi
MC 98000 Monaco
Tel +377-93-50-22-64
Fax +377-93-25-15-89
Em monaco@nigelburgess.com

Also:

Nigel Burgess Ltd.
16/17 Pall Mall
London SW1Y 5LU
Great Britian
Tel +44 (0) 171-766-4300
Fax +44 (0) 171-766-4329
Em london@nigedlburgess.com

C

C & L Insurance
7301 W. Palmetto Park Road
Boca Raton, FL 33433
Tel (561) 395-3730
Fax (561) 395-4239

Marine insurance including, yachts, marinas, boat builders, ship yards, dealers and marine-related industries.
YS

CBI Navi SpA
Via Giannessi-via Pescatori
55049 Viareggio
Lucca
Italy
Tel +39 (0) 584-388192
Fax +39 (0) 584-388060
Em info@cbinavi.com

**CMI
(California Multi-hull
International Yacht Sales)**
1235 Scott Street
San Diego, CA 92106
Tel (619) 222-9694
Fax (619) 222-9693
Em mail@cmiys.com

Consultants in the purchase of the world's finest luxury catamarans; and power, sail, and fast motorsail.
BR

CNB America, Inc.
2246 SE 17th Street
Fort Lauderdale, FL 33316
Tel (954) 763-9891
Fax (954) 763-9851
Em cnbusa@icaneat.net

US representation for the CNB Yard (Construction Navale Bordeaux), builder of aluminum and composite yachts 70 to 150ft. Also, international yacht brokers, specializing in the sale, management, and refit of sailing yachts 60ft plus.
BMA, BR

Also:

CNB
162 Quai De Brazza
Bordeaux 33100
France
Tel +33 (0) 557-80-8550
Fax +33 (0) 557-80-8551
Em cnb@cnb.fr

In 1996 CNB became the custom yachts and work boats division of the Beneteau Group including all custom naval construction such as motor and sailing yachts from 60 to 150ft, passengers ferry and fishing boats as well as catamarans. In 11 years, CNB has become a renowned builder for the quality of its aluminum construction and now is expecting the development of high-tech composite construction.
B, D

Cable & Wireless Caribbean Cellular
PO Box 1516, 1 Independence Drive
St. John's, Antigua
West Indies
Tel (268) 480-3650
Fax (268) 480-3614
Em info@caribcell.com
    www.caribcell.com

Cable & Wireless Caribbean Cellular is the premier cellular phone service provider throughout the Eastern Caribbean, Jamaica, and The Cayman Islands. The company offers cellular sales, service, and rentals at prices lower than satellite rates. Some locations offer professionally-installed cell phones, cable and antennas. For more information visit us at our web site.
YS

Camper & Nicholsons International
450 Royal Palm Way
Palm Beach, FL 33480
Tel (561) 655-2121
Fax (561) 655-2202
Em info@pal.cnyachts.com

Also:

Camper & Nicholsons International
The Courts
141 Alton Road
Miami Beach, FL 33139
Tel (305) 604-9191
Fax (305) 604-9196
Em: info@mia.cnyachts.com

Also:

Camper & Nicholsons International
25 Bruton Street
London W1X 7DB
Great Britain
Tel +44 (0) 171-491-2950
Fax +44 (0) 171-629-2068
Em info@loncnyachts.com

Also:

Camper & Nicholsons International
Les Princes
7 Avenue d'Ostende
MC 98000
Monaco
Tel +377 97.97.77.00
Fax +377 93.50.25.08
Em info@mon.cnyachts.com

Also:

Camper & Nicholsons International
Av. San Jeronimo 273, Local 21
Suite MX067-382
Tizapan San Angel
Mexico CP 10908
Tel +525 2814545
Fax. +525 2815926
Em al@mia.cnyachts.com

CNI'S global office network delivers its clients an unrivaled range of services in the most professional, ethical, and discreet manner possible. CNI is a full-service company, with emphasis on larger yachts. CNI's divisions interact to provide complete customer satisfaction.
YS, BR, C

Cantieri Di Pisa SpA
Via Aurelia Sud Km. 334
Pisa, 56121
Italy
Tel +39 050-500739
Fax +39 050-500799

M. Castedo Architects
307 Seventh Avenue, Suite 2406
New York, NY 10001
Tel (212) 255-4111
Fax (212) 929-7350
Em mcastedo@archonline.com

M. Castedo Architects is a New York City-based architecture and interior design firm involved with high-end residential projects and motoryacht styling/interior design. Recently completed projects include a total retrofit of a 150ft Benetti consisting of redesigned new interiors and a 20ft fishing cockpit extension.
D

Castlemain Yachts Inc.
757 SE 17th Street #780
Fort Lauderdale, FL 33316
Tel (954) 760-4730
Fax (954) 760-4737
Em charter@castlemain-yachts.com

Chartering yachts worldwide to discerning clients. Yacht management.
YS, C

Caterpillar Inc.
PO Box 610
Mossville, IL 61552-0610
Tel (800) 321-7332
Tel (309) 578-2559
Fax (309) 578-2559
Em Cat-Power@Cat.com
    www.Cat-Engines.com

Caterpillar has been manufacturing marine diesels since 1939. Caterpillar offers 27 different engine models, 12 featuring state-of-the-art electronic engine control. Marine propulsion engines are rated from 85-9655 bhp (63-7200 bkW); marine generator sets from 50-5200 ekW; and marine auxiliary engines from 70-7200 bhp (50-5400 bkW) — all backed and serviced by the same company.
O

Cavendish White
4 Bramber Court
Bramber Road
London W14 9PW
Great Britain
Tel +44 171-381-7600
Fax +44 171-381-7601
Em sales@cavwhite.demon.co.uk

Cello Music & Film Systems
1535 SE 17th Street Suite 111
Fort Lauderdale, FL 33316
Tel (954) 525-4877
Fax (954) 525-2087
Em greg.mcintyre@cello-us.com

Cello Music & Film Systems, Inc. designs and develops theater, audio, entertainment and integration systems for luxury yachts, homes, and professional entertainment/communications applications. Included in their service is complete architectural drawings and installation of turnkey custom audio, video, and automation systems. They also manufacture and distribute some of the visual components of the systems related to their projects.
O

Cheoy Lee Shipyards North America
1497 SE 17th Street
Fort Lauderdale, FL 33316
Tel (954) 527-0999
Fax (954) 527-2887
Em sueg@cheoyleena.com

New yacht construction, custom and production up to 200ft. Brokerage sales.
B, BMA, BR

Christensen Shipyards
4400 SE Columbia Way
Vancouver, WA 98661
Tel (360) 695-3238
Fax (360) 695-3252
Em info@christensenyachts.com

Christensen has established itself as the world leader by building more composite megayachts over 120ft than any other shipyard in the world. All are built on-site and comply with ABS Classification, AMS and European MCS.
B

Codecasa
Via Amendola
Viareggio
Lucca 55049
Italy
Tel +39 (0) 584-383221
Fax +39 (0) 584-383531

Concord Marine Electronics
2233 South Federal Highway
Fort Lauderdale, FL 33316
Tel (954) 779-1100
Fax (954) 779-7090
Em info@concordelectronics.com

Sales, service, and installation of marine electronics — navigation, communication and entertainment. Specializing in computer integration and data transfer.
YS

Guy Couach
Rue de I'Yser
Gujan Mestras, 33470
France
Tel +33 55-622-3550
Fax +33 55-666-0820
Em couach@couach.com
www.couach.com

Cox Marine
PO Box 1479
Newport, RI 02840
Tel (401) 845-9666
Fax (401) 845-2666
Em cox-marine@edgenet.net

Cox Marine has two main focuses: charter broker for power and sail yachts in cruising destinations worldwide, and charter marketing and management for a select group of large luxury-crewed charter yachts.
C

Cramm America, Inc.
PO Box 460520
Fort Lauderdale, FL 33346-0520
Tel (954) 462-3650
Fax (954) 462-3620

Hydraulic cranes, steering, windlasses, passarelles, boarding ladders, watertight doors.
YS

Crescent Custom Yachts, Inc.
111 Avenue C, Suite 101
Snohomish, WA 98290
Tel (360) 563-0567
Fax (360) 563-0403
Em brent_murphy@bc.symptico.ca
www.crescent-custom-yachts.com

Crescent Custom Yachts is a manufacturer of custom fiberglass motoryachts from 95 to 140ft. As a builder of custom yachts, Crescent has been called upon to build full-classed vessels by both the American Bureau of Shipping and Bureau Veritas. The manufacturing and repair/refit site is located just 10 minutes from Vancouver International Airport and is the newest shipyard in North America.
B, YS, BMA

Crestar Yachts Ltd.
Colette Court
125 Sloane Street
London SWIX 9AU
Tel +44 (0) 171-730-9962
 Toll free from US (800) 222-9985
Fax +44 (0) 171-824-8691
Em crestaryachts@mail.com

The sale and charter of yachts from 70ft in worldwide destinations including the Mediterranean, Caribbean, Bahamas, Indian Ocean, Australasia, the Far East, etc.
C

Crown Ltd.
1001 Staley Avenue
Savannah, GA 31405
Tel (912) 352-0715
Fax (912) 352-0726
Em malcolm@crownltd.com
www.crownltd.com

Since 1981 Crown Ltd. had been the world leader in design and fabrication of helm chairs, stools, table tops, and pedestals for the megayacht industry. Our products are the perfect blend of handcrafted quality and beautiful styling that can be customized according to your needs. Our service is second to none. Our website has 30 pages of downloadable autocad drawings of products.
O

Cruisair
PO Box 15299
Richmond, VA 23227
Tel (804) 746-1313
Fax (804) 746-7248

In 1999 Cruisair merged with Marine Air to form a new company, Taylor Made Environmental Systems.

Custom Boat Blinds, Inc.
2955 State Road 84, Suite I
Fort Lauderdale, FL 33312
Tel. (954) 583-3997
Fax (954) 583-3689
Em boatblinds@boatblinds.com

World leader in custom wood and exotic-wood blinds, plantation shutters for yachts. AC Louvers in exotic wood with exclusive system patented. Manufacture for Palmer Johnson, Bertram, Ronin, Buddy-Davis, Broward, etc. with offices in São Paulo, Brazil, and Nice, France.
YS

D

DMP America
PO Box 460520
Fort Lauderdale, FL 33346-0520
Tel (954) 462-3650
Fax (954) 462-3620
Em dmpamerica@dmpamerica.com

Marine electronic monitoring, safety, and control systems. Marine computers with LCD Displays.
YS

Dahlgren Duck & Associates
2554 Tarpley, Suite 110
Carrollton, TX 75006
Tel (972) 478-5991
Fax (972) 478-5996

DD&A specializes in special dinner services for the yachting industry that includes china, crystal, flatware and table, bed and bath linens. Also, custom sun care and bath care amenities. DDA represents most of the world's finest manufacturers, as well as highly-skilled artisans in Europe.
YS

Darling Yachts, Inc.
3732 Utica Pike
Jeffersonville, IN 47130
Tel (812) 288-8997
Em lamp1020@aol.com

Datastar Marine Products, Inc.
Yacht Harbor 100
18 Gostick Place
North Vancouver, BC
Canada
Tel (604) 990-6900
Fax (604) 990-6890

Luiz DeBasto Design, Inc.
444 Brickell Avenue, Suite 828
Miami, FL 33131
Tel (305) 373-1500
Fax (305) 377-0900
Em luizbasto@aol.com

Our office, based in Miami, specializes exclusively in the design of luxury yachts — custom, production and commercial boats. Over the years we have been commissioned to design a wide variety of vessels in terms of size, styling and type.
NA, D

Guido De Groot Design
Hogeword 122 2311 HT
Leiden
Holland
Tel +31 (0) 715663040
Fax +31 (0) 715663039

DeJong & Lebet, Inc.
1734 Emerson Street
Jacksonville, FL 32207
Tel (904) 399-3673
Fax (904) 399-1522
Em dejlebna@southeast.net

DeJong & Lebet, Inc. is a full service naval architecture company, best known for its passenger vessel designs. The 31-year old company also designs large yacht and yacht conversions. SWATH vessels are a specialty.
NA

Delta Marine
1608 South 96th Street
Seattle, WA 98108
Tel (206) 763-2383
Fax (206) 762-2627
Em info@deltamarine.com

As specialists in large yacht (100 to 200ft) fiberglass and metal construction, Delta combines new technologies and creative ideas with proven building techniques. All yachts are custom-designed, engineered and constructed on-site in full-service facilities including mechanical, electrical, composite, metal cabinet and paint workshops.
B

Delta Marine International
PO Box 22070
Fort Lauderdale, FL 33335-2070
Tel (954) 791-0909
Fax (954) 321-8145

Delta "T" Systems
PO Box 9159
Jupiter, FL 33468-9159
Tel (561) 694-2252
Fax (561) 694-2214
Em info@deltatsystems.com

Delta "T" Systems produces custom-designed engine compartment ventilation systems that improve engine performance and extend engine life. The systems include fans, moisture eliminators, fire dampers, and controls. The company offers a compact computerized control unit that automatically regulates and optimizes air intake and exhaust, and provides warnings of dangerous conditions.
YS

Derecktor Gunnell, Inc.
775 Taylor Lane
Dania, FL 33004
Tel (954) 920-5756
Fax (954) 925-1146
Em maidgi@aol.com

Derecktor Gunnell, Inc. was founded in 1967 and has grown to be one of the premier yacht facilities in the world. For yachts from 60 to 175ft, whether it be painting the bottom, adding a winged keel, or fine tuning your recently purchased megayacht (from a hull extension to complete interior design package to suit your tastes), Derecktor Gunnell, Inc. has the facilities, manpower, and experience to do it right.
YS

Derecktor Shipyards
311 East Boston Post Road
Mamaroneck, NY 10543
Tel (914) 698-5020
Fax (914) 698-6596
Em general@derecktor.com
www.derecktor.com

Since 1947 Derecktor has been building yachts of the highest quality. From America's Cup Racers to today's superyachts, Derecktor-built yachts can be found all over the world.
B

Design Alliance Ltd.
3911 Southridge
West Vancouver, BC,
Canada V7V 3H9
Te (604) 926-9408
Fax (604) 926-9405
Em designalliance@home.com

Design Alliance's activities cover the following areas: interior design, exterior design and styling, construction consultation, concept development, new and refit yachts and charter vessels, and on occasion will take-on residential commissions.
D

Destiny Yachts
1445 SE 16th Street
Fort Lauderdale, FL 33301
Tel (954) 462-7424
Fax (954) 462-0756

DETCO Marine (Sterling Coatings)
Box 1246
Newport Beach, CA 92659
Tel (800) 845-0023
Fax (949) 548-5986
Em detcomar@aol.com

DETCO/STERLING markets premier liner/polyurethane coatings, crystal varnish, and caulking compounds worldwide for megayacht application. High gloss, gloss retention, and primers for every surface are product highlights.
O

Detroit Diesel Corporation
13400 Outer Drive, West
Detroit, MI 48239-4001
Tel (313) 592-5000
Fax (313) 592-8176

Detroit Diesel is engaged in the design, manufacture, sale and service of heavy-duty diesel engines. Detroit Diesel offers a complete line of diesel engines from 28 to 10,000 horsepower for the on-highway truck, construction, mining and industrial, automotive coach and bus, marine, power generation, and military market. These markets are serviced directly through a worldwide network of more that 2500 authorized distributors and dealers.
O

Devonport Yachts
Devonport Royal Dockyard
Pylmouth, DevonPL1 4SG
Great Britain
Tel +44 (0) 1752-553311
Fax +44 (0) 1752-554883
Em devonport.co.uk
B

Diaship North America, Inc.
1535 SE 17th Street, Suite 103
Fort Lauderdale, FL 33316
Tel (954) 459-9996
Fax (954) 459-9997
Em diaship@gate.net
BMA, BR

Doyle Sailmakers, Inc.
89 Front Street
Marblehead, MA 01945
Tel (781) 639-1490
Fax (781) 639-1497
Em doyle@doylesails.com

Doyle Sailmakers is a worldwide sail loft specializing in the manufacture and service of megayacht sails. Our experience with a wide range of megayachts, including the classic J-Class, enables Doyle Sails to offer knowledgeable advice in design, cloth selection, and construction detailing. Contact Robbie Doyle to discuss your requirements.
O

Dynasea International, Inc.
511 Rutile Drive
Ponte Verde Beach, FL 32082
Tel (904) 356-0604
Fax (904) 543-0836

E

Espinosa
1320 South Federal Highway, Suite 216
Stuart, FL 34994
Tel (561) 287-4925
Fax (561) 287-4858

F

Bruce Farr & Associates, Inc.
613 Third Street, Suite 20
PO Box 4964
Annapolis, MD 21403-0964
Tel (410) 267-0780
Fax (410) 268-0553
Em info@farrdesign.com

Feadship America
801 Seabreeze Avenue
Bahia Mar
Fort Lauderdale, FL 33316
Tel (954) 761-1830
Fax (954) 761-3412

Feadship
PO Box 70
2110 AB Aerdenhout
Netherlands
Tel +31 23524 7000
Fax +31 23524 8639
Em info@feadship.nc

Design and build the most perfect luxury yachts in the world.
B, NA

Ferretti of America
2300 E. Las Olas Blvd.
Fort Lauderdale, FL 33301
Tel (954) 527-1126
Fax (954) 527-5809

Also:

Ferretti
Via Ansaldo 5
Forli, 47100
Italy
Tel +39 (0) 543-474411
Fax +39 (0) 543-782410

Ferretti Custom Line
Via Ansaldo 5
Forli, 47100
Italy
Tel +39 (0) 543-474411
Fax +39 (0) 543-782410

Tom Fexas Yacht Design Inc
333 Tressler Drive, Suites B & C
Stuart, FL 34994
Tel (561) 287-6558
Fax (561) 287-6810

Filtration Concepts, Inc.
2226 South Fairview
Santa Ana, CA 92706
Tel (714) 850-0123
Fax (714) 850-0955
Em info@filtrationconcepts.com
www.filtrationconcepts.com

Superyacht and commercial applications to 26,275 gallons/day. All stainless steel high pressure pumps and fittings—the highest rated pressure vessels in the marine industry. Over 2000 installations in the world. The finest yachts on the water use FCI watermakers.
O

First New England Financial
1600 SE 17th Street Suite 300
Fort Lauderdale, FL 33316
Tel (800) 380-6644
(954) 763-1089
Fax (954) 763-1055
Em www.firstnewengland.com

First New England Financial is one of the nations leaders in marine financing. We have been an active participant for over twenty years and have assisted buyers in the purchase of over a billion dollars in pleasure boat transactions.
O

Flagship Marine, Inc.
2427 SE Dixie Highway
Stuart, FL 34996
Tel (561) 283-1609
Fax (561) 283-4611
Em email@flagshipmarine.com

Manufacturer of marine air-conditioning, alarm systems, CCTV, and marine pumps. The Flagship Marine air-conditioning systems are the quietest, most efficient, and easiest to start available and are standard issue for the US and Canadian Coast Guard survival craft, the 47 MLB.
YS

Franck's Boat Company
1109 N. Northlake Way
Seattle, WA 98103
Tel (206) 632-7000
Fax (206) 632-0627

Founded in 1926. Company is now being run by the third generation of the Franck family. Our expertise is building and repairing wood and fiberglass boats.
B, YS

Fraser Yachts Worldwide
3471 Via Lido
Newport Beach, CA 92663
Tel (949) 673-5252
Fax (949) 673-8795
Em fraser@frasernb.com

Fraser Charters, Inc.
3471 Via Lido
Newport Beach, CA 92663
Tel (949) 673-5252
Fax (949) 673-8795
Em fraser@frasernb.com

Fraser Yacht Insurance Services, Inc.
3471 Via Lido
Newport Beach, CA 92663
Tel (949) 673-5252
Fax (949) 673-8795
Em fraser@frasernb.com

Fraser Yacht Management
3471 Via Lido
Newport Beach, CA 92663
Tel (949) 673-5252
Fax (949) 673-8795
Em ricks@frasernb.com

Fraser Yachts
2230 SE 17th Street
Fort Lauderdale, FL 33316
Tel (954) 463-0600
Fax (954) 763-1053
Em fraser@fraserfl.com

Also:

Fraser Yachts
1500 Westlake Avenue, North
Seattle, WA 98109
Tel (206) 282-4943
Fax (206) 285-4956

Also:

Fraser Yachts
2353 Shelter Island Drive
San Diego, CA 92106
Tel (619) 225-0588
Fax (619) 225-1325
Em frasersd@frasersd.com

Also:

Fraser Yachts
320 Harbor Drive
Clipper Yacht Harbor
Sausalito, CA 94965
Tel (415) 332-5311
Fax (415) 332-7036

Also:

Fraser Yachts
8, Quai des Sanbarbani
Port Fontvieille
MC 98000
Monaco
Tel +377 93-10-04-50
Fax +377 93-10-04-51
Em sales@frasermc.com

Fredericks/Power & Sail
201 Shipyard Way, Suite A/3
Newport Beach, CA 92663
Tel (949) 723-5330
Fax (949) 723-5332
Em fredericks@mall.com

Specialize in brokerage of yachts, both power and sail, as well as project coordination and management for new yacht construction.
YS, BR

Freeman Marine Equipment, Inc.
28336 Hunter Creek Road
Gold Beach, OR 97444
Tel (541) 247-7078
Fax (541) 247-2114

Freeman Marine is recognized worldwide as the leader in the design and manufacture of marine closures, supplying premium quick-acting hatches and custom lens hatches, as well as custom and standard portlights, windows, and doors. Freeman's broad product line includes hinged weather-tight and watertight single, Dutch and French doors, as well as pantograph doors, and single and dual axis sliding doors. Freeman Marine provides marine closures to the finest fast ships, megayachts, commercial workboats, and government vessels worldwide.
O

Ken Freivokh Design
Ash Studio, Crocker Hill
Fareham
Hampshire PO17 5DP
Great Britain
Tel +44 (0) 1329-832514
Fax +44 (0) 1329-833326
Em all@freivokh.com

FRY Associates, Inc. (FRYCO)
5420 Waddell Hollow Road
Franklin, TN 37064-9422
Tel (615) 591-8455
Fax (615) 591-8485
Em frycomar@aol.com

Edward D. Fry, Marine Engineer license 3833473, BSBA, Southern Illinois University. FRYCO designs vessels up to 300ft and specializes in megayachts. Computer models are used for speed production and hydrostatics. Ed Fry's building background assures practical, economic designs with emphasis placed on reliability and serviceability. Worldwide clientele.
NA

G

GMC Marine Ltd.
Seestr. 15
Kilchberg-Zurich
Switzerland CH-8802
Tel +41 1-715-0400
Fax +41 1-715-0480
Em gmc@pop.agri.ch

Yacht consultants for sale and charter of megayachts worldwide. New building supervision, insurance surveyors. Consultants for yacht designs and interior decoration.
NA, YS, D, BR, C

GTH Design Techniques, Inc.
17791 Fjord Drive, Suite Z
Poulsboro, WA 98370
Tel (360) 779-1909
Fax (360) 779-6133
Em gth@tscnet.com
www.gthdesign.com

GTH Design Techniques, Inc. is a full service interior design firm marketing services to the marine industry and owners of fine yachts. GTH Services include interior architecture, space planning, styling, joiner detailing, systems integration, lighting design, exterior styling and detailing, and supply of finishes, furnishings, materials and accessories.
D

Gerard's Service en Mer
Bahia Mar Yachting Center
801 Seabreeze Boulevard
Fort Lauderdale, FL 33316
Tel (954) 523-0465
Fax (954) 523-6156
Em gerard-s@ix.netcom.com

Gerard's Service en Mer is the answer for one-stop shopping when it comes to outfitting a yacht. Gerard's has assembled and currently shows the finest merchandise from some of the world's leading manufacturers such as: Baccarat, Lalique, Christofle, Haviland & Rosenthal. Leave the details to us when selecting the perfect table setting to compliment an existing or new interior décor. For information please call 1.877.GERARDS
YS

Global Power Systems
1500 Westlake Avenue North, Suite 4
Seattle, WA 98109
Tel (206) 301-0515
Fax (206) 301-0660

We manufacture voltage, phase, and frequency converters in sizes for 8-120KVA, single or three-phase AC power.
YS

Timothy Graul Marine Design
211 North Third Avenue
PO Box 290
Sturgeon Bay, WI 54235
Tel (920) 743-5092
Fax (920) 743-7936

TGMD serves owners by designing able, no-nonsense yachts with a commercial/workboat heritage. Don't come to us for swoopy styling, but for yards and owners who demand rugged good looks and dependability, call us.
NA

Greenbay Marine
4, Pioneer Sector 1
2262 Singapore
Tel +65 861-4178
Fax +65 861-8109

Guido Perla & Associates, Inc.
720 Third Avenue, Suite 1200
Seattle, WA 98104
Tel (206) 382-3949
Fax (206) 382-2090
Em gpa@gpai.com

Guido Perla & Associates is a leading naval architecture and marine engineering firm. We provide conceptual and detail designs, shipyard and construction support, and project management for all types of vessels, from passenger to industrial and service vessels.
NA

Gulf Craft Yachts, Inc.
1846 Mooring Line Drive
Vero Beach, FL 32963
Tel (561) 745-2087
Fax (561) 745-2087

H

HMY Yacht Sales
850 NE Third Street, Suite 213
Dania Beach, FL 33004
Tel (954) 926-0400
Fax (954) 921-2543
Em hmyyachtsales@att.net

Also:

HMY Yacht Sales
2401 PGA Blvd., Suite 182
Palm Beach Gardens, FL 33410
Tel (561) 775-6000
Fax (561) 775-6006
Em hmy@flinet.com

Also:

HMY Yacht Sales
24 Patriot Point Road
Mt. Pleasant, SC 29464
Tel (843) 971-2555
Fax (843) 971-2508
Em hmysc@infoave.net

HMY has been serving the yachting world from South Florida since 1979. In addition to brokerage sales, we are new boat dealers for Cabo, Post and Viking Yachts, Viking Sport Cruisers, Cigarette by Otam, and San Lorenzo American Series. It seems like every business says "Customer Service is our number one priority." But then they aren't able to prove it to their customers. Well, at HMY we say it, too, but the difference is, we mean it and we'll prove it!
YS, BR

Hall of Fame Marina
435 Seabreeze Blvd.
Fort Lauderdale, FL 33316
Tel (954) 764-3975
Fax (954) 779-3658

Open slip dockage for boats from 40 to 135ft with 50amp, 220v and 100amp 208v single and 3 phase electricity. We accommodate up to 9ft depth and are adjacent to the beach shopping.
YS

Halter Marine Group
13085 Seaway Road
Gulfport, MS 39503
Tel (252) 638-5550
Fax (252) 638-6844

Harbour Towne Marina
801 NE Third Street
Dania Beach, FL 33004
Tel (954) 926-0300
Fax (954) 922-5485
Em hrbrtowne@aol.com

One and a half miles from Fort Lauderdale International Airport, located just south of Port Everglades Inlet in South Florida, Harbour Towne is easily accessible, with no bridge between the inlet and the marina. Harbour Towne can accommodate yachts to 120ft. There are complete marine service facilities on the premises extending from maintenance and repair service to bottom work, rigging, painting, refinishing, custom woodwork and engine service. Ship store, fuel dock, with pump-out facilities, and restaurant.
YS, D, BR

Hargrave Yacht Design, J.B.
205 1/2 Sixth Street
West Palm Beach, FL 33401
Tel (561) 833-8567
Fax (561) 833-7791
Em jbhyacht@bellsouth.net

Hatteras Custom Yacht Sales
2501 SE Aviation Way, Suite D
Stuart, FL 34996-1903
Tel (561) 220-0707
Fax (561) 220-3002

Sale of new and brokerage Hatteras yachts to 130ft.
BR

Also:

Hatteras
110 North Glenburnie Road
New Bern, NC 28560
Tel (252) 633-3101
Fax (252) 633-2046

Heesen Shipyards BV
Rynstraat 2
PO Box 8
OSS-Holland 534022
Tel +31 412-665544
Fax +31 412-665566
Em info@heesenshipyards.nl
Builder of durable high-quality yachts with exclusive styling
B

Heinen & Hopman
PO Box 460520
Fort Lauderdale, FL 33346-520
Tel (954) 462-3650
Fax (954) 462-3620
Marine air-conditioning systems.
YS

Hinckley Company
130 Shore Road
Southwest Harbor, ME 04679
Tel (207) 244-5531
Fax (207) 244-9833
Em sales@thehinckleyco.com
www.thehinckleyco.com

Hodgdon Yachts
Murray Hill Road
East Boothbay, ME 04554
Tel (207) 633-4194
Fax (207) 633-4668

Ron Holland Design
PO Box 23
Kinsale County Cork
Ireland
Tel +353 2177 4866
Fax +353 2177 4808
Em rhd@iol.ie
Designers of high performance cruising yachts. Current projects range from 42 to 210ft.
NA

Jeff Homchick, Inc.
7531 19th Street NE
Seattle, WA 98115
Tel (206) 985-2160
Fax (206) 985-2257

Ted Hood Design Group
1 Little Harbor Landing
Portsmouth, RI 02871
Tel (401) 683-7003
Fax (401) 683-7029
Em inquiries@thco.com
For over 40 years Ted Hood Design Group has designed every type of sail and power yacht from 12ft sail-training vessels to 220ft luxury sailing yachts. Primarily known for designing very fast, shallow draft sailing yachts with classical American styling. Over 2,500 boats have been built to Hood designs by the world's most respected builders such as Little Harbor, Hinckley, Bristol, Alloy yachts and Royal Huisman.
NA

Huckins Yacht Corporation
3482 Lakeshore Blvd.
Jacksonville, FL 32210
Tel (904) 389-1125
Fax (904) 388-2281

Hunt Design
69 Long Wharf
Boston, MA 02110
Tel (617) 742-5669
Fax (617) 742-6354
Em CRHunt@tiac.net

Ideal Windlass Company
5810 Post Road, PO Box 430
East Greenwich, RI 02818
Tel (401) 884-2550
Fax (401) 884-1260
Em idlwindlas@aol.com
Since 1936 Ideal Windlass has been building rugged, dependable anchor windlasses and accessories for boats up to 200ft. Our Custom Division specializes in planning and manufacturing windlass systems for yachts 70 to 200ft. Because we manufacture our own gear boxes, we have the capacity to offer a wide range of customized units.
O

Inace
Av President Kennedy 100
60060-610, Fortaleza CE
Brazil
Tel +55 85-2314287
Fax +55 85-2319110

Injoi
4651 SW 72nd Avenue
Miami, FL 33155
Tel (305) 667-4656
Fax (305) 667-4636
Em wjoimiami@aol.com
Manufacturer of Premium Teak dock, deck, interior and garden furniture. Marine, residential, commercial applications. Miami-based company owner, Synthia David.
D

Intelect Integrated Electronics
2500 NW 55th Court, Suite 210
Fort Lauderdale, FL 33309
Tel (954) 739-4449
Fax (954) 739-4342
Em enquiries@intelect-electronics.com
Intelect designs and installs integrated electronic systems exclusively for the superyacht market. Our designs include but are not limited to distributed audio and video entertainment, home theater, satellite television, touchscreen automation control systems, computer display distribution, security systems and the integration of any and all of the above. We utilize the latest in display technology, especially plasma and LCD flat screen monitors.
O

Interlux Yacht Finishes
2270 Morris Avenue
Union, NJ 07083
Tel (908) 964-2374
Fax (908) 686-8545
YS

Intermarine
301 North Lathrop Avenue
Savannah, GA 31402
Tel (912) 234-6579
Fax (912) 239-1306
Em webmaster@intermarineyachting.com
Intermarine is a full-service ship building and repair facility located on the Savannah River 22 miles up river from the Atlantic Ocean. Specializing in large-scale fiberglass composite construction Intermarine has delivered eight of the Osprey Class Minehunters to the US Navy and has underway eight custom motoryachts ranging in size from 95 to 142ft. In addition to these new construction efforts, Intermarine provides repair and refit services to the yachting, commercial, and government markets.

International Yacht Collection
1515 SE 17th Street, Suite 125
Fort Lauderdale, FL 33316
Tel (954) 522-2323
Fax (954) 522-2333
Em yachtcollection.net
IYC is an international yacht brokerage firm specializing in the sale and purchase of new and late-model motor and sportfishing yachts. IYC was created to address the needs of the experienced and demanding yachtsman. IYC has brought together an experienced, effective, and honest team of brokers that represent the "Boutique" brokerage organization of the 1990s and beyond.
BR

Interphase Technologies, Inc.
2880 Research Park Drive
Soquel, CA 95073
Tel (831) 477-4944
Fax (831) 462-7444
Em timw@interphase-tech.com
Interphase Technologies is the leading supplier of forward-scanning sonar electronics for pleasure boaters, cruisers, and sportfishermen worldwide, as well as light commercial fleets. First introduced in 1991, the company's patented phased-array technology has set the standard for affordable high-performance sonar systems.
YS

Charles P. Irwin Yacht Brokerage, Inc.
2400 East Las Olas Blvd., Suite C
Fort Lauderdale, FL 33301
Tel   (954) 463-6302
Fax   (954) 523-0056
Em   cpirwin@msn.com

Charles P. Irwin Yacht Brokerage, Inc. has the finest reputation for honesty and straight forwardness for over 30 years. We have been closely connected with most major boat companies. Our sales staff of highly qualified and motivated brokers have an expertise in motoryachts, sportfishermen, trawlers and sailboats.
BR

Isotta Fraschini Motori
800 Principal Court, Suite C
Chesapeake, VA 23320
Tel   (757) 548-6000
Fax   (757) 548-6012
Em   cbiggs@fdgm.com

Isotta Fraschini: a name that has always been synonymous with advanced technology in the history of Italian industry. A past of excellence, of quality, and of international renown that has led to specialization in the production of high-performance diesel engines for pleasure crafts, sportfishing, patrol, and work boats.
O

Italian Trade Commission
PO Box 56689
Atlanta, GA 30343
Tel   (404) 525-0660
Fax   (404) 525-5112
Em   itc@italtrade.atlanta.com

A commercial agency of the Italian government that can provide US businesses with information on Italian firms specializing in yacht building and design, suppliers of furnishings, equipment, accessories and services.
O

J

J Class Management
32 Church Street
Newport, RI 02840
Tel   (401) 849-3060
Fax   (401) 849-1642
Em   mjw@jclass.com

Project management, yacht management, crew hire and training, yacht insurance, payroll management, systems interior and deck design, specification, bidding and new build oversight and restoration oversight, yacht brokerage and charter brokerage — All for classic yachts.
YS, D, BR, C

JRC
1011 SW Klickitat Way # B-100
Seattle, WA 98134
Tel   (206) 654-5644
Fax   (206) 654-7030
Em   rossflett@jrcamerica.com

Sales and service of marine electronic equipment.

Lynn Jachney Charters
PO Box 302
Marblehead, MA 01945
Tel   (781) 639-0787
Fax   (781) 639-0216
Em   ljc@boston.sisna.com

Jackson Marine Sales, Inc.
1915 SW 21st Avenue
Fort Lauderdale, FL 33312
Tel   (954) 792-4900
Fax   (954) 587-8164
Em   jmsboats@aol.com

Full service marine/boatyard. 70-ton marine travel-lift. 15 specialty marine businesses on-site.
YS, BR

Glade Johnson Design, Inc.
11820 Northup Way, Suite 220
Bellevue, WA 98005
Tel   (425) 827-1600
Fax   (425) 827-2147
Em   gjdi@blarg.net

Glade Johnson Design, Inc. has designed thirteen new yachts, three of which were Feadships, and seven refits (three were Feadships). We offer exterior styling and complete interior design and outfitting services for yachts over 100ft. Our experienced team of 12 produces artistic conceptual work, as well as highly-detailed control drawings that only the latest AutoCAD systems can realize.
D, O

K

KVH Industries, Inc.
50 Enterprise Center
Middletown, RI 02842
Tel   (401) 847-3327
Fax   (401) 849-0045
Em   info@kvh.com
       www.kvh.com

KVH Industries utilizes its proprietary fiber optic, auto-calibration, and sensor technologies to produce navigation and mobile satellite communications systems for commercial, military, and marine applications. KVH is the world leader in providing stabilized satellite TV and communication systems for marine use. They produced the first Inmarsat type-approved, stabilized maritime antenna for Inmarsat-phone mini-M service.
O

Bruce King Yacht Design
PO Box 599, Newcastle Square
Newcastle, ME 04553
Tel   (207) 563-1186
Fax   (207) 563-1189
Em   kingydes@lincoln.midcoast.com

We are a yacht design firm that is able to provide complete naval architecture and design services for any type of yacht, for both production and custom projects. We have become known as a leader in modern retro-style yacht design.
NA, D

Knight & Carver Yacht Center, Inc.
1313 West 24th Street
National City, CA 91950
Tel   (619) 336-4141
Fax   (619) 336-4050
Em   kcyachts@aol.com

Knight & Carver is a builder of composite boats, both custom and production, ranging in size from 33 to 150ft. Knight & Carver also operates a marine repair facility with a 300-ton lifting capacity.
B, YS

Patrick Knowles Designs
1650 SE 17th Street Suite 210
Fort Lauderdale, FL 33316
Tel   (954) 832-0108
Fax   (954) 832-9951

Primarily focused on the designs of custom yacht interiors; other strengths include exterior styling, interior arrangements, technical interior drawings and specifications, as well as complete décor selection and coordination.
D

Koch, Newton & Partners
1700 E. Las Olas Blvd.
Fort Lauderdale, FL 33301
Tel   (954) 525-7080
Fax   (954) 525-7095
Em   KnandP@aol.com

L

Langan Design Associates
17 Goodwin Street
Newport, RI 02840
Tel   (401) 849-2249
Fax   (401) 849-3288

Lazzara International Yacht Sales
5300 West Tyson Avenue
Tampa, FL 33611
Tel   (813) 835-5300
Fax   (813) 835-0964
Em   lazzarayachts.com

Combining their family legacy of 50 years of master yacht building with the latest advances in computer and marine technology has resulted in a new and imaginative company that produces yachts in a class by themselves. The Lazzara Motor Yacht is the most technically innovative production yacht ever created. To produce this brilliantly conceived yacht, they began by asking yacht owners who cruised extensively what they wanted in a yacht.
B, BMA, NA, D, BR

LeClercq Marine Construction
1080 West Ewing
Seattle, WA 98119
Tel   (206) 283-8555
Fax   (206) 286-1726
Em   leclercq@leclercqmarine.com

LeClercq Marine Construction specializes in new construction and refit of custom fiberglass composite luxury motoryachts in size ranges from 60 to 130ft in length.
B

★ DIRECTORY

Legendary Yachts, Inc.
PO Box 206
2902 Addy Street
Washougal, WA 98671
Tel (360) 835-0342
Fax (360) 835-5052
Our wooden classics fill a critical void in yachting by offering a unique, high-quality product that is simply not available anywhere else. Like great music, our boats are masterworks, testaments to the creativity, perseverance, and talent of designers such as Herreshoff, Stephens, Alden, Fife and Rhodes, to mention only a few.
B

Liebowitz & Pritchard Architects & Yacht Designers
86 Thomas Street, Loft 2
New York, NY 10013
Tel (212) 240-9000
Fax (212) 240-9006
Em LPARCH@mindspring.com

Linn Products
Floors Road, Waterford
Glascow G76 0ED
Great Britian
Tel +44 (0)141-307-7777
Fax +44 (0)141-644-4262

Little Harbor Custom Yachts
1 Little Harbor Landing
Portsmouth, RI 02871
Tel (401) 683-7000
Fax (401) 683-7029
Em inquiries@thco.com
    www.thco.com

Little Hoquiam Shipyard
Hoquiam, WA
SALES: Fraser Yachts Worldwide
1001 Fairview Avenue North, #1300
Seattle, WA 98109
Tel (206) 382-9494
Fax (206) 382-9480

Living Color Enterprises, Inc.
6850 NW 12th Avenue
Fort Lauderdale, FL 33309
Tel (954) 970-9511
Fax (954) 978-3811
Em gperez@livingcolor.com
Living Color Enterprises specializes in custom-built, museum-quality exhibitry, themed environments, and architectural aquarium systems. Fabricated natural elements include geological sculpture, coralscapes, rainforest, ancient ruins, trees, rock and waterscapes. These features include: stage sets, props, and special effects engineered and developed for theme parks, museums, zoos, casinos, retail and hospitality worldwide.
B, YS, D

Lurssen Werft
Friedrich-Klippert Strasse 1
28759 Bremen
Germany
Tel +49 (0) 421-6604-166
Fax +49 (0) 421-6604-170
Em breman@lurssen.com

M

MacDougall's Cape Cod Marine Service, Inc.
145 Falmouth Heights Road
Falmouth, MA 02540
Tel (508) 548-3146
Fax. (508) 548-7262
Em ccmarine1@capecod.net
Full-service yacht yard with electronics, canvas, ezzcy, 80-ton railway, and 50-ton travel lift. Located halfway between Newport and Nantucket.
YS

Maiora Yachts
Via Scorzanese
Massaros-Zona Industriale
Viareggio,
Italy
Tel +39 0584-93353
Fax +39 0584-93118

Marine Design International
3821 NE 12 Terrace
Pompano Beach, FL 33064
Tel (954) 785-6893
Fax (954) 785-0233

Marine PartsFinders Plus
224 Datura Street, Suite 207
West Palm Beach, FL 33412
Tel (561) 655-4218
Fax (561) 655-7545
Em partsplus@marineparts.com
International marine supply company sourcing all major systems and their component parts.
YS

Maritech Marine Electronics
3 Yacht Haven Marine Center
Stamford, CT 06902
Tel (203) 323-2900
Fax (203) 967-9717
Em info@maritech.com
Sales of navigation, communications, computer networking, and entertainment systems for yachts worldwide.
YS

Mars Metal Company
4130 Morris Drive
Burlington, Ontario
Canada L7L 5L6
Tel (800) 381-5335
Tel (905) 637-3862
Fax (905)637-8841
Em mars@bserv.com
    www.marsmetal.on.ca
Produces custom and production keel configurations from 1,000 pounds to over 100,000 pounds. Company's capabilities include pattern-making, mold-making, stainless steel fabrication, and specialized finishing areas. The company also specializes in custom bulb additions for draft reduction and added stability. Constant testing and upgrading advancements have made the company the leader in keel technology, servicing customers worldwide.
YS

Gregory Marshall
4700 42nd Avenue SW, Suite 553
Seattle, WA 98116
Tel (206) 937-4977
Fax (206) 937-4377

Jerry Martin Associates
PO Box 360
Gurnee, IL 60031
Tel (847) 662-9070
Fax (847) 336-7126

Rodger Martin Yacht Designs
PO Box 242
Newport, RI 02840
Tel (401) 849-9850
Fax (401) 848-0119

Maxwell Winches
1610 Babcock Street
Costa Mesa, CA 92627
Tel (949) 631-2634
Fax (949) 631-2846

McQueen's Boatworks Ltd.
11571 Twigg Place
Richmond, BC
Canada V6V ZK7
Tel (604) 325-4544
Fax (604) 325-4516
Em mcqueens@uniserv.com
Custom yacht builder specializing in Ed Monk-designed fiberglass motoryachts and sportfishers. Renowned for quality of work and customer satisfaction on a "one-on-one" basis.
B

MedLink, Inc.
1301 E. McDowell Road, Suite 204
Phoenix, AR 85006
Tel. (602) 452-4300
Fax (602) 252-8404
Em Info@medaire.com
MedLink provides Emergency Tele-medicine at sea with access to emergency room physicians 24 hours a day, 7 days a week; coordination of land-based emergency medical resources, health advisories, and immunization recommendations. Maritime-specific training for management of onboard illness and injury; automated external defibrillator, blood-borne pathogens prevention. Maritime kits for harsh environments and treatment of various injuries including lacerations, burns, and venomous bites.
YS

Megayacht Services International
5410 West Tyson Avenue
Tampa, FL 33611
Tel (561) 573-6415
Fax (813) 835-7372

Merrill-Stevens Dry Dock
1270 NW 11th Street
Miami, FL 33125
Tel (305) 324-5211
Fax (305) 326-8911
Em jeffs@alt545.com

Merrill-Stevens Yacht Sales
1270 NW 11th Street
Miami, FL 33125
Tel (305) 547-2650
Fax (305) 547-2660

Metalnave
Estaleiro Italjai S/A
Rua Mario Trilma 271
Ilha da Conceicao
Nitero
RJ24050-190
Brazil
Tel +55 21-620-1414
Fax +55 21-620-8017

Ed Monk
PO Box 10397
Bainbridge Island, WA 98110
Tel (206) 842-2167
Fax (206) 842-3182

Monte Fino Custom Yachts
901 SE 17th Street, Suite 203
Fort Lauderdale, FL 33316
Tel (954) 463-0555
Fax (954) 463-8621

Mulder Design
Appeldijk 33, 4201 AE Gorinchem
PO Box 444, 4200 AK Gorinchem, Holland
Tel +31 183-692001
Fax +31 183-692002
Em info@mulderdesign.nl
Conceptual design, design, naval architecture, and engineering of high-speed, semi-displacement luxury motoryachts and commercial boats.
NA

Murray & Associates, Inc.
705 SE 24th Street
Fort Lauderdale, FL 33316
Tel (954) 527-5505
Fax (954) 527-5504

N

Naiad Marine Florida, Inc.
Broward Business Park
3650 Hacienda Blvd., Suite D
Fort Lauderdale, FL 33314
Tel (954) 797-7566
Fax (954) 791-0827
Em nmfl@nmfl.com
www.nmfl.com
Also:

Naiad Marine Systems
50 Parrott Drive
Shelton, CT 06484
Tel (800) 760-naiad
Fax (203) 929-3594
Em naiadvdm@aol.com
Naiad Marine Systems designs and manufacturers Naiad Roll Stabilization Systems, Stabilizer Controllers, Bow Thrusters and Integrated Hydraulic Systems for vessels from 35 to 300ft. Naiad Marine Systems also installs, services and repairs our systems through our worldwide dealer network.
YS

Nautor AB
Box 10, 68601 Pietarsaari
Finland
Tel +358 6 7601 111
Fax +358 6 7667 364
Em swan.yachts@nautor.inet.fl
Nautor has been building Swan yachts since 1966. Considered the world's premier production yachts, the current range comprises 9 models including the Swan 80 and the 112ft Swan 100 Plus. The principle for Swans is seaworthiness, built to cross oceans, proving safe, comfortable accommodations, with Whitbread race winning pedigree, performance is as vital as the luxurious interiors.
B

Nautica International, Inc.
6135 NW 167 Street Suite E-17
Miami, FL 33015
Tel (305) 556-5554
Fax (305) 557-0268
Em www.nauticaintl.com
Our deluxe rigid inflatable boats are tenders to many exclusive yachts worldwide. Featuring faster, better-planing hulls for optimum performance and luxurious, well-appointed deck plans with emphasis placed on comfort. Entirely constructed using only top materials in our Miami, Florida plant, each 9 to 36ft RIB boasts a 10-year warranty.
B

Nordlund Boat Co.
1626 Marine View Drive
Tacoma, WA 98421
Tel (206) 627-0605
Fax (206) 627-0785

**Nortek Group
(Custom Navigation South)**
3200 South Andrews Avenue
Fort Lauderdale, FL 33316
Tel (954) 761-3678
Fax (954)522-5526
Em nortekgrp@nortek.net
1. **Custom Navigation South, Inc.**— *communication and navigation systems.*
2. **Nortek Entertainment Inc.**— *Audio/Video entertainment systems*
3. **Cole Marine Distributing, Inc.**— *mechanical and finished goods.*
YS

Northcoast Yachts, Inc.
401 Alexander Avenue, Suite 407
Tacoma, WA 98421
Tel (253) 627-2503
Fax (253)272-0306
Em ncyachts@ix.netcom.com
Northcoast Yachts is a custom boatbuilder of yachts from 80 to 145ft in our own one-piece tooling molds that we can build to any design and specification level.
B

Northern Marine
1920 R Avenue
Anacortes, WA 98221
Tel (360) 299-8400
Fax (360) 299-2600

Northrop & Johnson, Inc.
5 Marina Plaza
Newport, RI 02840
Tel (401) 848-0120
Fax (401) 849-0620
Em yachts@nandj.com
Also:

Northrop & Johnson, Inc.
1901 SE 4th Avenue
Fort Lauderdale, FL 33316
Tel (954) 522-3344
Fax (954)522-9500
Em njyachts@aol.com
Northrop & Johnson Yacht-Ships, Inc. is committed to providing clients with the best brokerage experience possible, whether listing a yacht, purchasing a yacht, choosing a builder, finding the right crew, or anything in between. With nearly 50 years of experience and 5 offices worldwide, there's no facet of the business we don't know.
BR

Notika Teknik Yacht Construction
Tersaneler Cad. G. 50 Sok. No. 3
Tuzla - Instanbul - Turkey 81700
Tel +90 216-493-6227
Fax +90 216-493-6228
Notika Teknik, in its thirteenth year of production, is currently building its new "Centaurian" series of large 100 to 115ft motoryachts in epoxy/composite for the European and US markets.
B, NA, YS, D

Novurania of America, Inc.
2105 South US 1
Vero Beach, FL 32962
Tel (561) 567-9200
Fax (561) 567-1056
Em novuraniainc@novurania.com
Novurania Rib manufacturer. Featuring luxury yacht tender 10 to 36ft outboards/inboards, gas or diesel.
B

Nuvolari-Lenard
39a via Della Chiesa
31020 Zerman
Italy
Tel +39 041-457272
Fax +39 041-457393
Em nlyachts@mpbnet.it

O

Oceanco
1650 SE 17th Street, Suite 200
Fort Lauderdale, FL 33316
Tel (954) 522-4155
Fax (954) 522-5363
Em oceanco@aol.com
Also:

Oceanco International
Gildo Pastor Center
7 Rue du Gabian
MC 98000 Monaco
Tel +377 93-10-02-81
Fax +377 92-05-65-99
Em Oceanco@aol.com

Offer & Associates International, Inc.
2945 State Road 84, Suite A-1
Fort Lauderdale, FL 33312
Tel (954) 587-0935
Fax (954) 587-8272
Em offerinc@worldnet.att.net

We sell and consult on the sale of large, custom yachts throughout the world — including extensions, refits, charters, and yacht management.
BMA, YS, BR, C

Offshore Yachts
1011 Brioso Drive #102
Costa Mesa, CA 92672
Tel (949) 645-4159
Fax (949) 645-0250

For over 50 years Offshore has been a leader in high-performance luxury yachts, ranging from 48 to 90ft. Offshore is renowned for the highest standards in quality, craftsmanship, safety, and innovative design by famed naval architect William Crealock, putting them in a class by themselves.
B

Omega Marine
470 Camino Elevado
Bonita, CA 91902
Tel (619) 421-3427
Fax (619) 482-1226\

Overing Yacht Design
998 Robinson Avenue
Ocean Springs, MI 39564
Tel (601) 872-1881
Fax (601) 875-2862
Em overing@datasync.com

P

Pacific Coast Marine Industries, Inc.
4314 Russell Road
Mukilteo, WA 98275
Tel (425) 743-9550
Fax (425) 348-3767
Em pcmii@compuserve.com

Pacific Coast Marine Industries, Inc. (PCM) fabricates custom doors, hatches, windows, and related marine hardware for both commercial and leisure vessels. PCM maintains a large inventory of a wide variety of aluminum extruded shapes. Coupled with our customized fabrication processes, this large inventory results in an irrefutable fit for our customers, regardless of the application or vessel type. Pacific Coast Marine Industries is noted for its leadership in ingenuity and for consistently providing high-quality products.
O

Pacific Custom Interiors, Inc.
2601 West Marina Place, Suite P
Seattle, WA 98199
Tel (206) 282-5540
Fax (206) 282-2803
Em paccustom@aol.com

Located in a corner of Elliott Bay Marina in Seattle, Washington, Pacific Custom Interiors, Inc. continues to grow in 1999. With over 14 years experience in yacht upholstery and design, President Sheryl McLaughlin recently married and is now Sheryl Guyon. We have expanded our interior design services and added 2 additional designers to the office. Currently PCI is responsible for the interiors of over twenty, 65ft plus yachts with an aggregate project value of over $65 million.
D

Pacific Mariner
PO Box 1382
La Conner, WA 98257
Tel (360) 466-1189
Fax (360) 466-1189
Em pacmar@ncia.com

Pacific Mariner builds a 65ft raised pilothouse motoryacht. It is cruise-ready upon completion with a full electronics package, 2 Gensets, watermaker, reverse cycle air. Davit bow thruster and tender. It is a three-stateroom three-head layout with two crew bunks aft in the lazarette. Power is 2x 800hp 3406E caterpillars Mathers controls and 5-blade Nibral props.
B

Pacific Rim Yachts, Inc.
2850 John Stevens Way
Hoquiam, WA 98550
Tel (360) 532-9338
Fax (360) 533-1009
Em shawboat@techline.com

Pacific Rim Yachts was established in 1990. The company specializes in custom composite construction and has delivered new vessels ranging from 31 to 119ft. Recently the yard has created tooling for a series of fiberglass motoryachts. The Northern Pacific model line includes a 64ft PHMY, a 68ft Sportfisher, and a 70ft PHMY.
B

Padanaram Yachts Company
1601 Trapelo Road
Waltham, MA 02451
Tel (781) 890-5511
Fax (781) 890-1512
Em info@w-class.com

Palm Beach Yacht Crew
4200 Poinsettia Avenue
West Palm Beach, FL 33407
Tel (561) 863-0082
Fax (561) 863-4406
Em Palmbeachcrew@flinet.com
www.yachtcrew.com

Yacht Crew Placement & Management Agency provides professional qualified yacht crew for all vessels, power and sail, reference checks, longevity and commitment goals. Also offers worldwide yacht charters and global crew medical insurance. Other locations in Antibes, France and Queensland, Australia.
YS

Palmer Johnson Incorporated
61 Michigan Street
Sturgeon Bay, WI 54235
Tel (920) 743-4412
Fax (920) 743-3381

Custom yacht builders, service and refit yards.
B, YS

Paradigm Yacht Sales & Brokerage, Inc.
15065 McGregor Blvd., Suite 104
Fort Myers, FL 33908
Tel (941) 454-8484
Fax (941) 454-8485
Em marina@peganet.com
paradigmyachts.com

Experience, integrity, and service guarantee each client the ultimate satisfaction when buying or selling your next yacht.
BR, C

Pavlik Design Team
1301 East Broward Blvd.
Fort Lauderdale, FL 33301
Tel (954) 523-3300
Fax (954) 525-9501

Pavlik Design Team's mission is to develop planning and design solutions that serve the client's strategic objectives. Under the direction of President Seann Pavlik, the yacht division is backed by over 25 employees and specializes in both new construction and vessel refitting. The company has consistently been ranked as one of the top ten design firms in the country for the past decade.
D

Pedrick Yacht Design, Inc.
3 Ann Street
Newport, RI 02840
Tel (401) 846-8481
Fax (401) 846-0657
Em: pedrickyacht@compuserve.com

Pedrick Yacht Designs is a progressive naval architecture and marine engineering firm offering exceptional quality and diversity of design services. Established in Newport, Rhode Island in 1977, Pedrick Yacht Designs works in both power and sail, being best known for creating extraordinary sailing yachts. From Grand Prix racers to the world's finest, high-performance cruising yachts, the firm's designs maximize performance, comfort, and beauty to the particular requirements of each client.
NA

Performance Paint Yacht Refinishing
275 SW 33rd Street
Fort Lauderdale, FL 33315
Tel (954) 462-1080
Fax (954) 462-2244

Perini Navi USA, Inc.
One Maritime Drive
Portsmouth, RI 02871
Tel (401) 683-5600
Fax (401) 683-5611
Em perininaviuse@efortress.com

Also:

Perini Navi SpA
Via Coppino, 114
55049 Viareggio
Italy
Tel   +39 (0) 584-4241
Fax   +39 (0) 584-424200
Em   sales@perininavi.it

This company was founded by Fabio Perini in 1984 and has focused on the engineering, design, and construction of large sailing yachts capable of being handled by a reduced crew. In its brief history, the yard has, to date, 23 yachts cruising the worlds oceans and an additional three under construction.
B, NA, D

Michael Peters Yacht Design
47 South Palm Avenue, Suite 202
Sarasota, FL 34236
Tel   (941) 955-5460
Fax   (941) 957-3151
Em   mpyd@aol.com

MPYD provides complete naval architecture, design, and engineering for powerboats and motoryachts to 160ft. Specializing in advanced hull designs, MPYD has designed vessels to speeds of 140 knots in wood, aluminum, FRP, and advanced carbon composites. MPYD currently has projects from 25 to 117ft under construction on four continents.
NA

Phantom Marine
2801 Carleton Street
San Diego, CA 92106
Tel   (619) 221-8184
Fax   (619) 221-8051

Specializing in sales, service and installation of marine electronics. Factory authorized dealers for Furuno, Simrad, Raytheon, ICOM, and many more. Serving Southern California's boating industry from Marine del Ray to Ensenada. Showrooms located in Newport Beach and San Diego.
YS

Philbrook's Boatyard, Ltd.
2324 Harbour Road
Sidney, BC V8L 2P6
Canada
Tel   (250) 656-1157
Fax   (250) 656-1155

Philbrook's Boatyard has been building, repairing, and renovating motor and sail yachts since 1950. It is the largest yacht repair facility in the Victoria area with two enclosed work areas accessed by two marine railways for vessels up to 120ft or 150 tons in capacity. Over seventy qualified tradesmen make up the Philbrooks crew. They include marine mechanics, shipwrights, metal fabricators, marine electricians, painters, fine woodworkers and composite craftsmen.

Pokela Design
4015 Ruston Way
Tacoma, WA 98402
Tel   (253) 752-9704
Fax   (253) 752-9705
Em   pokeladesign@compuserve.com

International yacht styling and interior design.
D

Puleo International Designs
733 West Las Olas Blvd.
Fort Lauderdale, FL 33312
Tel   (954) 522-0173
Fax   (954) 761-3216
Em   slpuleo@aol.com

Premise: "Never say never." Extend the clients dream. Complete renovations and new construction. Exceptional space planning and use. Original architectural designs. Thorough experience in yacht projects internationally. Project problem-solving a specialty.
D

Q

Quantum Marine Engineering of Florida
4350 West Sunrise
Plantation, FL 33313
Tel   (954) 587-4205
Fax   (954) 587-4259
Em   qmeflorida@aol.com

Precision design and manufacturing of marine hydraulics and control systems. Sales, service, and repair of stabilizers, deck cranes, thrusters.
YS

Queenship
23352 Fisherman Road
Maple Ridge, BC V2X 7E6
Canada
Tel   (604) 466-0695
Fax   (604) 466-0689

R

Rayburn Custom Yachts Canada
32860 Mission Way
Mission, BC V2V 5X9
Canada
Tel   (604) 820-9153
Fax   (604) 820-2457

Raytheon Marine Company
676 Island Pond Road
Manchester, NH 03109-5420
Tel   (603) 634-4716
Fax   (603) 634-4756
Em   michael-j-mitchell@raytheon.com

Raytheon Marine Company manufacturers a complete line of professional maritime navigation and communication equipment; including ARPA Radar, ECDIS, Gyrocompass, autopilot, Depth Sounders, GMDSS, Steering Systems and Integrated Bridge Systems. All products are backed by a world-wide factory authorized service network.
YS

Rex Yacht Sales
2152 SE 17th Street
Fort Lauderdale, FL 33179
Tel   (954) 463-8810
Fax   (954) 462-3640
Em   rexyachts@worldnet.att.net
      www.rexyachts.com

Rex Yacht Sales has been a continuing yacht brokerage and new-build agent for the past 24 years. Well known for its introduction and development of the Cheoy Lee Yacht line, Rex now concentrates on new-build representation, coordinating clients' wishes with naval architects, suppliers, and shipyards. Projects currently under construction at Sensation Yachts (New Zealand), Trinity Yachts (Louisiana), Guy Couach Yachts (France) and INACE (Brazil). The firm is distributor for the semi-custom Guy Couach Yachts. Rex is an excellent source for assistance in new-building or brokerage.
BMA, BR

Rikki Davis Inc.
1323 SE 17th Street, Suite 209
Fort Lauderdale, FL 33316
Tel   (954) 761-3237
Fax   (954) 764-0497
Em   rikkid@bellsouth.net
C

Ritchie Navigation
243 Oak Street
Pembroke, MA 02359
Tel   (781) 826-3131
Fax   (781) 826-7336
Em   sales@ritchienavigation.com

Manufacturers of magnetic and electronic compasses for the marine industry since 1950.
O

Rivolta Marine
1741 Main Street, #101
Sarasota, FL 34236
Tel   (941) 9540355
Fax   (941) 954-0111
Em   rrivolta@gte.net

Rivolta Marine is a full-service design-build shipyard, providing high technology construction and architectural services for both sailing boats and power boats, and for private individuals, designers, and manufacturers. Rivolta Marine brings the best in European design and American technology to each project, treating every client individually.
B, NA

Dee Robinson Interiors, Inc.
2755 East Oakland Park Blvd., Suite 301
Fort Lauderdale, FL 33306
Tel   (954) 566-2252
Fax   (954) 566-2044
Em   deerob@bellsouth.net

Specializes in superyacht interior design and execution of all phases of pre-construction and refits.
D

★ DIRECTORY

Robinson Hallen-Berg
2894 South Coast Highway
Laguna Beach, CA 92651
Tel (949) 494-9951
Fax (949) 494-6281

Roscioli International, Inc.
3201 State Road 84
Fort Lauderdale, FL 33312
Tel (954) 581-9200
Fax (954) 791-0958

Robin M. Rose & Associates
1500 Cordova Road, Suite 312
Fort Lauderdale, FL 33316
Tel (954) 525-6023
Fax (954) 525-0010
Em rroseyacht@worldnet.att.net
home.att.net/robinrose

Robin M. Rose & Associates, Inc. was started in May of 1989. We specialize in project management, space planning, furniture design, and execution which all go hand-in-hand. We are proud of the fact that over 90 percent of our business is repeat clientele and referrals.
D

Royal Huisman Shipyard BV
PO Box 23
8325 ZG Vollenhove
The Netherlands
Tel +31 (0) 527-243131
Fax +31 (0) 527-243800
Em yachts@royalhuisman.com

Royal Marine Insurance Group
8300 Executive Center Drive #102
Miami, FL 33166
Tel (305) 477-3755
Fax (305) 477-3858
Em info@royalmarine.com

From initial consultation to complete administration, Royal Marine provides an entire range of products and services to the yachting industry: yacht management, luxury yachts, charter operations, fleet and owner associations, and many more coverages.
O

Rybovich Spencer
4200 Poinsettia Avenue
West Palm Beach, FL 33407
Tel (561) 844-1800
Fax (561) 844-8393
Em service@rybovich.com

A world-renowned service and repair yard with capabilities including a 300-ton and 70-ton travelift and 120-ton syncrolift. Areas of expertise include carpentry, metal and mechanical, diesel and generator, paint and electrical, and yard crews. A 22-acre facility with over 50 years of experience in refits, extensions, reconstruction, and repairs. With no bridges to sea—an easy destination from the Palm Beach Intercoastal.

S

Sacks Yacht Charters, Inc.
1600 SE 17th Street, Suite 418
Fort Lauderdale, FL 33316
Tel (954) 764-7742
Fax (954) 523-3769
Em info@sycinfo.com

Jack Sarin Naval Architects, Inc.
382 Wyatt Way, NE
PO Box 10151
Bainbridge Island, WA 98110
Tel (206) 842-4651
Fax (206) 842-4656
Em jsarin@worldnet.att.net

Jack W. Sarin Naval Architects, Inc. is a full-service naval architectural firm in operation since 1980. In addition to hull design and engineering, the firm provides an in-house staff and facilities to include a full range of interior and lighting design, styling, and complete ship's system coordination during construction.
NA

Bob Saxon Associates, Inc.
1500 Cordova Road, Suite 314
Fort Lauderdale, FL 33316
Tel (954) 760-5801
Fax (954) 467-8909
Em yachts1@bobsaxon.com

Private yacht management, charter yacht management, professional crew placement, charter brokerage.
YS, C

SEA
7030 220th Street SW
Mountlake Terrace, WA 98043
Tel (425) 771-2182
Fax (425) 771-2650
Em salesmktg@sea-ami.com

SEA is an American manufacturer of marine electronics including VHF and SSB radiotelephones, satellite products, and GMDSS equipment. SEA has received an award for best of its category from the National Marine Electronics Association 17 out of the past 18 years.
O

Sea Tel, Inc.
1035 Shary Court
Concord, CA 94518
Tel (925) 798-7979
Fax (925) 798-7986
Em jcaulfield@seatel.com

Sea Tel is the world's leading manufacturer of marine stabilized antenna systems for satellite communications and satellite television at sea. Sea Tel markets its products globally and has a responsive worldwide service support network. With dishes ranging from 13 inches to 12ft, Sea Tel provides all types and sizes of vessels with the right antenna system for their applications.
YS

Seaward Marine Insurance
1001 West 46th Street #32
Miami Beach, FL 33140
Tel (800) 831-8304
Fax (305) 538-9421

Seaward Marine has been in business eight years, providing marine coverage for: yachts, multi-hulls, charter vessels, marinas and marine artisans.
YS

Setzer Design Group
1149 Executive Circle, Suite C
Cary, NC 27511
Tel (919) 319-0559
Fax (919) 319-0557
Em setzerdesign@mindspring.com

Setzer Design is a full-service naval architecture and design office. We specialize in custom yachts from 70 to 200ft. Our focus for the motoryacht has been on classic and expedition yachts, of which we have 5 under construction. Our focus remains to create designs that can be built, and are meant to go to sea with style and comfort.
NA, D

Seven Seas Communications, Inc.
1700 East Las Olas Blvd.
Fort Lauderdale, FL 33301
Tel (954) 761-7671
Fax (954) 761-7668
Em sales@sevenseascom.com

Seven Seas Communications is a leading provider of global mobile satellite communications services and equipment to the yachting and marine industries. Seven Seas offers a full site of services for remote and offshore communications including voice, data, and fax through iridium, Mini-phone, Inmarsat A, B, M, and Oceancell.
YS

Sharp Design, Inc.
5030 Camino De La Siesta, Suite 405
San Diego, CA 92108
Tel (619) 220-4860
Fax (619) 220-4890
Em sharp.design@worldnet.att.net

George J. Shull & Associates
801 Seabreeze Blvd.
Fort Lauderdale, FL 33316
Tel (954) 463-4546
Fax (954) 463-5531
Em tcshull@aol.com

George J. Shull & Associates specializes in placing multi-million dollar loans on megayachts and aircraft for distinguished clientele. The firm has relationships with some of the world's most respected lending and private banking institutions. With offices at Bahia Mar Marina in Fort Lauderdale, Shull is committed to your service.
O

Siewert Design
PO Box 601
Charlestown, SC 29402
Tel (843) 853-6154
Fax (843) 577-4234
Em siewertdesign@mindspring.com

Siewert Design provides its clients with innovative, cost-effective and enduring yacht design. The office is primarily concerned with the conceptual and detail design of both exterior styling and interior arrangements. It also offers services in illustration and project planning to clients who need assistance in guiding their project to completion.
NA, D

Skaf Interiors, Inc.
Bahia Mar Yachting Center
801 Seabreeze Blvd.
Fort Lauderdale, FL 33316
Tel (954) 523-6155
Fax (954) 532-6156
Em suzanne@skafinteriors.com

Skaf Interiors, Inc. specializes in yacht refits and new construction projects, offering a "turn-key" interior with timeless details designed for both beauty and practicality. On-site management allows us to maintain the maximum level of quality control all the way through to the project's completion. Dedicated to excellence, we offer the finest customer service in the field of interior design.

Larry Smith Electronics
1619 Broadway
Riviera Beach, FL 33404
Tel (561) 844-3592
Fax (561) 844-1608
Em lsei@gate.net

With over 40 years in the marine industry, factory-trained technicians and in-house CADD department, we provide sales, custom installations, and service for discriminating owners of custom-built boats and megayachts. To serve our customers worldwide we have offices in South Florida, the Pacific Northwest, and Europe.
YS

Paola D. Smith & Associates
300 Northeast 3rd Avenue
Fort Lauderdale, FL 33301
Tel (954) 761-1997
Fax 954) 767-6270
Em pds@aksi.net

Paola D. Smith & Associates is among the top leading interior design firms in the industry of megayachts. With over 25 years of experience, their firm's technical support team is classified among the finest in the industry, providing complete interior design services, including exterior styling and space planning for both customized new construction and refits.
D

South Florida Yacht, Inc.
66 Blue Heron Blvd.
Riviera Beach, FL 33004
Tel (954) 925-7177
Fax (954) 927-7331

Sovereign Yachts, Inc.
23511 Dyke Road
Richmond, BC V6V 1E3
Canada
Tel (604) 515-0992
Fax (604) 515-0994

Sparkman & Stephens, Inc.
529 Fifth Avenue, 14th Floor
New York, NY 10017
Tel (212) 661-1240
Fax (212) 661-1235
Em design@sparkmanstephens.com
   brokerage@sparkmanstephens.com

Naval architecture, marine engineering, yacht brokers, marine insurance, worldwide. From 16 to 250ft sail and power.
NA, BR, C

Sponberg Yacht Design, Inc.
PO Box 661
8 Fair Street
Newport, RI 02840
Tel (401) 849-7730
Em ewsponberg@cs.com

Naval architects and marine engineers-designers of offshore racing and cruising sailboats, mono-hulls and multi-hulls, powerboats and motoryachts. Specialists in high-performance wing-masts, free-standing rigs, and engineered boat structures. Service provided in repair engineering and supervision.
NA

St. Augustine Marine, Inc.
404 South Riberia Street
St. Augustine, FL 32084
Tel (904) 824-4394
Fax (904) 824-9755
Em stauqmar@atlantic.com

We are a full service yacht yard that can handle up to 150-ton on the railway and 50-ton on a mobile hoist —both are new. Services include: painting, extensions, interiors, repowering and full restorations. Electronics and air-conditioning, and canvas work are available as well.
YS

Sterling Lacquer Manufacturing Co.
3150 Brannon Avenue
St. Louis, MO 63139
Tel (314) 776-4450
Fax (314) 771-1858

Also:

Sterling Europe NV
Hoek 76, Unit 55
2850 Boom
Belgium
Tel +32 38 44 59 35
Fax +32 38 44 60 36

Sterling Lacquer Manufacturing Company first began manufacturing and marketing commercial and industrial coatings in 1907 and is still owned by the same family. Our history is one of total dedication and development of environmentally-friendly and user-friendly coatings that will meet the demand of the future.
YS

Striker Pacific Corporation
2170 8th Avenue North, Suite 301
Seattle, WA 98109
Tel (206) 301-0864
Fax (206) 301-0170

Summit Furniture
5 Harris Court
Monterey, CA 93940
Tel (408) 375-7811
Fax (408) 375-0940

Sunseeker USA, Inc.
2175 N. Andrews Avenue Ext., Unit 7
Pompano Beach, CA 33069
Tel (954) 984-2911
Fax (954) 984-2913

Sunseeker USA, Inc. is the American distributor for British-based Sunseeker International, a family-owned company founded in 1962. Sunseeker International is the world's largest privately-owned motoryacht manufacturer. This award-winning company has received the Queen's award for Export Achievement three times, the only marine company to have ever gained this honor.
BR

Superyacht Services Atlantic Ltd.
70 Hazelholme Drive
Halifax, Nova Scotia, B3M-1N5
Canada
Tel (902) 461-4271
Fax (902) 445-3311
Em ssatlantic@hotmail.com

Superyacht Services Atlantic Ltd. has assembled an international team of yachting professionals to paint, fair and refit large yachts. Working closely with the renowned Lunenburg Foundry Shipyard, we are capable of servicing vessels up to 240ft.

Superyacht Technologies
757 SE 17th Street, Suite 760
Fort Lauderdale, FL 33316
Tel (954) 614-8917
Fax (954) 761-3192
Em info@super-yachts.com

Project management firm active in new construction, refitting and vessel operations, marine engineering, MCA surveys and regulation consultants, superyacht surveys, and safety management.
YS

Swiftships, Inc.
PO Box 1908
Morgan City, LO 70381
Tel (504) 384-1700
Fax (504) 380-2591

T

Tarrab Yachts
1535 SE 17th Street, Suite 109
Fort Lauderdale, FL 33316
Tel (954) 462-0400
Fax (954) 462-4968
   www.tarrabyachts.com

Tarrab Yachts, Argentina's premier builder of semi-custom fiberglass yachts from 60 to 125ft and above, has been producing yachts of quality for nearly forty years. Company founder Alberto Tarrab has built the operation from a vacant lot in Tigre, a suburb of Buenos Aires, slowly and carefully into a complex that today encompasses a half-million square feet under one roof.
B

Taylor Made Environmental Systems, Inc.
PO Box 15299
Richmond, VA 23227
Tel (804)746-1313
Fax (804) 746-7248

Taylor Made Environmental Systems, Inc. (TMES), a member of the Taylor Made Group, Inc. was created in 1999 by the merger of Marine Development Corporation, Richmond, Virginia, and Marine Air Systems, Pompano Beach, Florida. TMES is the world's leading supplier of environmental control systems, battery chargers, and refrigeration products for the recreational and commercial marine industry and vehicular markets. The company's products are built at plants in Virginia and Florida and sold under the Cruisair, Marine Air, Sentry, and Grunert brand names.
NA, O

The Marina at Atlantis
PO Box N-4777
Nassau, The Bahamas
Tel (242) 363-6068
www.sunint.com

The Marina at Atlantis is a centerpiece of Atlantis, Paradise Island, a unique celebration of the legends of the lost continent of Atlantis. The marina has 63 megayacht slips accommodating yachts from 40 to 220ft. The facilities, services, and attractions of the spectacular Atlantis resort, only steps away and fully available to all marina guests, put the marina in a class all by itself.
O

Triconfort
PO Box 1558
Huntersville, NC 28070
Tel (704) 875-8787
Fax (704) 875-1104
Em triconfort@aol.com

Architects of luxury outdoor living for more than 56 years, Triconfort designs and manufactures distinctive wood, resin, and aluminum furnishings for exclusive environments. Select design showrooms display Triconfort products, and Triconfort furniture can be found worldwide on the finest yachts.
YS

Trinity Yachts
4325 France Road, Box 8001
New Orleans, LA 70182
Tel (504) 283-4050
Fax (504) 284-7179
Em B.smith@haltermarine.com
www.haltermarine.com

U

US Paint
831 S. 21st Street
St. Louis, MO 63103
Tel (314) 621-0525
Fax (314) 621-0722
Em info@uspaint.com

Universal Aqua Technologies, Inc.
2660 Colombia Street
Torrance, CA 90505
Tel (562) 944-4121
Fax (562) 941-9633
Em uat1sy@aol.com

UAT manufactures high-quality reverse osmosis sea water desalination systems for yachts, ships, oil rigs, and land-based applications. Equipment sizes range from 200 gallon/day to 16,000 gpd. All sizes are available in framed and modular configurations and include a patented Digital Diagnostic Control Panel.
YS

V

Vectorworks International, Inc.
805 Marina Road
Titusville, FL 32796
Tel (407) 269-8444
Fax (407) 269-8483
Em hopfk@vectorworks.com

Vectorworks International provides design, engineering, tooling, and FRP production services to the marine industry. Our backbone, however, is production of plugs and moulds, utilizing two large CNC 5-axis routers.
B, NA, YS

Vintimar, Inc.
2420 140th Place SE
Mill Creek, WA 98012
Tel (425) 485-1203
Fax (425) 316-0250
Em vinit@gte.net

Vintimar provides custom shipboard monitoring and control systems, including graphical user interfaces. Our systems interface with fire, security, CCTV, HVAC, lighting, paging, and other shipboard monitoring systems. We also develop custom computer applications, program PLC's, and implement computer networks.

W

Wally Yachts
Seaside Plaza
8 Avenue Des Ligures
Monaco MC 98000
Tel +377 93100093
Fax +377 93100094
Em Info@wallyyachts.com

Wally Yachts creates distinctive custom sail yachts, acting as a general contractor: the company is responsible for the entire conception of the project, the choice and the coordination of all the suppliers, the supervision of the work, quality control, and the "turn-key" delivery of the boat.
B

Wayne C. Group
625 Lucerne Avenue, 2nd floor
Lake Worth, FL 33460
Tel (541) 588-8135
Fax (541) 588-8136

Webster Associates
PO Box 30038
Fort Lauderdale, FL 33303
Tel (954) 525-5101
Fax (954) 525-5103
Em jim@jimwebster.com

Yacht and charter brokers providing clients with intensive, confidential services.
BR, C

West Bay SonShip Yachts, Ltd.
8295 River Road
Delta, BC V4G 1B4
Canada
Tel (604) 946-6226
Fax (604) 946-8722
Em marketing@west-bay.com
www.west-bay.com

Westerbeke Corporation
41 Ledin Drive
Avon Industrial Park
Avon, MA 02322
Tel (508) 588-7700
Fax (508) 559-9323
Em wtbk@aol.com

Manufacturer of marine engines, generators, and air climate control systems.
O

Westport Shipyard, Inc.
PO Box 308
1807 Nyhus Street
Westport, WA 98595
Tel (360) 268-1800
Fax (360) 268-1900
www.westportshipyard.com

Westport Shipyard has been building fiberglass yachts since 1977, having built more large FRP hulls than any other builder in the USA; currently building production 112ft and 128ft yachts on speculation, completing one every four months, providing high quality and proven value.
B

Westport Yacht Sales
2957 State Road 84
Fort Lauderdale, FL 33312
Tel (954) 316-6364
Fax (954) 316-6365

Westship, Inc.
1535 SE 17th Street, # 205
Fort Lauderdale, FL 33316
Tel (954) 463-0700
Fax (954) 764-2675
Em inquire@westshipyachts.com

Westship builds and markets custom fiberglass yachts 98 to 165ft under the direction of Herb Postma. All Westship yachts encompass advanced composite technology, innovative designs, contemporary exterior styling, and luxurious custom interiors. Each Westship echoes the philosophy of minimum maintenance, maximum luxury, with unequalled sea-keeping characteristics. Full marine support services available worldwide.
B, BMA

Wilson Management Ltd.
2506 Tortugas Lane
Fort Lauderdale, FL 33312
Tel   (954) 584-6187
Fax (954) 584-1014
Em   greg@wilson-management.com
Also:
Wilson Management Ltd.
16a Hull Road
Hessle
HU13 OAH
England
Tel   +44 1482-648-322
Fax +44 1482-648-277
Em   allan@wilson-management.com
Also:
Wilson Management Ltd.
77 Impasse des Cabrieres
06250 Mougins
France
Tel   + 33 (0) 492-92-16-09
Fax + 33 (0) 493-75.89.69
Em   yachts@wilson-management.com
Also:
Wilson Management Ltd.
Le Port 06320 Cap d'Ail
France
Tel   +33 (0) 492-107979
Fax +33 (0) 492-107979
Em   ibt@wilson-management.com
Also:
Wilson Management Ltd.
Ataturk Cad. Belvu Sit, C Blok
Kat 3, No. 19 Kusadasi
Turkey
Tel   +90 256-613-2679
Fax +90 256-613-2977
We are worldwide agents for: Tecnomar Offshore & Steel Yachts, Predator Marine, Dauphin Marine, ARC 2000 and Libertas. Yacht sales and charter brokers. Management of large yachts. Consultancy and project management for the construction of large yachts.
C, BR

Andrew Winch Designs Ltd.
The Old Fire Station
123 Mortlake High Street
London SW14 8SN
Great Britain
Tel   +44 (0) 20-8-392-8400
Fax +44 (0) 20-8-392-8401

Y

Yacht Design Associates
1535 SE 17th Street, #205
Fort Lauderdale, FL 33316
Em   ydainc@aol.com
Yacht Design Associates is a fully-licensed interior design firm bringing innovative ideas and unique design concepts to the creation of the finest quality and personalized environment for each client. Projects include new construction, renovations, and consultation.
D

Yachting Partners International
28/29 Richmond Place
Brighton, East Sussex BN2 2NA
Great Britain
Tel   +44 (0) 1273-571722
Fax +44 (0) 1273-571720
Em   ypi@ypi.co.uk
Also:
Yachting Partners International
Avenue de 11 Novembre
06600 Antibes
France
Tel   +33 (0) 493-34-01-00
Fax +33 (0) 493-34-20-40
Em   ypifr@ypi.co.uk

Yachts East, Inc.
2955 State Road 84 Bay B-4
Fort Lauderdale, FL 33312
Tel   (954) 584-6666
Fax (954)584-0335
Em   boatpdlr@aol.com
Service work, bottom jobs, paint, engine work, rebuild and replace, woodwork, interiors, monthly maintenance, electrical, and electronics. We specialize in refits and rebuilds. We are also the warranty center for Neptunus and Ocean Yachts.
YS

Yacht Equipment & Parts
3330 SW 3rd Avenue
Fort Lauderdale, FL 33315
Tel   (954)463-7222
A full-service sales, installation, service of all components and equipment found on megayachts including: stabilizers, bow thrusters, watermakers, controls air conditioning, electrical systems and hydraulic systems.
YS

Yacht Link Engineering
PO Box 7078
Fort Lauderdale, FL 33338
Tel   (954) 771-2489
Fax (954) 771-5837
Em   sales@yachtlinkpro.com
We sell vessel management programs called Yacht Link Pro, which keeps track of inventory, maintenance, purchasing, MCA compliancy, crew suppliers, and custom boat drawings. Another product is called Yacht Link Manager. This is for use in the office of yacht suppliers for inventory, investing, purchasing, and accounting.
O

Yukon Trawlers
9067 Sunrise Road
Custer, WA 98240
Tel   (360) 366-3486
Fax (360) 366-3985

Z

Zurn Yacht Design
PO Box 110
Marblehead, MA 10945
Tel   (617) 561-3999
Fax (617) 561-9222

Zodiac of North America
PO Box 400
Stevensville, MD 21666
Tel   (410) 643-4141
Fax (410) 643-4491
Em   info@zodiac.com
US distributor of Zodiac inflatable boats, semi-rigid yacht tenders, life rafts, and marine evacuation slides. Standard production of semi-rigid inflatable boats from 11 to 24ft. Inboard and outboard power, including water jets and marine diesel. Custom boats of any size, including "aluminum hulls" USCG and SOLAS approved liferafts.
B, YS

DEVONPORT
YACHTS

elegance

Devonport Yachts - specialists in
new builds, conversions, refits

DEVONPORT
YACHTS

Devonport Management Limited,
Devonport Royal Dockyard,
Plymouth, England PL1 4SG
Telephone 44 1752 553311
Facsimile 44 1752 554883

INDEX

INDEX

A
A.J. Originals, 172
Abeking & Rasmussen, 232
Acubens Design, 235
Admiral Marine, 232, 258
Admiralty/Queenship, 241
Aegean Sea, 208
Aerie, 36-41, 253
Aerodyne Yachts, 257
AeroRig, 253
Affinity, 235, 253, 255
Airex, 82, 154
Akhir Yachts, 233
Alaskan Yachts, 252
Al Riyadh, 236
Alden, John Design, 252
Alfa Laval Fuel Systems, 107
Allegra, 42-49, 242, 260
Allen, Taylor 183
Alloy Yachts, 256, 261
Alpha Marine, 232
Alumercia, 235
American Bow Thruster, 49, 65
American Marine, 256
Andrawis, Phil, 257
Andromeda, 50-57
Anita, 238
Anita's Interiors, 252
Ansul Fire Systems, 87
Antares Star, 234
Antonisa, 237, 256
Apollonio, 241, 252, 254
Aqua Air, 177
Aquasition, 237
Aquatech Propellers, 49
Aquedelo-Botero, Orlando, 108, 109
Araminta, 238
Ardeo Design, 253
Arrabito, Giovanni, 235
Artese, Joe, 253
Atlantide, 254, 255
Atlas Energy Systems, 105, 107
Avalon, 240, 261
Awlgrip, 82
Azimut, 232

B
Baglietto, 232, 260
Baker Furniture Co., 102
Balleri Chairs, 98
Barbeito Design, 253
Barnett, Jonathan Quinn, 66, 238, 253
Be Mine, 208
Beeldsnijder, Pieter, 81, 241
Belleza, 237
Bellini, 242, 259, 260
Benedetta II, 232
Beneteau, 233
Benetti, 232, 253
Benson, Tom/Grace, 102
Berretta/Queenship, 232, 241
Bertram Yachts, 236
Bertram, Richard Yacht Sales, 58
Big Bad John, 234
Blue Ice, 232
Blue Moon, 236
BOC Around Alone Race, 257
Bonita, 254
Bonville, Claudette, 108, 115
Borkumriff IV, 252
Bounty, 238
Branagh, Capt. Steve, 198
Braveheart, 254
Breeze, 256
Brooklin Boatyard, 183
Broward, 162, 170, 233, 254, 256, 258
Bubba Too, 233, 254
Burger, 102, 233
Byrne, Brindan Design, 57

C
Cable Marine, 25
Cabo Yachts, 253
Cabon Design, 233
Cakewalk, 236, 261
Camper & Nicholson International, 140, 254
Cantieri Di Pisa, 233
Card, Capt. Stephen, 66
Caribe/Queenship, 241, 252, 254
Castedo, M., 253
Caterpillar, 48, 49, 57, 84, 87, 93, 96,101, 152, 238, 241, 254
CBI Navi, 232, 233
Cecilia Marie, 256
Charlie's Angel, 242
Cheoy Lee Shipyards, 82, 233, 254
Cherosa, 242
Christensen Yachts, 170, 234, 241, 259
Christina, 258
Christofle, 55, 159
Cichero Design, 235
Cigarette, 170
Clark, Dr. Jim, 9, 72, 241
CNB, 233
Codecasa, 234
Cole, Scott, 253
Concordia Custom Yachts, 141
Constellation, 239, 240
Crescent Custom Yachts, 58, 234, 243, 256, 259, 260
Crescent Lady, 234
CRN Ancona, 236
Crosser, 259
Crystal, 252
Crown Ltd, 176
Custom Line S.p.A., 236
Custom Navigation, 86, 166
Custom Surface Wall Coverings, 166
Cutting Edge, 241

D
Dacor Radiant Heat Cooktop, 38
Dare To Dream, 58-65, 234, 256
De Basto, Luiz, 122,123, 127, 237, 253
De Groot, Guido, 92
De Voogt, Frits, 88, 93, 235
De Vries, 88, 235
Delfield Refrigerators, 46
Delta Marine, 108, 115, 234, 235, 253, 254, 255
Delta-T Systems, 157
Denison Yachts, 252
Derecktor Shipyards, 207, 235, 256, 261
Destiny Yachts, 235
Detroit Diesel/MTU, 41,106,115,130,133, 147, 157,169,176, 236, 237, 241, 255, 258
Detroit Eagle, 236
Diaship, 235, 254
Dini, Luca, 233
Discovery, 66-71
Discovery Shipbuilders, 71
Divinycell, 60, 82
Dixon, Bill, 239
Donghia Furniture, 159
Donna C III, 242
Donzi, 126
Dragos Shipyard, 255
Duracell, 257
Dynasty, 233

E
E.A.R. Soundproofing, 177
Eastbay, 256
Edwin Fields Carpet, 176
Electronics Unlimited, 105
Encore, 237
Endless Summer, 259
Enterprise Diesel, 69
Equinoccio, 259
Erica XII, 255, 261
Erte, 150, 151
Escape, 234, 259
Eskimo Ice Chipper, 168
Espinosa Design, 238, 254, 258
Evviva, 232
Excellence II, 236
Explorer Yachts, 261

F
Fabrica Carpet, 85
Farr, Bruce, 255
Fae Lon, 233
Feadship, 88, 93, 235, 261
Felicity, 232
Ferretti, 128, 133, 236
Fexas, Tom, 82, 83, 84, 87, 233, 241, 253, 254
Fleming Yachts
Forbes Cooper Yachts, 241
Fountain Boats, 170
Franck's Boat Co., 236
Fraser Yachts, 232, 236, 237, 238
Fredrikstad, 254
Freivokh, Ken, 254, 255,
Frers, German, 75, 77, 81, 239, 241
Fry, Edward, 255
Fryco, 255

Furuno, 151

G
Gaarden Party, 239
Gaggenau, 39, 104, 106, 148, 151, 175
Gallant Lady, 235, 260
Garden, Bill, 259
Garlington Landweer, 258
Genmar Yacht Group, 236
Genuwood, 86, 111
Georgia, 256
Gershowitz, Sam/Marlena, 116
Gino Yachting, 211, 219
Giusti, Capt. Paul, 162
Glendinning, 168
Golden Bay IV, 232
Gorg, Jurgen, 112, 113
Grady White, 39
Gran Finale, 235, 254
Green Marine, 207
Greenbay Marine, 236, 260
Grohe, 54, 56
Guy Couach, 234

H
Halter Marine, 236, 242
Hammen Waste Treatment, 93
Hana How, 259
Harken, 138, 181, 182
Harrison Robbins, 153
Hatteras Yachts, 142, 170, 236, 256, 259
Heesen Shipyard, 235, 260
Heikel, Rod, 214
Hermes, 91
Herreshoff, L. Francis, 238
Hetairos, 256
High End Speakers, 54
Hodgdon Yachts, 237, 256, 261
Holland, Ron, 235, 255
Holly Belle, 258
Home James, 258
Honda, 65
Hood, Ted, 255, 261
Hood Sailmakers, 183
Horizons, 260
Horizon Watermakers, 87
Horvath, Tom, 58
Huckins Yachts, 237
Huisman, Wolter, 9
Hunt Design, 235, 254, 255
Hunter Dougless, 85
Hyperion, 72-81, 241

I
Illusion, 148, 253
Imron, 57
Inace, 237
In Full Bloom, 254
Ingram, Nigel, 134
Inspiration, 254
Intermarine Yachting, 237, 254, 258
International Paint, 82
Iroquois, 235

J
Jacuzzi, 41, 47, 48, 54, 56, 57, 62, 65, 86, 87, 91, 92, 100, 111, 124, 127, 144, 168, 171, 175, 176
Janet, 82-87
Jennaire, 83, 87, 168
Joel, Billy, 261
John Deere Diesel, 57
Johnson, Glade, 256

Jubilee, 233
Karadon, 151, 152
Katrion, 88-93, 236
Kilopak, 48
King, Bruce, 237, 256, 261
Kirschstein, Michael, 237
Kisses, 236
Kitchen Aid, 104
Klegecell, 148
Knowles, Patrick, 104, 256
Kubota Diesel, 57
KVH TracVision, 153

L
La Baronessa, 94-101, 240, 261
Lad, 233
Lady Grace Marie, 102-107
Lady Linda, 108-115
Land Rover, 255
Langan, Bill, 256, 261
Lange, Capt. Alan, 101
Lazzara Yachts, 237
LeClercq Marine, 237, 258
Legacy, 237
Legendary Yachts, 238, 253
Lenox China, 44
Leopard 2000, 255
Lewmar, 135, 138
Liebowitz & Pritchard, 253, 256, 257
Lima Generators, 57
Limitless, 238
Little Hoquiam Shipyard, 238, 253, 260
Lloyds Ship, 259, 260
Lucy Design, 71
Lurssen Yachts, 238
Lyman-Morse, 260

M
Maclear, Frank, 55
Magic One, 254
Magnum Marine, 258
Maiora, 238
Majilite, 60, 85, 122, 124, 176
Majka, Bruce
Maloekoe, 236
MAN, 141
Man, Kertz, 168
Marala, 208
Marco Polo, 238
Margueritte, 261
Marine Air, 87, 106
Marine Construction Management, 134, 207
Marine Design International, 257
Marlena, 116-121, 242
Marquipt, 65, 126
Marshall, Evan K., 235, 239
Marshall, Greg, 243, 258
Martin, Rodger, 257
Mathers Controls, 151
Matrix Watermakers, 107
Maxwell Winches, 121, 147
McKinna Yachts, 252, 258
McLaughlin, Sheryl, 159, 160
McMullen & Wing, 258, 260
McQueen's Boatworks, 148, 153, 238, 253, 257, 259
McQuiston, Michael, 91
Mea Culpa, 259
Meduse, 235
Merritt-Knowles Design, 162, 163
Merritt Yachts, 260
Metalnave, 259
Mia Elise, 122-127, 237

Michaels, Marc, 122
Micro Eye, 124
Midnight Lace, 254
Miele Appliances, 46, 69
Mistral, 238
Misty One, 241
Mitsubishi, 174
MonArk Vessel Monitor System, 69
Monitor, 258
Monk, Ed, 36, 37, 41, 148, 153, 238, 239, 257, 259
Montana, 128-133
Monte Fino Yachts, 238
MTU, 62, 80, 81, 127, 160
Mulder Design, 234
Munford, John, 88, 93, 134, 234
Murray, Bill, 239, 258

N
Naiad Stabilizers, 49, 65, 84, 87, 115, 153
Nassa Too, 254
Nautor Swan, 238, 239
Nautica, 152
Nautical Structures, 87, 106, 115
Nautico Submersibles, 162
Navtec, 141
Nectar of the Gods, 234
Negro, Lopez, 46
Neptunus Yachts, 255
Nettinga, Paul, 53
New Century, 208
New England Ropes, 141
Nina, 252
Nirvana, 233
Nissan Pacific, 55
Nobletec, 151
Nolan, Tim, 148, 153, 257
Nordlund Boat Co., 148, 153, 238, 239, 256, 257, 259
Nordlund, Gordon/Sally, 36
North Coast Lady, 239
North Sails, 55, 72, 81
Northcoast Yachts, 239, 253
Northern Lights, 65, 87, 107, 115, 121, 127, 141, 152, 160, 177
Northern Marine, 239
Northrop Pacific, 232
Northstar, 151
Norwegian Queen, 243
Notika Teknik Yachts, 239
Nova Spirit, 242, 259
Novurania, 65, 87, 91, 106, 107, 126, 162, 176, 236
Nuvolari-Lenard, 94, 97, 101, 255

O
O'Keefe, Don, 107
Obsessions, 235
Oceanco, 239, 259, 261
Octopussy, 235
Offshore Spars, 141
Omega Marine Developers, 50
Onan, 147
Oregon Mist, 241

P
Pacific Custom Interiors, 160, 257
Pacific Mariner Yachts, 258
Packard Boats, 45
Padanaram Yachts, 183, 240
Palmer Johnson, 94, 101, 240, 256, 260, 261
Pamina, 255
Paragon Design, 42, 49, 122, 127

Pavlik Design, 258
Paxman Engines, 121
Pedigree Cats, 253
Pedrick, David, 134, 232, 258
Perini Navi, 240, 241, 255
Perkins, Capt. Jack, 102
Perry, Robert, 241
Pershing Yachts, 236
Peters, Michael, 257, 258, 259
Philbrook's Boatyard, 241
Phryne, 240
Picasso, Pablo, 259
Pipewelders, 166
Plum Duff, 232
Pokela Design, 36, 41, 148, 153, 257, 259
Posgay, John, 42, 49
Postma, Herb, 243
Predator Boats, 236
Premier Yachts, 254
Primadonna, 234
Princess Marla, 42

Q
Quantum Sails, 141
Que Linda, 236
Queenship, 232, 241, 253

R
Radiance, 238
Rayburn Yachts, 241
Rayburn, Ron, 241
Regency, 239, 253
Rekmann, 137
Remington, Frederick, 46
Rendova, 39
Resin Systems, 236
Rhodes 77 M/S, 253
Richey, Douglas, 102, 107
Rivolta Carmignani, 55
Robinson, Dee, 42, 118, 121, 259
Rochte, Carl, 53
Rockport Marine, 183, 240
Romsdal, 66, 71, 241
Rondal Spars, 77, 75
Rose, Robin, 174, 177, 259
Ross, David, 107
Royal Huisman Shipyard, 9, 72, 81, 241, 252, 255, 261
Rust, Randy, 154, 157
Rybovich Spencer, 148, 149, 241

S
Sabates, Carolyn, 42, 49
Sabates, Felix, 42
Sagamore, 256
Samantha Lin, 236
Sander, Per Magnus, 198, 207
Sarin, Jack, 58, 60, 234, 238, 243, 258, 259
Savannah, 134-141, 237
Savio Design, 87, 233
Savio, Melody, 82
Scales, Bill, 234
Scheherazade, 256, 261
Sciomachen Design, 57
Sea Hawk, 243
SeaDoo, 65, 176

Seaquester, 233
Sensation Yachts, 259
Serenity, 233
Setzer, Ward, 233, 236, 243, 260
Shaman, 198-207
Shamrock, 236
Sharp, Doug, 121
Shelter Island Runabout, 261
Sheriff, 142-147, 236
Shibumi, 241
Siesser's Palace, 242, 260
Siewert, Greg, 260
Signe, 253
Silicon Graphics Unix, 75
Silkline Creations, 239
Simaron, 233
Simrad, 48, 151, 169
Sinbad, 236
Smith, Paola, 242, 260
Solemates, 235
Sophie Blue, 233
Souvenir, 241
Sovereign Lady, 242
Sovereign Yachts, 242, 243, 258, 260
Sparkman & Stephens, 94, 101, 256, 260
Spectra Sails, 72
Spode, 91
St. Eval, 254
Star Light, 235
Starck, Phillipe, 122
Stargate II, 240
Stars & Stripes '87, 235
Starshine Studios, 165
Starship, 239
Steelhead Marine, 152
Stephens, Bob, 240
Stidd Seats, 83, 87, 152
Stultz Manufacturing, 46
SubZero, 38, 39, 104, 105, 165
Sundance Yacht Sales, 252
Sunseeker, 242, 255
Surprise, 260
Swan Plus, 239
SWATH, 252
Swiftships, 242
Syringa, 66

T
Tango, 241
Tarrab Yachts, 242, 260
TEC, 176
Teignbridge Propellers, 156, 160
Tempwise Controls, 166
The Dreamer, 232
Ticonderoga, 238
Tiffany, 91, 159
Tigress, 148-153, 238, 259
Tilman, H.W., 203, 207
Timeless, 172
Tofias, Donald, 178, 240
Treffers, John/Sandi, 66
Trick One, 240
Trident Yachts, 243, 254
Trinity Yachts, 42, 49, 121, 236, 242, 259, 260
Trintella Yachts, 255
Tripp Design, 207

Turquoise, 208-219
Twin Disc, 86
Twisted Pair, 240

U
U-Line Refrigeration, 85
Ubiquitous, 154-161
Ultima III, 232
Unfurled, 241, 261

V
Van Capellan Sound, 127, 177
Van Lent & Zonen, 235
Vanguard, 239
Vantage Lighting, 166
Vantage Marine, 153
Varsity Jacket, 162-169, 256
Vectran, 138, 178, 183
Vega, 254
Vermont Castings, 135
Victoria of Strathearn, 261
Victory Lane, 42
Victory Lane Enterprises, 49, 243, 260
Virgo II, 233
Vitters, 241, 261
Volrath Refrigeration, 57
Vosper Bow Thrusters, 127
Vripack, 235

W
W-Class, 178-183, 240
Waterford Crystal, 39, 44, 46
Watkins, Randolph, 134
Wehr Nuts, 170-177, 234, 259
West Bay SonShip, 243, 256, 259
West Epoxy, 181
Westinghouse, 151
Westport Shipyard, 58, 154, 234, 238, 243, 258, 259
Westship, 243
Westship One, 243
Whale Song, 236
White Star, 259
White Wings, 183, 240
White, Joel, 178, 240
White, Steve, 183
Whitefin, 253
Whitehawk, 256
Whitener, Gary/Sueannah, 148, 151
Wild Horses, 178-183, 240
Winch, Andrew, 207, 240, 255, 261
With Interest, 239
Wolf Two, 233

Y
Yamaha, 87, 106, 152, 176
Young, Capt. Raymond, 170
Yukon Trawler, 232

Z
ZF, 49, 65, 130, 152
Zodiac, 69, 96
Zuccon International, 128, 133
Zurn, Douglas, 261

ABSOLUTE INSPIRATION ABSOLUTE REWARD

A careful look at the Swan 60 Cruiser/Racer will dispel any misconceptions about her race bred origin. Her shape is clearly the result of the extensive research developing the Regatta version, which reaffirmed Nautor's ability to build a competitive grand-prix racer. Yet other tangible rewards are the uncluttered deck, the powerful, but manageable sail plan and the well thought interior. Her modern feel and outstanding sailing characteristics are matched by ocean going strength, quality of specification and versatility as a performance cruiser. The inspiration for a yacht design comes from many sources. For a company as experienced as Nautor, success on the race course is just one.

NAUTOR's SWAN 60

SWAN RANGE: 112 80 77 77DH 68 68CC 60 60R 57RS 57CC 56 56R 48 48R 44MKII 40

NEWPORT RI +1 (401) 846 8404	**NEW YORK** +1 (203) 425 9700	**ANNAPOLIS** +1 (410) 266 5455	**FORT LAUDERDALE** +1 (954) 462 1448	
MIAMI +1 (305) 673 4600	**CHICAGO** +1 (312) 755 9000	**SEATTLE** +1 (206) 447 7030	**SAN FRANCISCO** +1 (510) 235 5564	**NEWPORT BEACH** +1 (949) 645 9700

OY NAUTOR AB
P.O. BOX 10 FIN-68601
PIETARSAARI FINLAND
T. +358 6 7601 111
F. +358 6 7667 364
E. swan.yachts@nautor.inet.fi
www.nautors-swan.com

Photographers

Front Cover	Dana Jinkins	51-53	Dana Jinkins	88-101	Bill Muncke	143/Bottom	Bugsy Gedlek
Title Page	Dana Jinkins	54/Top	Dana Jinkins	102-107	Donna & Ken Chesler	144-147	Bugsy Gedlek
3	Dana Jinkins	54/Bottom	Sandra Williams	108	Dana Jinkins	148	Martin Fine
36-41	Neil Rabinowitz	55-57	Dana Jinkins	109/Top	Donna & Ken Chesler	149/Top	Mike Whitt
42	Shaw McCutcheon	58-66	Neil Rabinowitz	109/Bottom	Dana Jinkins	149/Bottom	Martin Fine
43/Top	Shaw McCutcheon	67	Martin Fine	110-115	Dana Jinkins	150-153	Martin Fine
43/Bottom	Dana Jinkins	68-71	Neil Rabinowitz	116-121	Shaw McCutcheon	154-161	Neil Rabinowitz
44/Top	Dana Jinkins	72	Dana Jinkins	122-127	Gary John Norman	162-169	Donna & Ken Chesler
44/Bottom	Shaw McCutcheon	73	Louis Psihoyos	128-133	Bugsy Gedlek		
45-47	Dana Jinkins	74-79	Dana Jinkins	134	Dana Jinkins	170-183	Dana Jinkins
48/Top	Shaw McCutcheon	80	Louis Psihoyos	135/Top	Guy Gurney	197	Dana Jinkins
48/Bottom	Dana Jinkins	82	Dana Jinkins	135/Bottom	Dana Jinkins	198-207	Onne Van Der Waal
49	Shaw McCutcheon	83/Top	Mike Whitt	136-141	Dana Jinkins	208-219	Roger Lean-Vercoe
50/Top	Dana Jinkins	83/Bottom	Dana Jinkins	142	Bugsy Gedlek	231	Dana Jinkins
50/Bottom	Sandra Williams	84-87	Dana Jinkins	143/Top	Bruce Miller	261	Dana Jinkins

Advertisers

Appollonio Naval Architecture	251	Ferretti	33	Linn	223	Philbrook's	18
Brunton Propellers	188	Fraser	10	Luiz de Basto	184	Pokela Design	188
Burger Boat	14	George Shull	25	Lurssen Werft	34	Richard Bertram	31
Camper & Nicholson	8	Global Power	249	Lynn Jachney	195	Rivolta	195
CBI Navi	28	Greg Marshall	186	Marine Medical	220	Robinson Hallenberg	220
Cheoy Lee	23	GTH Design	186	Maxwell Winches	244	Simrad	30
Christensen	19	Guido de Groot	192	Megayacht Services	16	Sovereign Yachts	245
Crestar	196	Hatteras	12-13	Merrill Stevens	262	Strida	246
Datastar	220	Heliyachts	193	Nautilus	288	Striker Pacific	27
Delta Marine	6-7	Holland Jachtbouw	191	OY Nautor	287	Summit	225
Delta Marine	190	Homchick	194	Nigel Burgess	3	Superyacht Technologies	229
Derecktor	230	Ideal Windlass	220	Nordlund	227	Swiftships	222
Design Alliance	193	Inace	228	Nuvolari Lenard	189	Sylvia Bolton	193
Devonport	282	Interlux	192	Overing Yacht Design	229	Tilse	229
Diaship	21	Intermarine	22	Pacific Custom	190	Tom Fexas	250
Dynasea	188	Jack Sarin	244	Padanaram	185	Triconfort	187
Eastbay	20	Ken Freivokh	250	Palmer Johnson	15	Trinity	26
Edmiston	4	Koch, Newton & Partners	221	Paola Smith	247	Van Cappellen	226
Feadship	17	Kusch	32	Patrick Knowles	29	Wayne C Group	24
				Pedrick	246	Wilson	224

NAUTILUS UNDERWATER SYSTEMS

TEL: 954.525.1566
FAX: 954.525.2366
NAUTILUSSYSTEMS.COM

**YACHT-BASED SUBMERSIBLES
RECOMPRESSION CHAMBERS
ADVANCED DIVING SYSTEMS**
SOURCING – CONSULTING – INTEGRATION

20 Old Time American Tunes Arranged for Ukulele

by Rob Mackillop

CD Contents

1	Angeline The Baker	11	Fire On The Mountain
2	Arkansas Traveller	12	Frosty Morning
3	Barlow Knife	13	Lonesome Injun
4	Belle Of Lexington	14	Man Of Constant Sorrow
5	Big Scioty	15	New River Train
6	Black Eyed Susan	16	Red Haired Boy
7	Breaking Up Christmas	17	Red River Valley
8	Cluck Old Hen	18	Whiskey Before Breakfast
9	Down In The Valley	19	Home Sweet Home
10	Ducks On The Mill Pond	20	Wildwood Flower

MEL BAY®

1 2 3 4 5 6 7 8 9 0

© 2012 BY MEL BAY PUBLICATIONS, INC., PACIFIC, MO 63069.
ALL RIGHTS RESERVED. INTERNATIONAL COPYRIGHT SECURED. B.M.I. MADE AND PRINTED IN U.S.A.
No part of this publication may be reproduced in whole or in part, or stored in a retrieval system, or transmitted in any form or by any means, electronic, mechanical, photocopy, recording, or otherwise, without written permission of the publisher.

Visit us on the Web at www.melbay.com — E-mail us at email@melbay.com

CONTENTS

Introduction 3

GCEA Tuning
   Angeline The Baker 4
   Arkansas Traveller 5
   Barlow Knife 6
   Belle of Lexington 7
   Big Scioty 8
   Black Eyed Susan 9
   Breaking Up Christmas 10
   Cluck Old Hen 11
   Down In The Valley 12
   Ducks On The Mill Pond 13
   Fire On The Mountain 14
   Frosty Morning 15
   Lonesome Injun 16
   Man Of Constant Sorrow 17
   New River Train 18
   Red Haired Boy 19
   Red River Valley 20
   Whiskey Before Breakfast 21

GCEG Tuning
   Home Sweet Home 23
   Wildwood Flower 24

About the Author 25

Welcome to
20 Old Time American Tunes
Arranged For Ukulele!

These arrangements were written for pick or plectrum technique, but are perfectly playable with a fingerstyle technique.

I have made the arrangements idiomatic to the instrument, as any folk music must be. Eighteen of the tunes are in regular ukulele tuning, but the last two – *Home Sweet Home* and *Wildwood Flower* – have the first string tuned down a tone, giving the same note as the fourth string. This tuning of GCEG is close to banjo tuning, which suits these two songs very well.

Just a little note about keys: Most of the songs are in their traditional key, but occasionally this could lead to problems for the ukulele player. So, my solutions are practical – I either change the key, or adapt one or two notes here and there, so as not to interrupt the flow of the music. With different-sized ukuleles, or the use of a capo, any key can be found. So if you want to play these tunes with other musicians, there should be no problem.

I really enjoyed doing these arrangements, and you will find videos of my playing some of them on my website, RobMacKillop.net – feel free to contact me through my website.

Rob MacKillop
Edinburgh

Angeline The Baker

Arr. Rob MacKillop

Traditional

Arkansas Traveller

Arr. Rob MacKillop

Traditional

Barlow Knife

Arr. Rob MacKillop

Traditional

Belle of Lexington

Arr. Rob MacKillop
Traditional

Big Scioty

Arr. Rob MacKillop

Traditional

Black Eyed Susan

Arr. Rob MacKillop

Traditional

Breaking Up Christmas

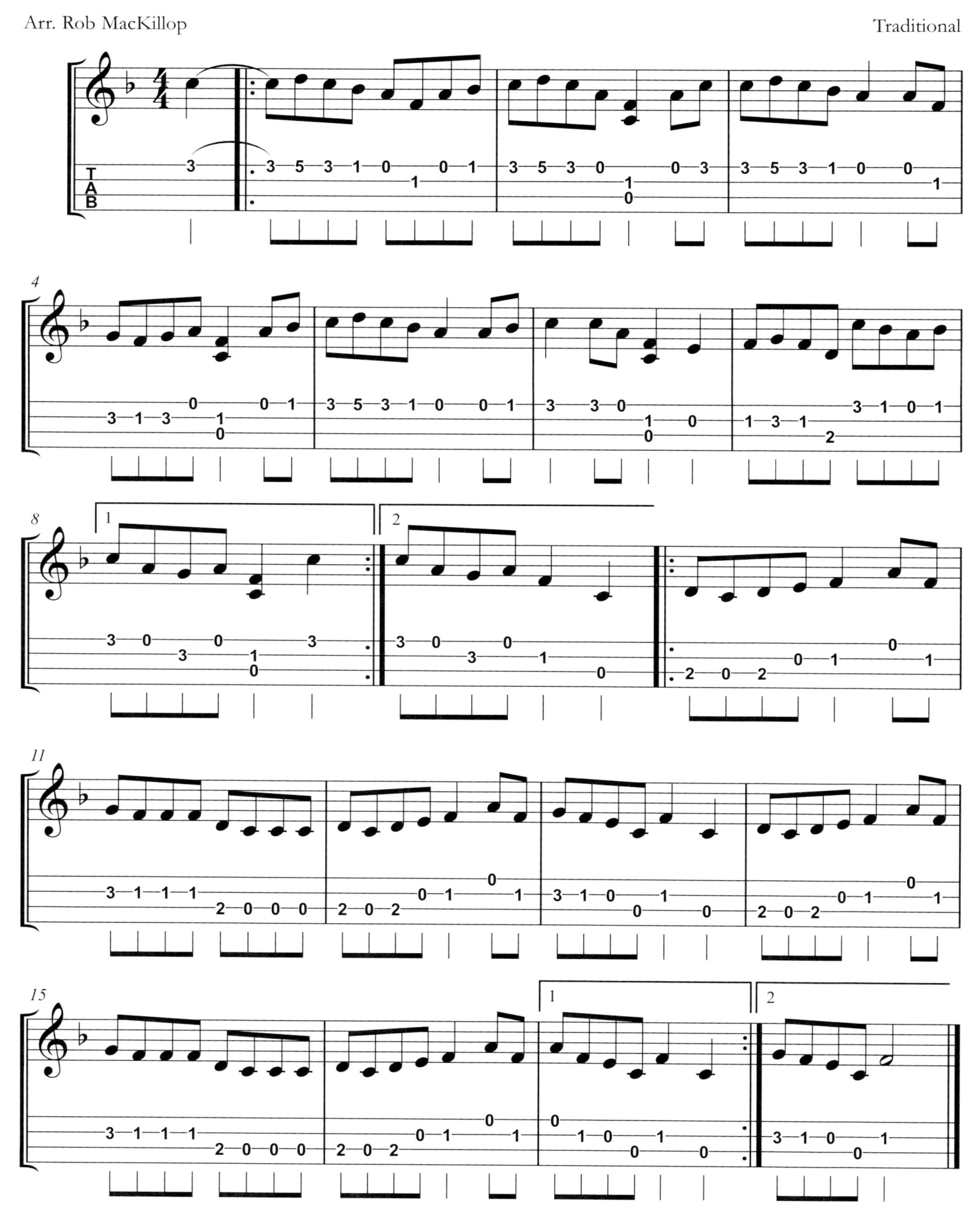

Arr. Rob MacKillop

Traditional

Cluck Old Hen

Arr. Rob MacKillop

Traditional

Down In The Valley

Arr. Rob MacKillop

Traditional

Ducks On The Mill Pond

Arr. Rob MacKillop

Traditional

Fire On The Mountain

Arr. Rob MacKillop

Traditional

Frosty Morning

Arr. Rob MacKillop

Traditional

Lonesome Injun

Arr. Rob MacKillop

Traditional

Man Of Constant Sorrow

Arr. Rob MacKillop

Traditional

New River Train

Arr. Rob MacKillop

Traditional

Red Haired Boy

Arr. Rob MacKillop

Traditional

Red River Valley

Arr. Rob MacKillop

Traditional

Whiskey Before Breakfast

Arr. Rob MacKillop

Traditional

The following two tunes require the first string of the ukulele to be tuned down by one tone, from A to G. Both the first and fourth strings now have the same note:

GCEG

Home Sweet Home

Arr. Rob MacKillop

Traditional

Wildwood Flower

Arr. Rob MacKillop

Traditional

Rob MacKillop

"One of Scotland's finest musicians" *Celtic World*

"A top-drawer player" *Early Music Today*

"A true champion of Scottish music" *The Herald*

"A player of real quality, with warmth of personality and communication skills to match...one of Scotland's top professionals" *Classical Guitar*

"MacKillop displays dazzling virtuosity...the playing is exceptionally musical" *Sounding Strings*

"a leading traditional talent who is single-handedly responsible for unearthing some of the nation's finest music" *The Scotsman*

Rob MacKillop has recorded eight CDs of historical music, three of which reached the Number One position in the Scottish Classical Music Chart. In 2001 he was awarded a Churchill Fellowship for his research into medieval Scottish music, which led him to studying with Sufi musicians in Istanbul and Morocco. He broadcast an entire solo concert on BBC Radio 3 from John Smith's Square, London.

He has presented academic papers at conferences in Portugal and Germany, and has been published many times. Rob has been active in both historical and contemporary music.

Three of Scotland's leading contemporary composers have written works for him, and he also composes new works himself. In 2004 he was Composer in Residence for Morgan Academy in Dundee, and in 2001 was Musician in Residence for Madras College in St Andrews. He created and directed the Dundee Summer Music Festival.

He worked as a Reader of schools literature for Oxford University Press, and as a reviewer for *Music Teacher*. He has also been Lecturer in Scottish Musical History at Aberdeen University, Dundee University, and at the Royal Scottish Academy of Music and Drama, and for six years worked as Musician In Residence to Queen Margaret University in Edinburgh. He has been a regular article writer for BMG magazine.

Rob plays lutes, banjo, guitar and ukulele with gut strings, plucking the strings with the flesh of his fingers, not the nails. This produces a warm and intimate sound, reminiscent of the old lute players.

RobMacKillop.net

Checkout www.melbay.com for more editions by Rob MacKillop

Notes

Notes